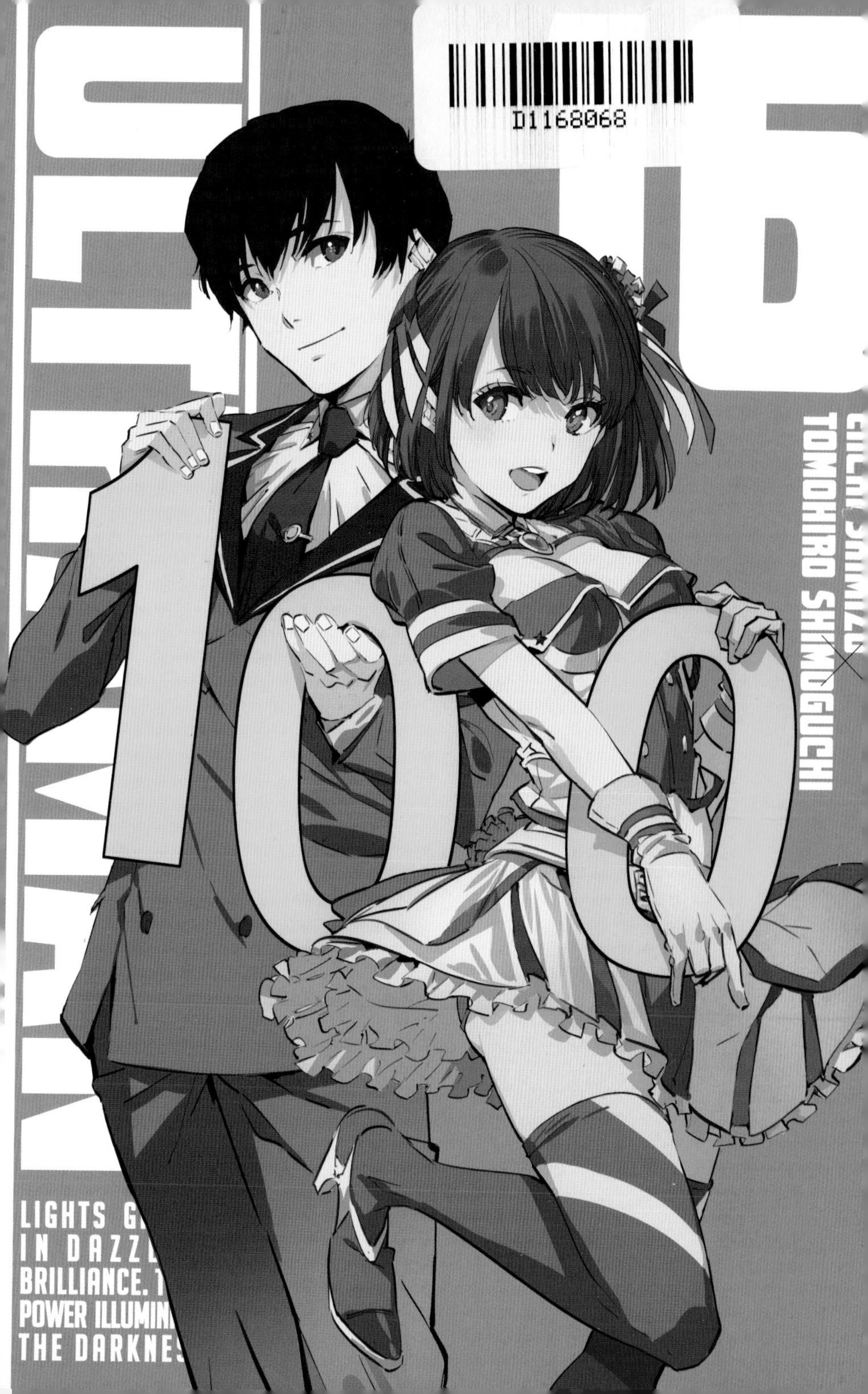

TOMOHIRO SHIMOGUCHI
100
LIGHTS G
IN DAZZL
BRILLIANCE. T
POWER ILLUMIN
THE DARKNES

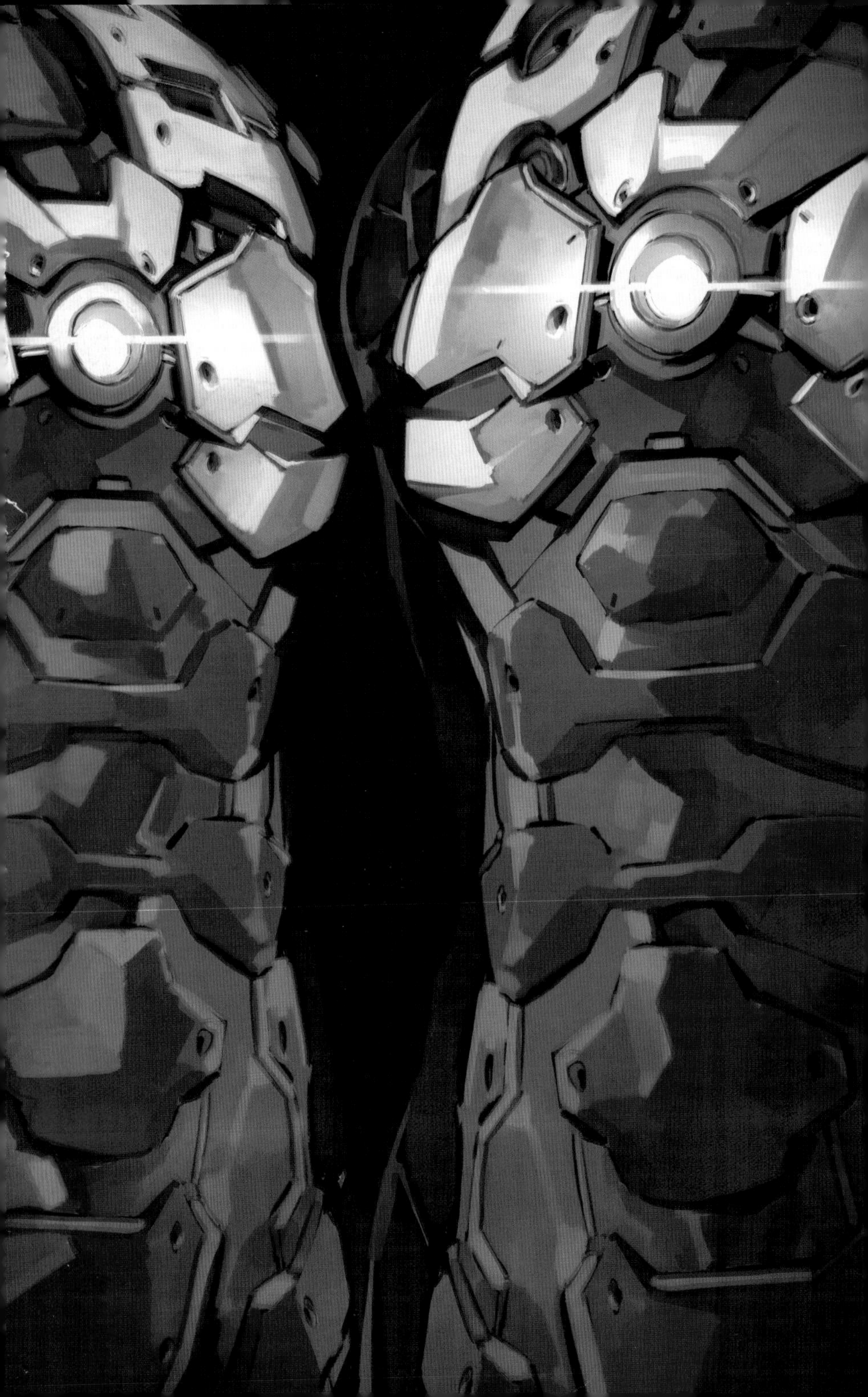

THIS IS THE BEGINNING OF A NEW AGE.

CONTENTS

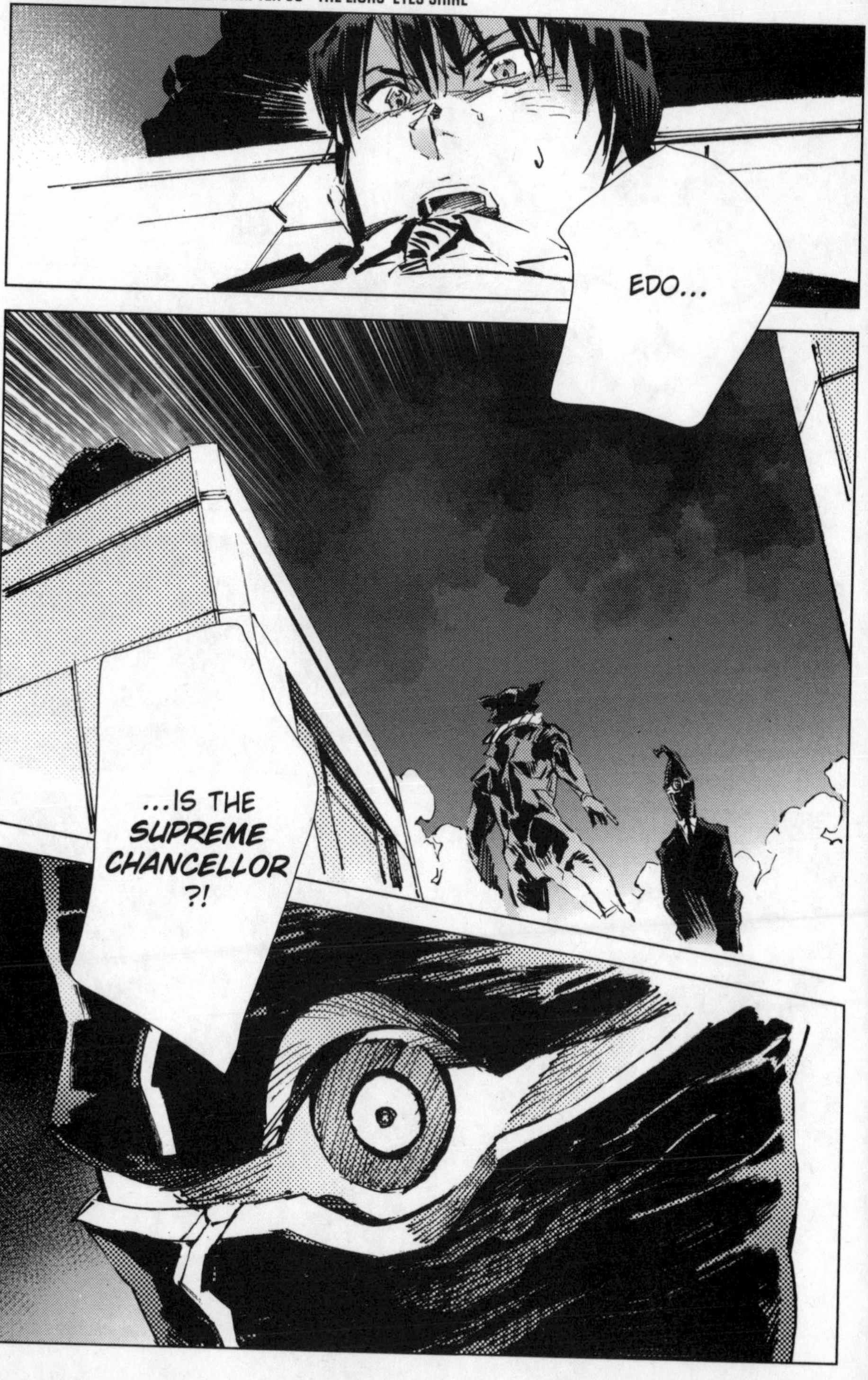
EDO...
...IS THE SUPREME CHANCELLOR ?!

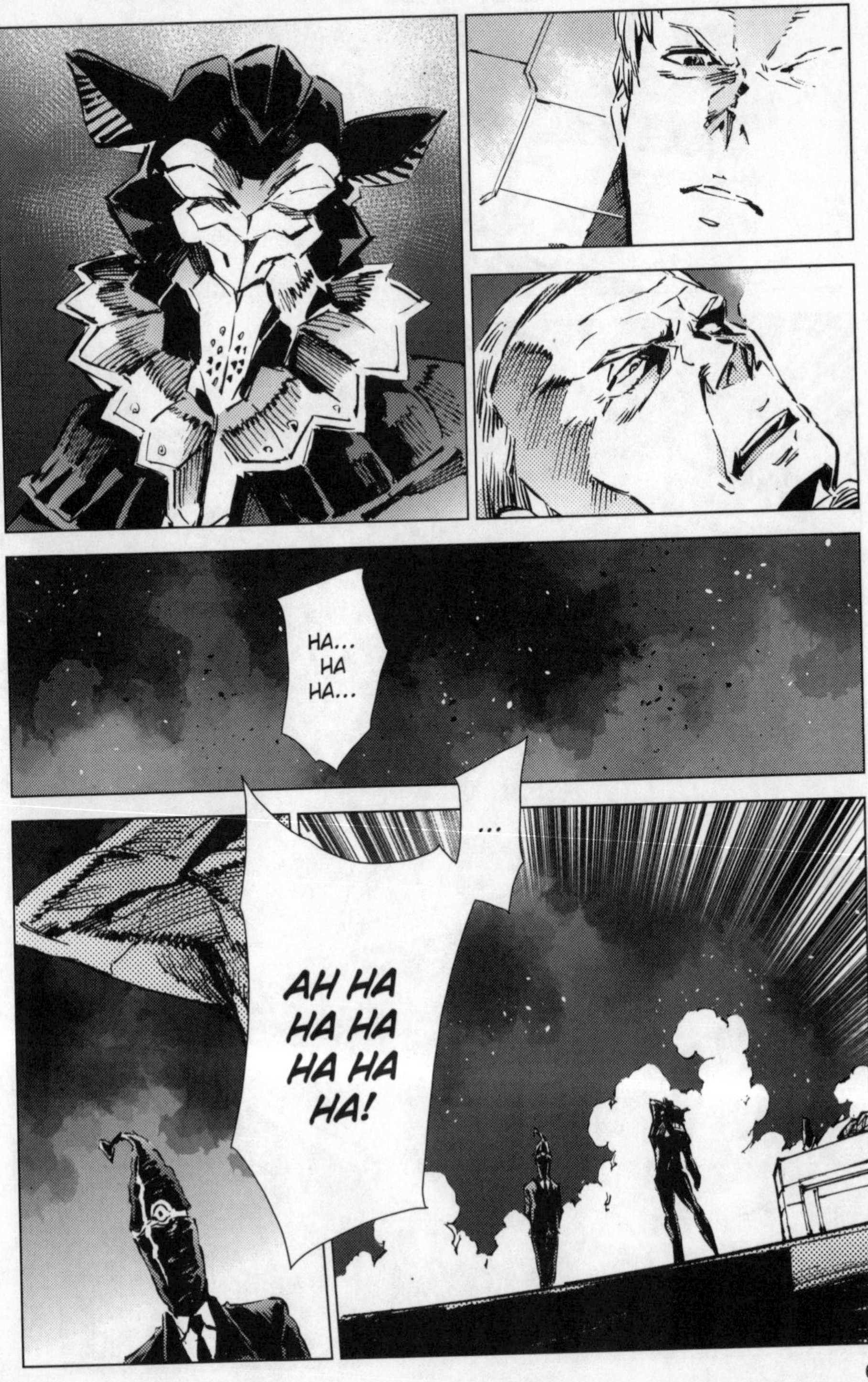
HA... HA HA...
...
AH HA HA HA HA HA HA!

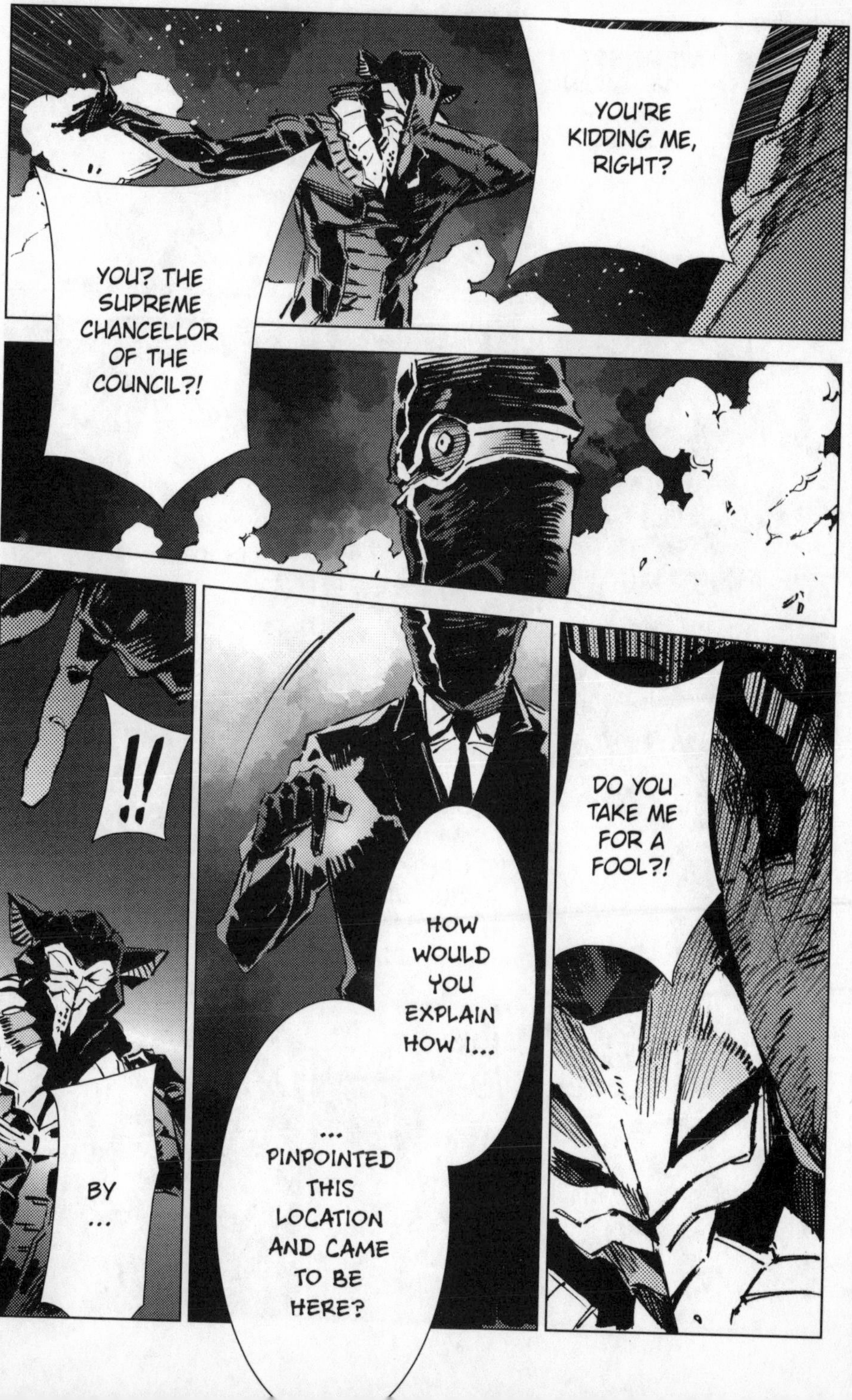
YOU'RE KIDDING ME, RIGHT?
YOU? THE SUPREME CHANCELLOR OF THE COUNCIL?!
DO YOU TAKE ME FOR A FOOL?!
HOW WOULD YOU EXPLAIN HOW I...
... PINPOINTED THIS LOCATION AND CAME TO BE HERE?
!!
BY ...

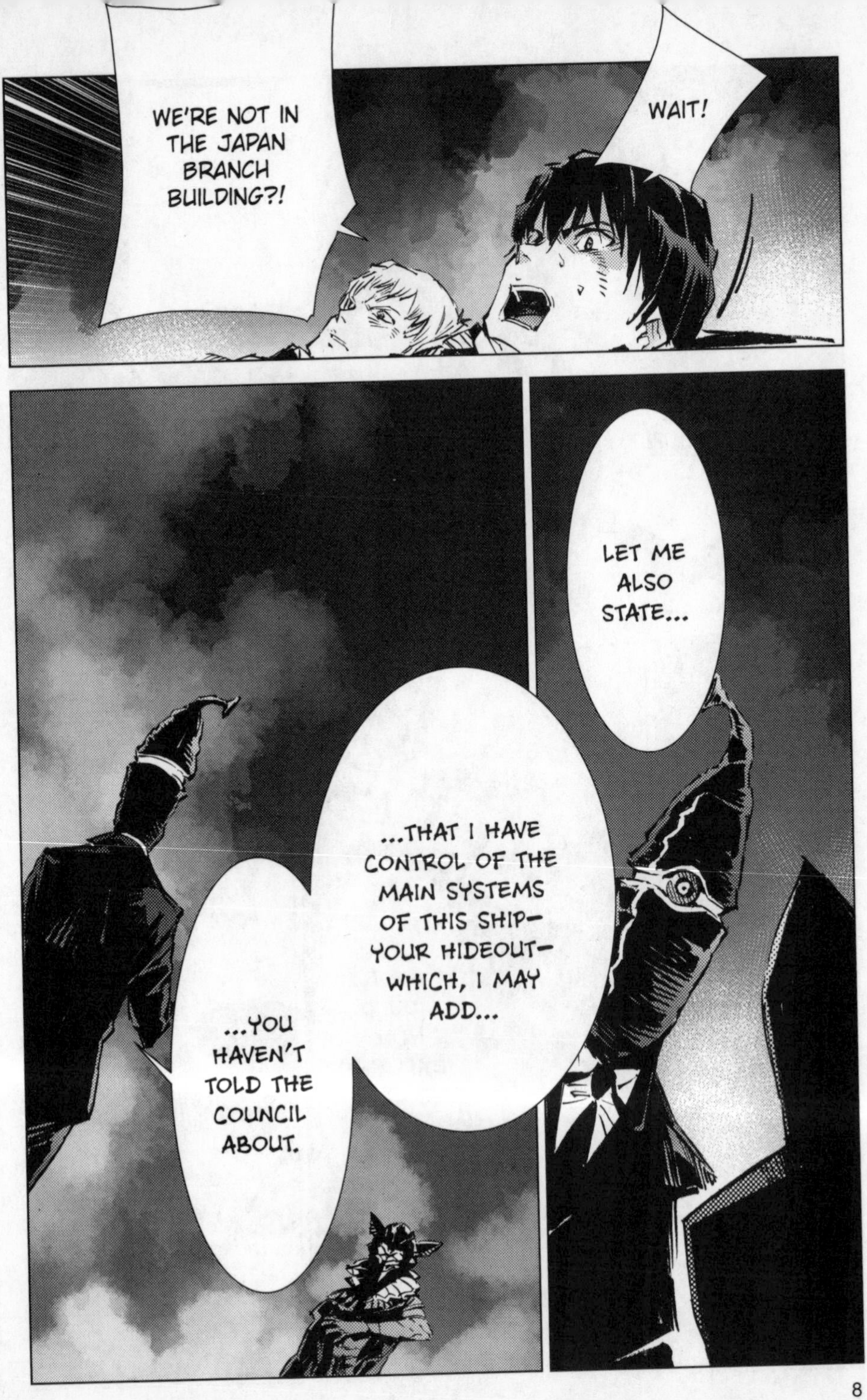
WAIT!
WE'RE NOT IN THE JAPAN BRANCH BUILDING?!
LET ME ALSO STATE...
...THAT I HAVE CONTROL OF THE MAIN SYSTEMS OF THIS SHIP—YOUR HIDEOUT—WHICH, I MAY ADD...
...YOU HAVEN'T TOLD THE COUNCIL ABOUT.

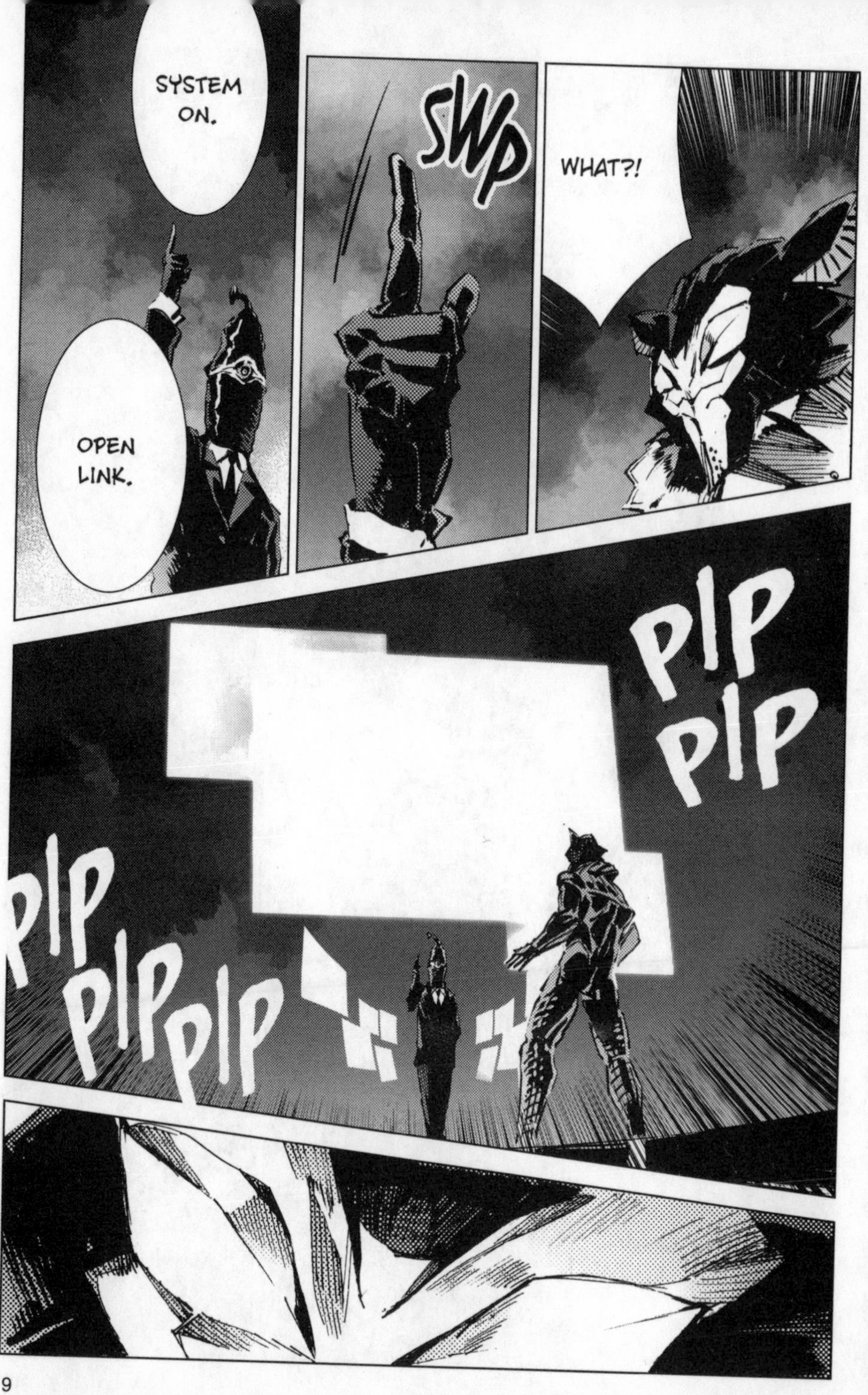
WHAT?!
SWP
SYSTEM ON.
OPEN LINK.
PIP PIP
PIP PIP PIP

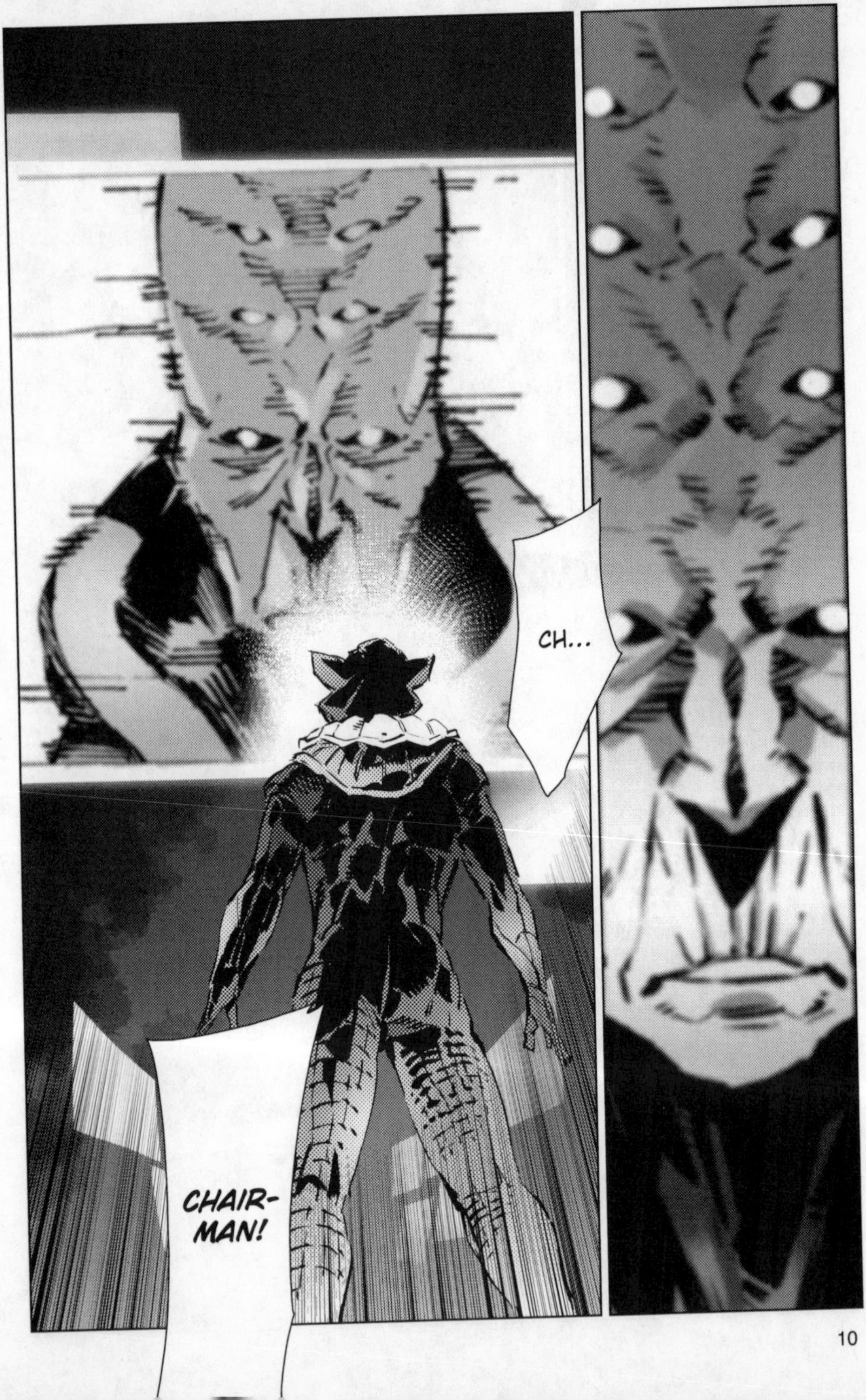
CH...
CHAIR-MAN!

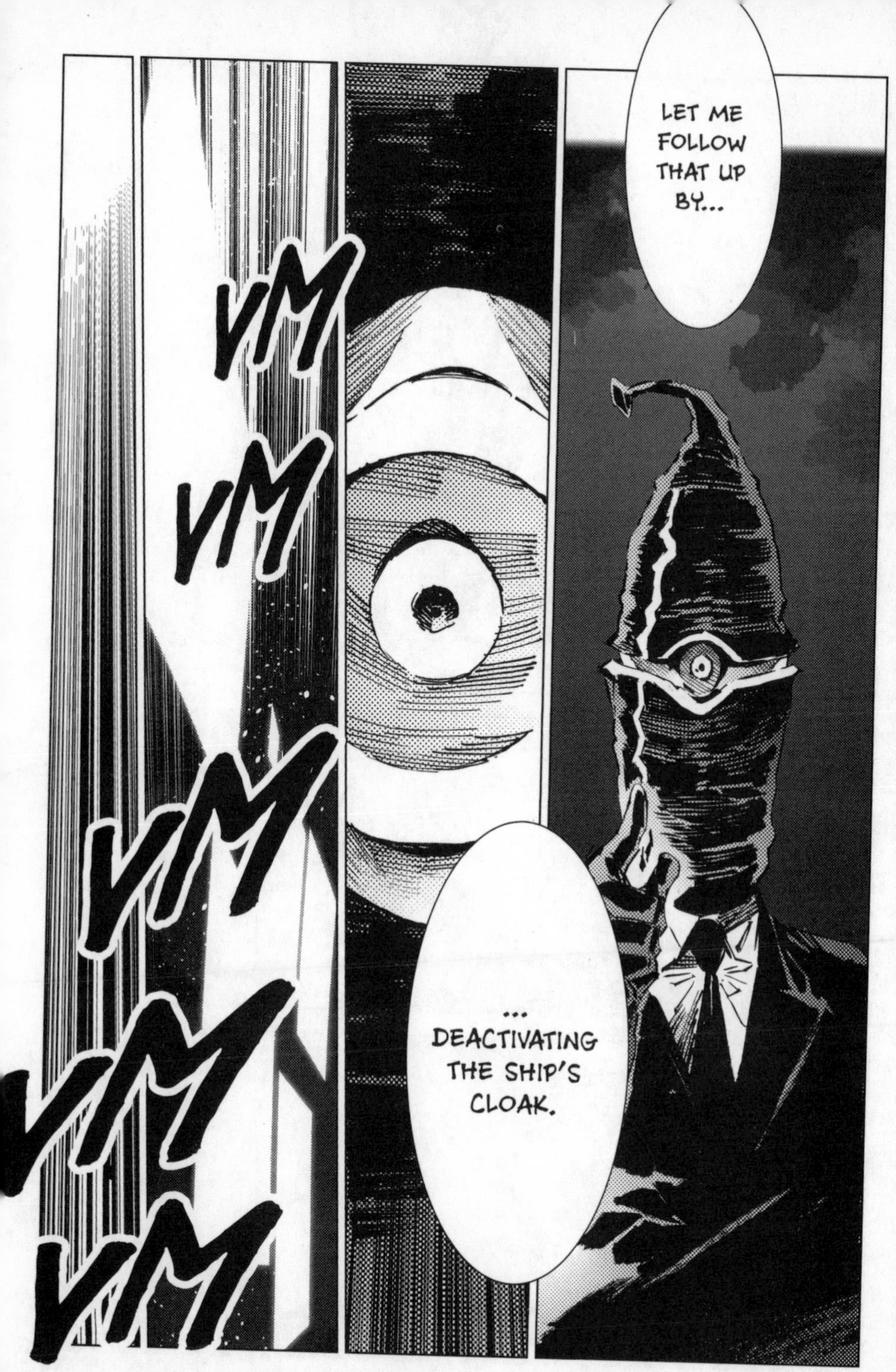
LET ME FOLLOW THAT UP BY...
...DEACTIVATING THE SHIP'S CLOAK.
VM
VM
VM
VM
VM

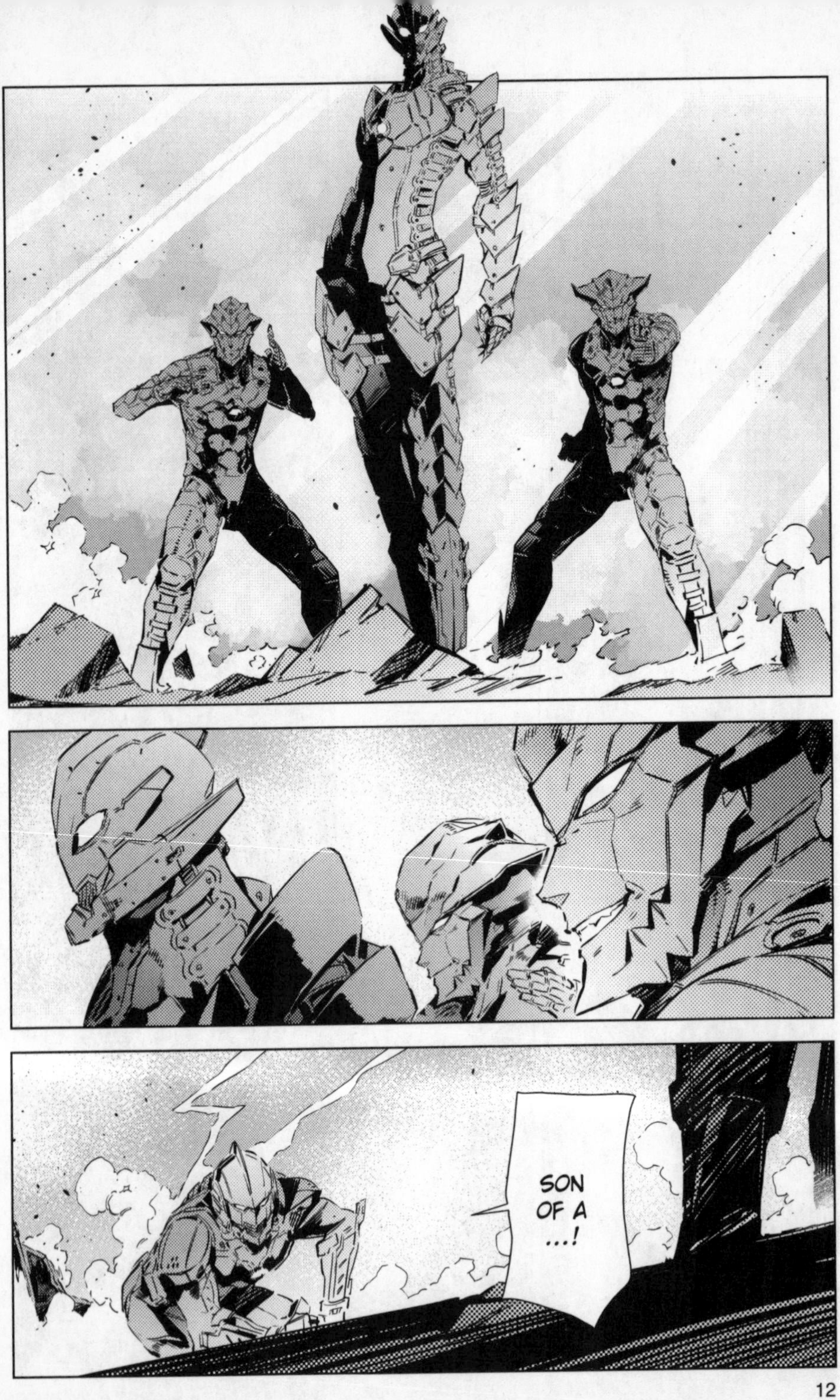
SON
OF A
...!

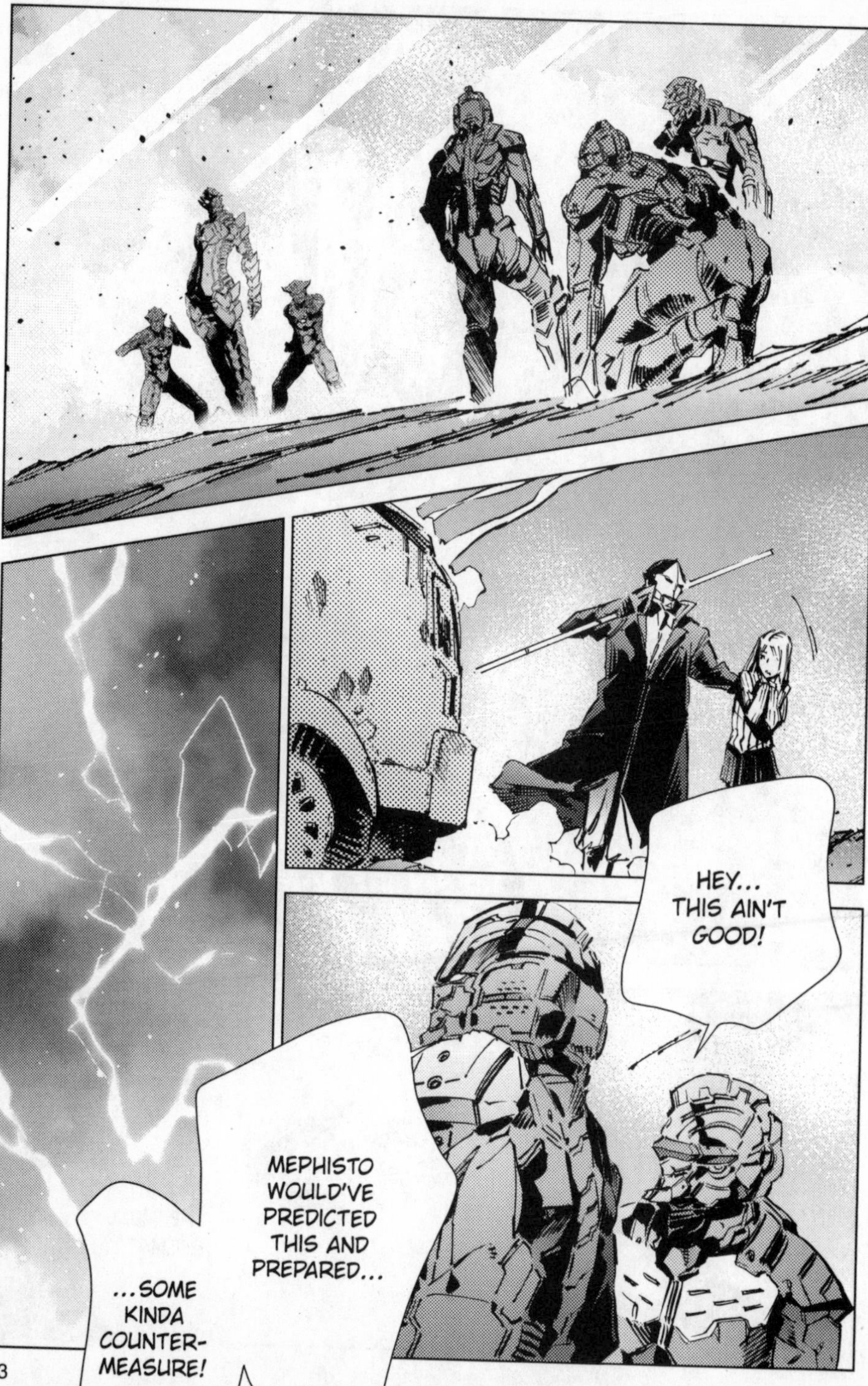
HEY... THIS AIN'T GOOD!
MEPHISTO WOULD'VE PREDICTED THIS AND PREPARED...
...SOME KINDA COUNTER-MEASURE!

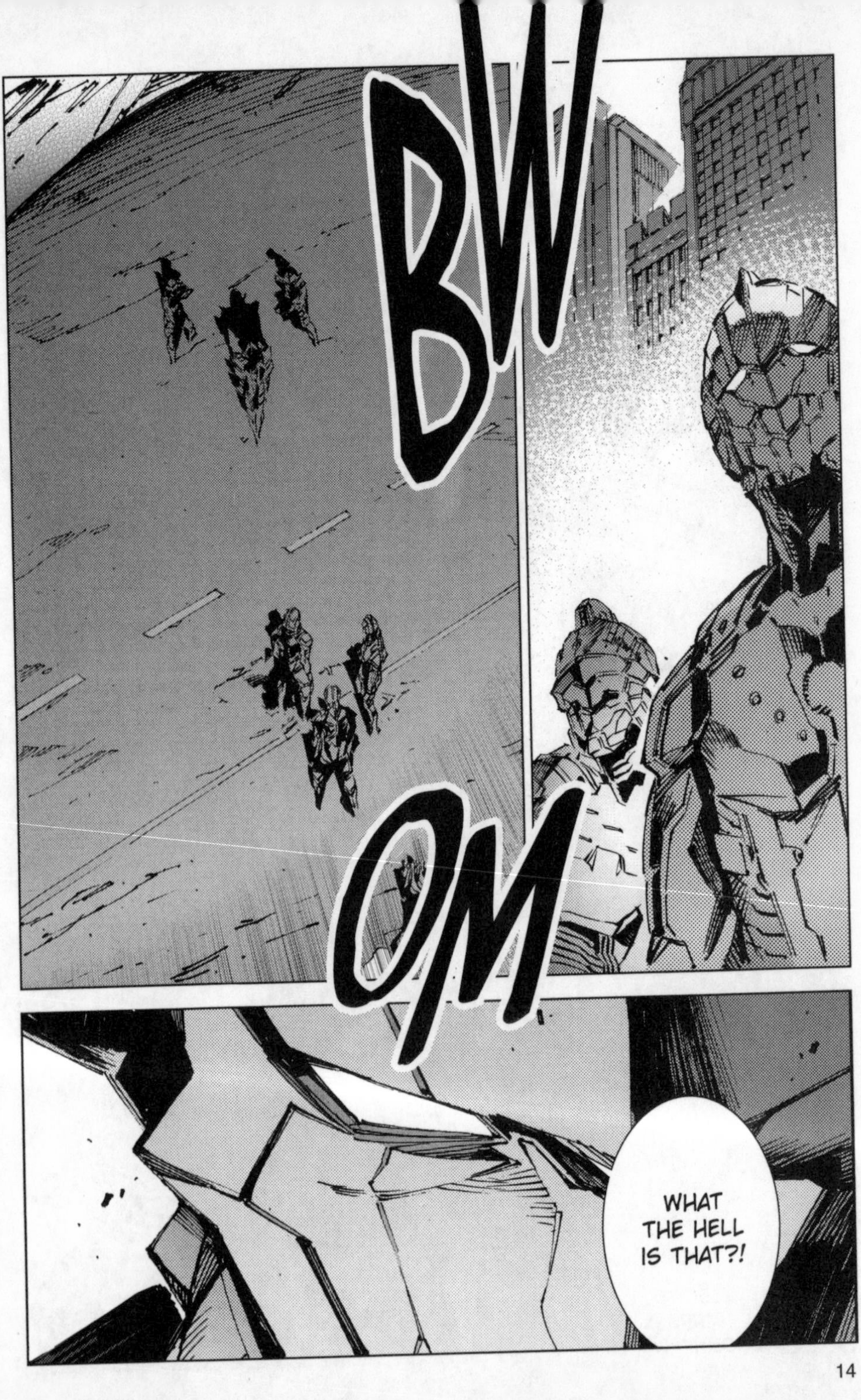
BWOM
WHAT THE HELL IS THAT?!

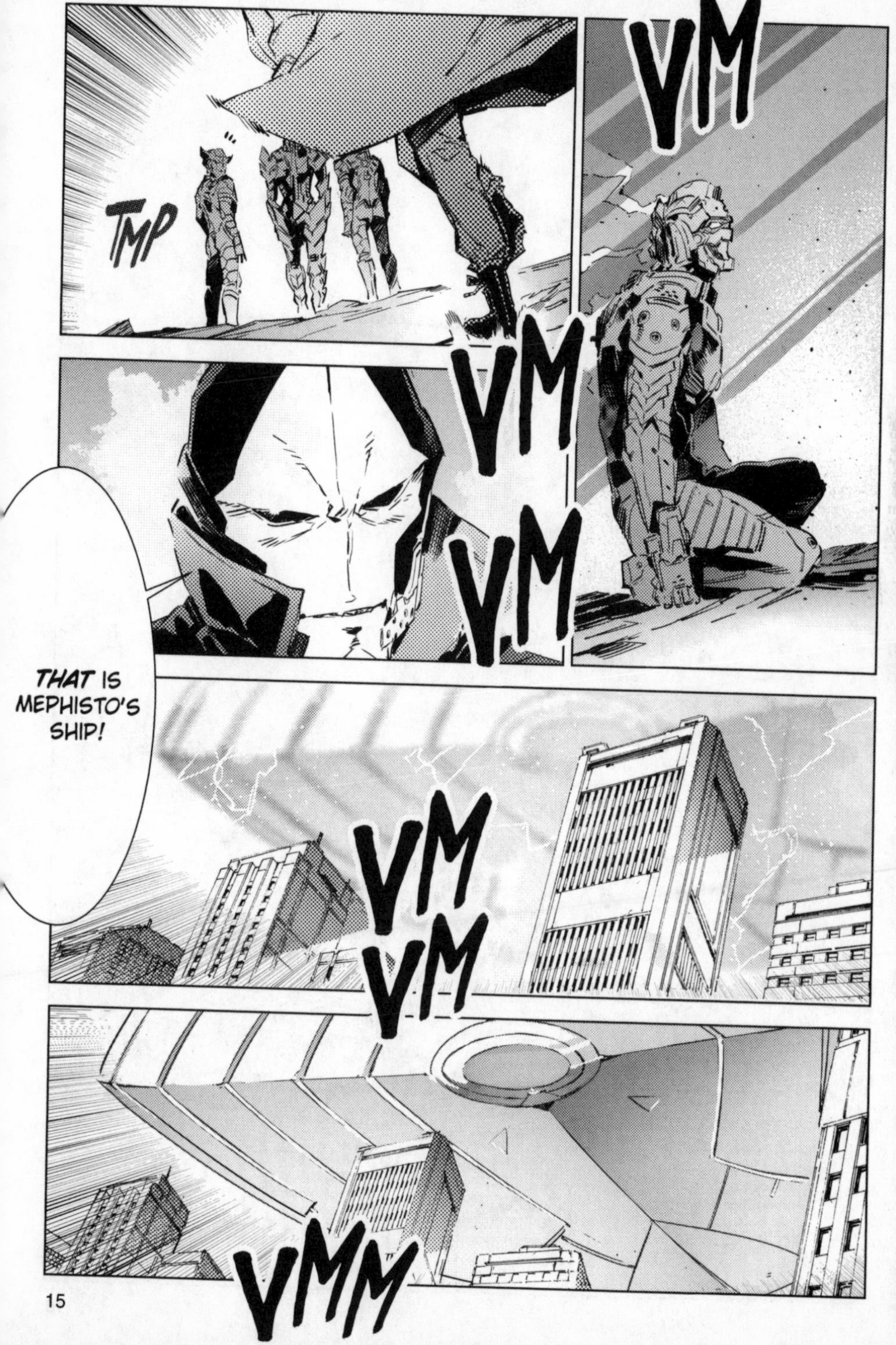
VM
TMP
VM
VM
THAT IS MEPHISTO'S SHIP!
VM
VM
VMM

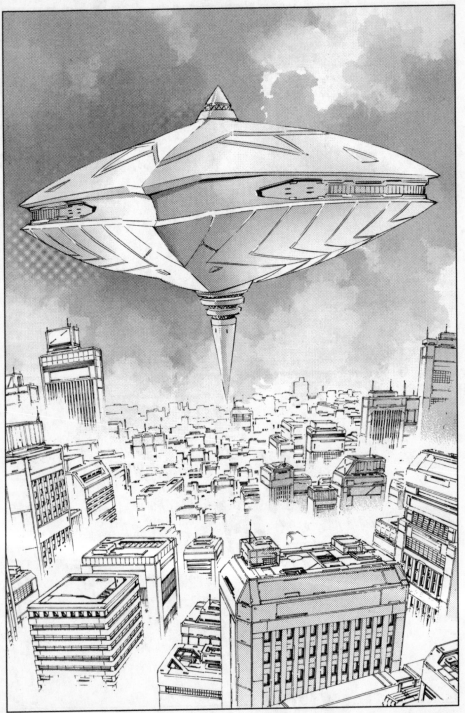

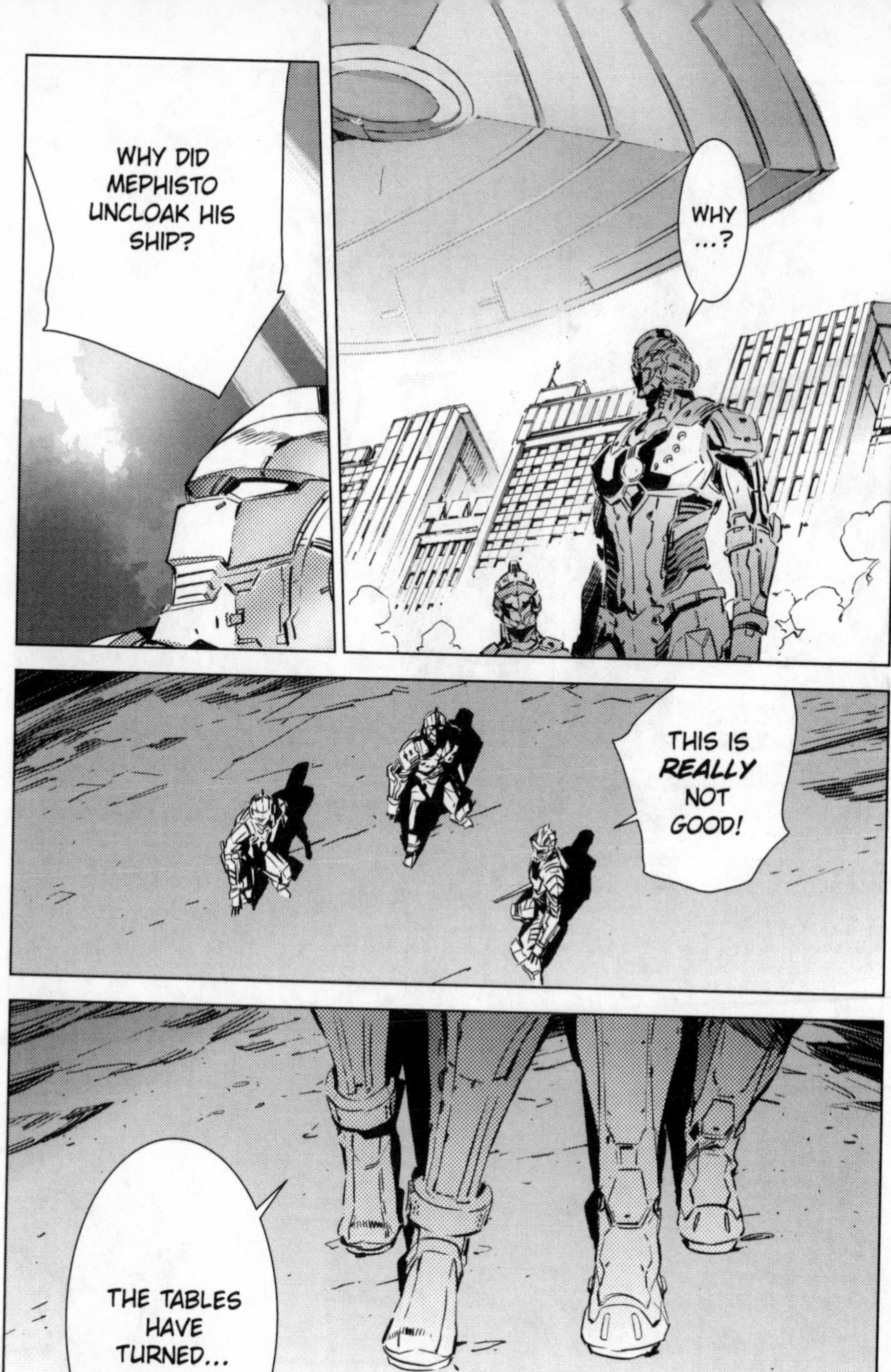
WHY ...?
WHY DID MEPHISTO UNCLOAK HIS SHIP?
THIS IS *REALLY* NOT GOOD!
THE TABLES HAVE TURNED...

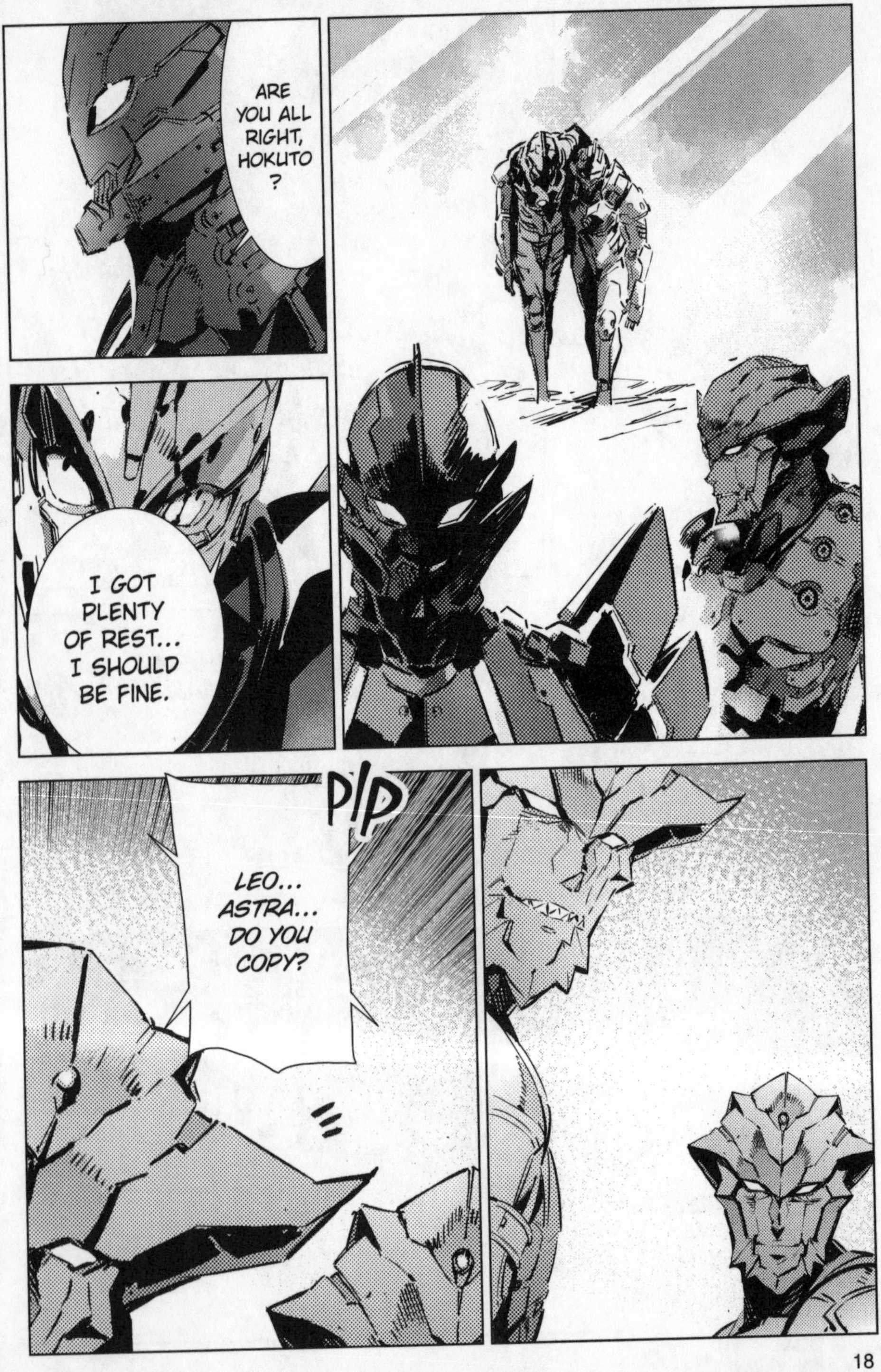
ARE YOU ALL RIGHT, HOKUTO?
I GOT PLENTY OF REST... I SHOULD BE FINE.
PIP
LEO... ASTRA... DO YOU COPY?

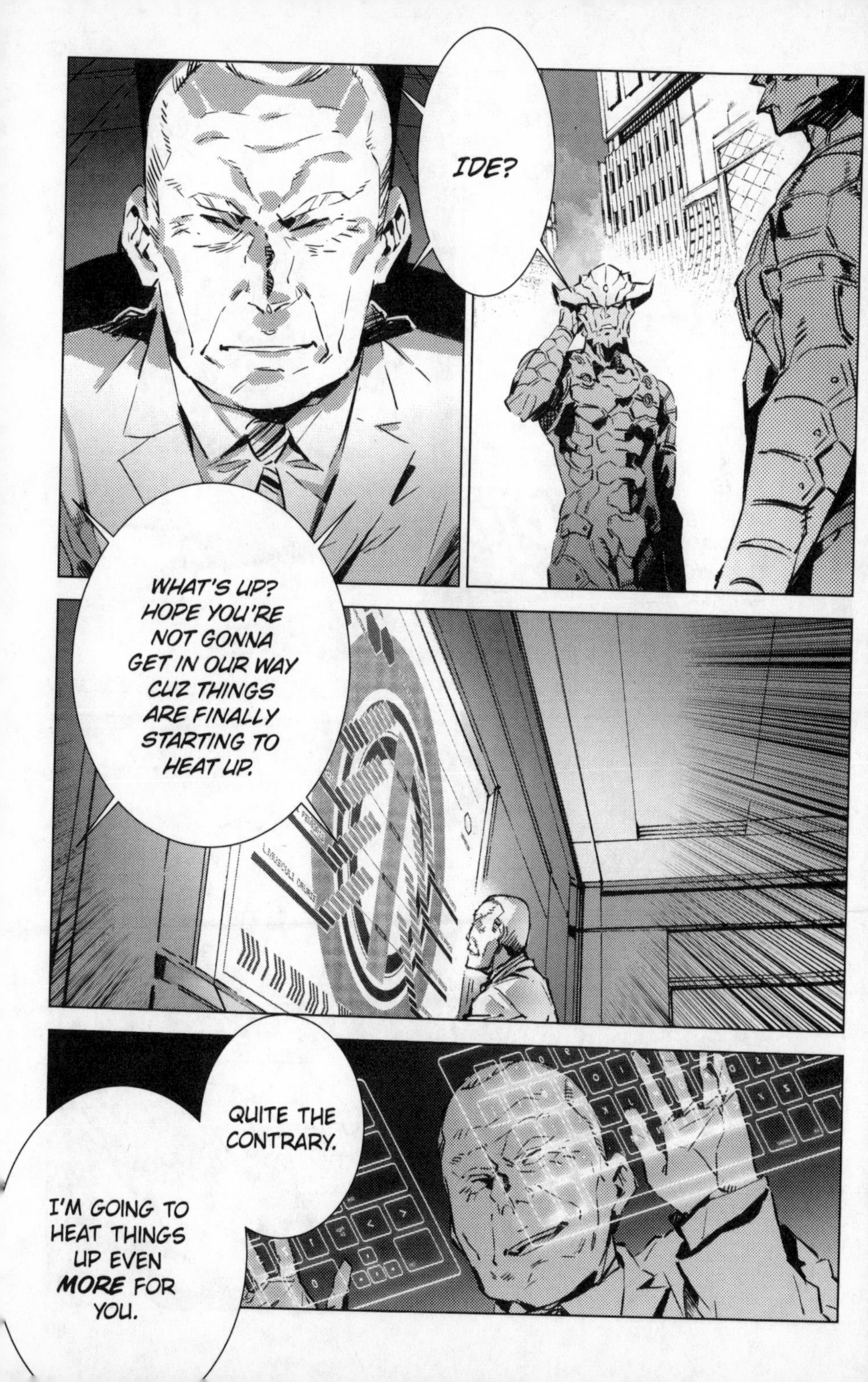
IDE?
WHAT'S UP? HOPE YOU'RE NOT GONNA GET IN OUR WAY CUZ THINGS ARE FINALLY STARTING TO HEAT UP.
QUITE THE CONTRARY.
I'M GOING TO HEAT THINGS UP EVEN **MORE** FOR YOU.

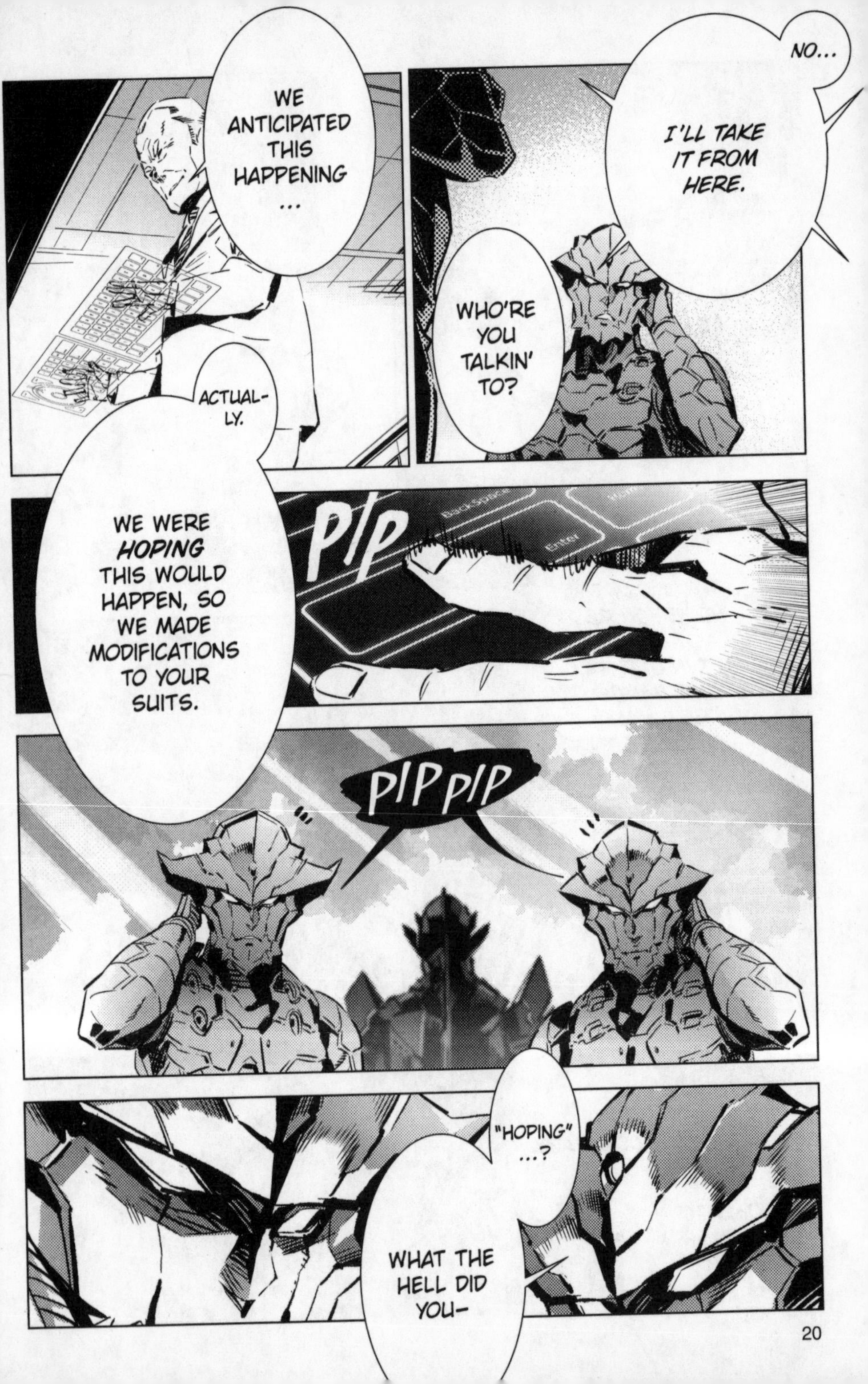
NO...
I'LL TAKE IT FROM HERE.
WHO'RE YOU TALKIN' TO?
WE ANTICIPATED THIS HAPPENING...
ACTUAL-LY.
WE WERE *HOPING* THIS WOULD HAPPEN, SO WE MADE MODIFICATIONS TO YOUR SUITS.
PIP
PIP PIP
"HOPING"...?
WHAT THE HELL DID YOU-

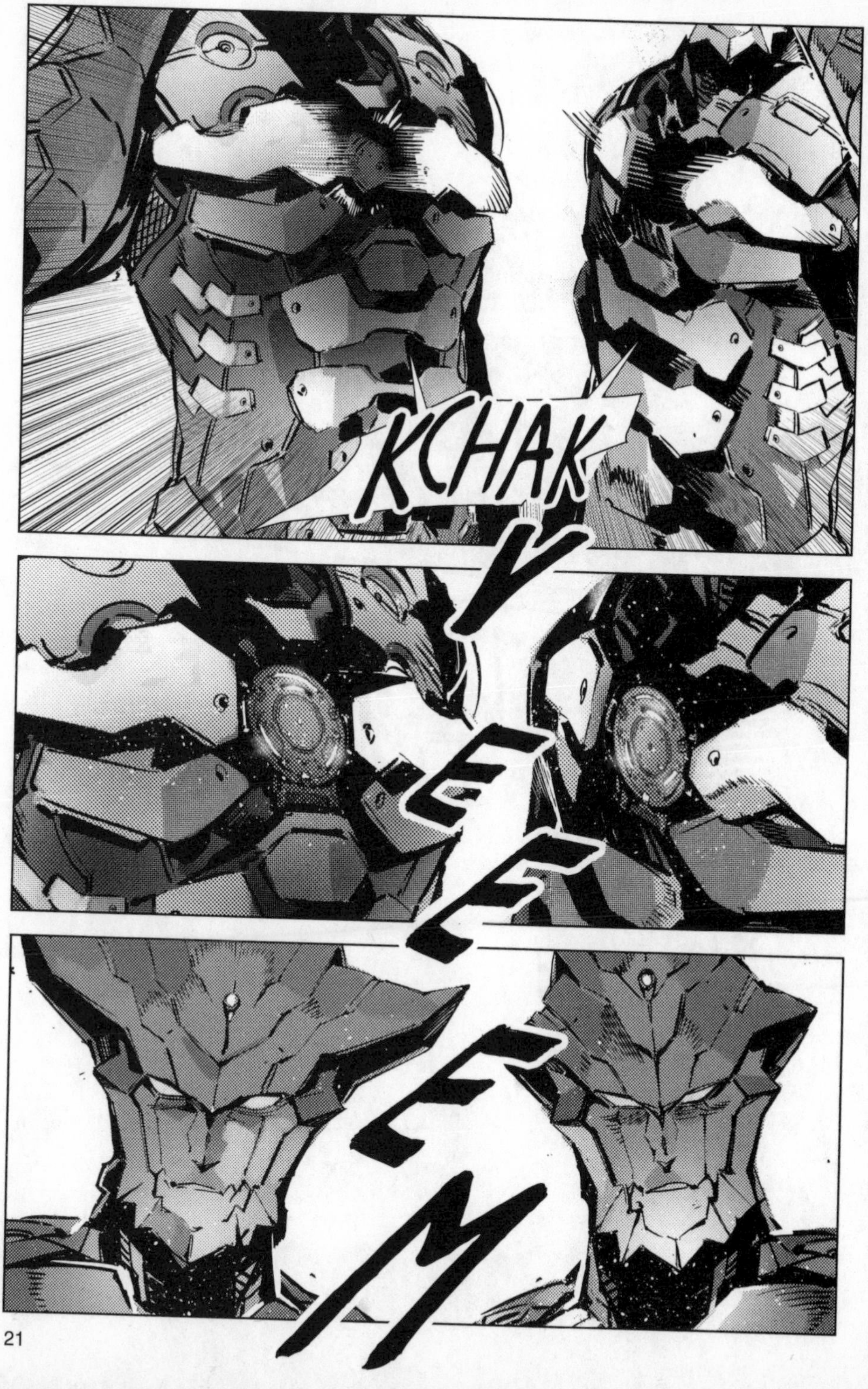
KCHAK
VEEEEM

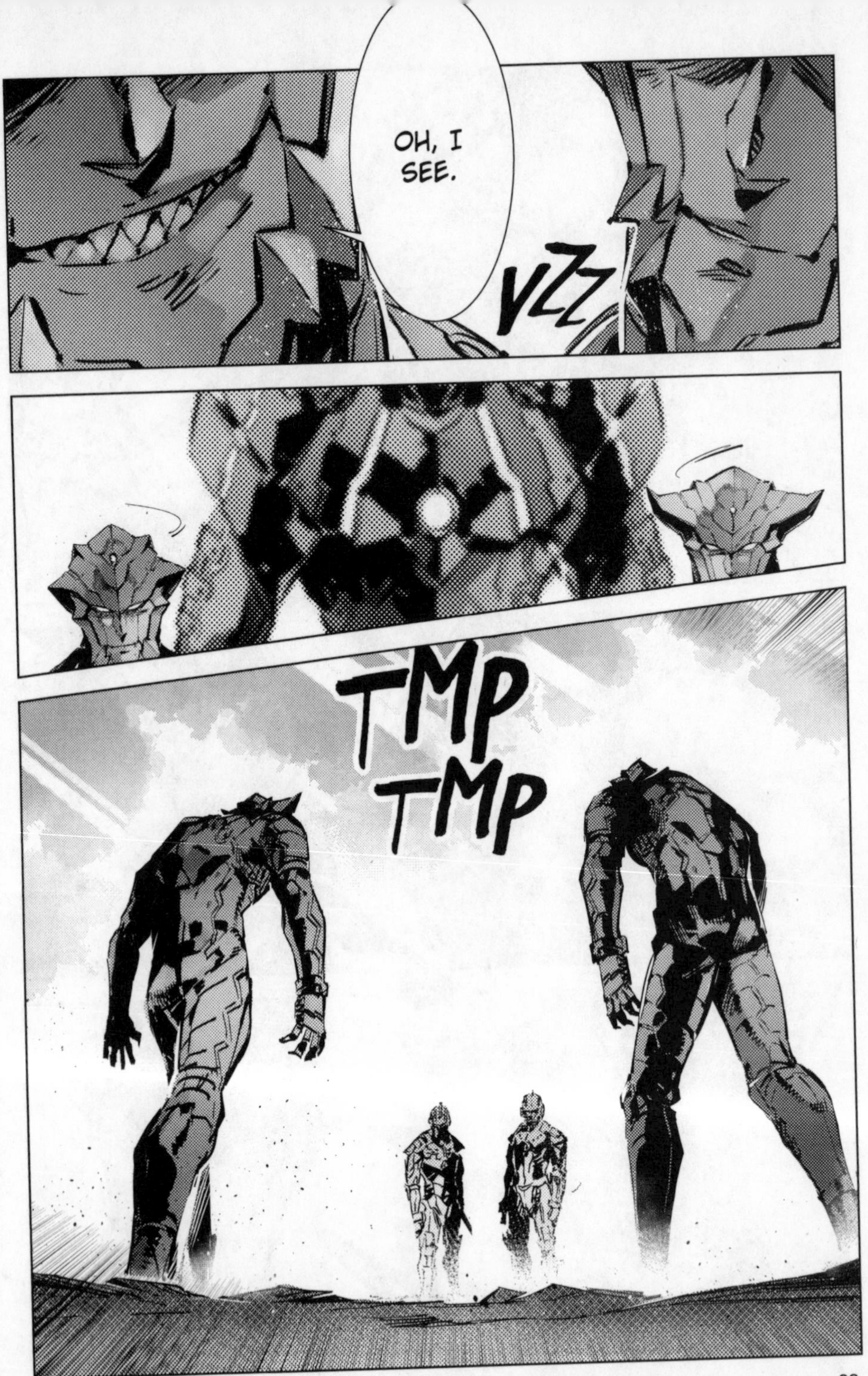

OH, I SEE.
VZZ
TMP TMP

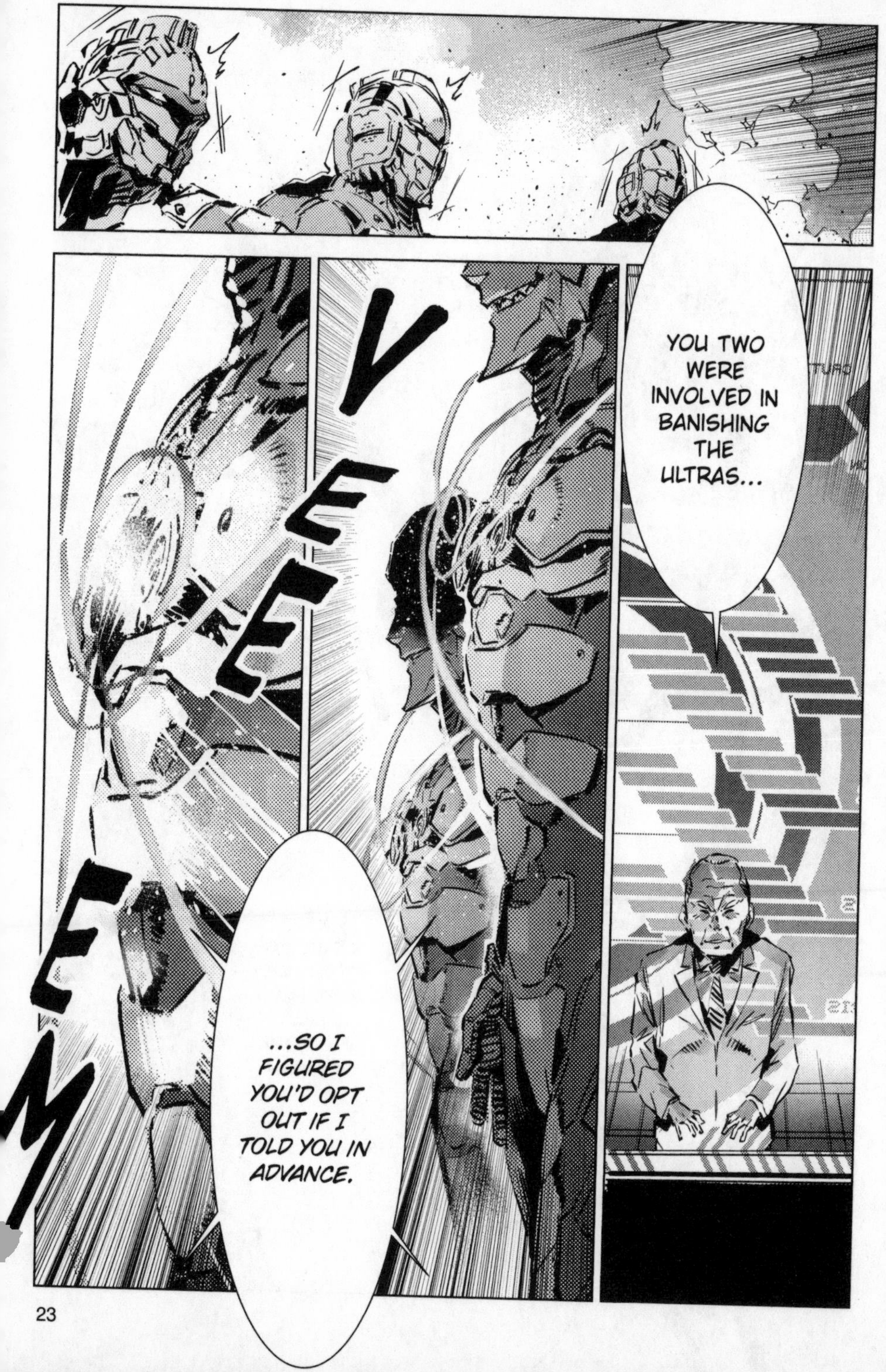
YOU TWO WERE INVOLVED IN BANISHING THE ULTRAS...
VEEEEM
...SO I FIGURED YOU'D OPT OUT IF I TOLD YOU IN ADVANCE.

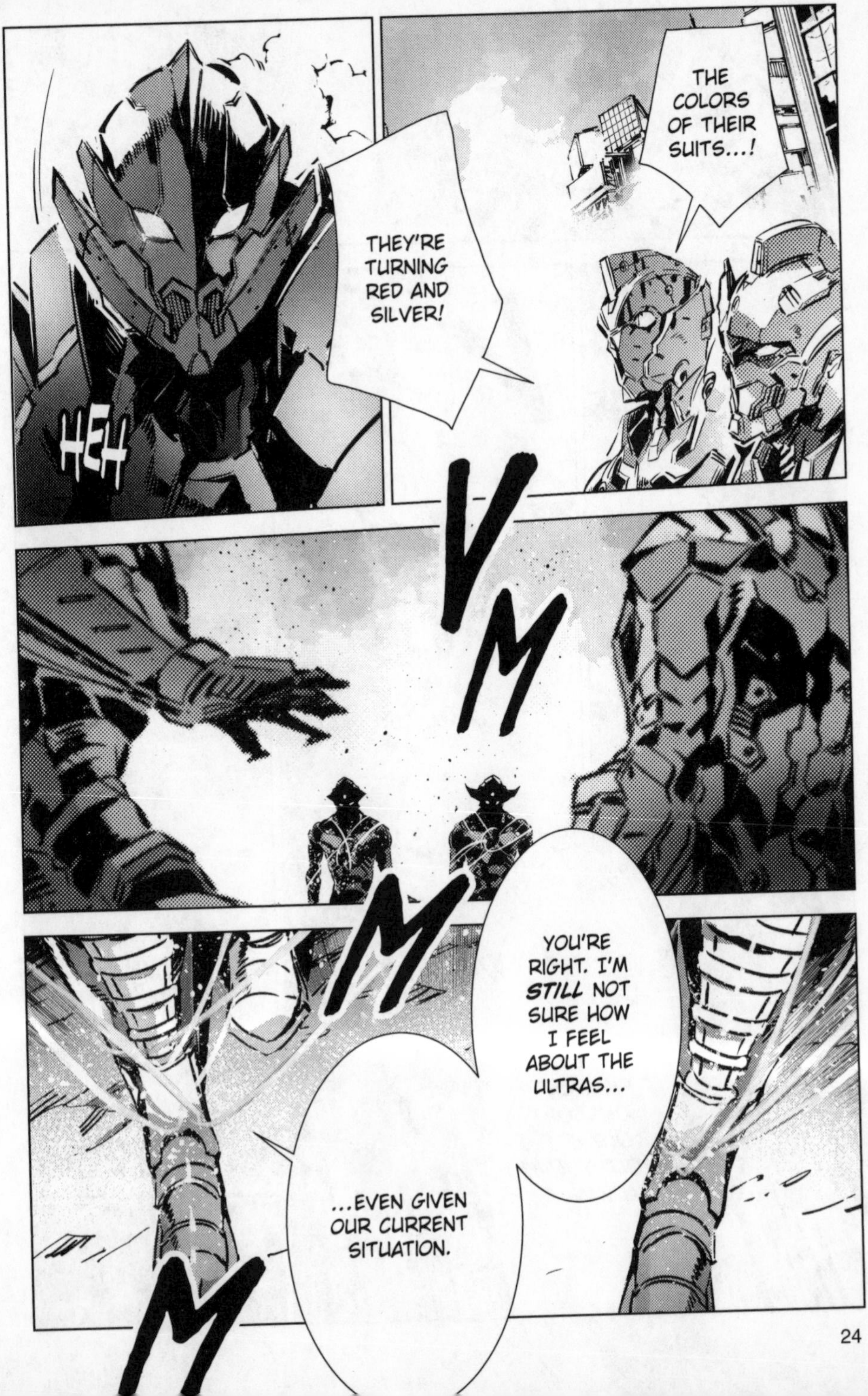
THE COLORS OF THEIR SUITS...!
THEY'RE TURNING RED AND SILVER!
HEH
VMMM
YOU'RE RIGHT. I'M *STILL* NOT SURE HOW I FEEL ABOUT THE ULTRAS...
...EVEN GIVEN OUR CURRENT SITUATION.

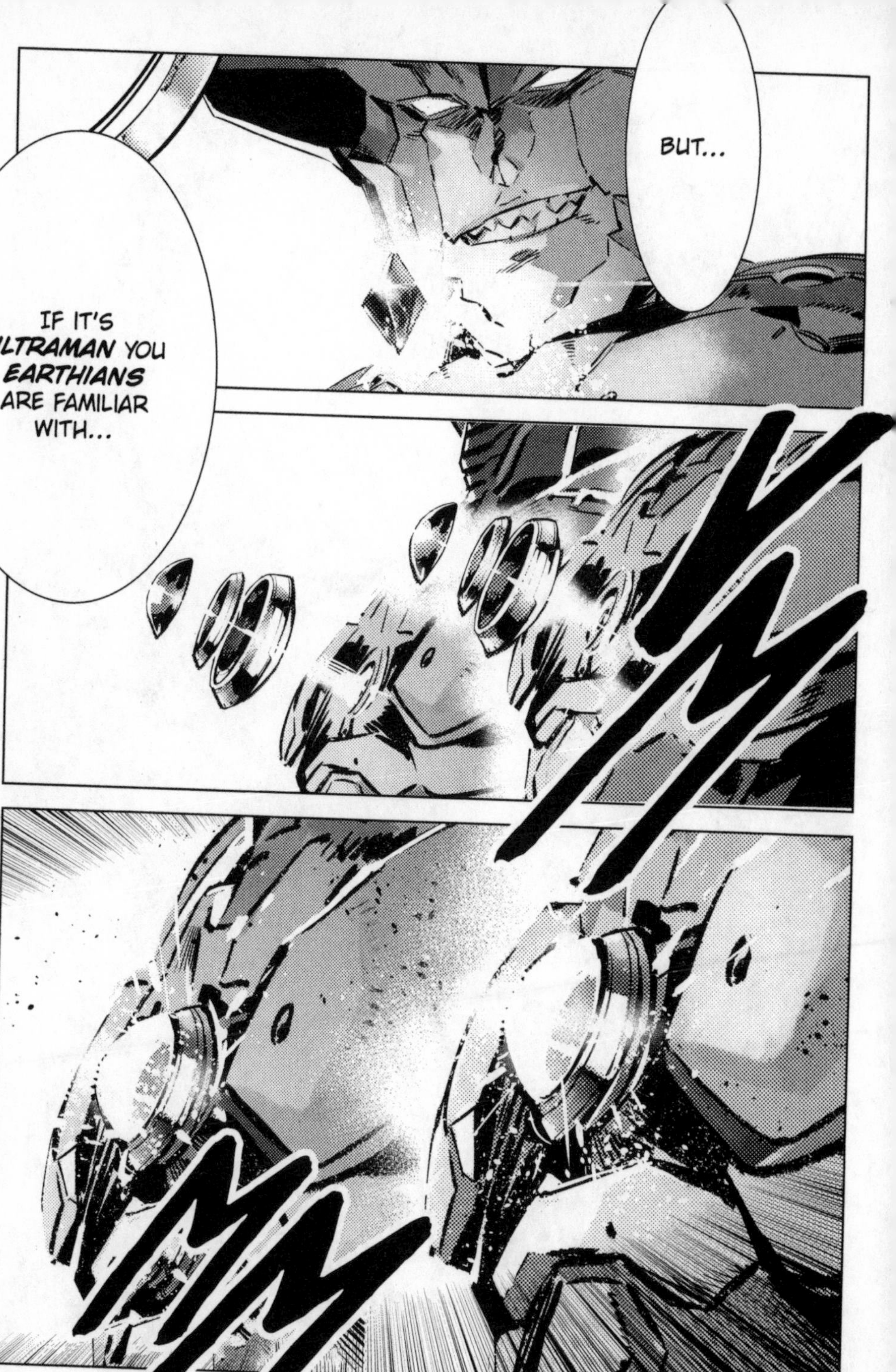
BUT...
IF IT'S ULTRAMAN YOU EARTHIANS ARE FAMILIAR WITH...

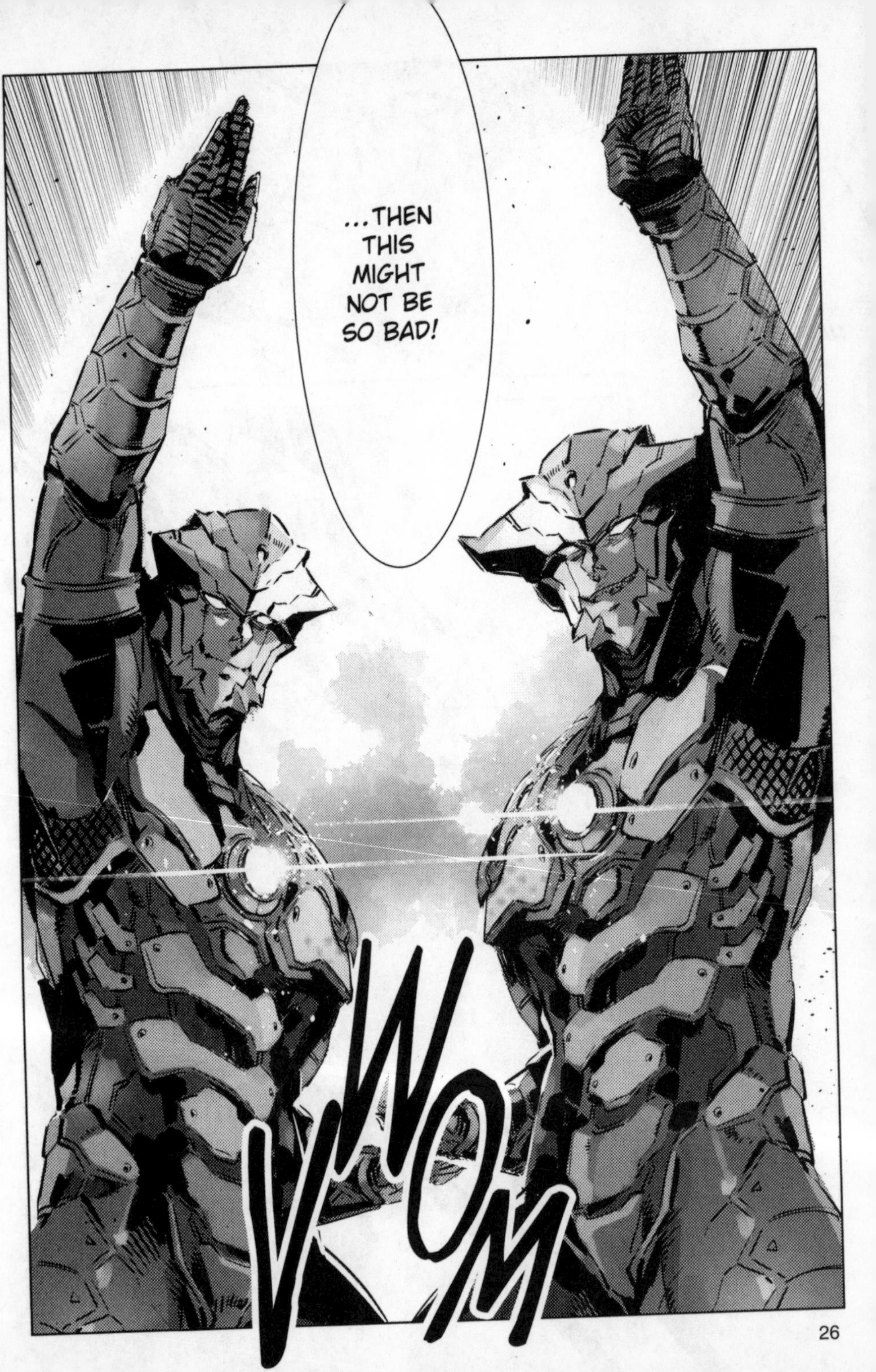
...THEN THIS MIGHT NOT BE SO BAD!
VWOM

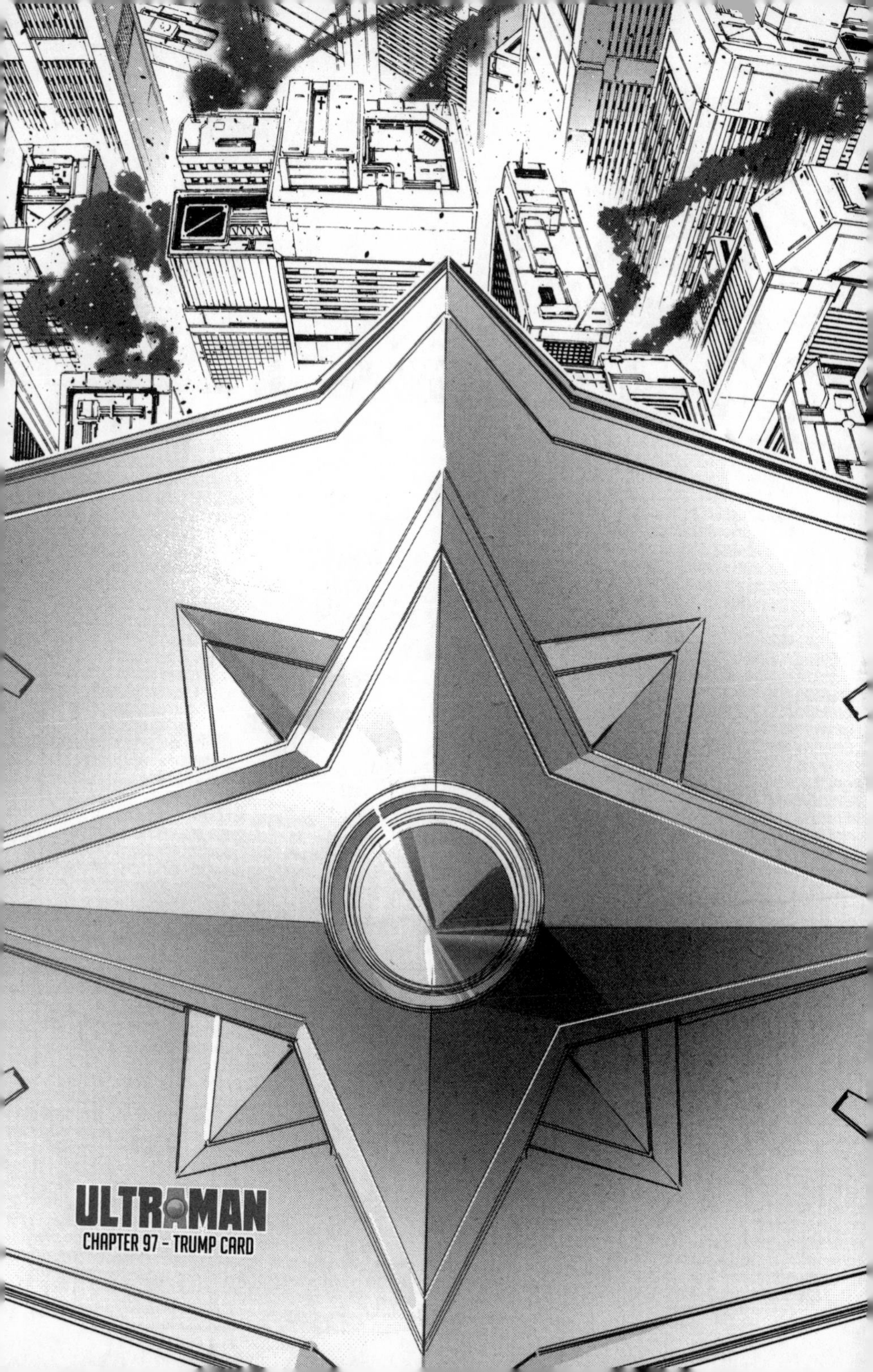
ULTRAMAN
CHAPTER 97 - TRUMP CARD

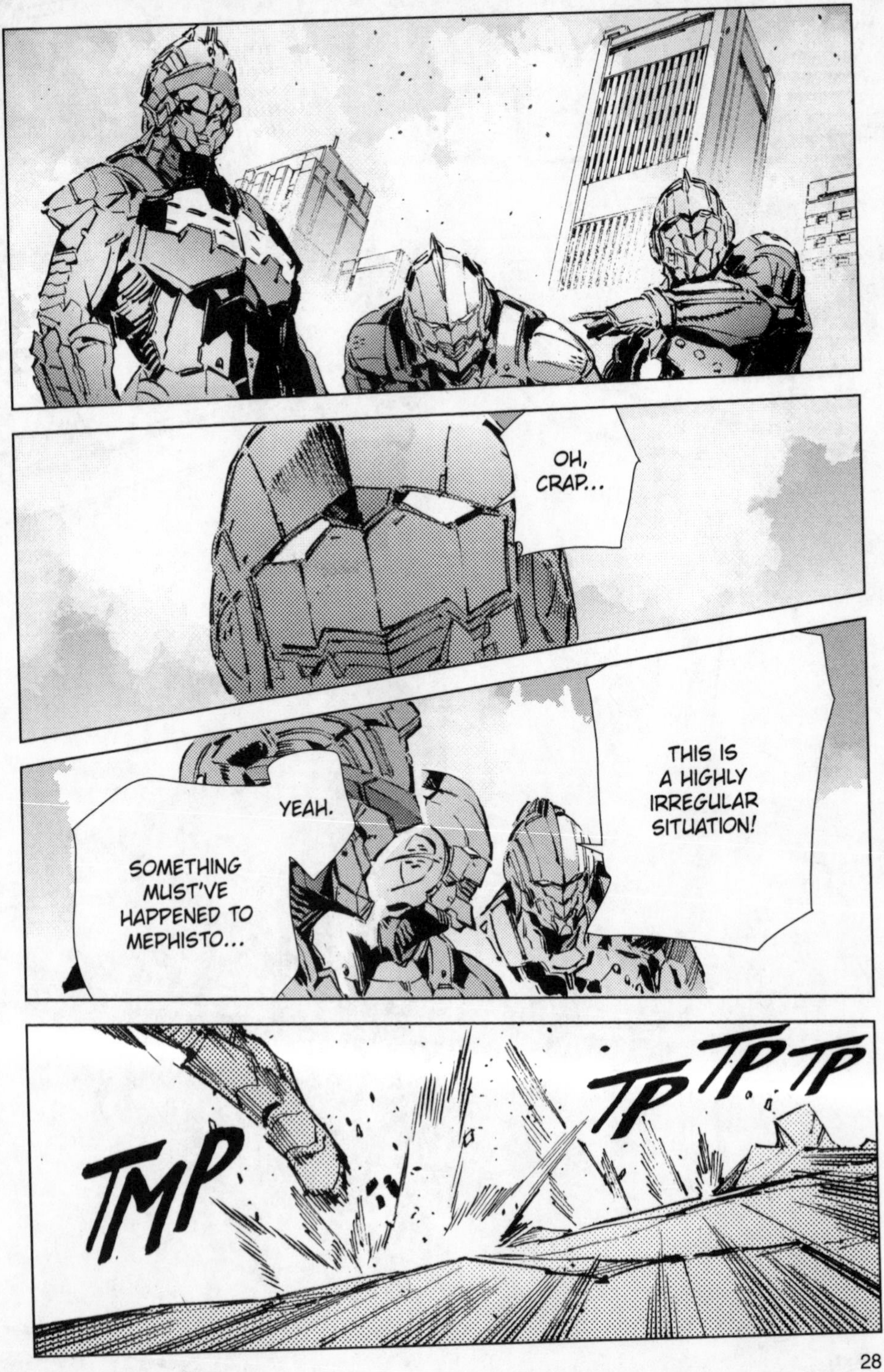
OH, CRAP...
THIS IS A HIGHLY IRREGULAR SITUATION!
YEAH.
SOMETHING MUST'VE HAPPENED TO MEPHISTO...
TP TP TP
TMP

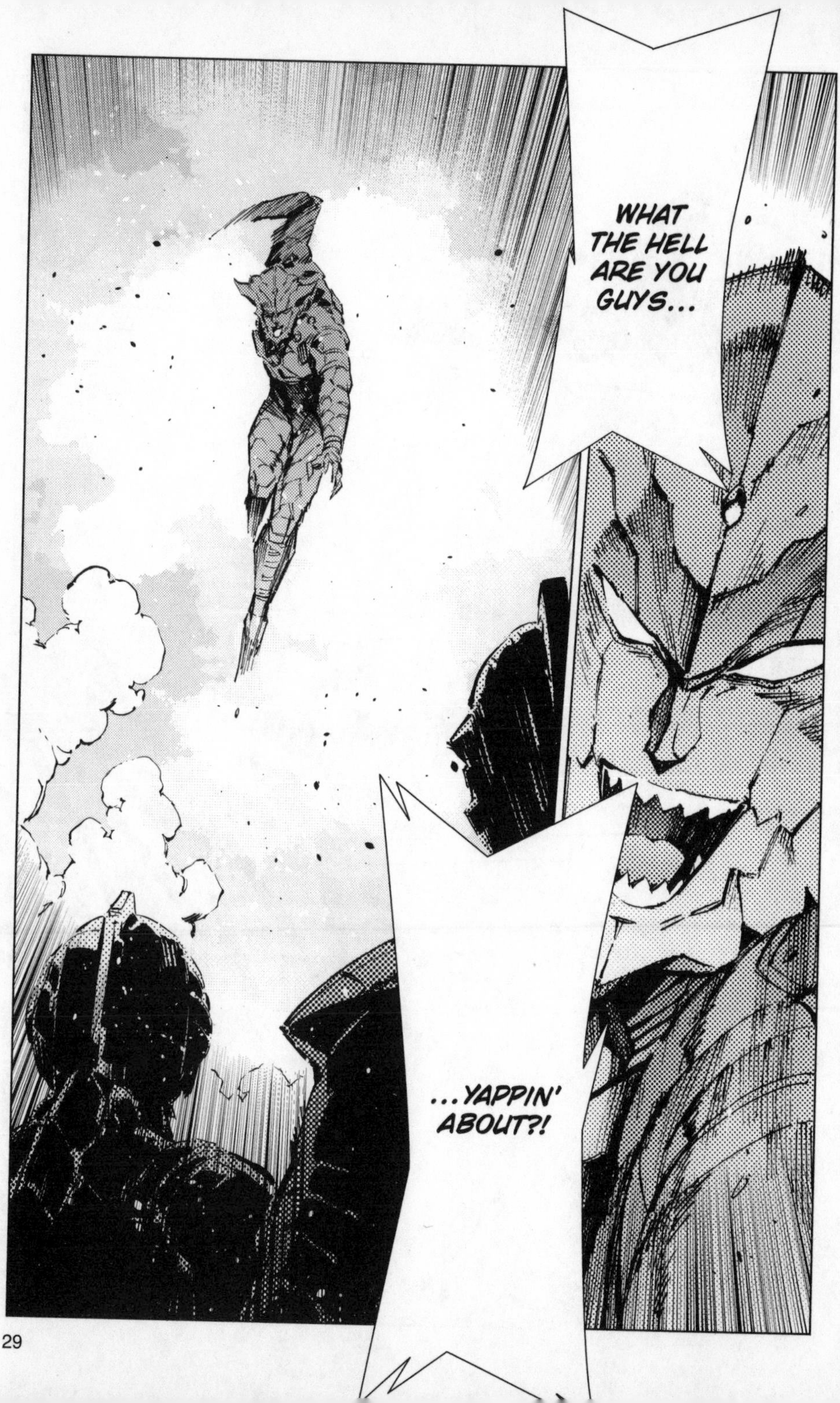
WHAT THE HELL ARE YOU GUYS...
...YAPPIN' ABOUT?!

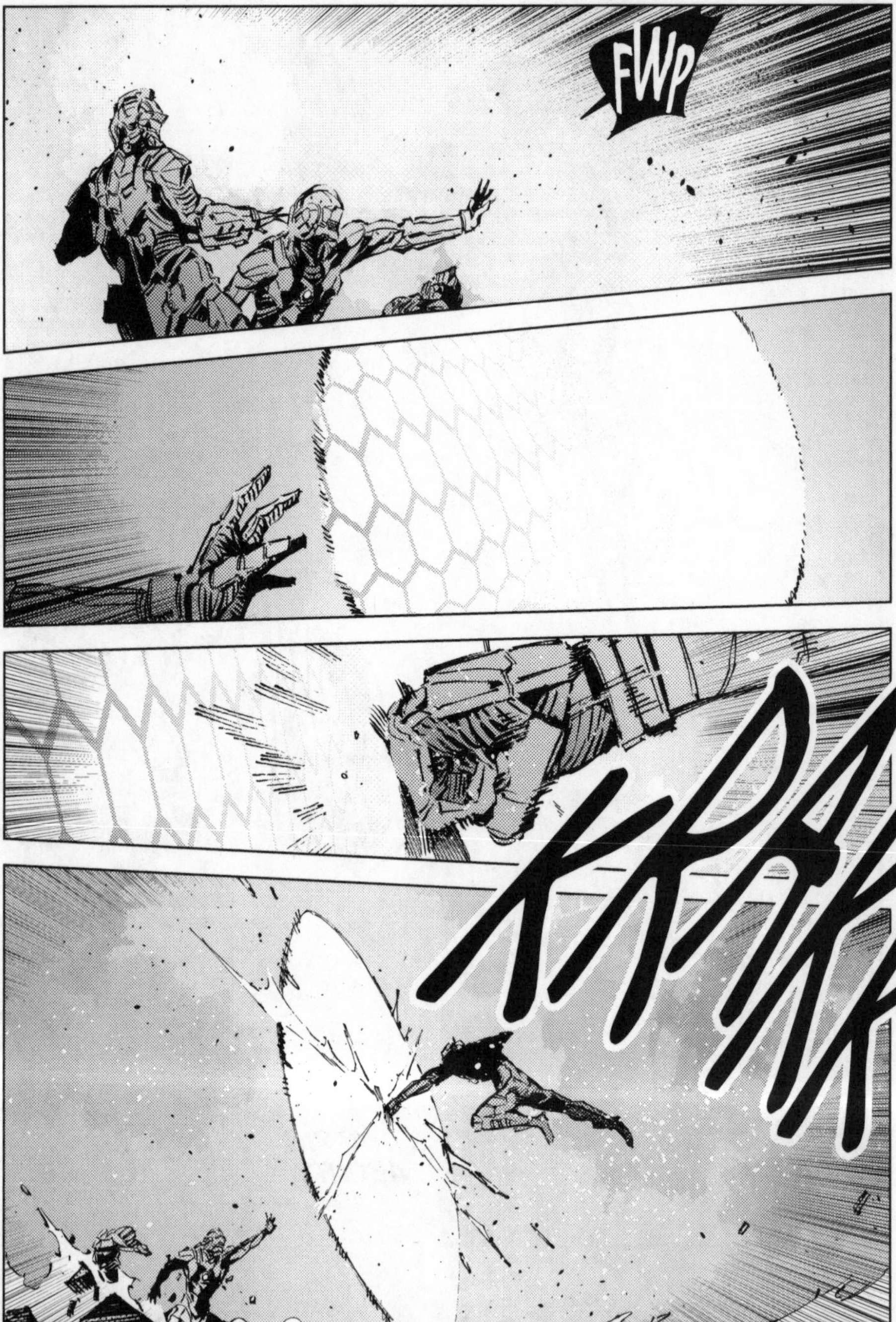
FWP
KRAKK

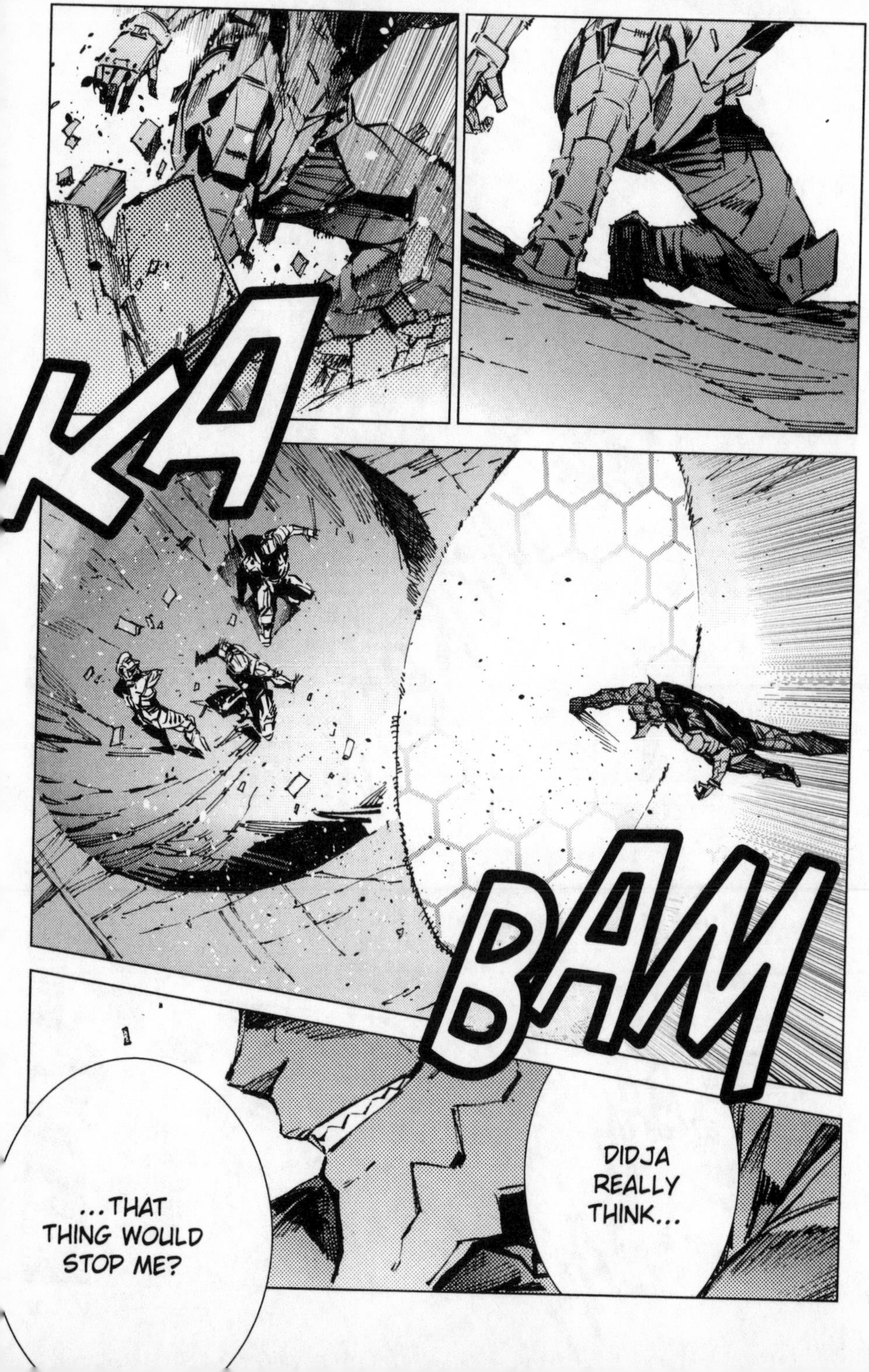
KA
BAM
DIDJA REALLY THINK...
...THAT THING WOULD STOP ME?

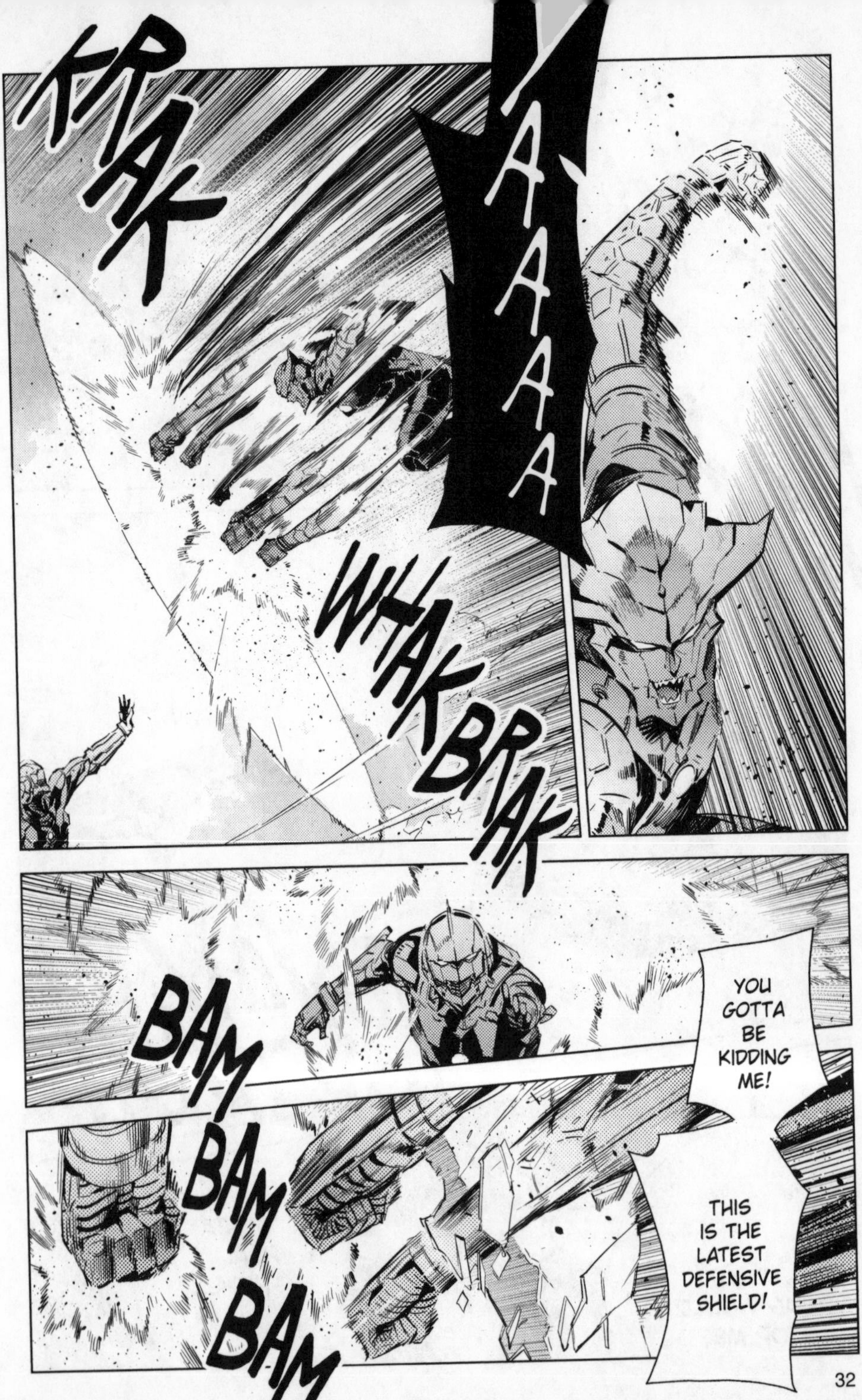
YAAAAAAA
KRAK
WHAKBRAK
YOU GOTTA BE KIDDING ME!
BAM BAM BAM BAM
THIS IS THE LATEST DEFENSIVE SHIELD!

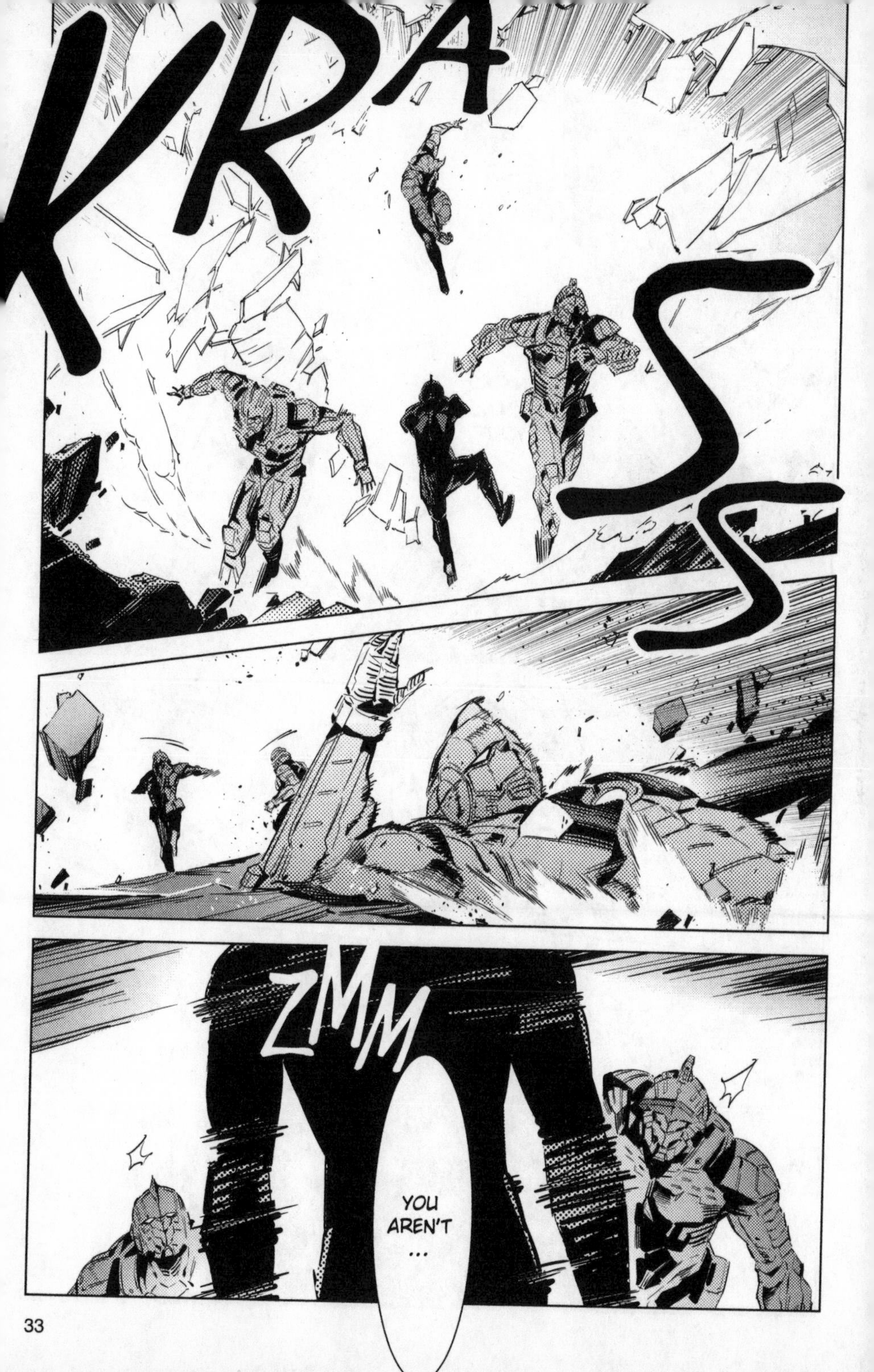
KRA
SS
ZMM
YOU AREN'T ...

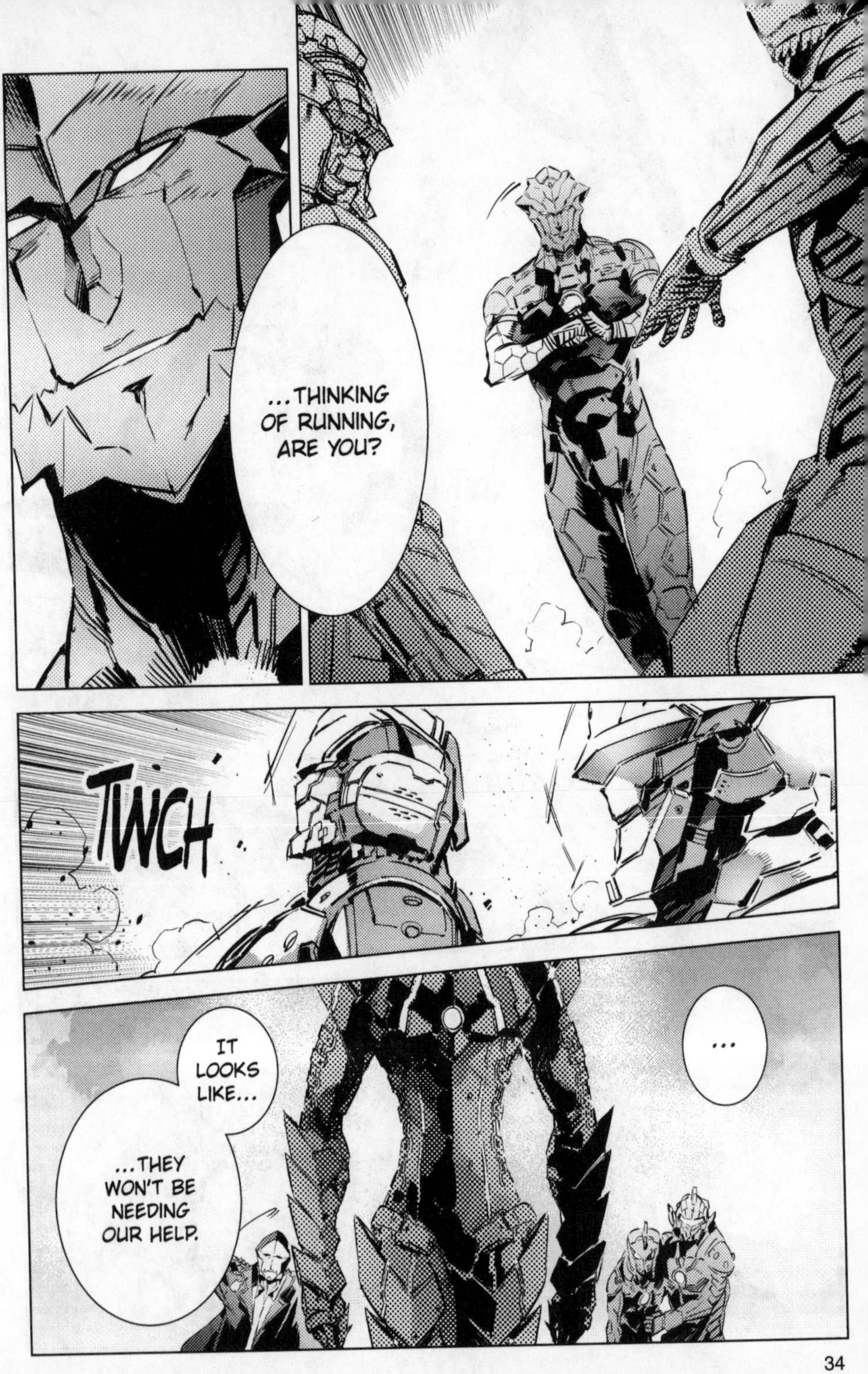
...THINKING OF RUNNING, ARE YOU?
TWCH
...
IT LOOKS LIKE...
...THEY WON'T BE NEEDING OUR HELP.

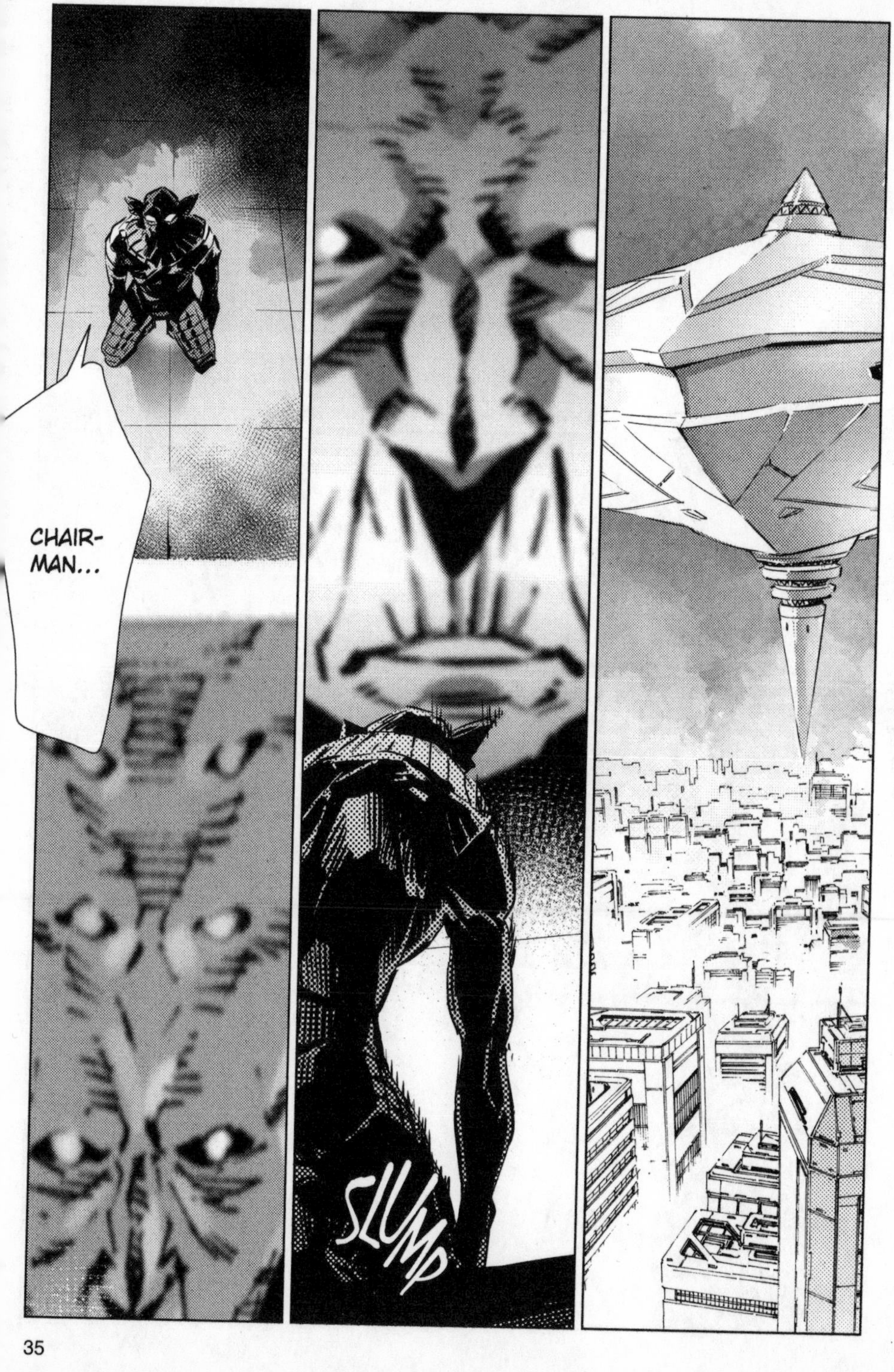
SLUMP
CHAIR-MAN...

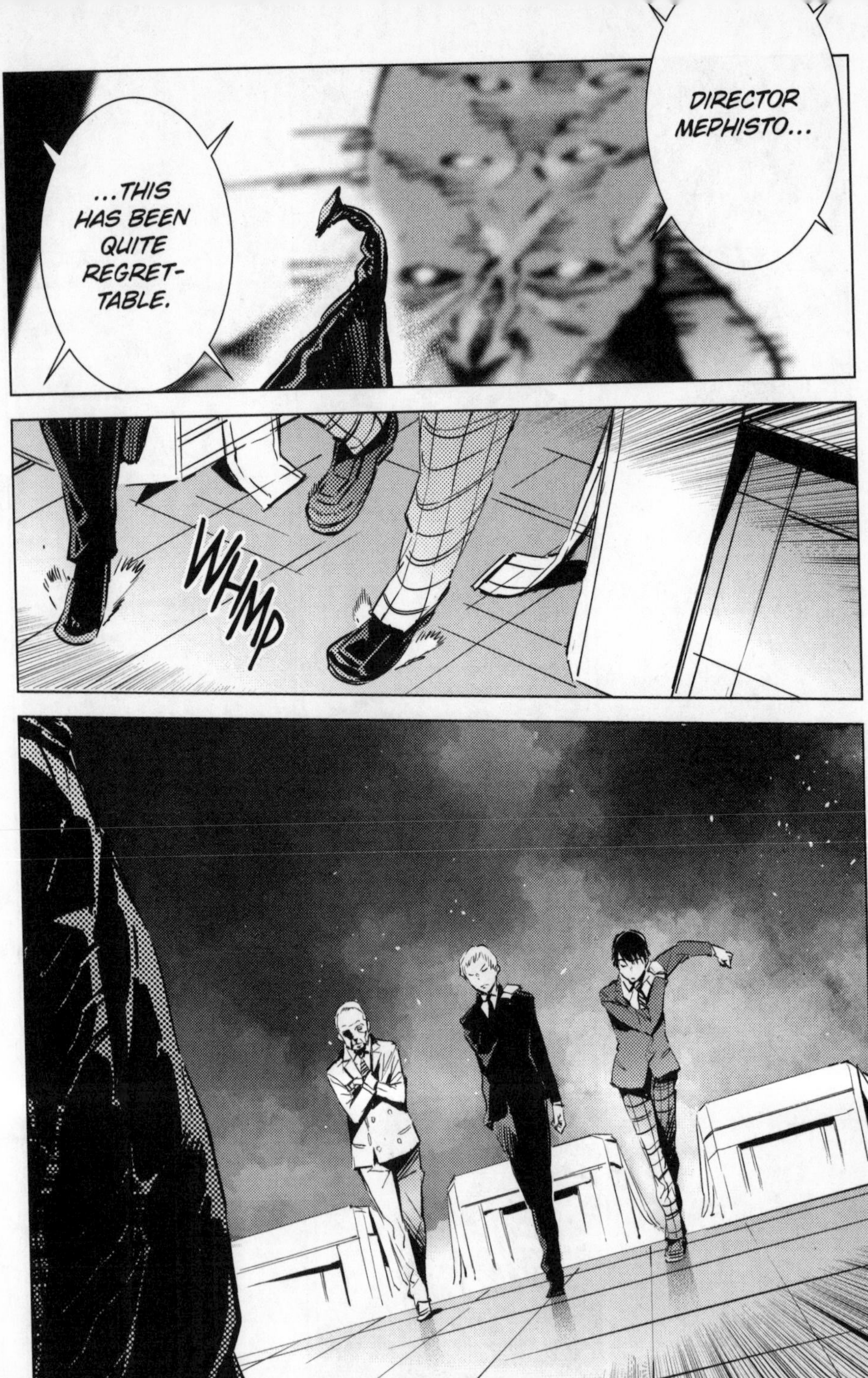
DIRECTOR MEPHISTO...
...THIS HAS BEEN QUITE REGRET-TABLE.
WHMP

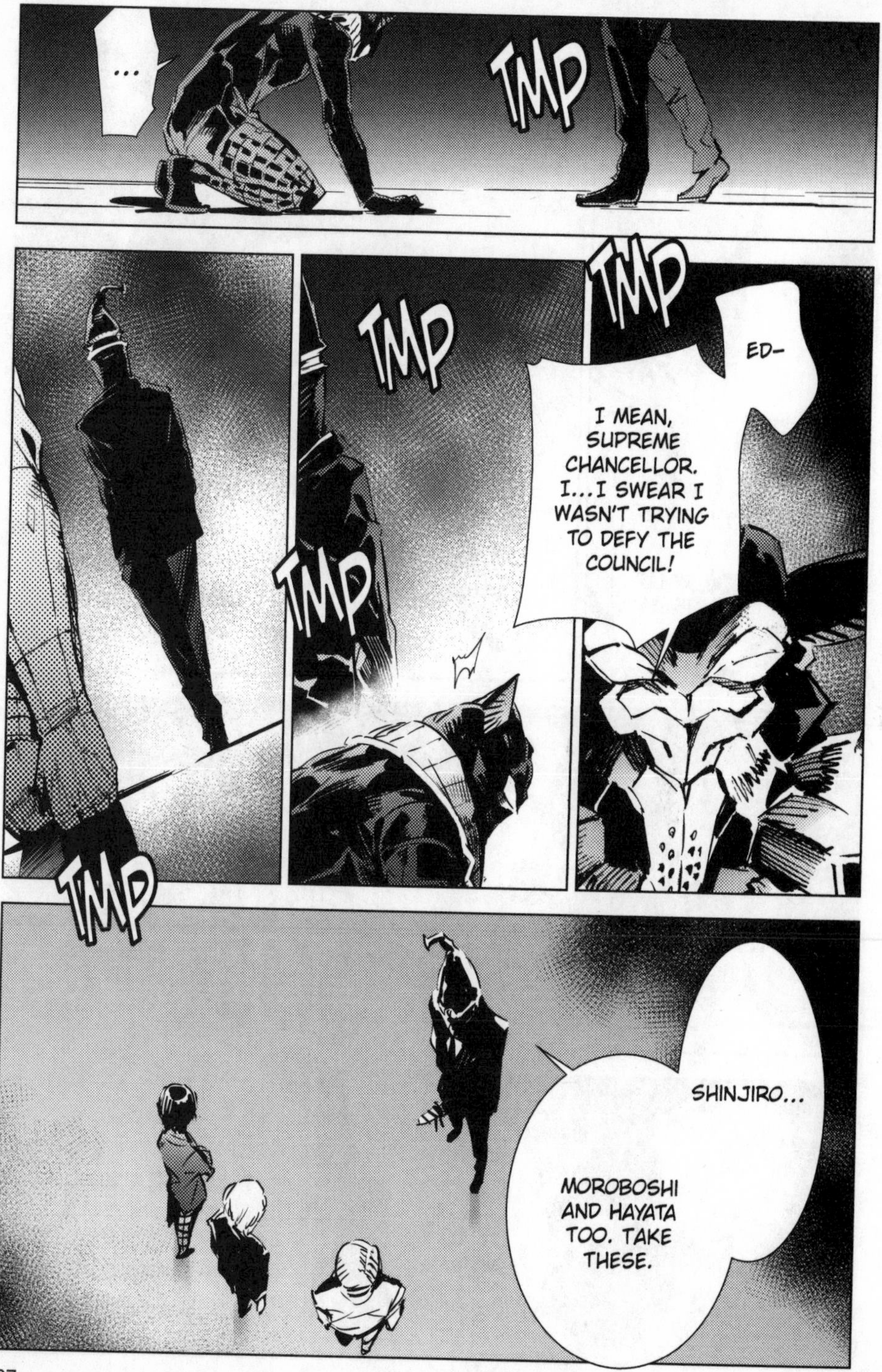
TMP
...
TMP
ED—
I MEAN, SUPREME CHANCELLOR. I...I SWEAR I WASN'T TRYING TO DEFY THE COUNCIL!
TMP
TMP
TMP
SHINJIRO...
MOROBOSHI AND HAYATA TOO. TAKE THESE.

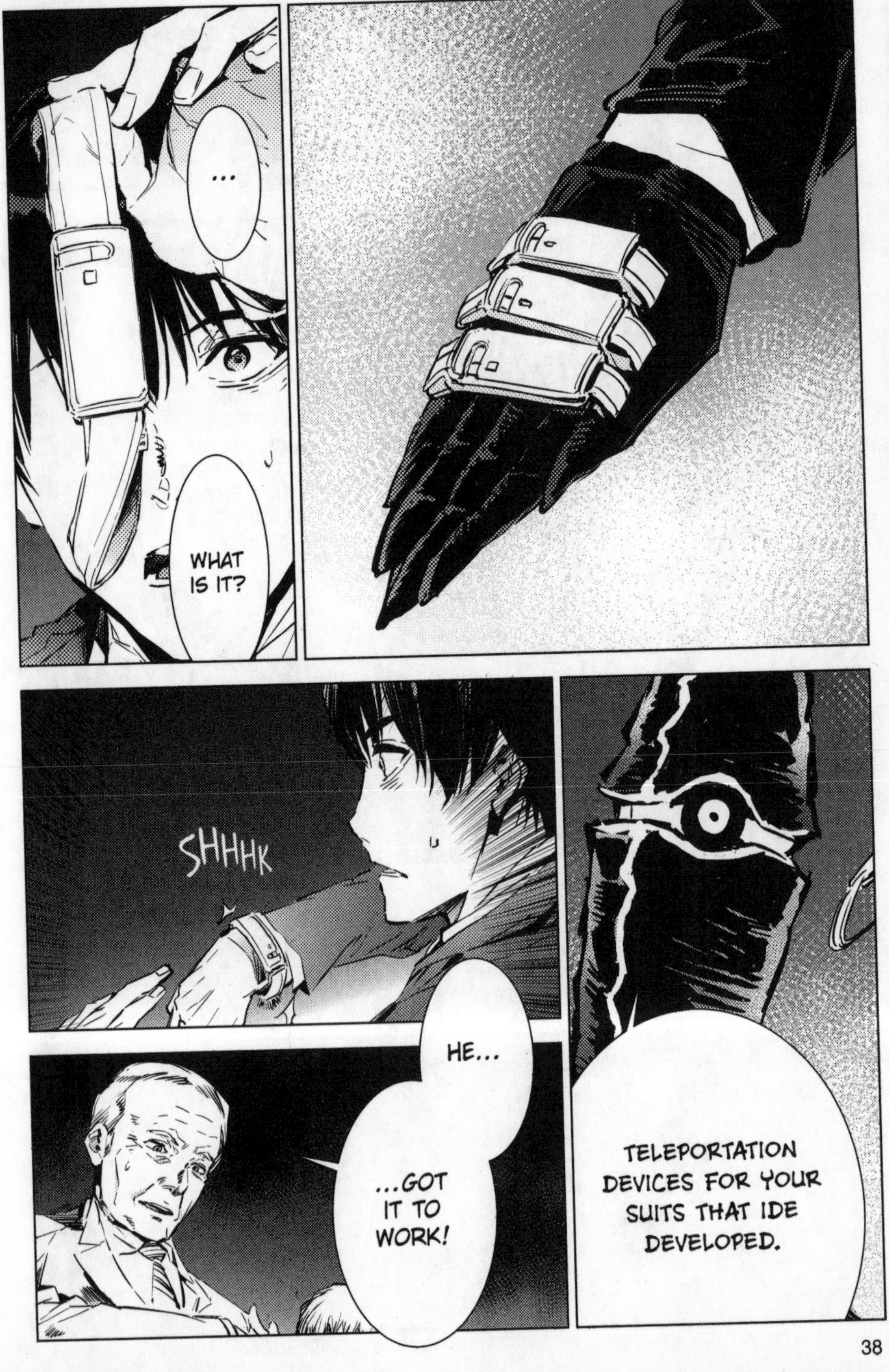
...
WHAT IS IT?
TELEPORTATION DEVICES FOR YOUR SUITS THAT IDE DEVELOPED.
SHHHK
HE...
...GOT IT TO WORK!

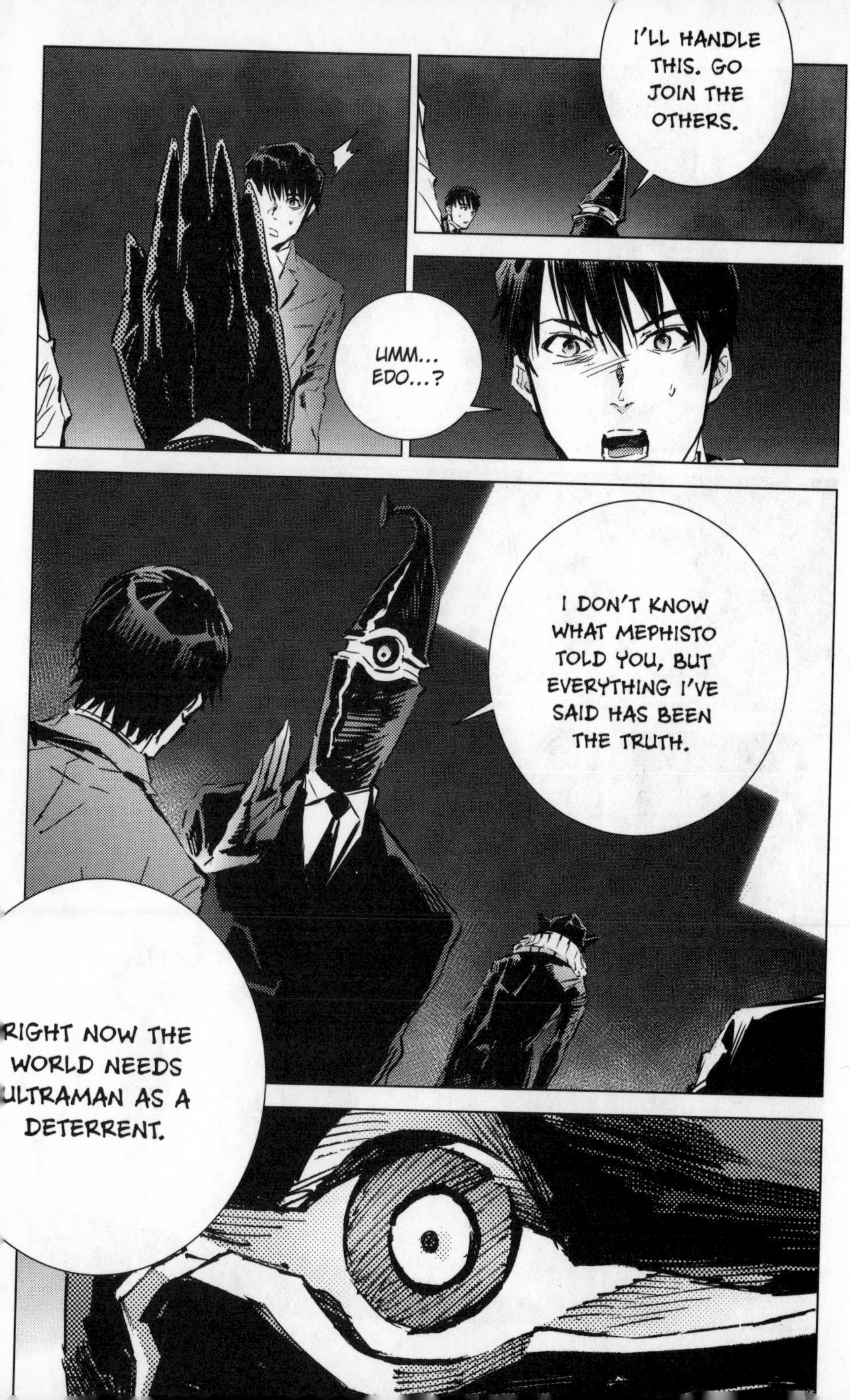
I'LL HANDLE THIS. GO JOIN THE OTHERS.
UMM... EDO...?
I DON'T KNOW WHAT MEPHISTO TOLD YOU, BUT EVERYTHING I'VE SAID HAS BEEN THE TRUTH.
RIGHT NOW THE WORLD NEEDS ULTRAMAN AS A DETERRENT.

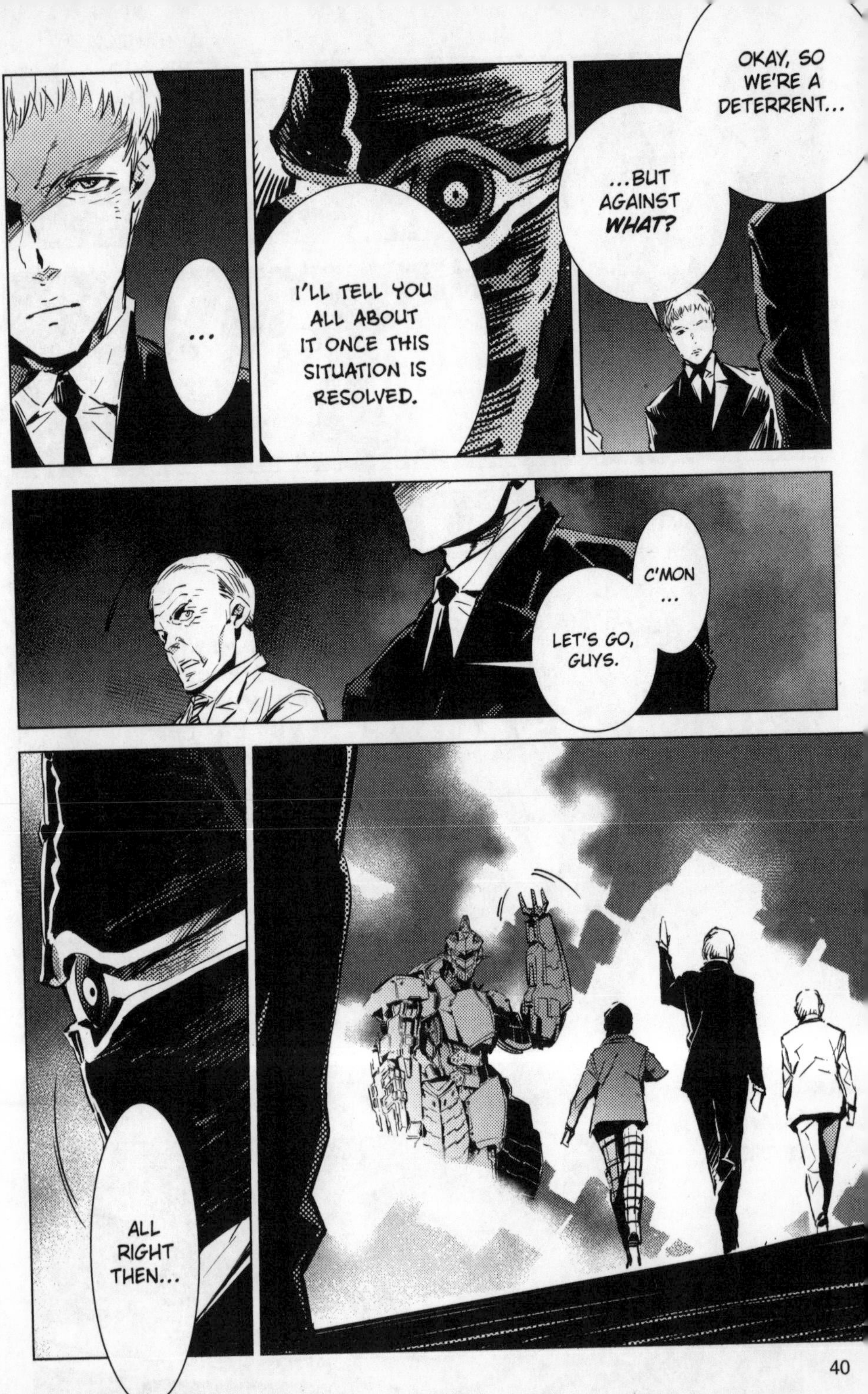
OKAY, SO WE'RE A DETERRENT...
...BUT AGAINST *WHAT?*
I'LL TELL YOU ALL ABOUT IT ONCE THIS SITUATION IS RESOLVED.
...
C'MON ...
LET'S GO, GUYS.
ALL RIGHT THEN...

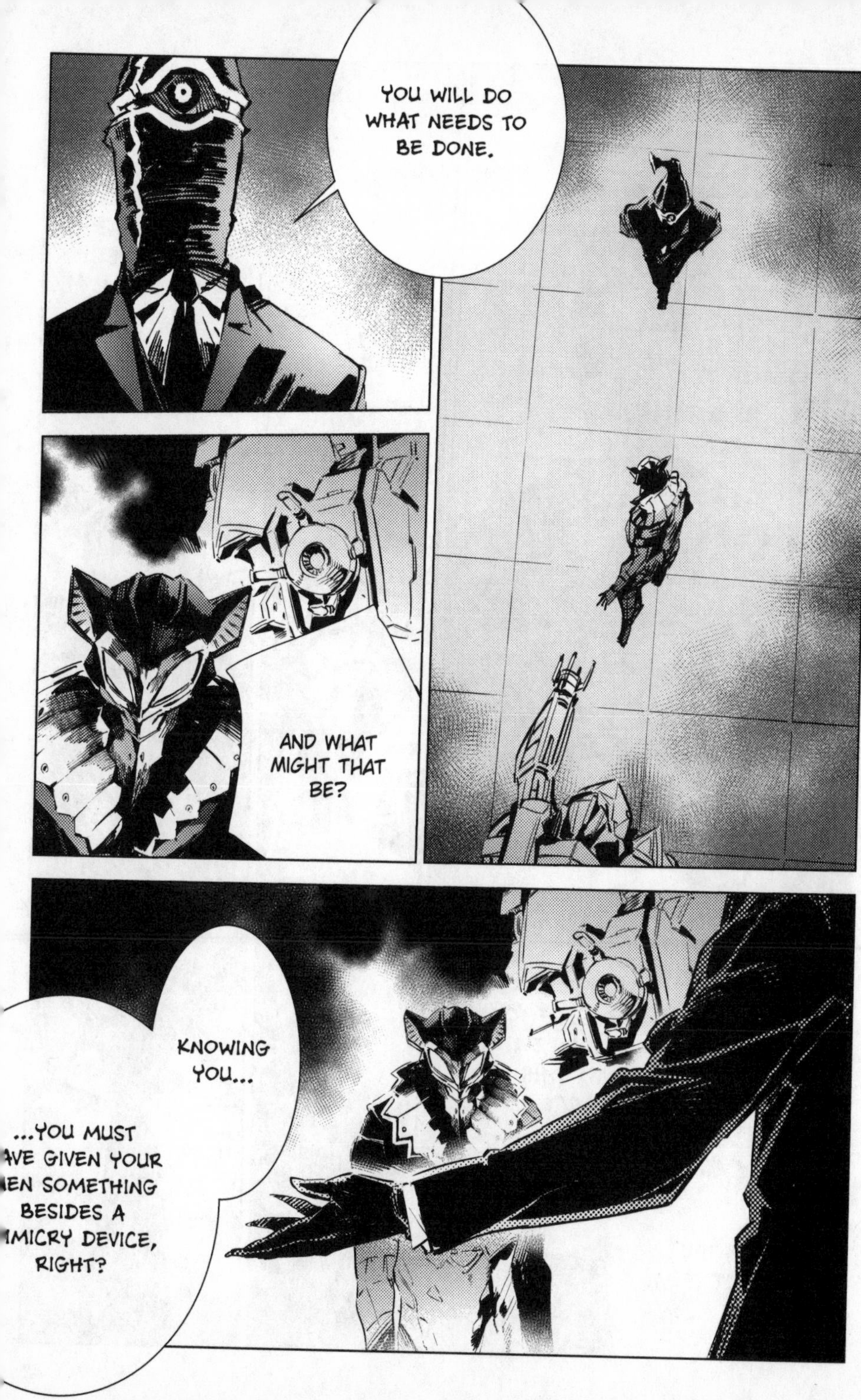
YOU WILL DO WHAT NEEDS TO BE DONE.
AND WHAT MIGHT THAT BE?
KNOWING YOU...
...YOU MUST AVE GIVEN YOUR EN SOMETHING BESIDES A IMICRY DEVICE, RIGHT?

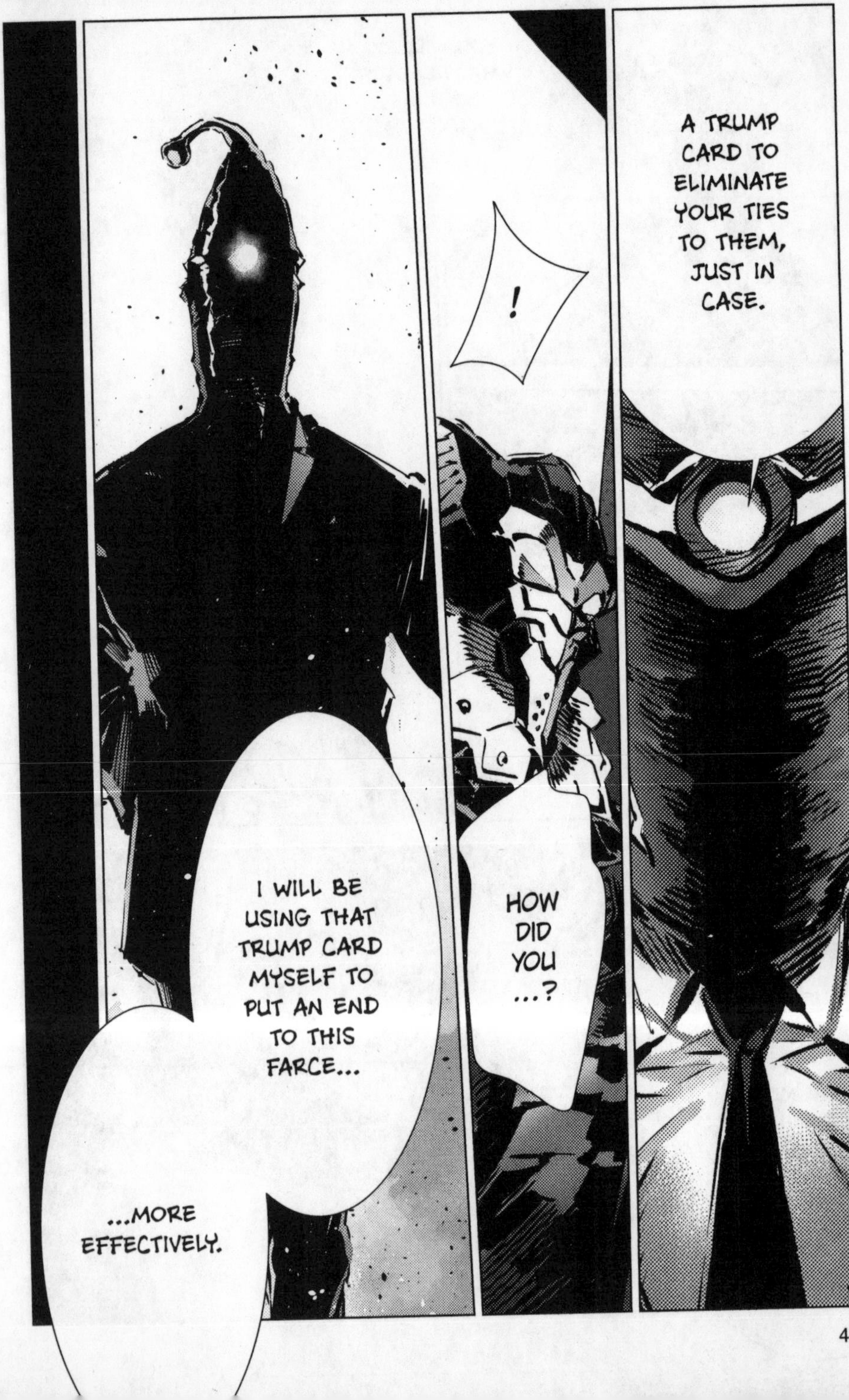
A TRUMP CARD TO ELIMINATE YOUR TIES TO THEM, JUST IN CASE.
!
HOW DID YOU ...?
I WILL BE USING THAT TRUMP CARD MYSELF TO PUT AN END TO THIS FARCE...
...MORE EFFECTIVELY.

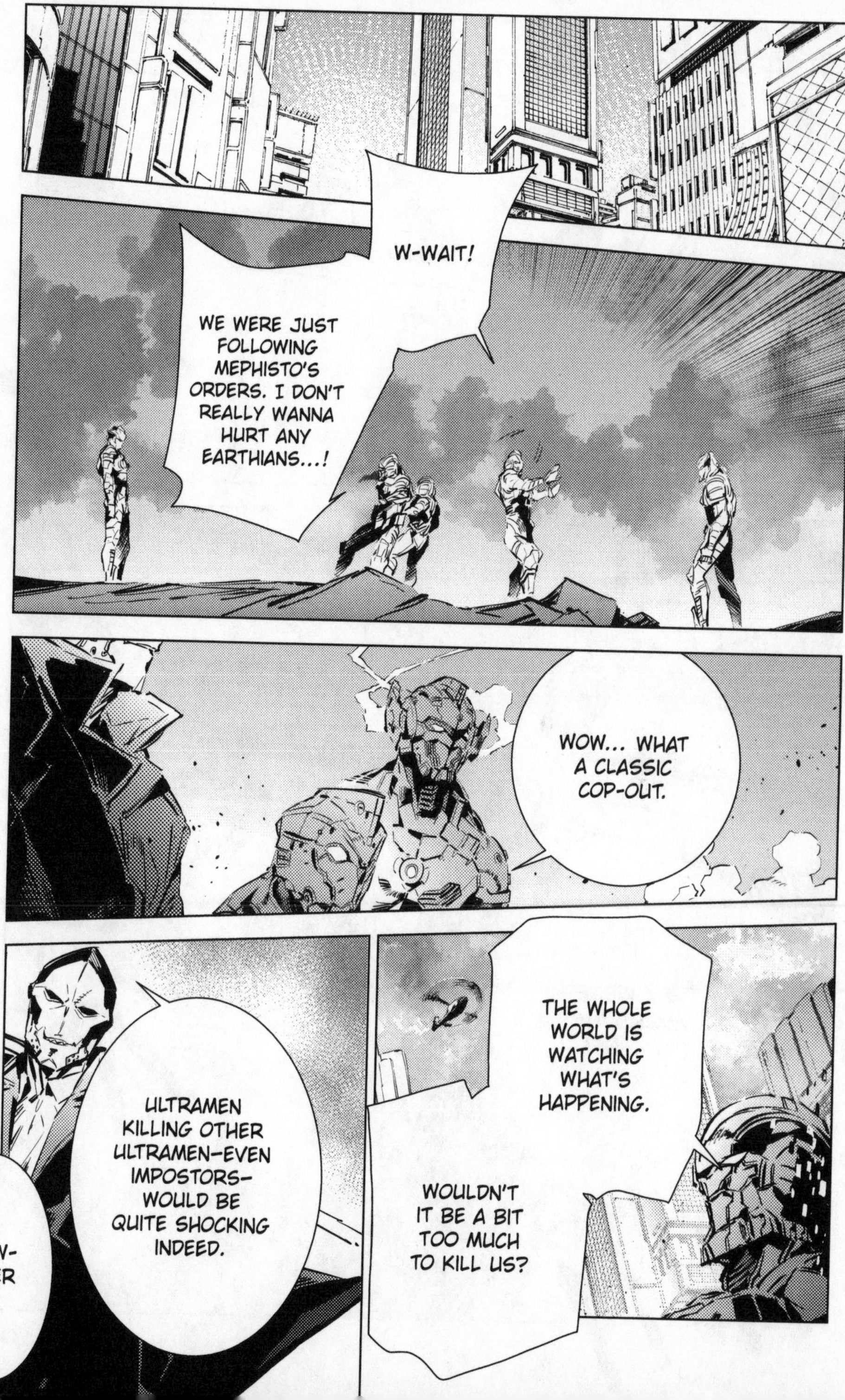
W-WAIT!
WE WERE JUST FOLLOWING MEPHISTO'S ORDERS. I DON'T REALLY WANNA HURT ANY EARTHIANS...!
WOW... WHAT A CLASSIC COP-OUT.
THE WHOLE WORLD IS WATCHING WHAT'S HAPPENING.
WOULDN'T IT BE A BIT TOO MUCH TO KILL US?
ULTRAMEN KILLING OTHER ULTRAMEN—EVEN IMPOSTORS—WOULD BE QUITE SHOCKING INDEED.
OW- VER ...

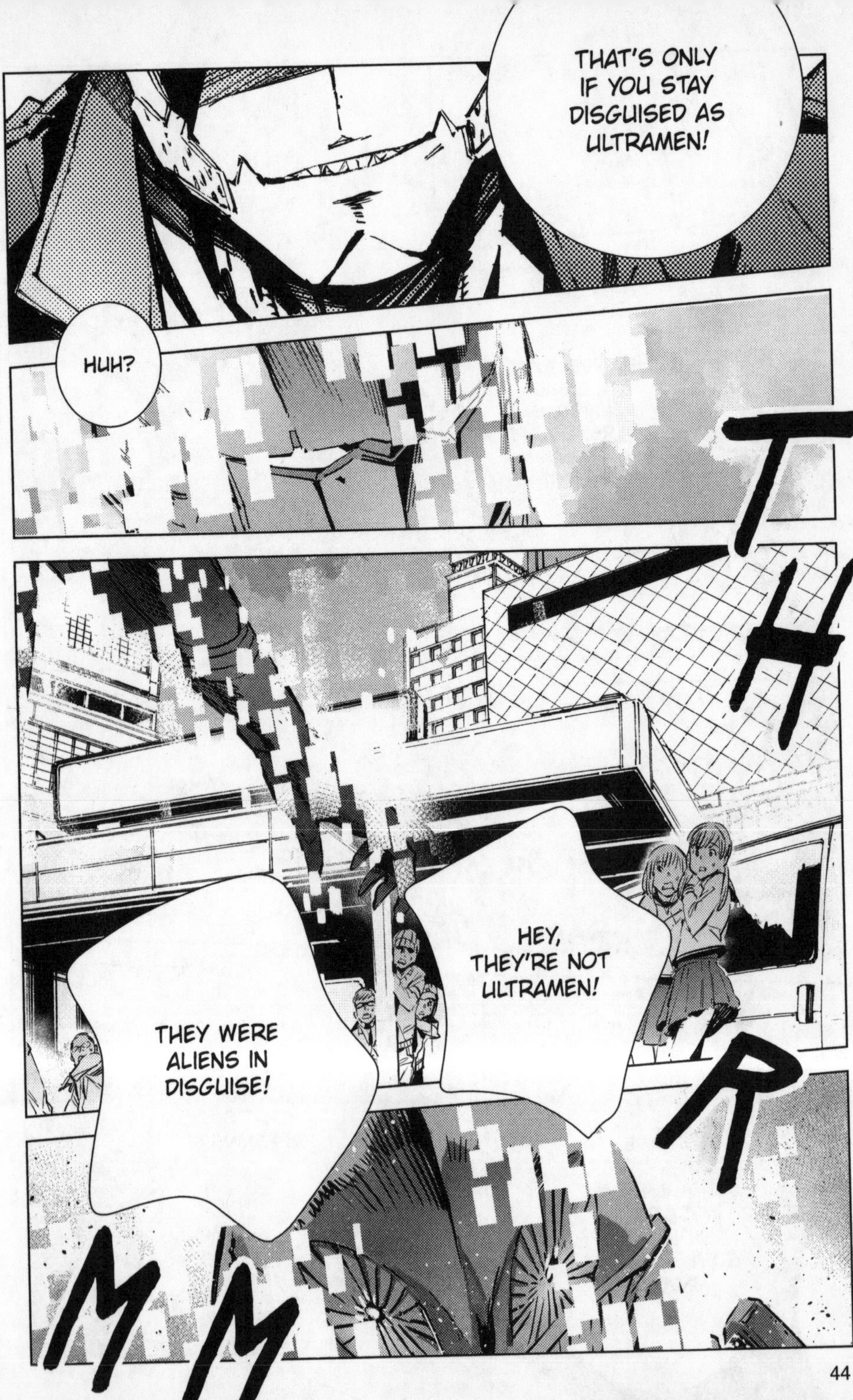
THAT'S ONLY IF YOU STAY DISGUISED AS ULTRAMEN!
HUH?
THRMM
HEY, THEY'RE NOT ULTRAMEN!
THEY WERE ALIENS IN DISGUISE!

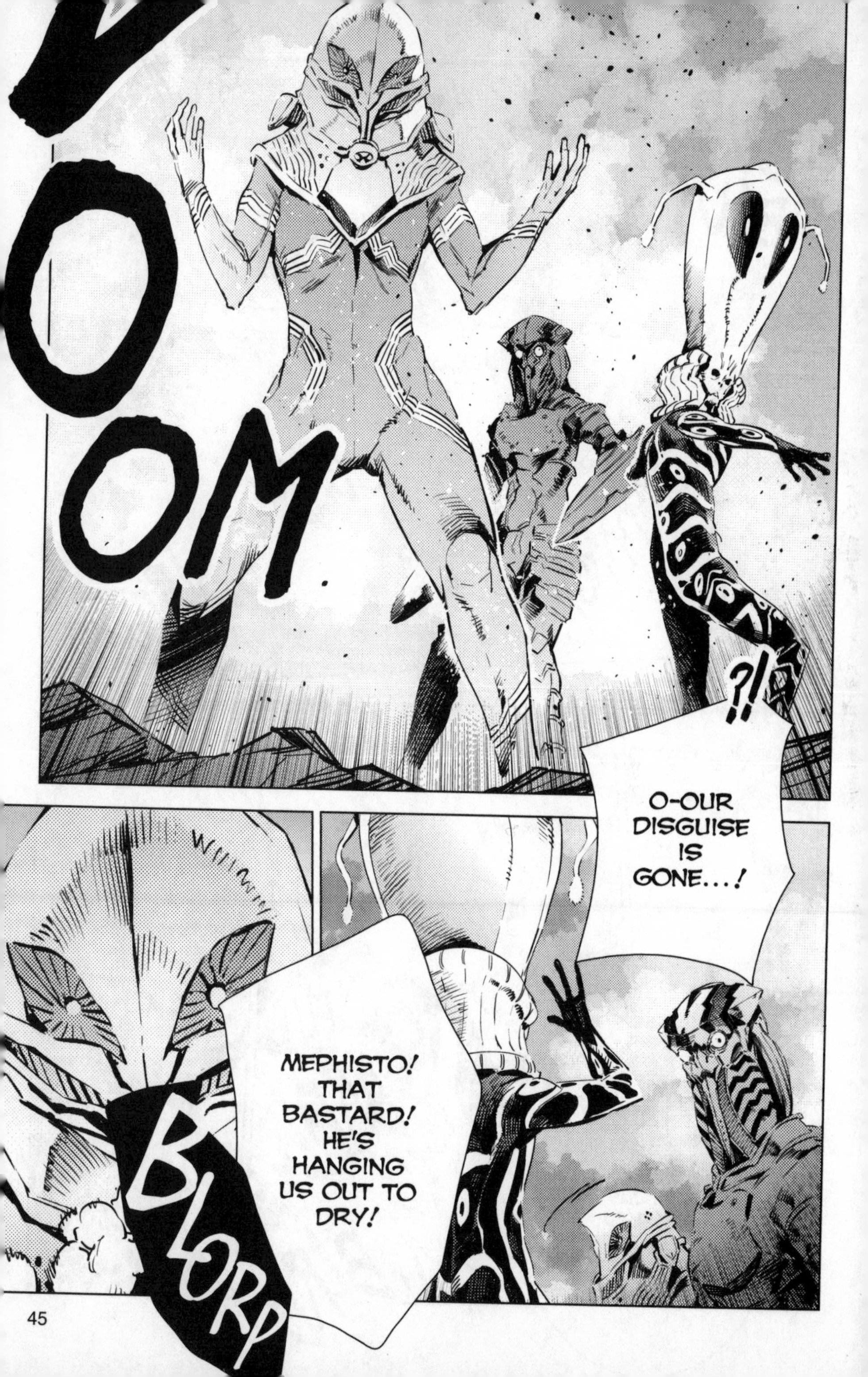
VOOM
?!
O-OUR DISGUISE IS GONE...!
MEPHISTO! THAT BASTARD! HE'S HANGING US OUT TO DRY!
BLORP

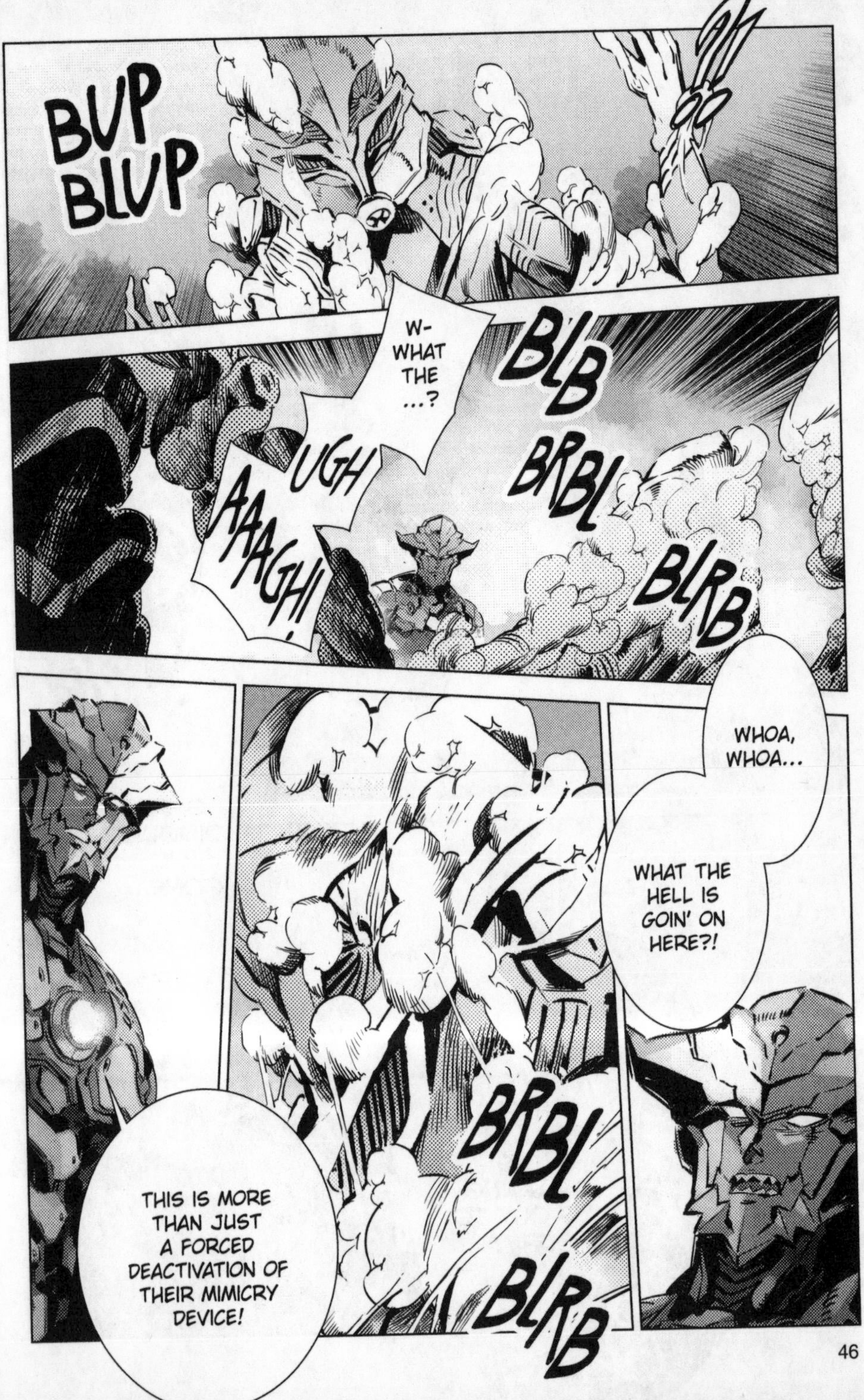
BUP BLUP
BLB
W-WHAT THE ...?
BRBL
BLRB
UGH
AAAAGH!
WHOA, WHOA...
WHAT THE HELL IS GOIN' ON HERE?!
BRBL
BLRB
THIS IS MORE THAN JUST A FORCED DEACTIVATION OF THEIR MIMICRY DEVICE!

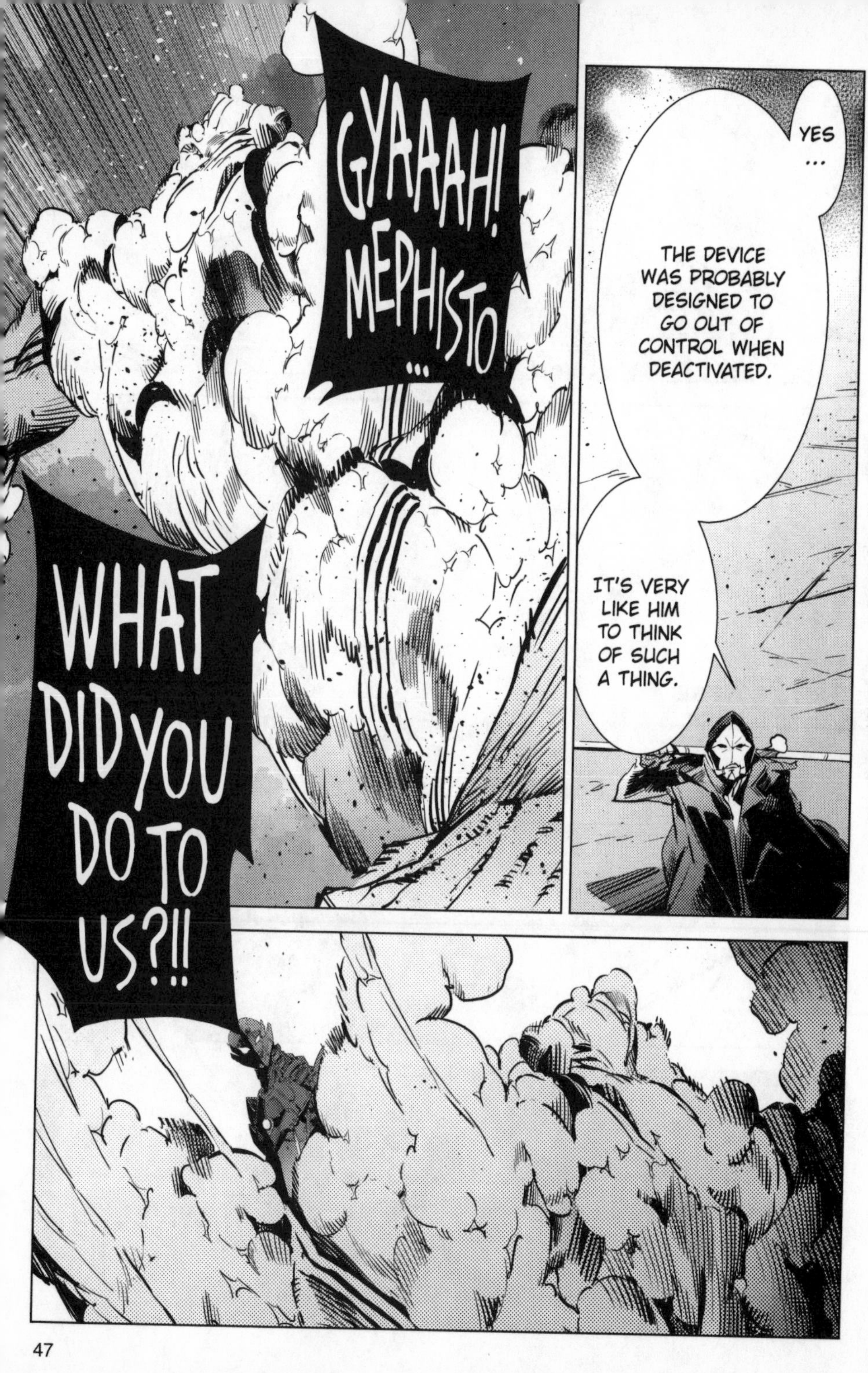
YES ...
THE DEVICE WAS PROBABLY DESIGNED TO GO OUT OF CONTROL WHEN DEACTIVATED.
IT'S VERY LIKE HIM TO THINK OF SUCH A THING.
GYAAAH! MEPHISTO ...
WHAT DID YOU DO TO US?!!

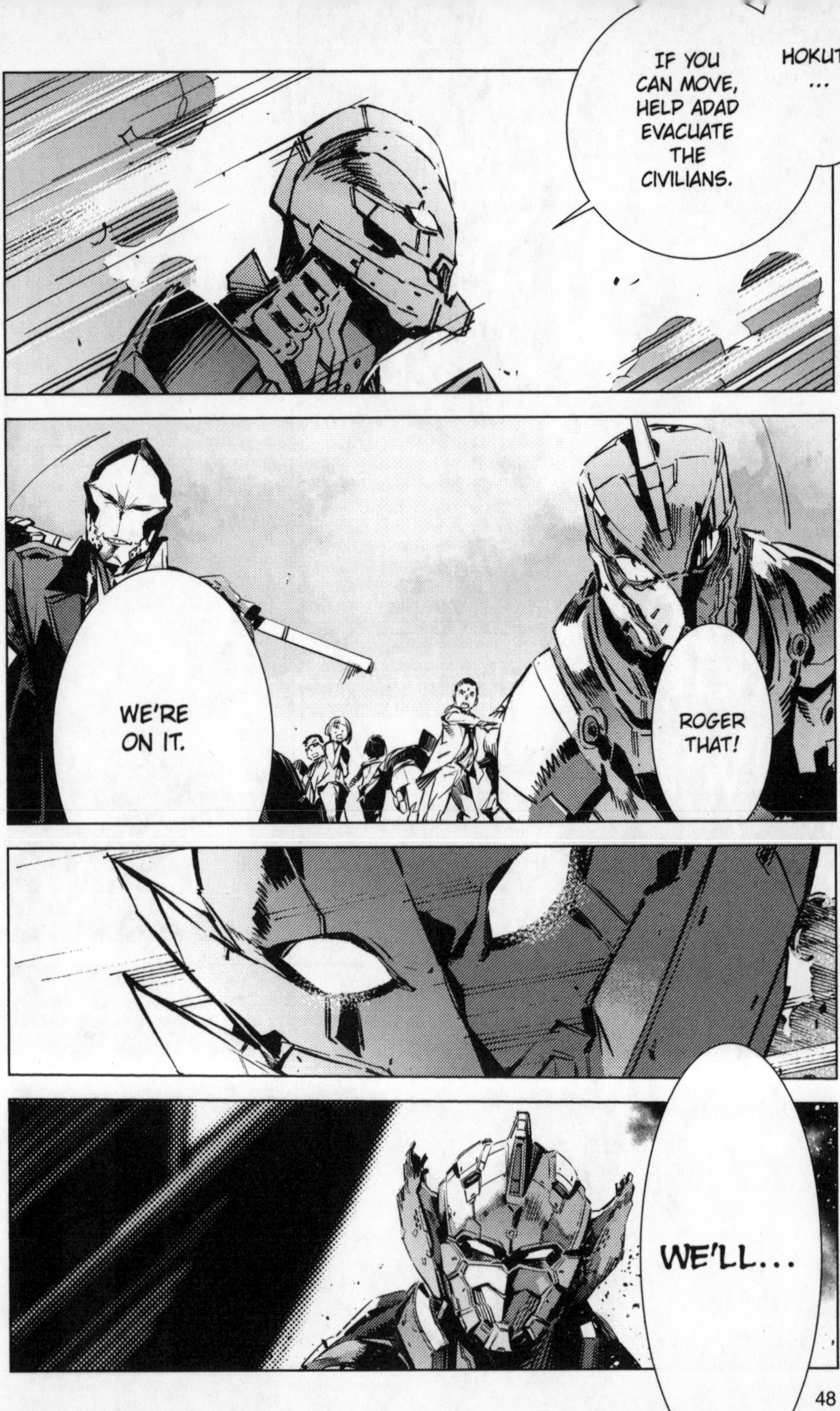
HOKUTO ...
IF YOU CAN MOVE, HELP ADAD EVACUATE THE CIVILIANS.
ROGER THAT!
WE'RE ON IT.
WE'LL...

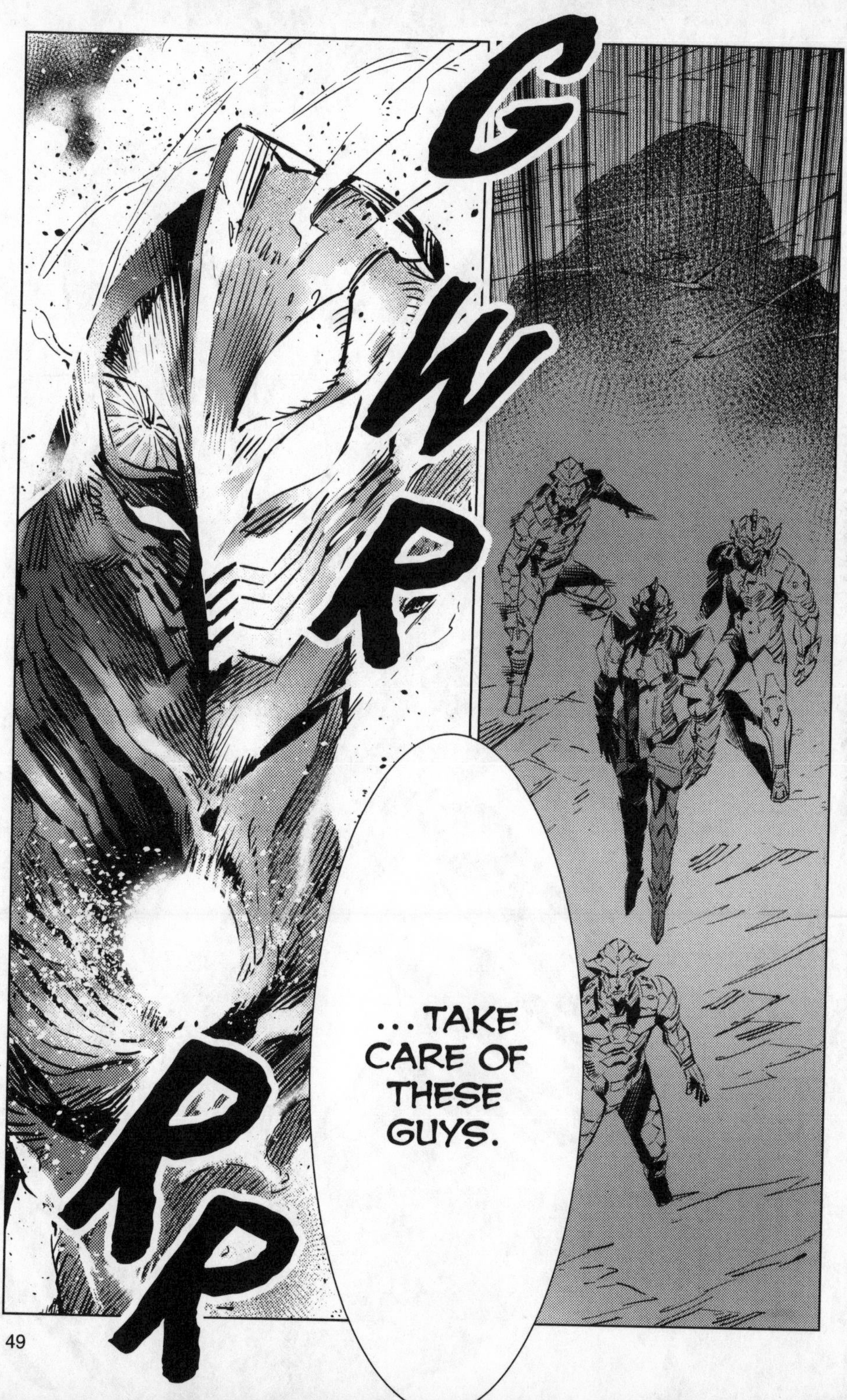
GWRRR
...TAKE CARE OF THESE GUYS.

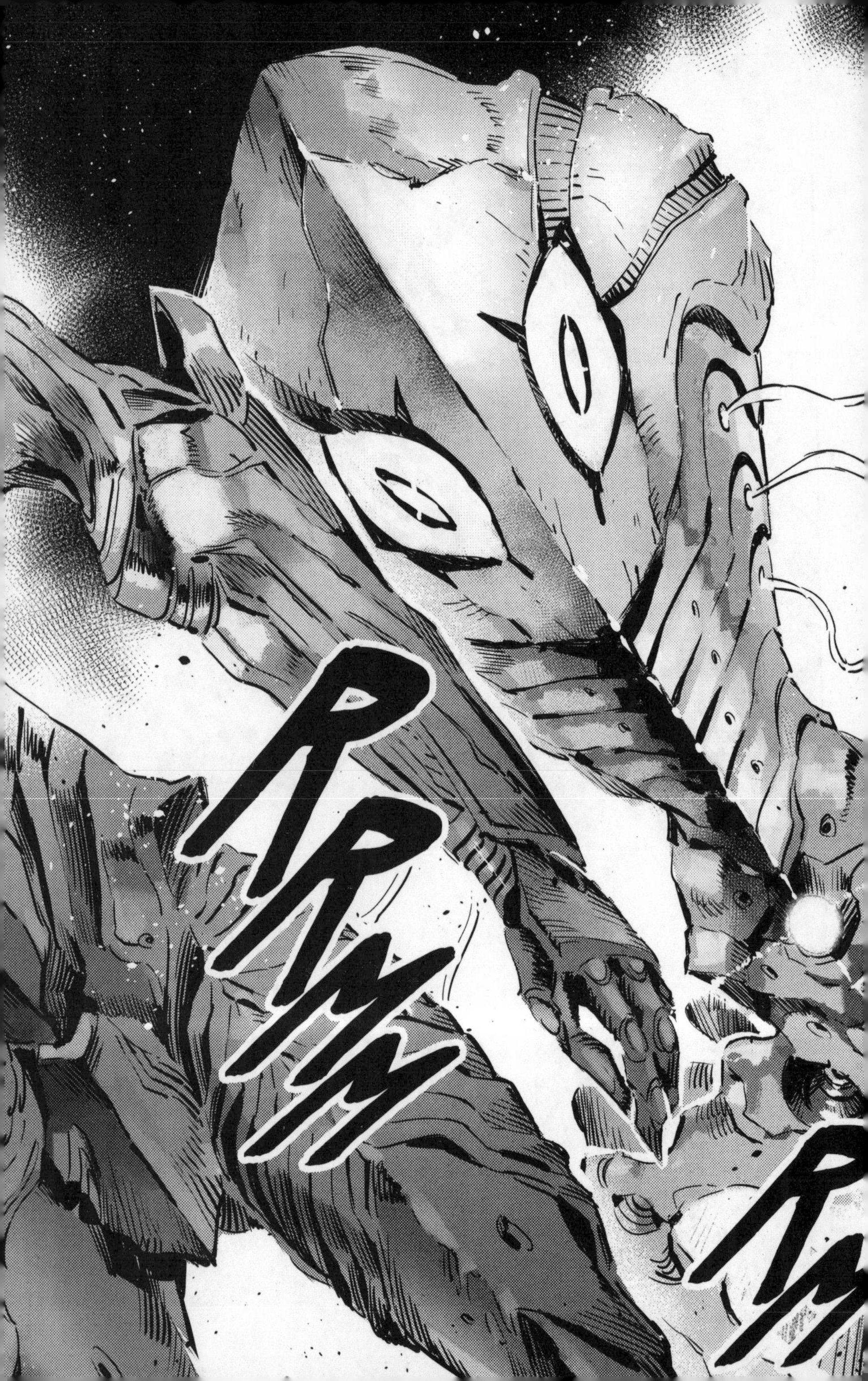
RR
RRMM

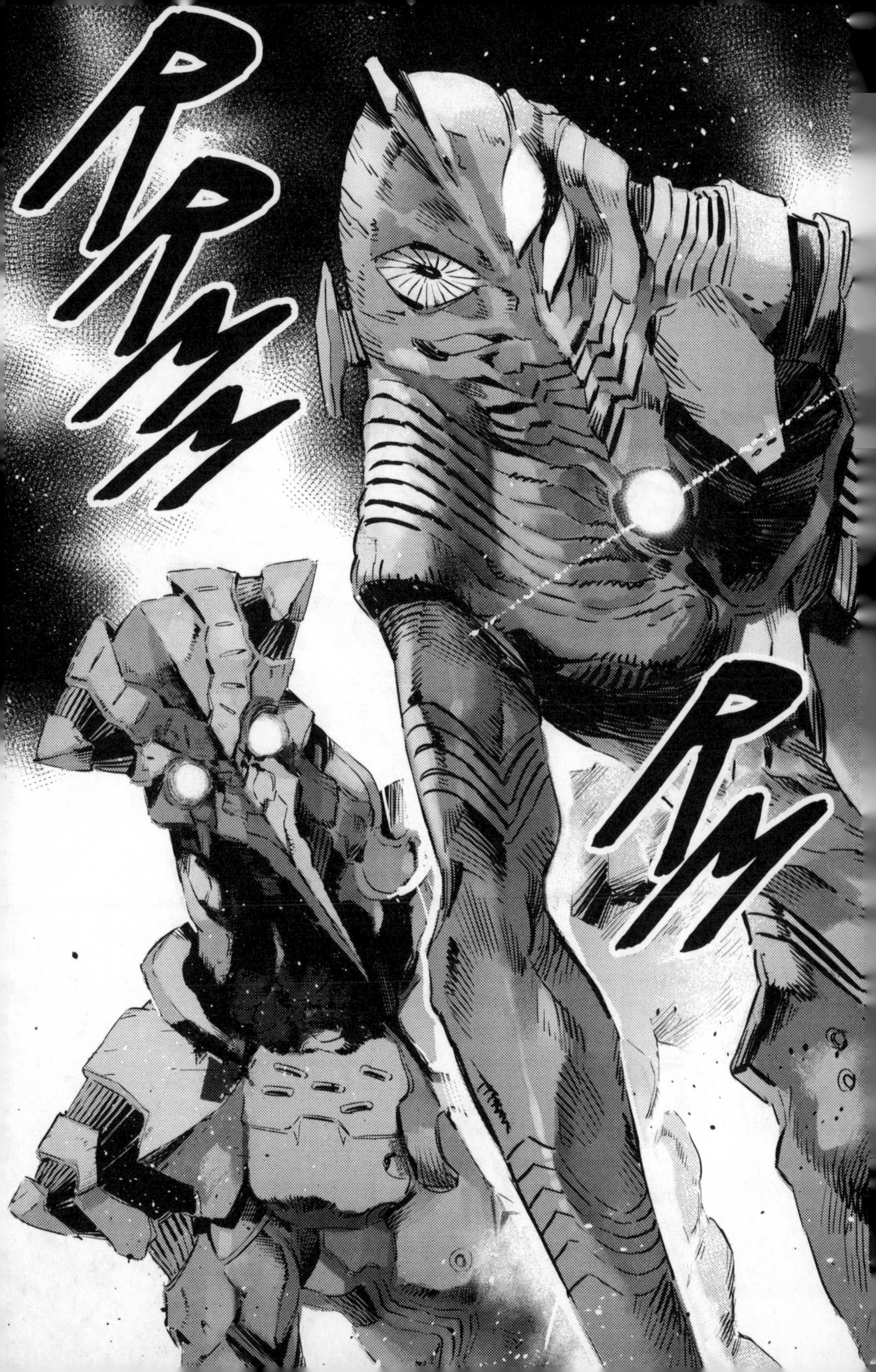
PRMMM
PRM

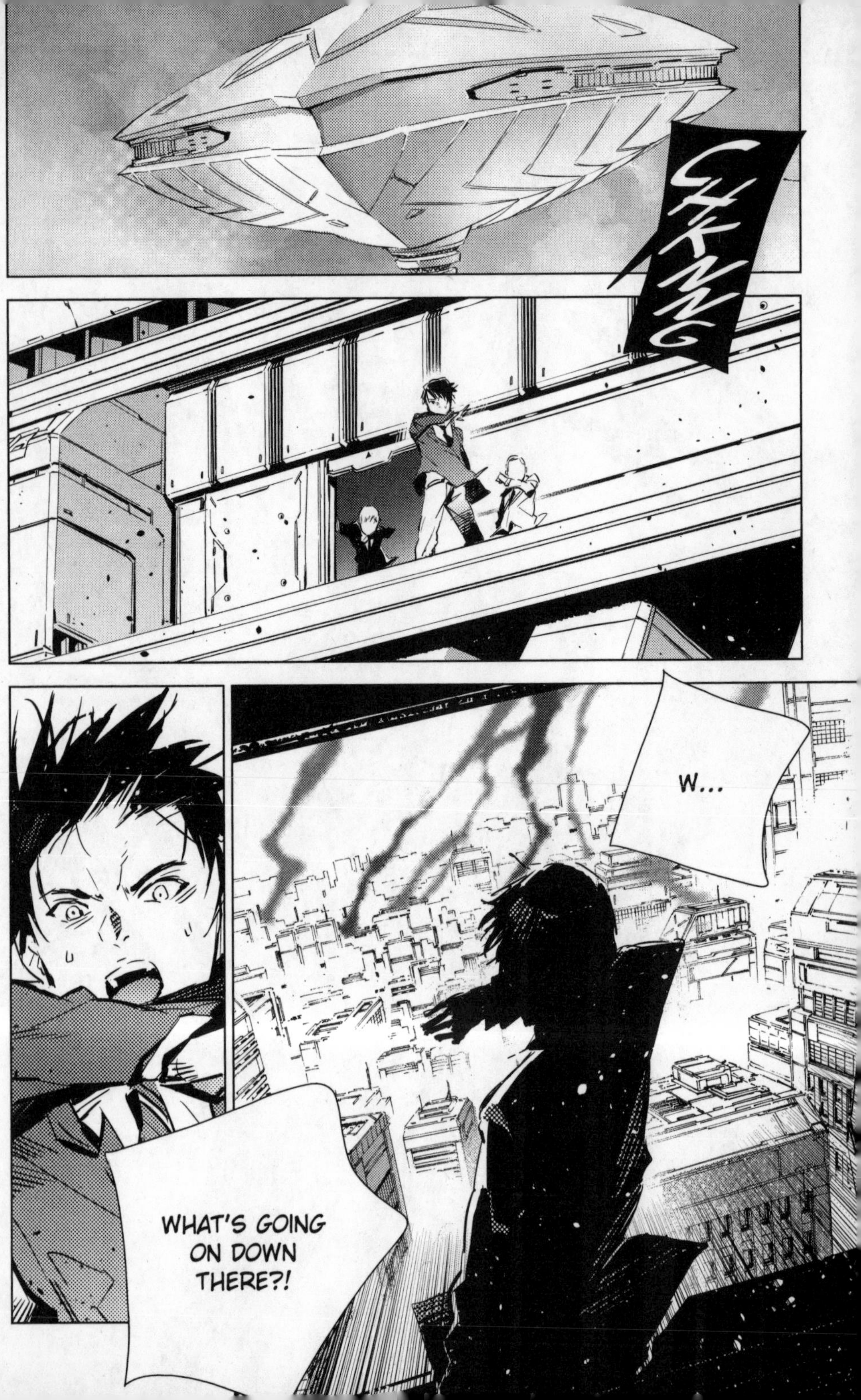
CHKNNG
W...
WHAT'S GOING ON DOWN THERE?!

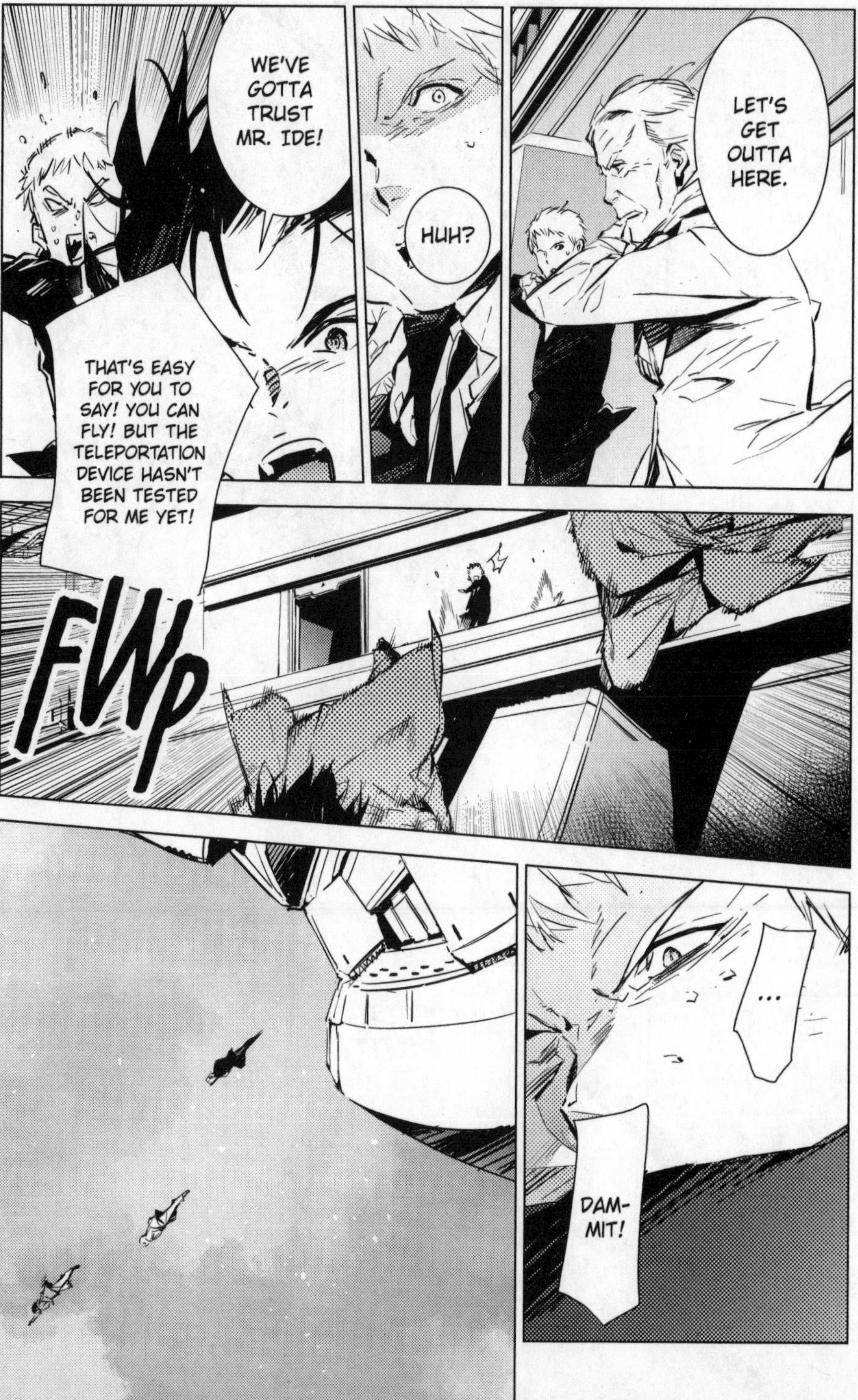
LET'S GET OUTTA HERE.
HUH?
WE'VE GOTTA TRUST MR. IDE!
THAT'S EASY FOR YOU TO SAY! YOU CAN FLY! BUT THE TELEPORTATION DEVICE HASN'T BEEN TESTED FOR ME YET!
FWP
...
DAM-MIT!

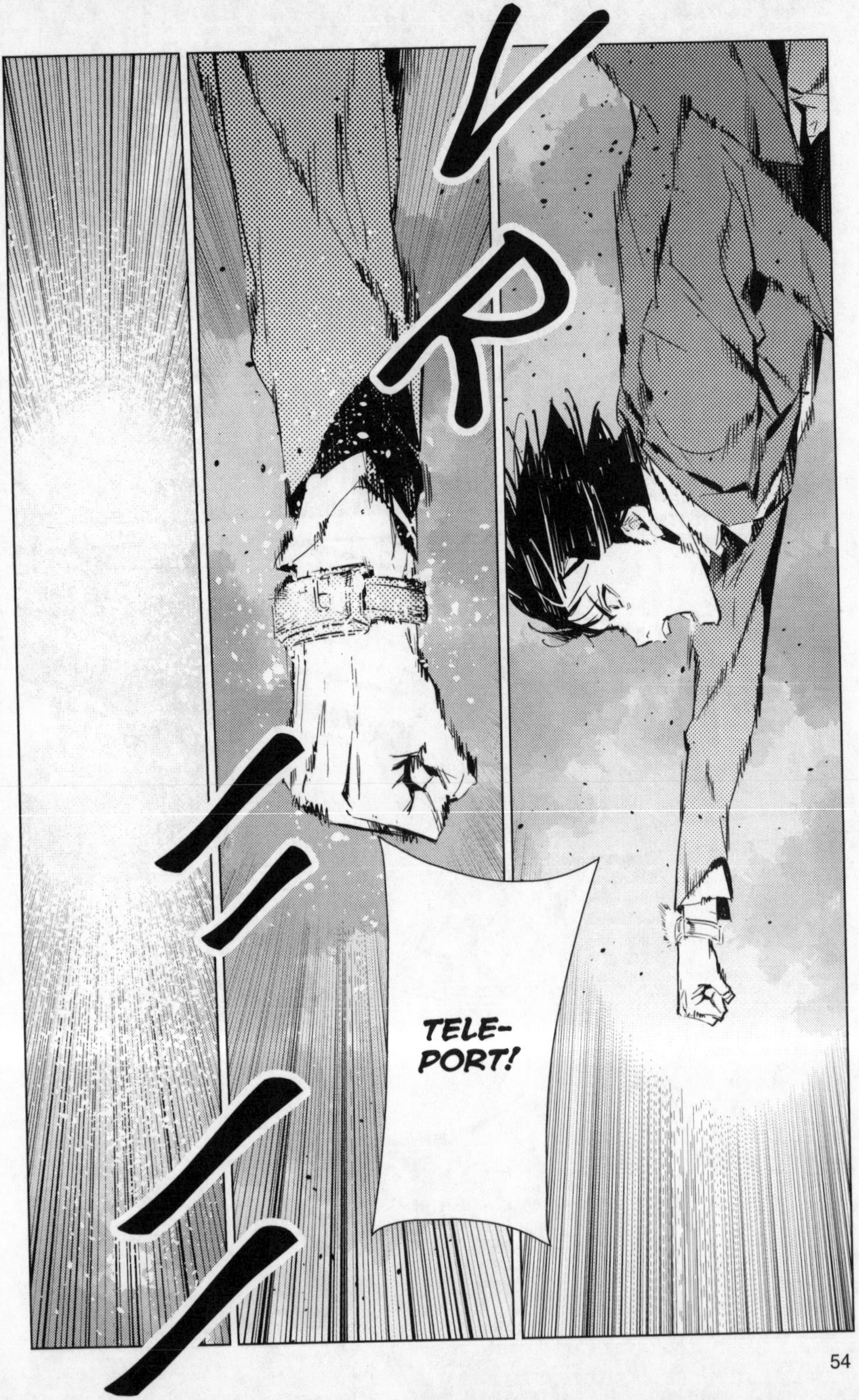
VR
TELE-
PORT!

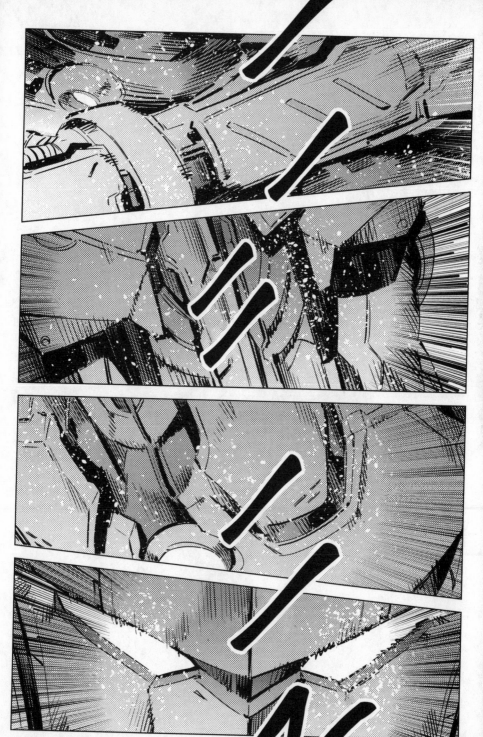

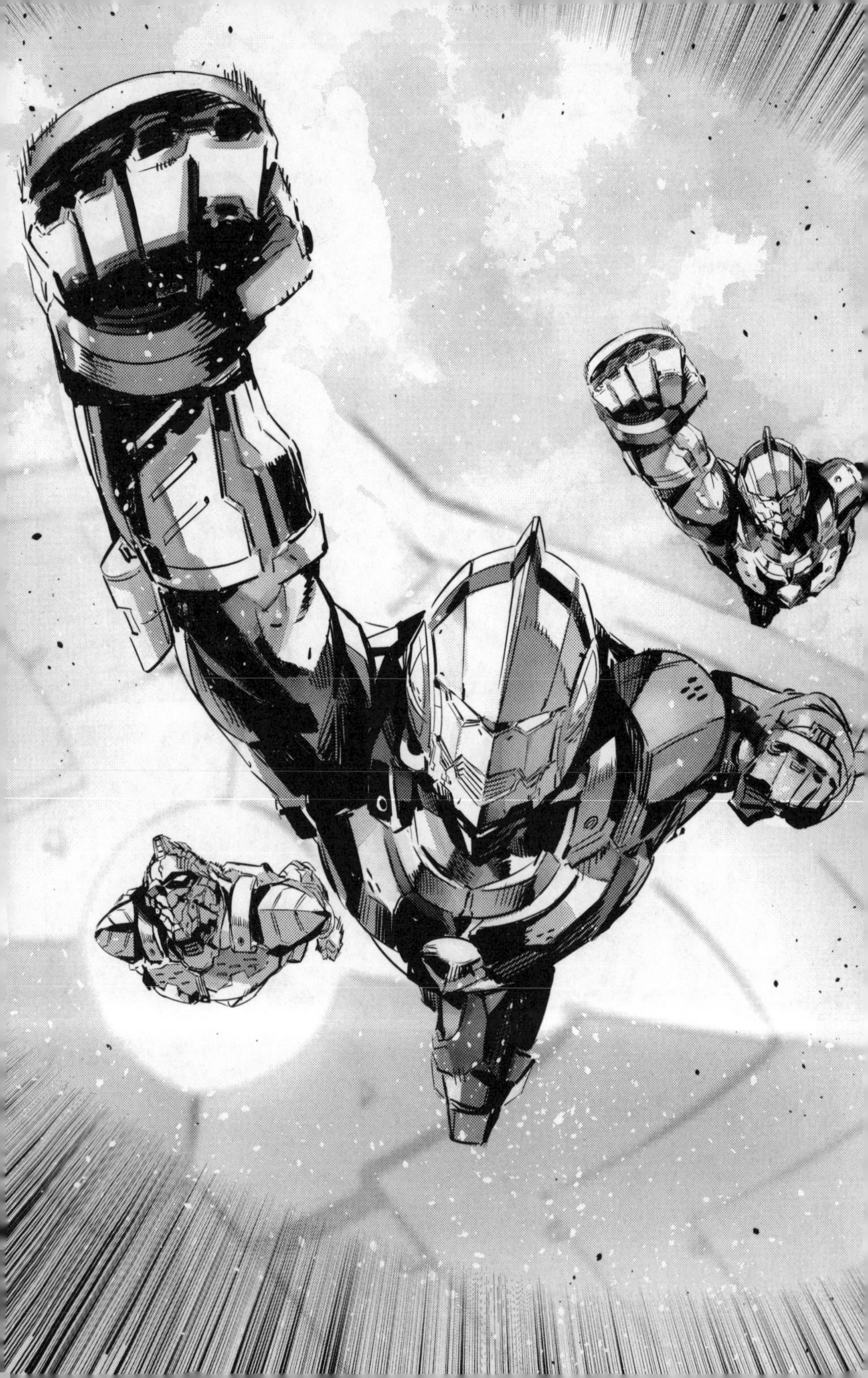

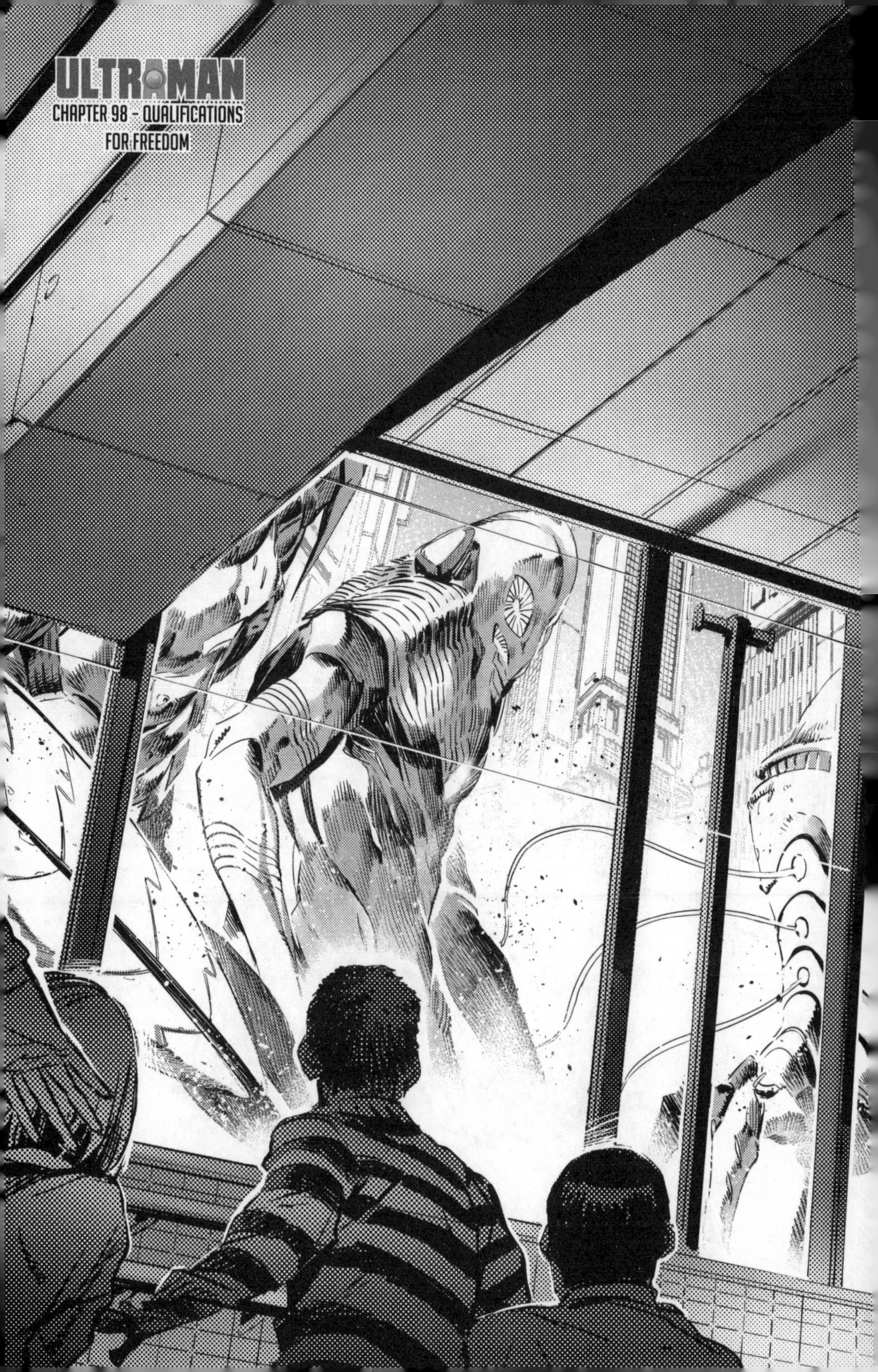
ULTRAMAN
CHAPTER 98 - QUALIFICATIONS FOR FREEDOM

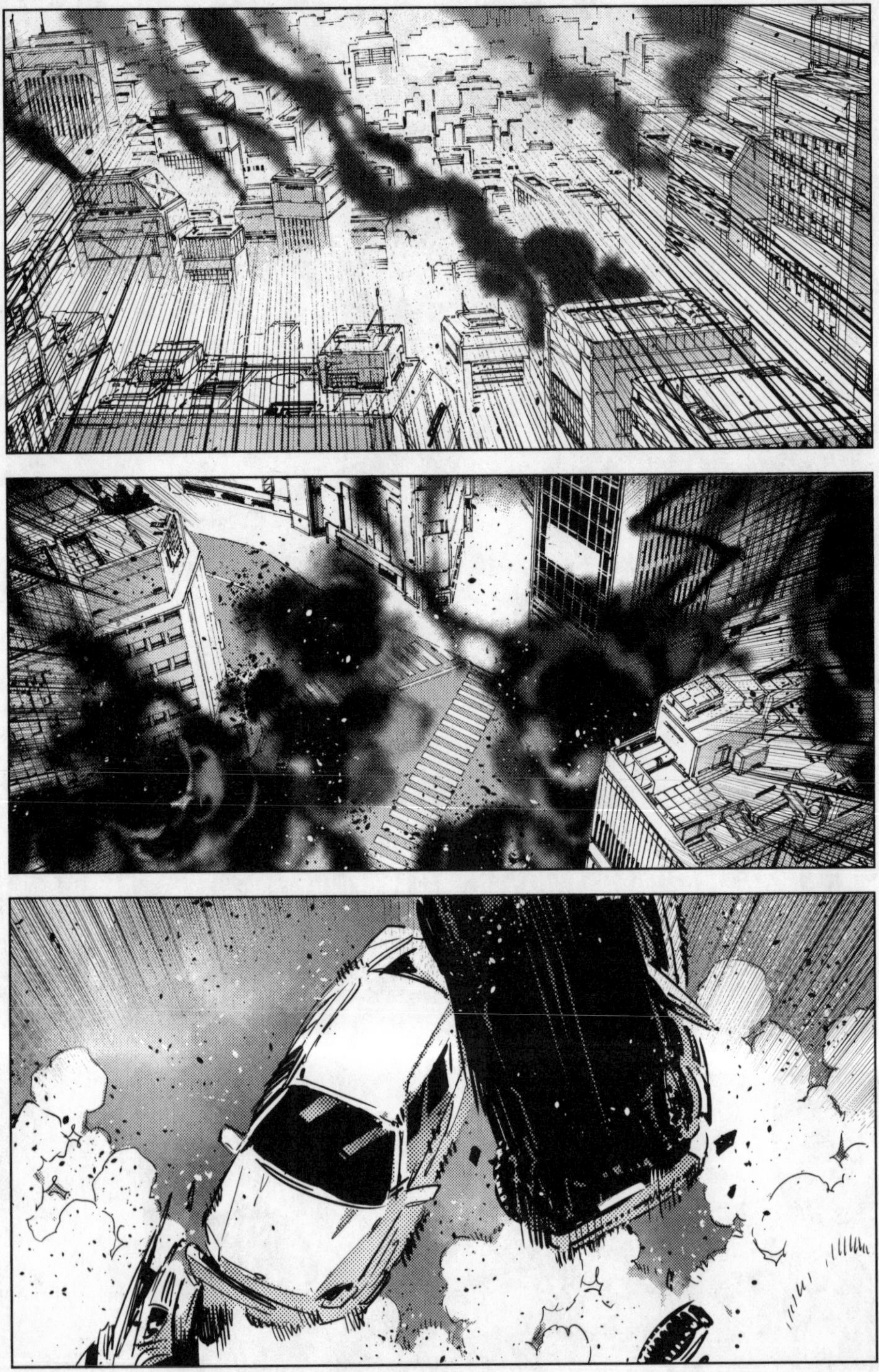

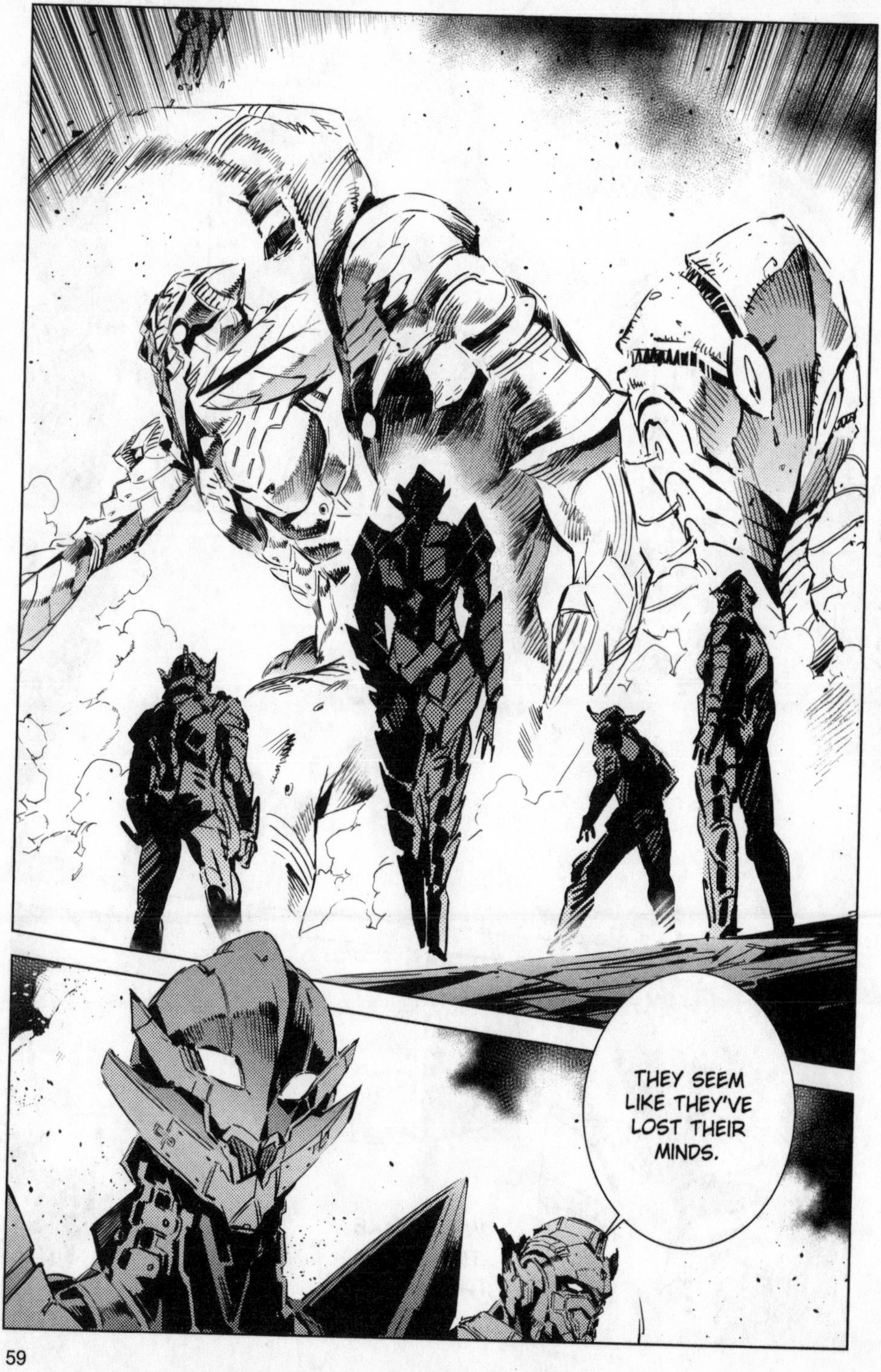
THEY SEEM LIKE THEY'VE LOST THEIR MINDS.

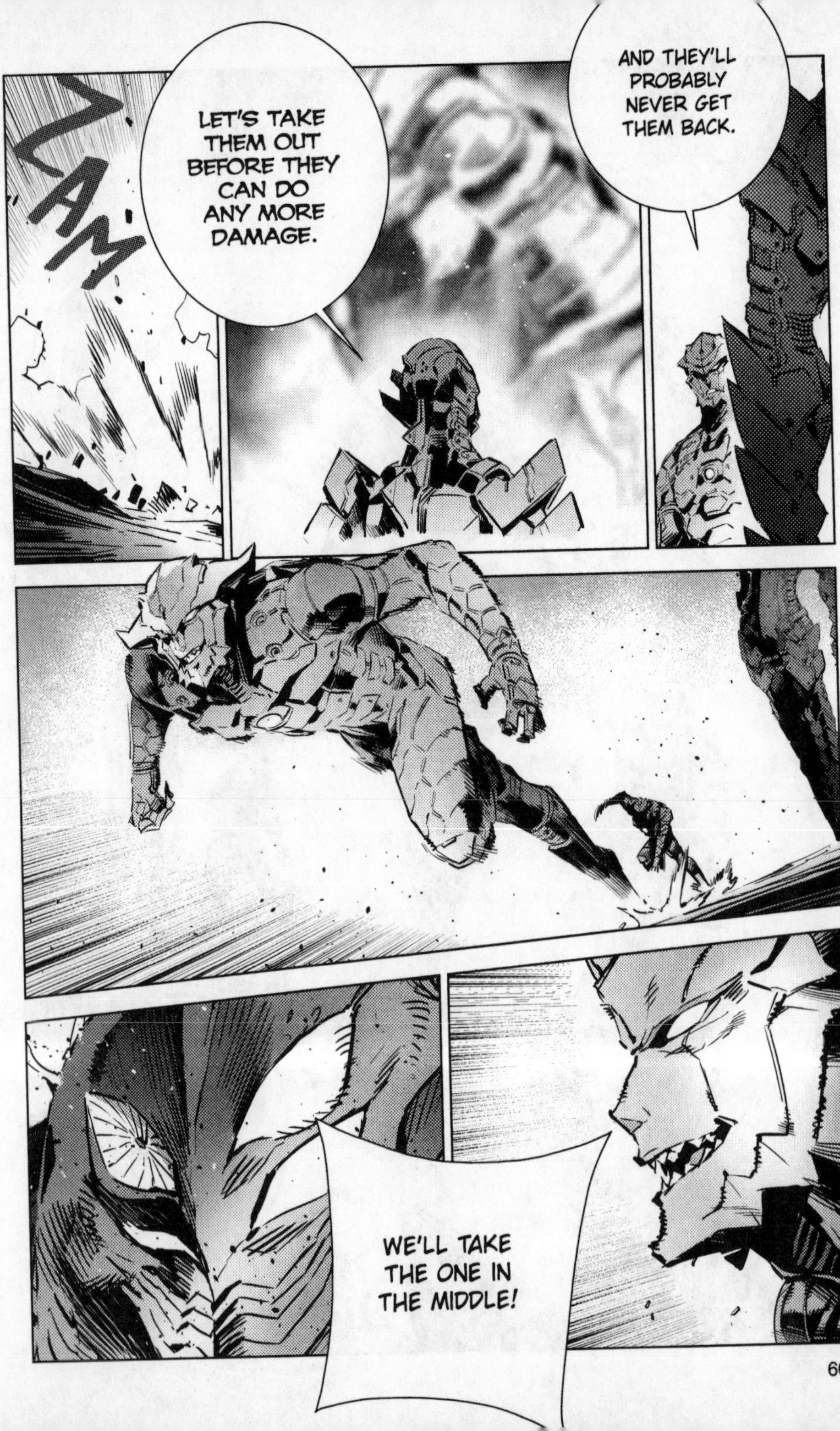
AND THEY'LL PROBABLY NEVER GET THEM BACK.
LET'S TAKE THEM OUT BEFORE THEY CAN DO ANY MORE DAMAGE.
ZAM!
WE'LL TAKE THE ONE IN THE MIDDLE!

I'LL TAKE THAT GUY.

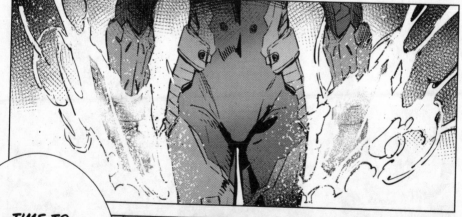

TIME TO GET A LITTLE PAYBACK FOR EVERYTHING YOU DID TO ME.

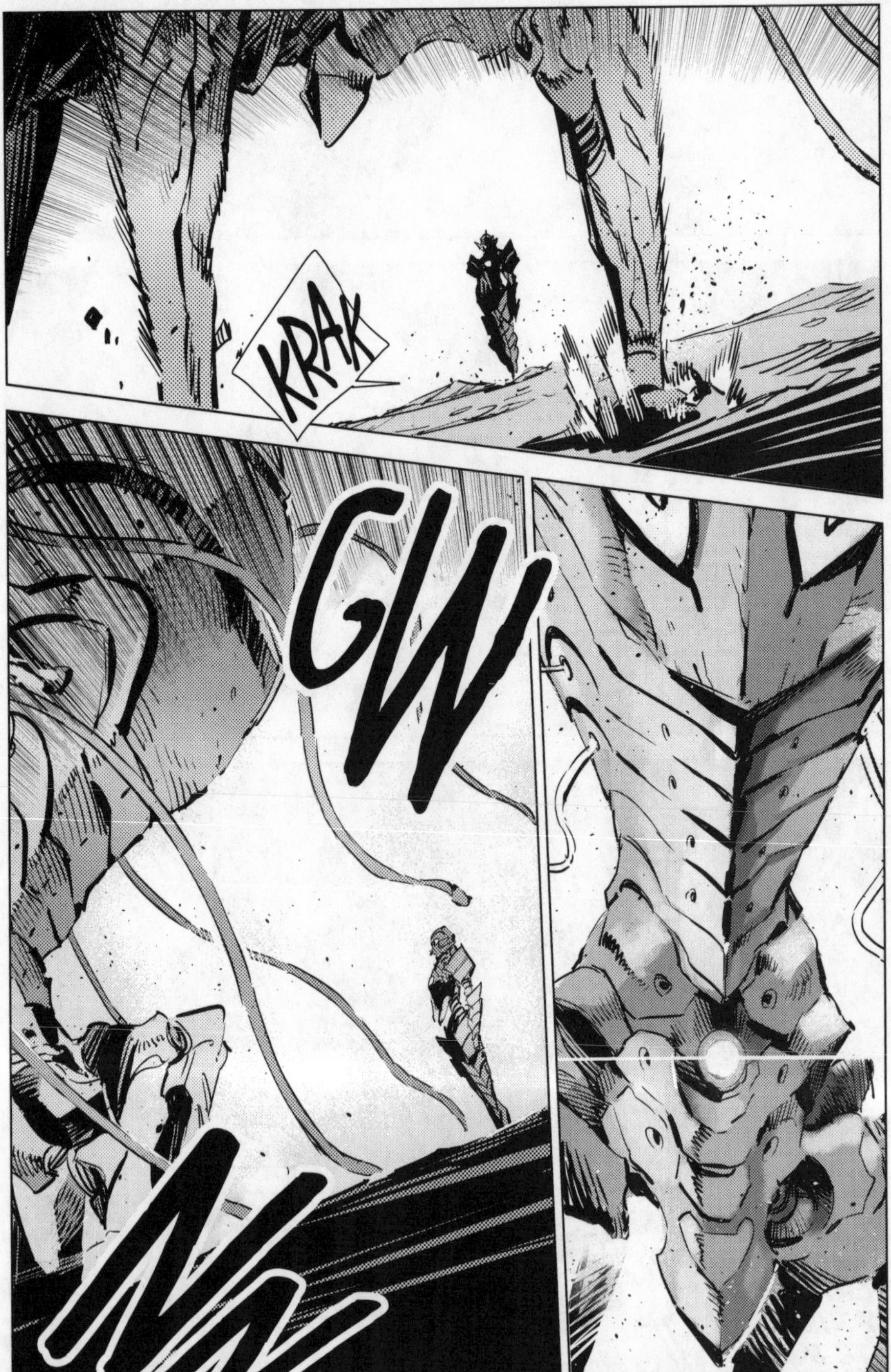
KRAK
GW
MM

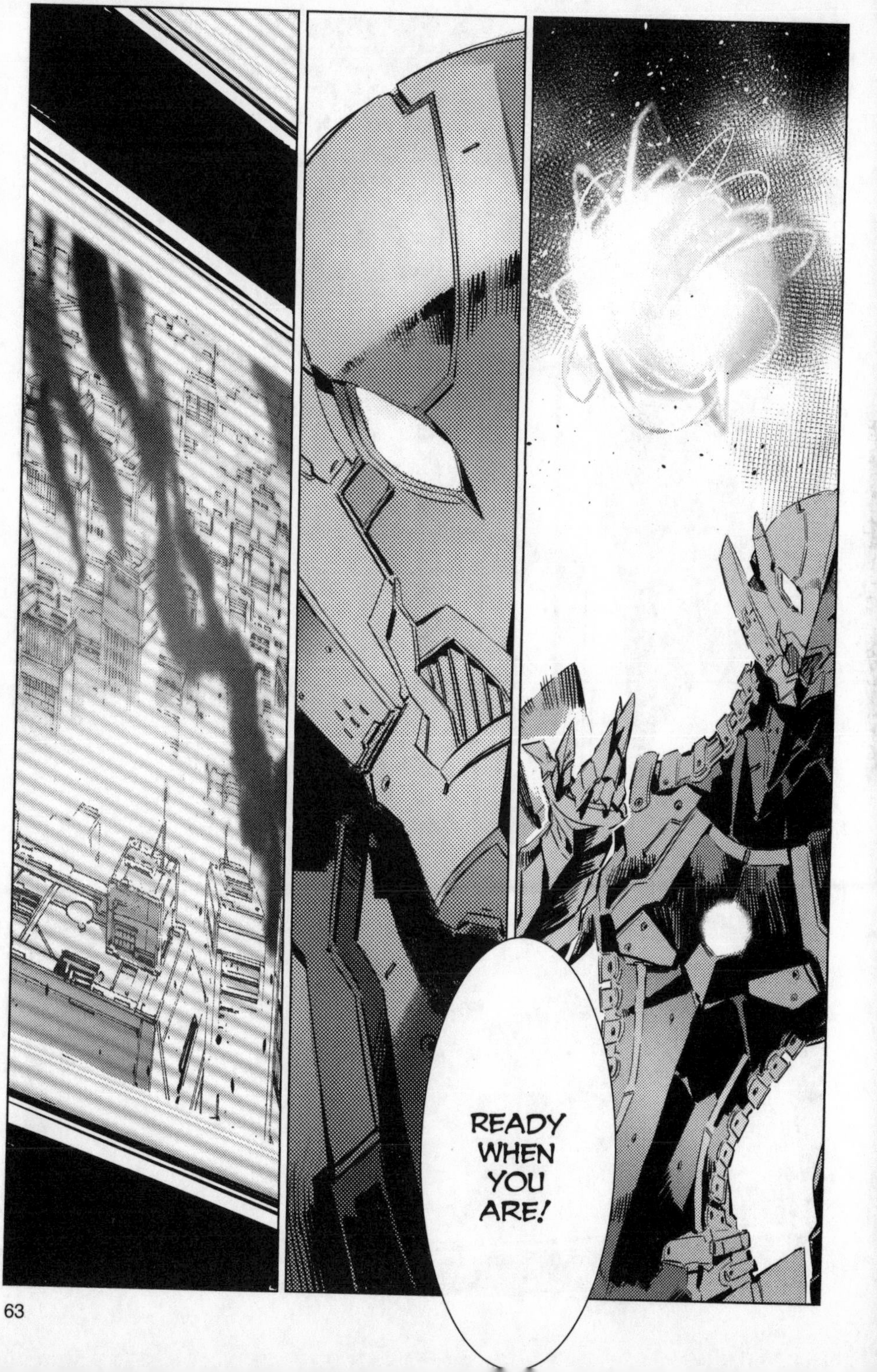
READY WHEN YOU ARE!

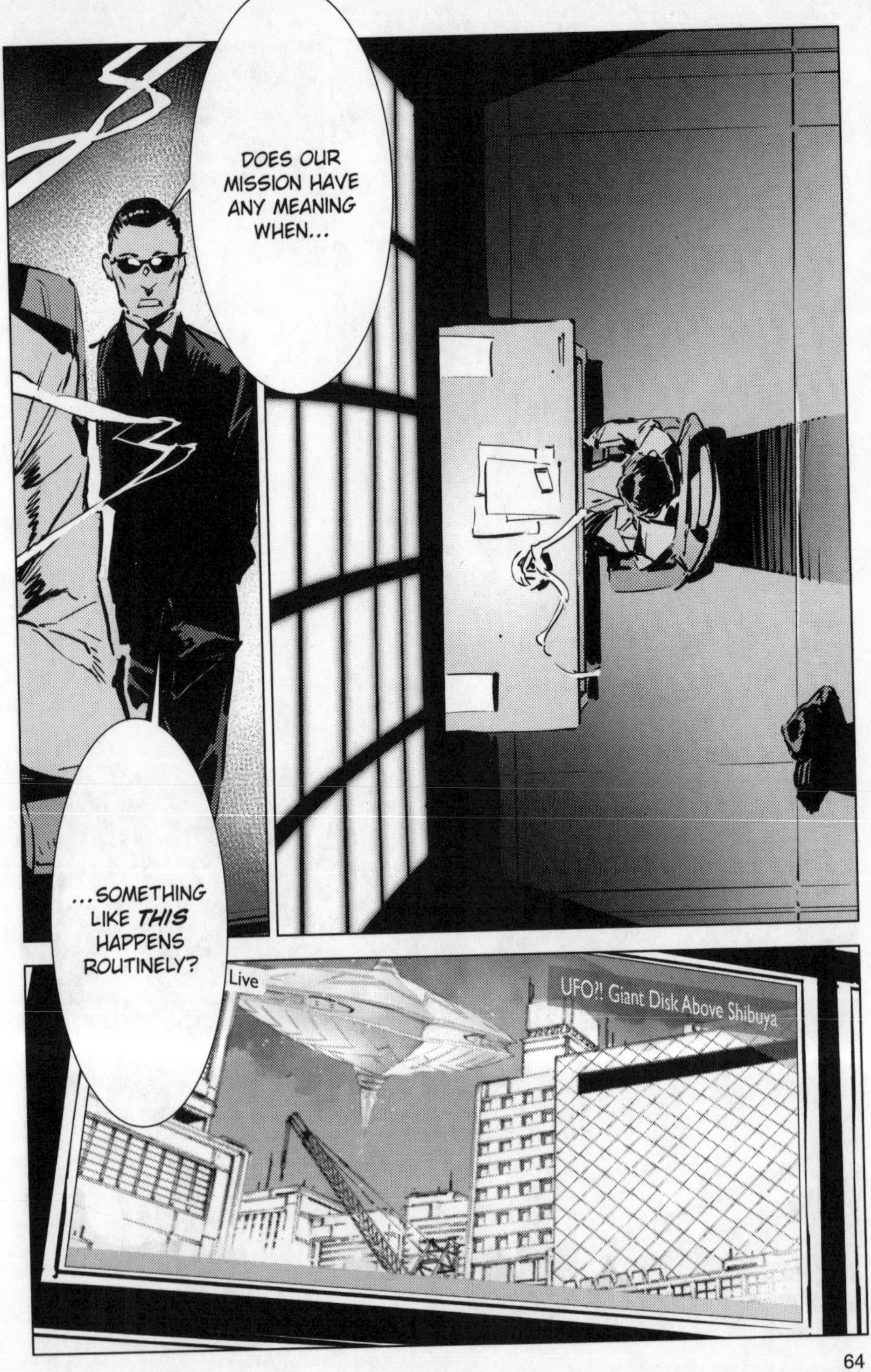
DOES OUR MISSION HAVE ANY MEANING WHEN...
...SOMETHING LIKE *THIS* HAPPENS ROUTINELY?
Live
UFO?! Giant Disk Above Shibuya

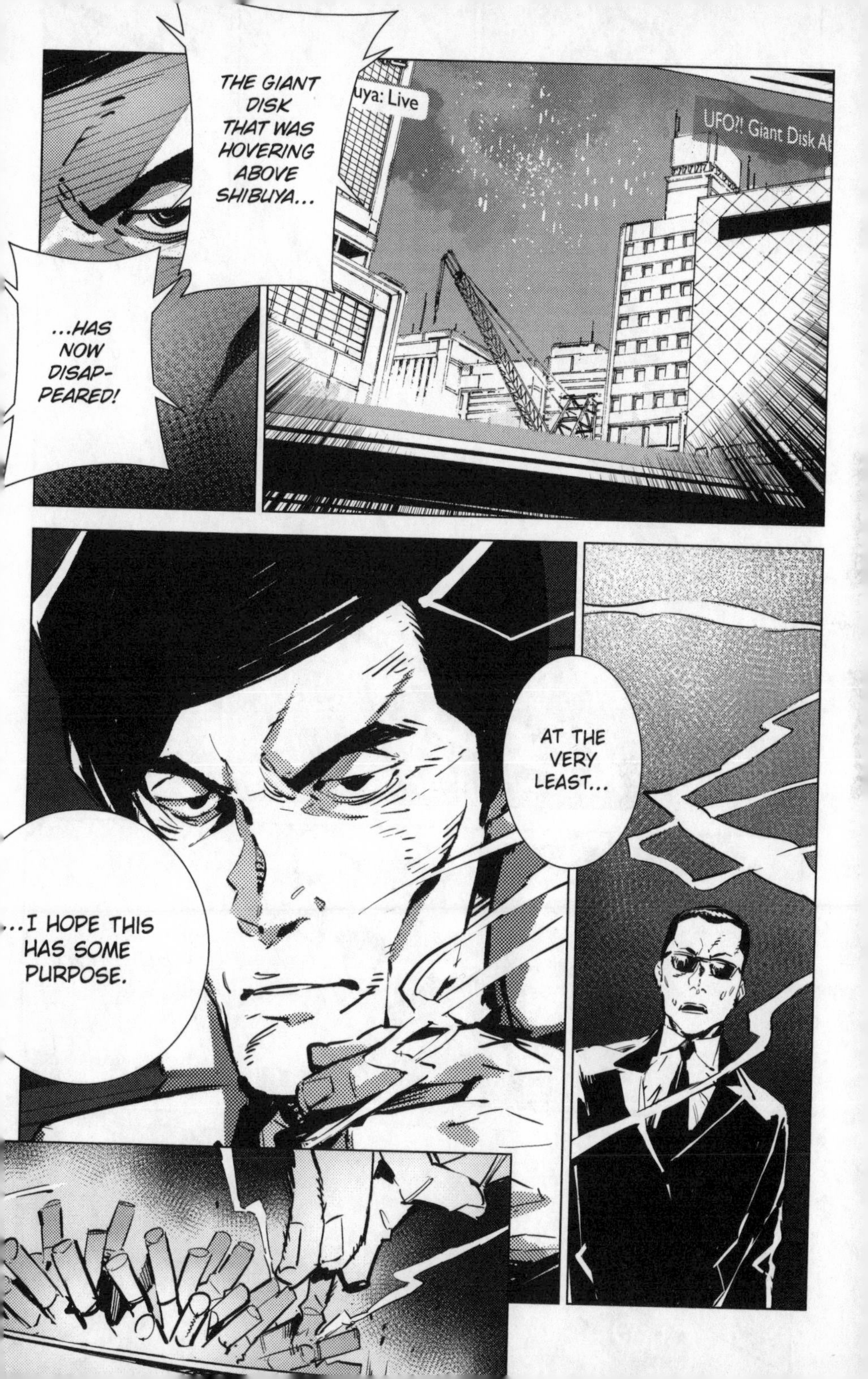
uya: Live
UFO?! Giant Disk A
THE GIANT DISK THAT WAS HOVERING ABOVE SHIBUYA...
...HAS NOW DISAP-PEARED!
AT THE VERY LEAST...
...I HOPE THIS HAS SOME PURPOSE.

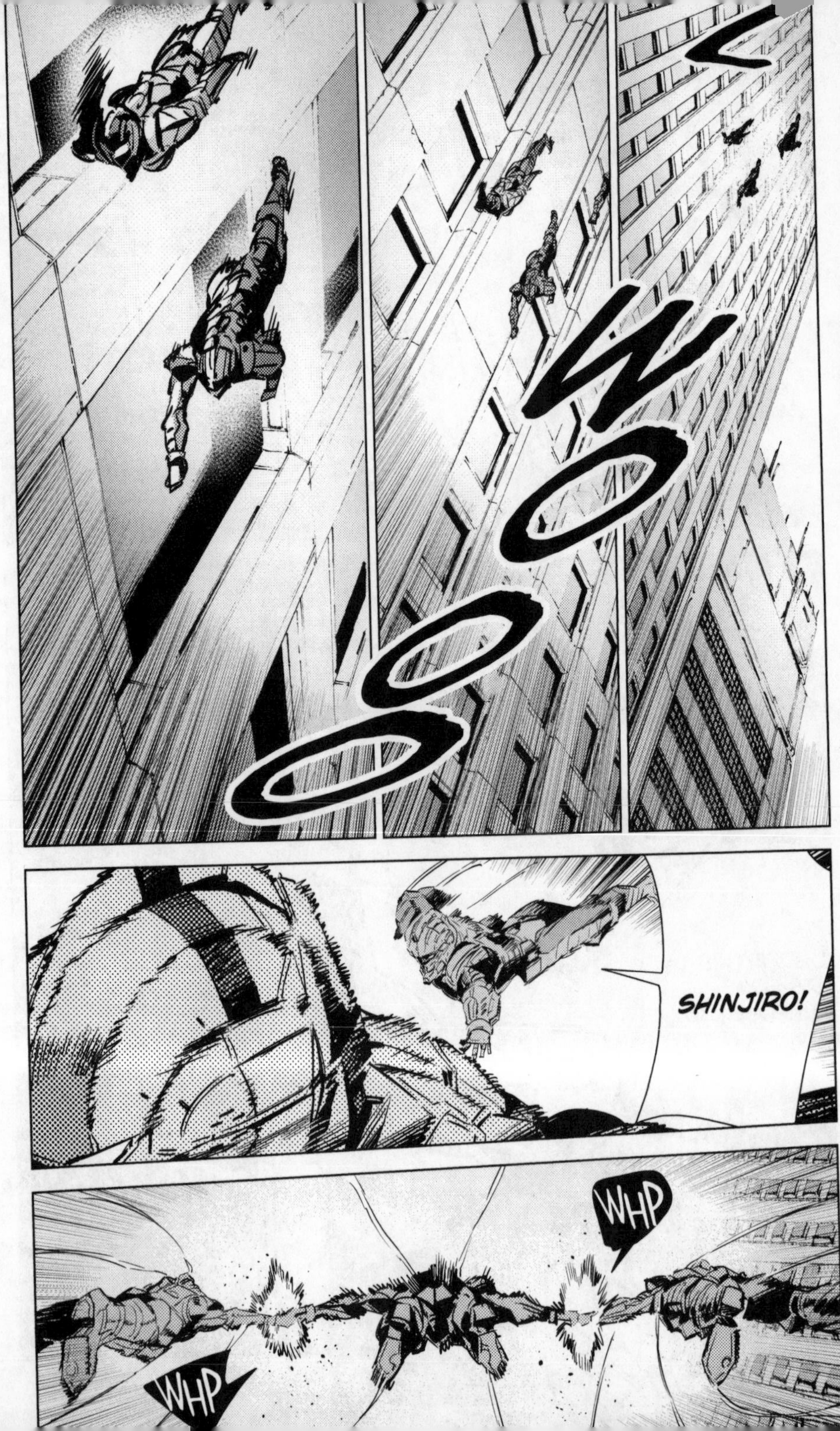
SHINJIRO!
WHP
WHP

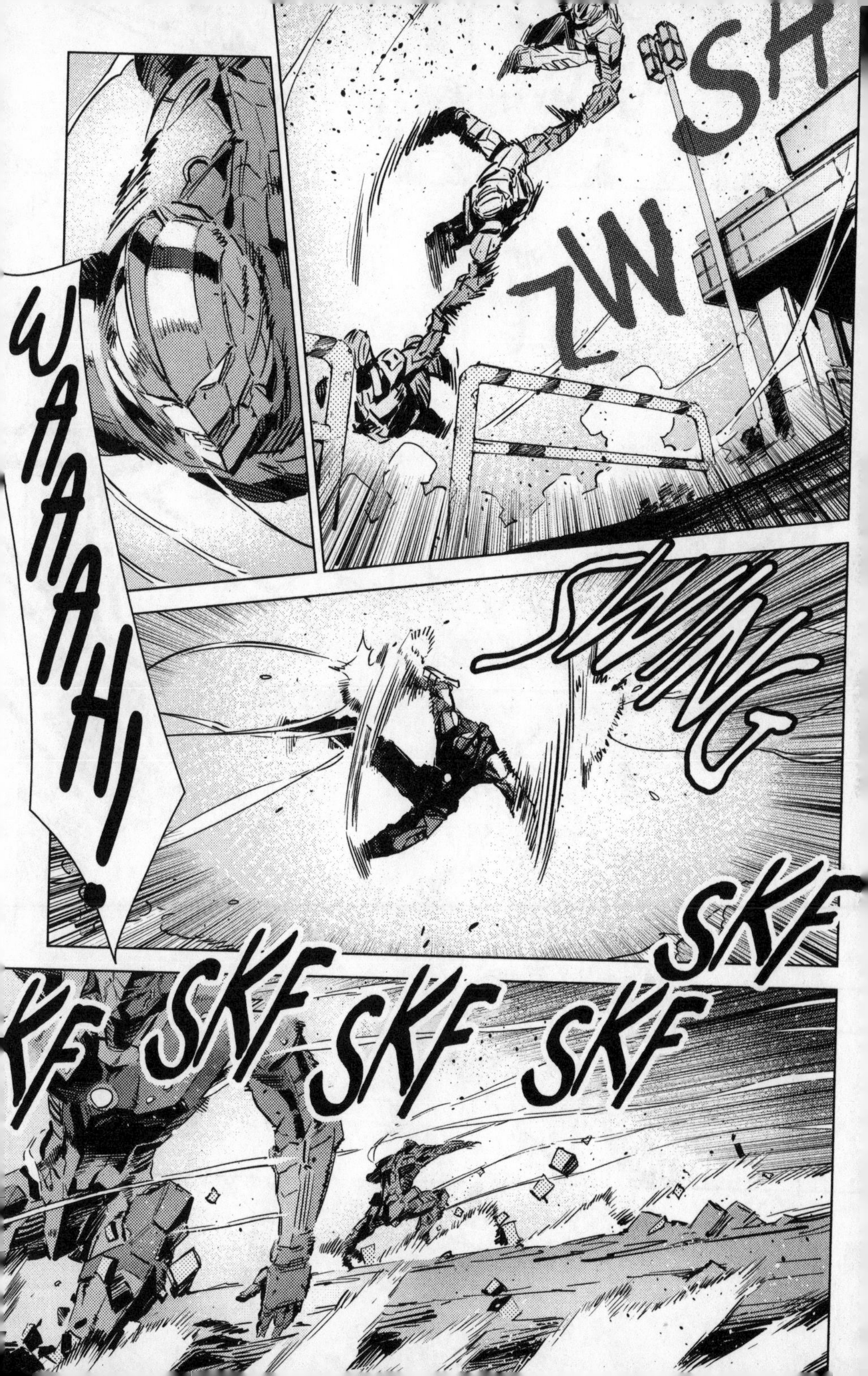
ZWSH
WAAAH!
SWING
SKF
SKF
SKF
SKF
SKF

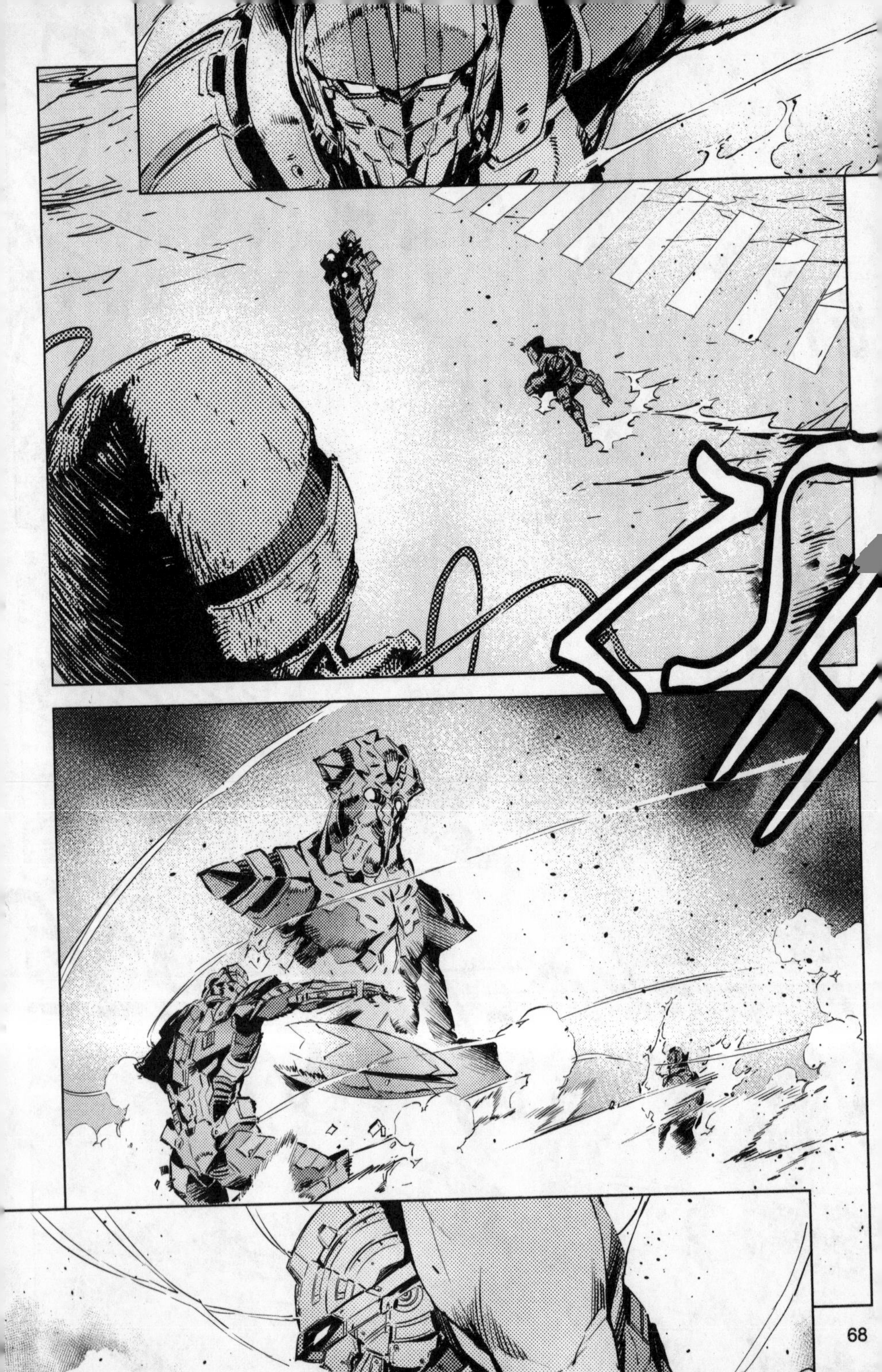

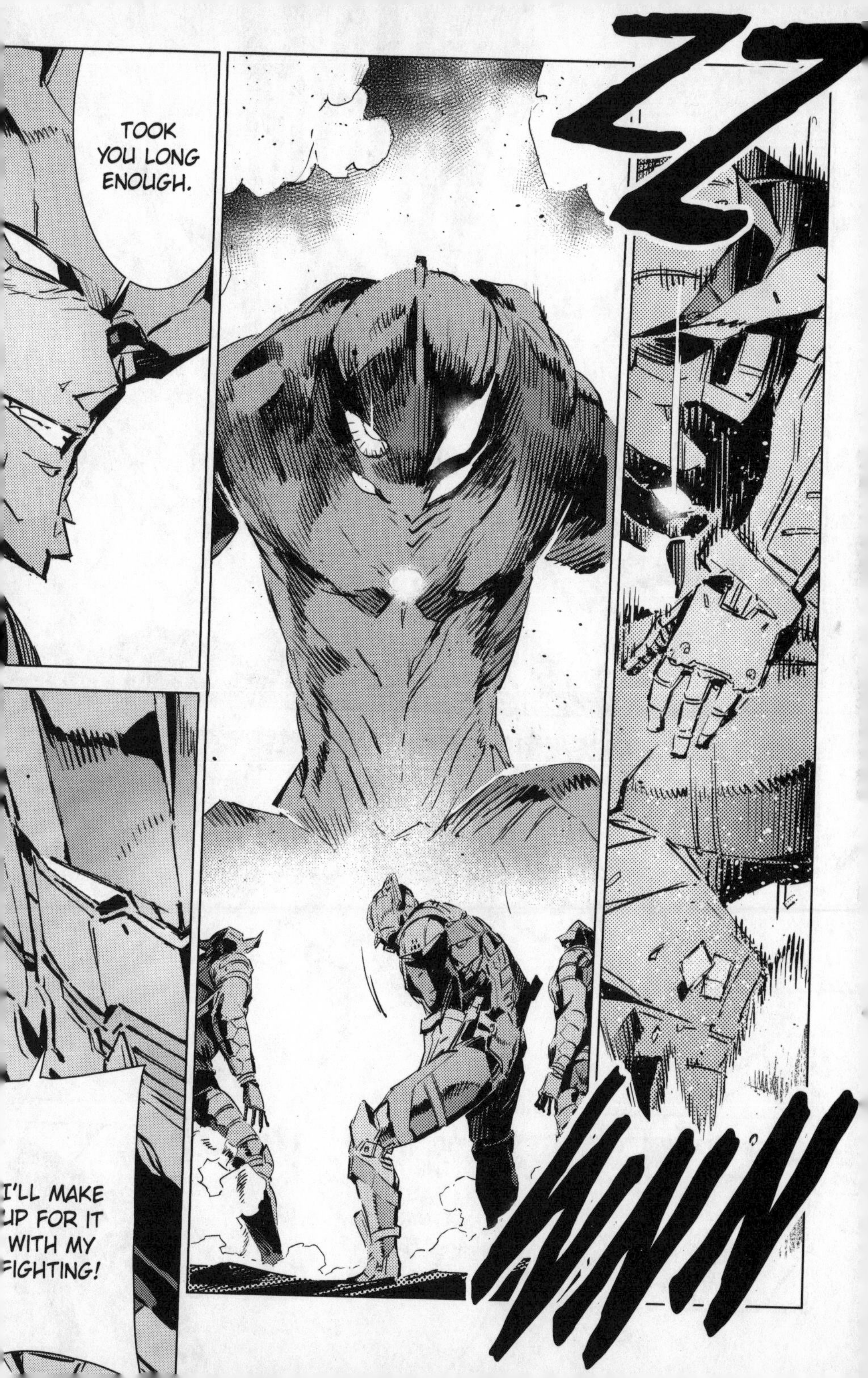
ZZ
TOOK YOU LONG ENOUGH.
I'LL MAKE UP FOR IT WITH MY FIGHTING!

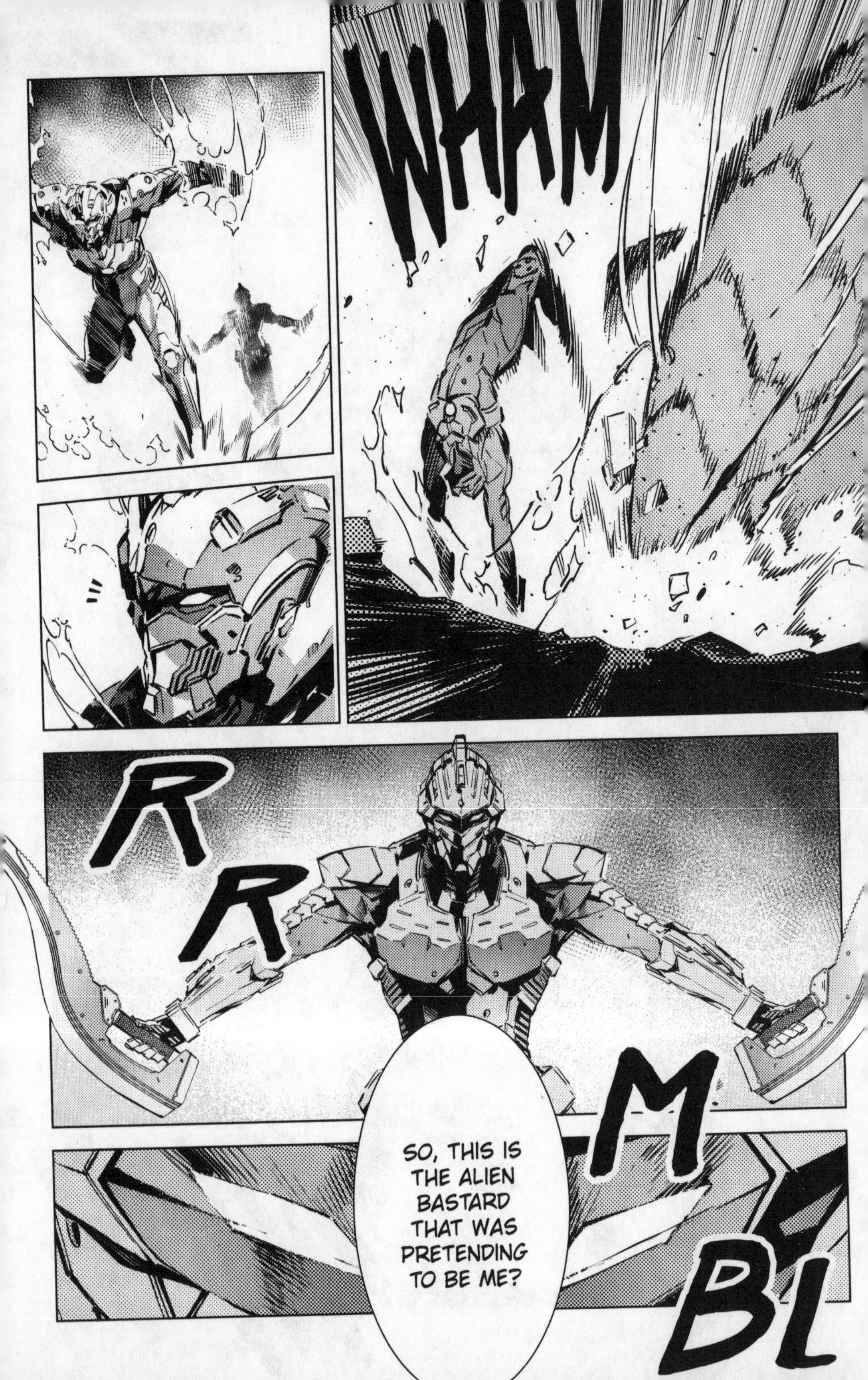
WHAM
RR
M
BL
SO, THIS IS THE ALIEN BASTARD THAT WAS PRETENDING TO BE ME?

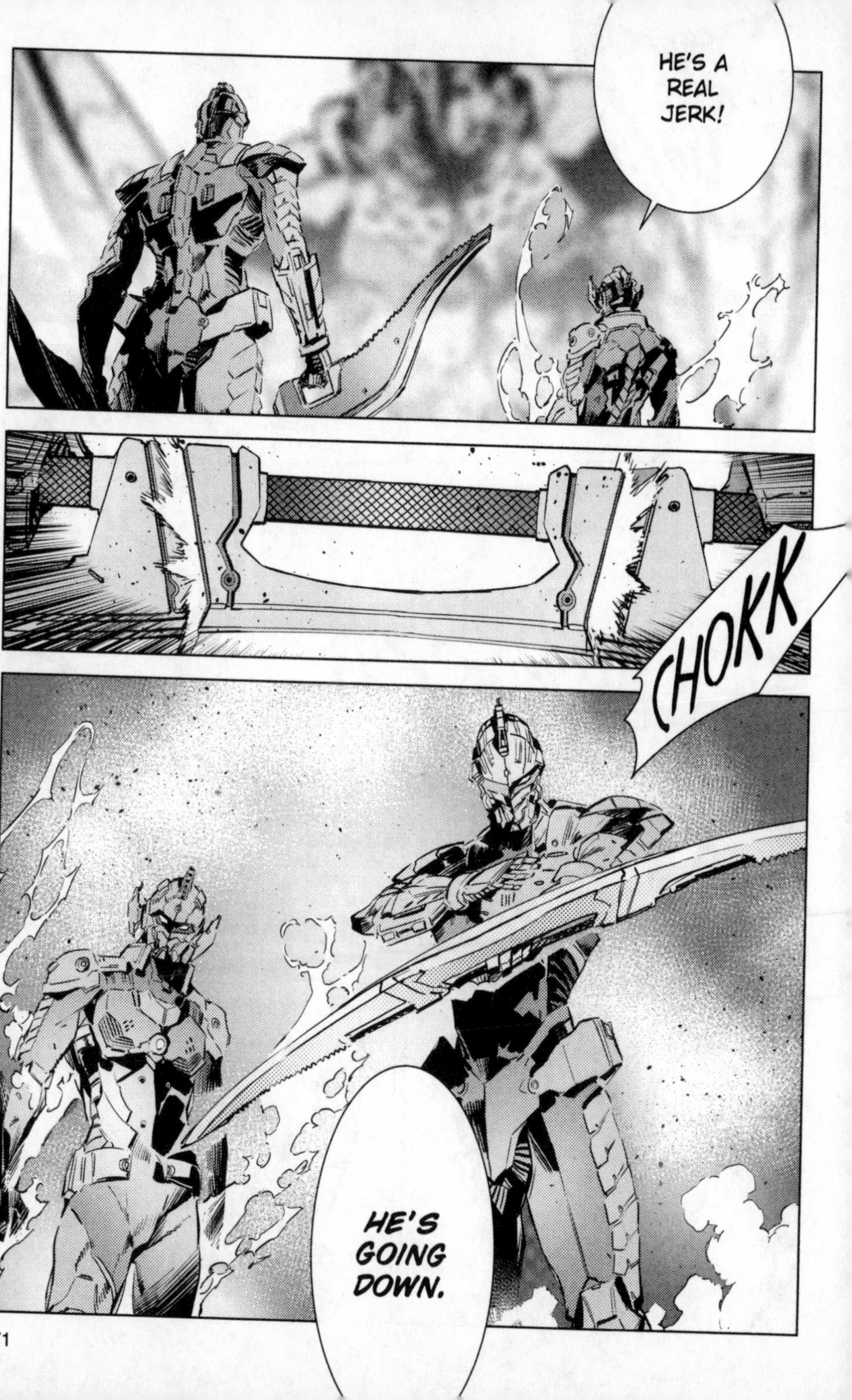
HE'S A REAL JERK!
CHOKK
HE'S GOING DOWN.

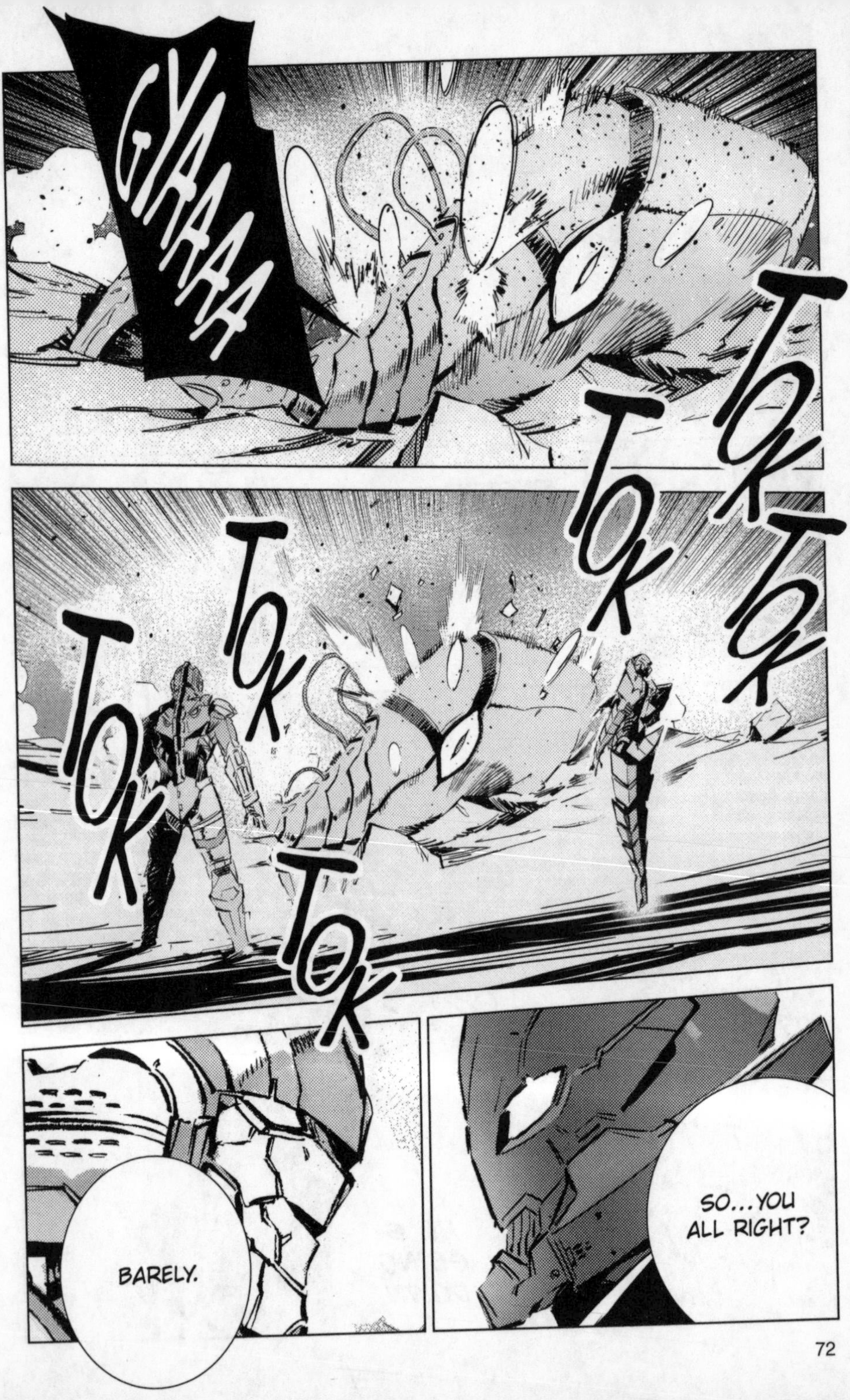
GYAAAA
TOK
TOK
TOK
TOK
TOK
SO...YOU ALL RIGHT?
BARELY.

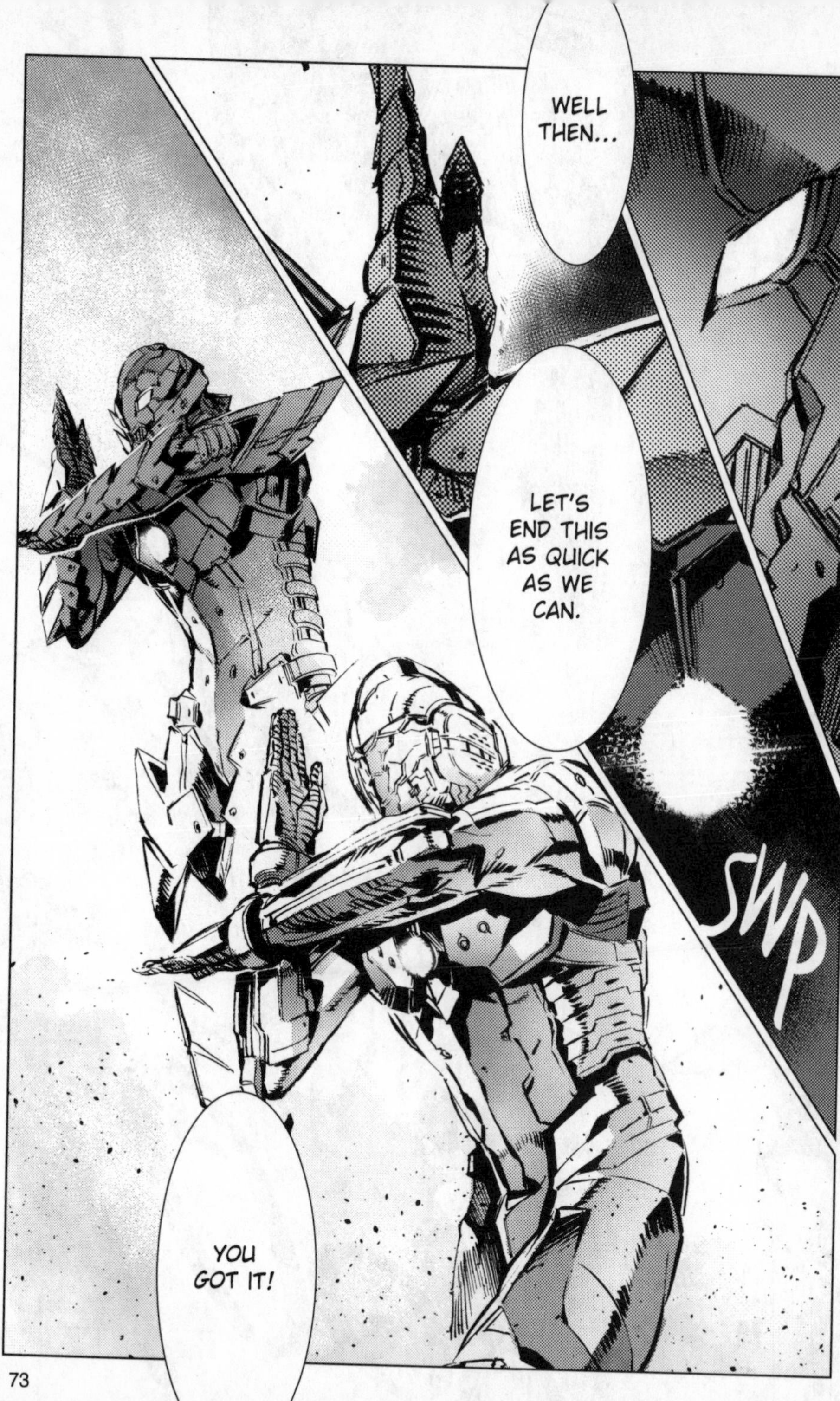
WELL THEN...
LET'S END THIS AS QUICK AS WE CAN.
SWP
YOU GOT IT!

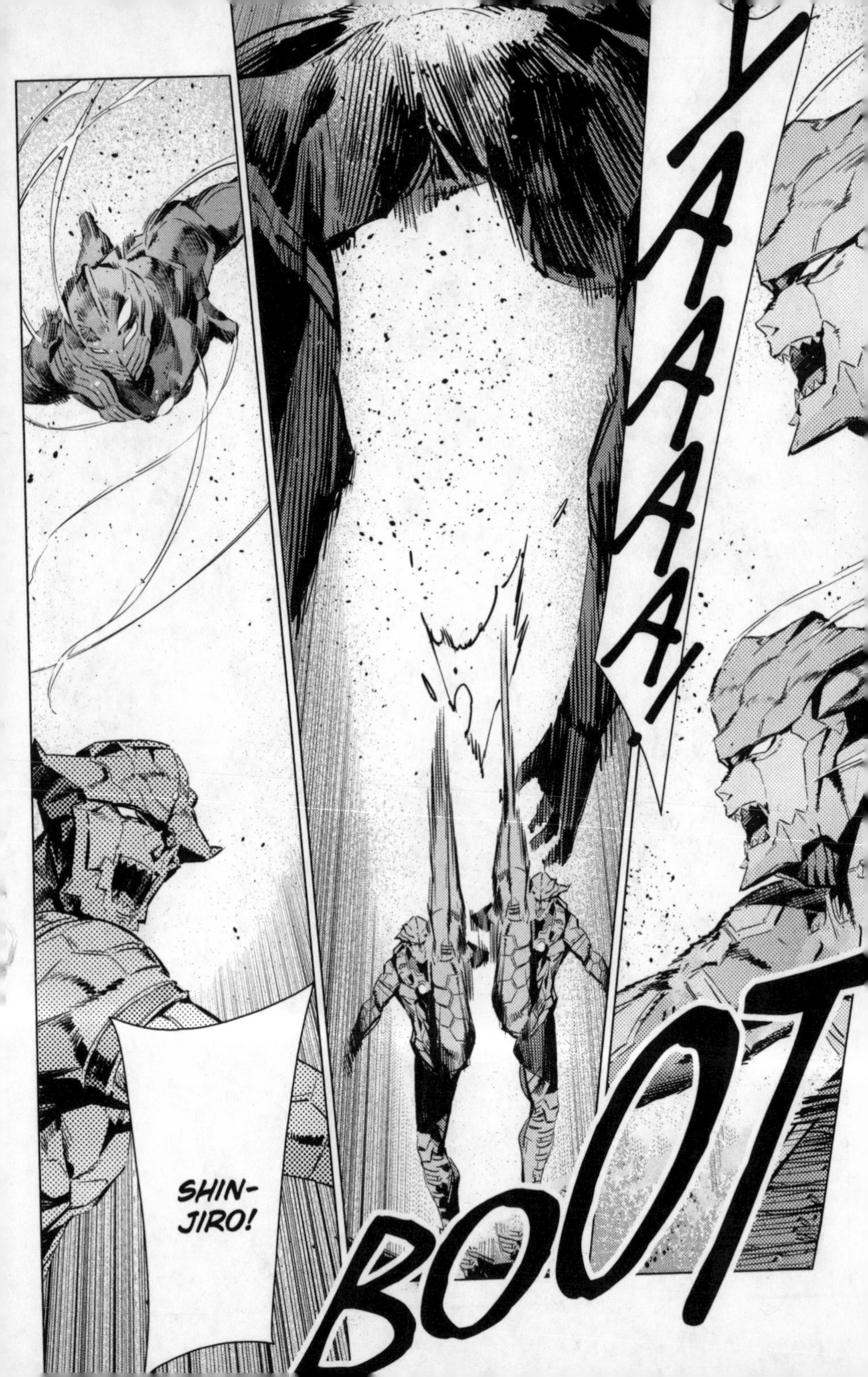
YAAAAAI!
BOOT
SHIN-
JIRO!

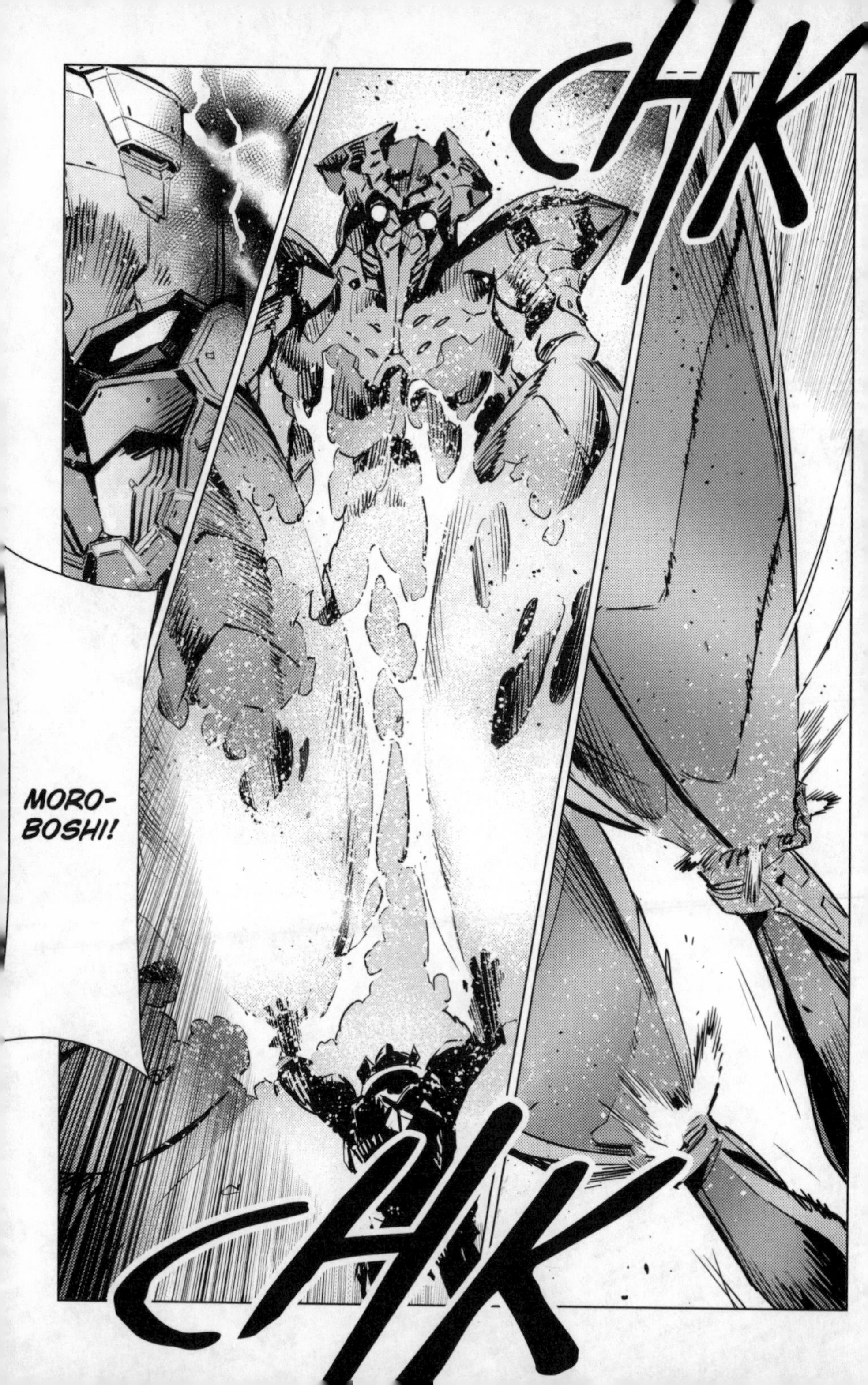
CHK
CHK
MORO-BOSHI!

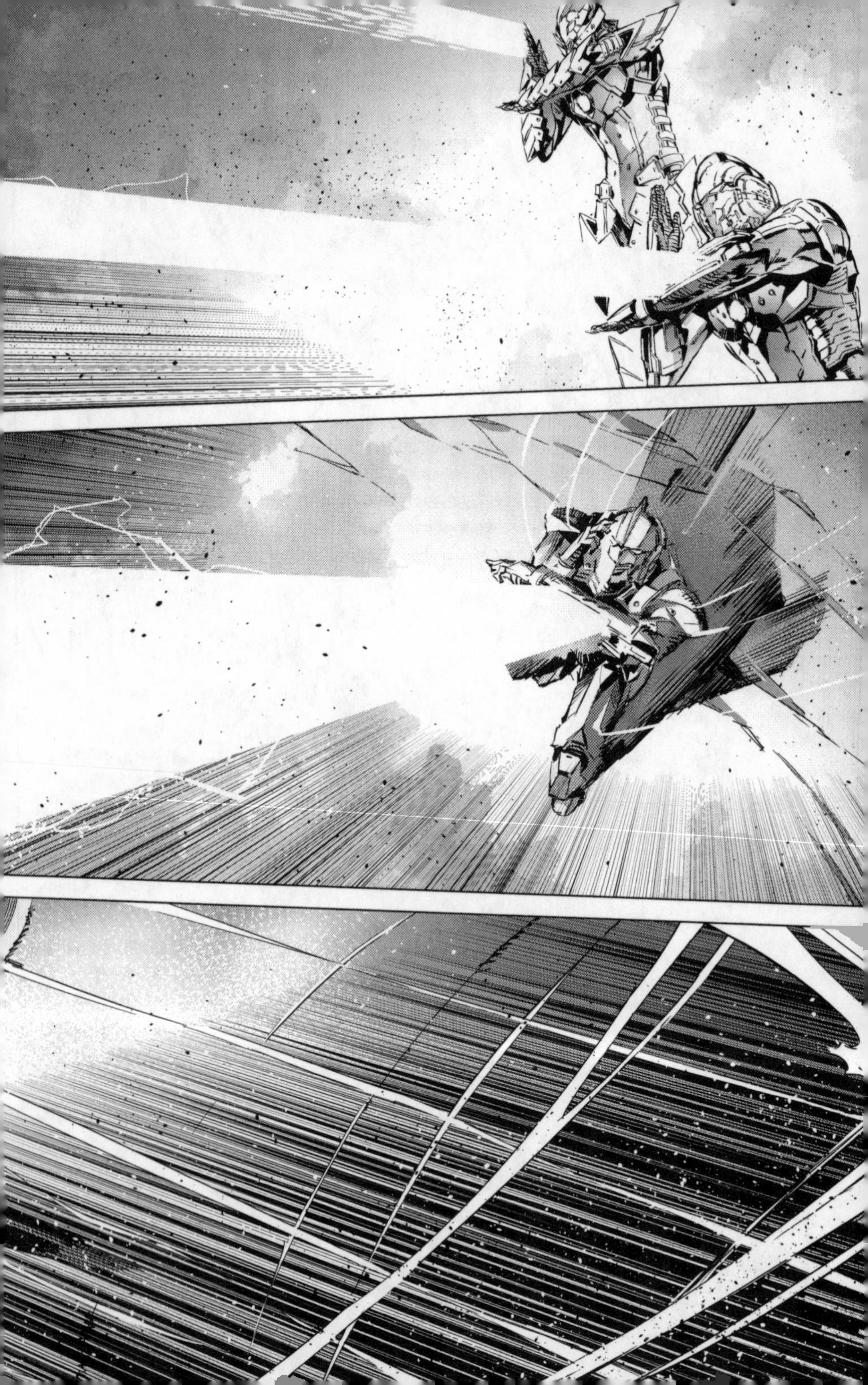

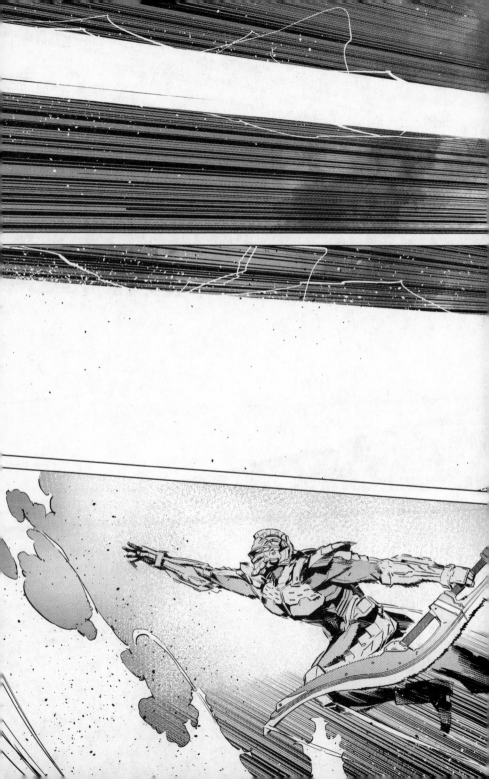

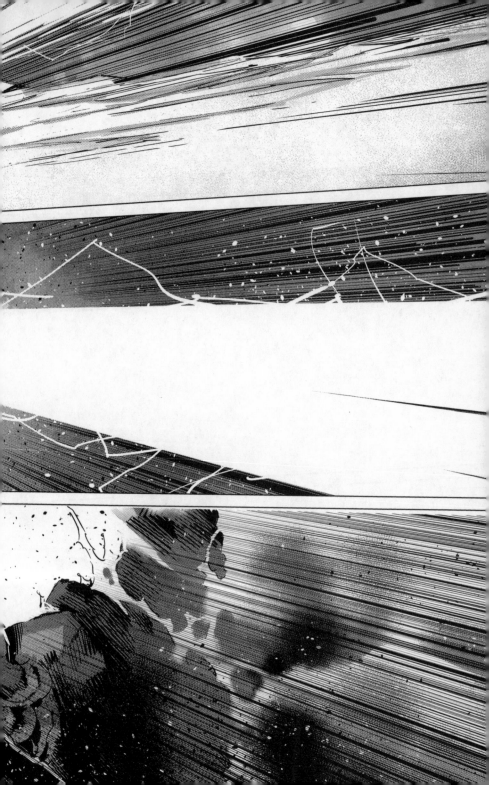

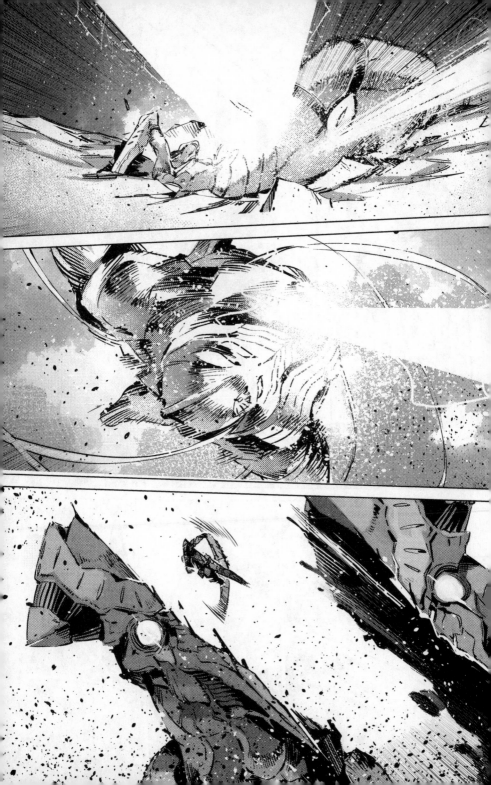

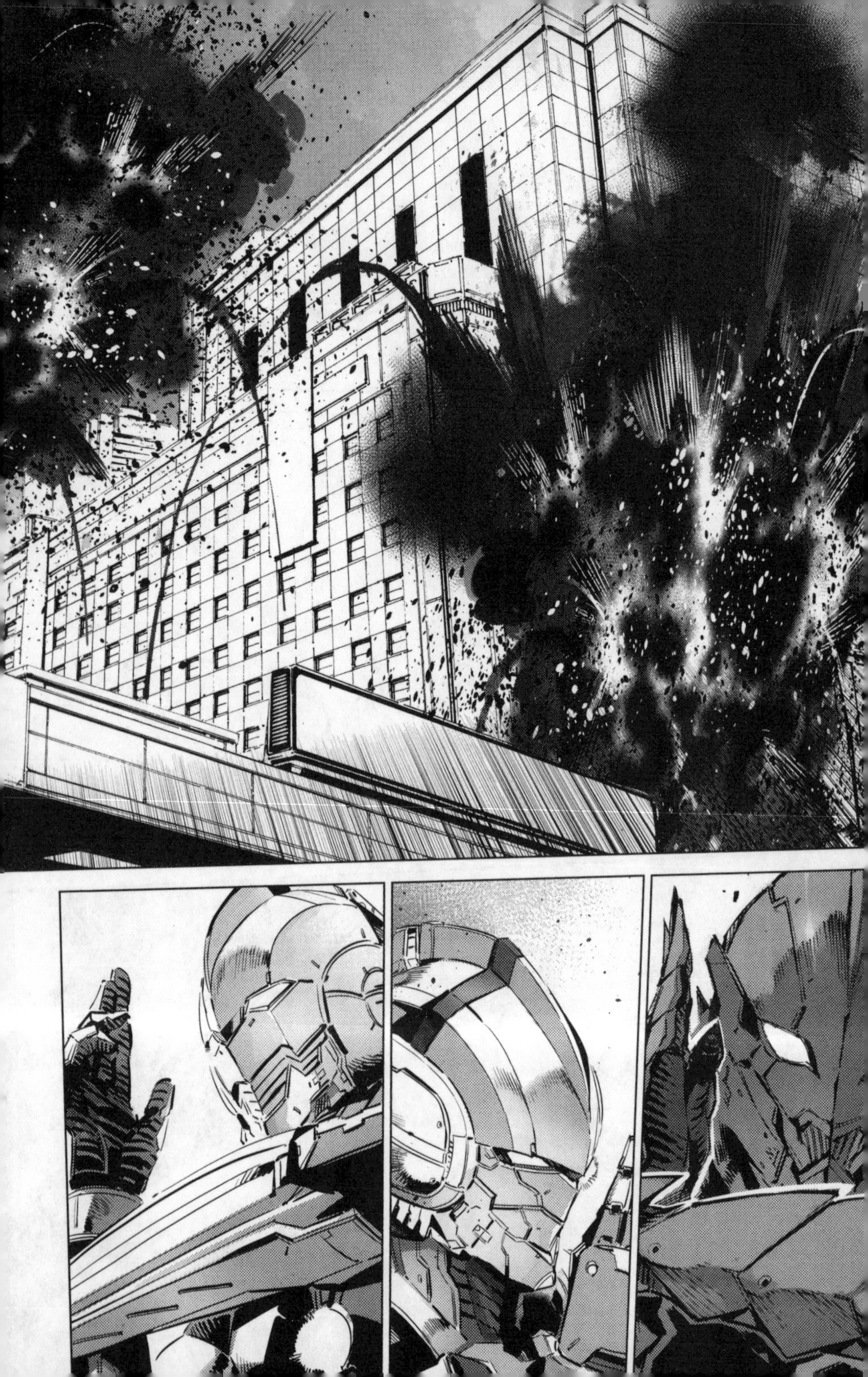

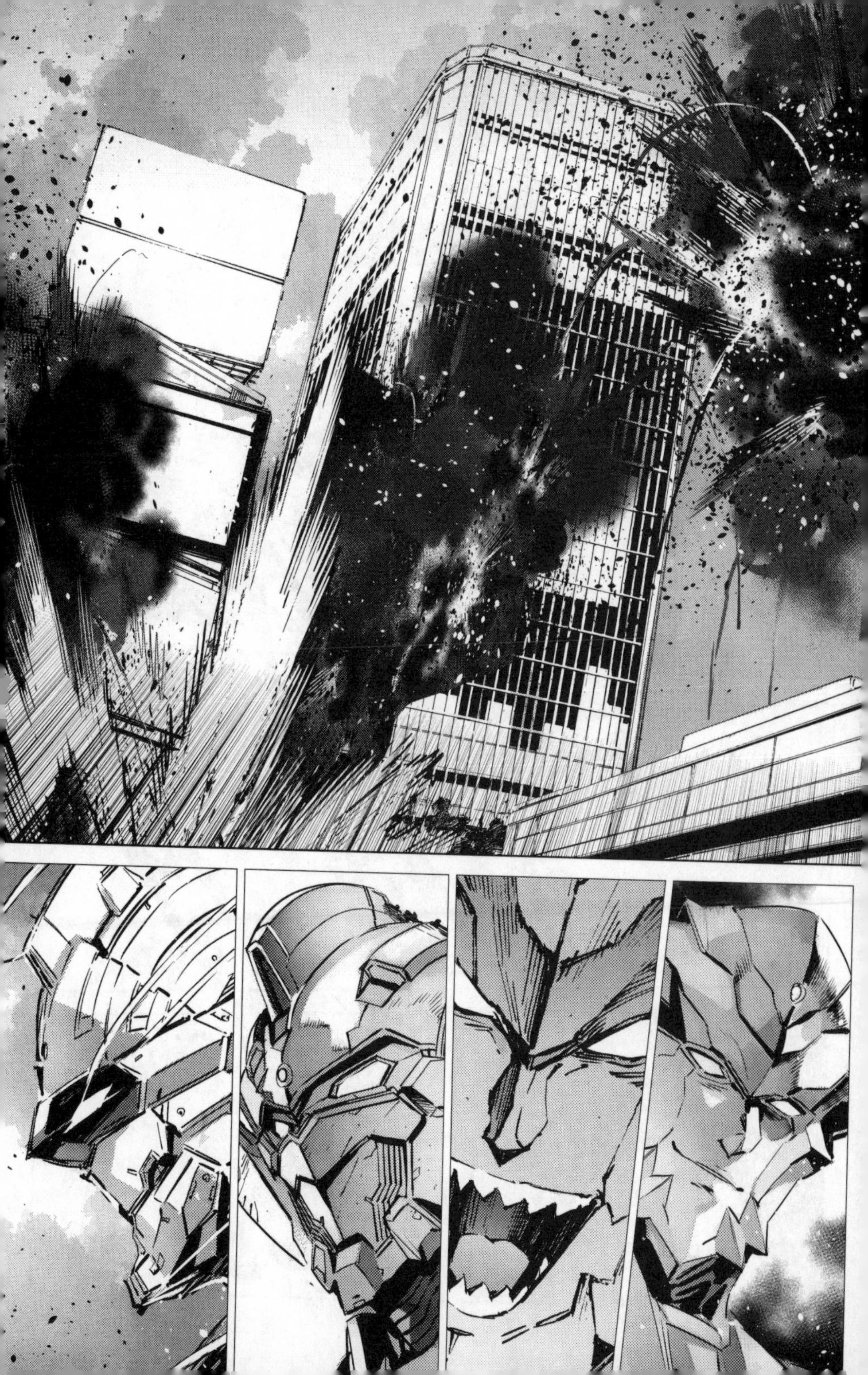

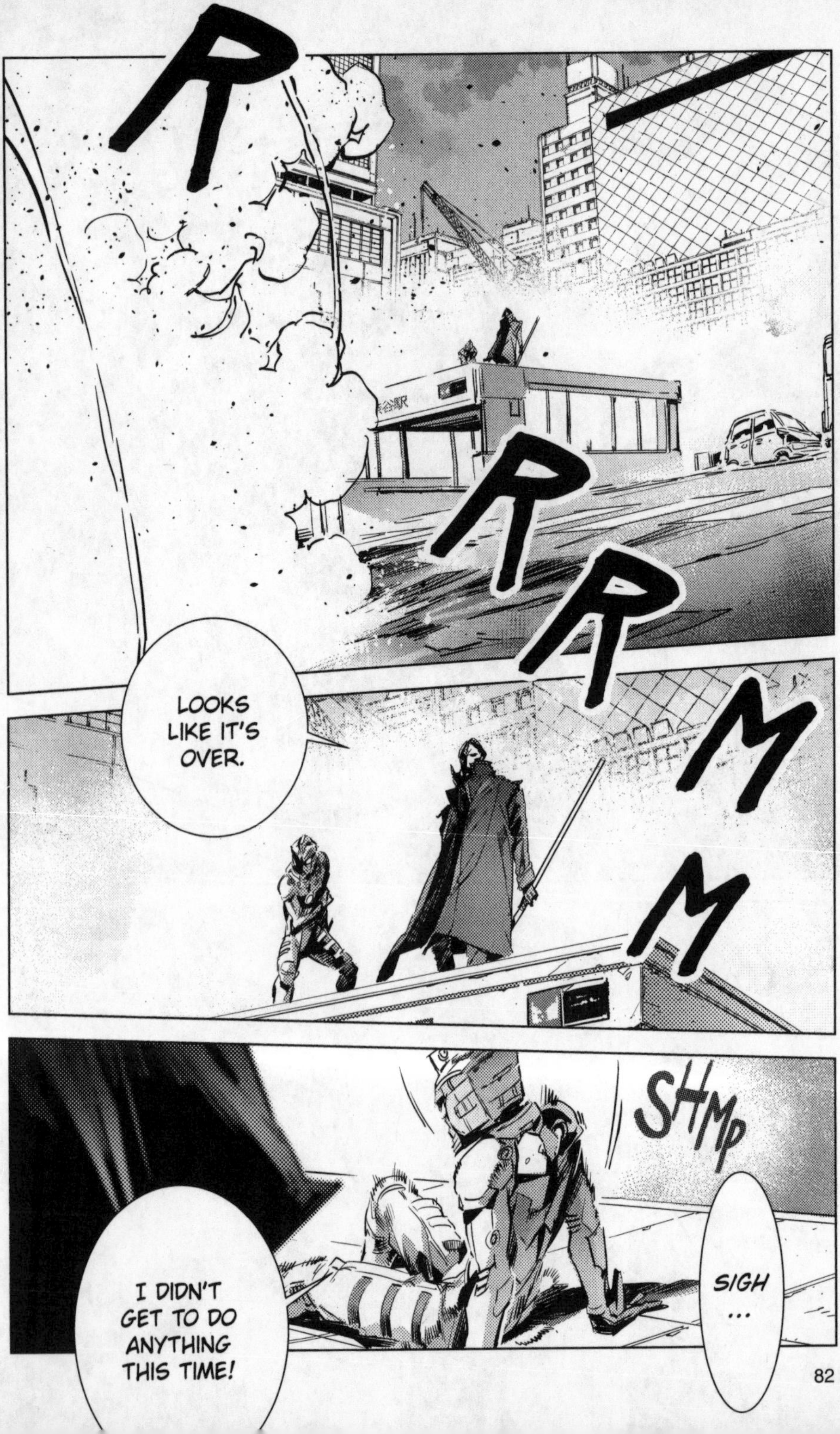
R—RRMM
LOOKS LIKE IT'S OVER.
SHMP
SIGH...
I DIDN'T GET TO DO ANYTHING THIS TIME!

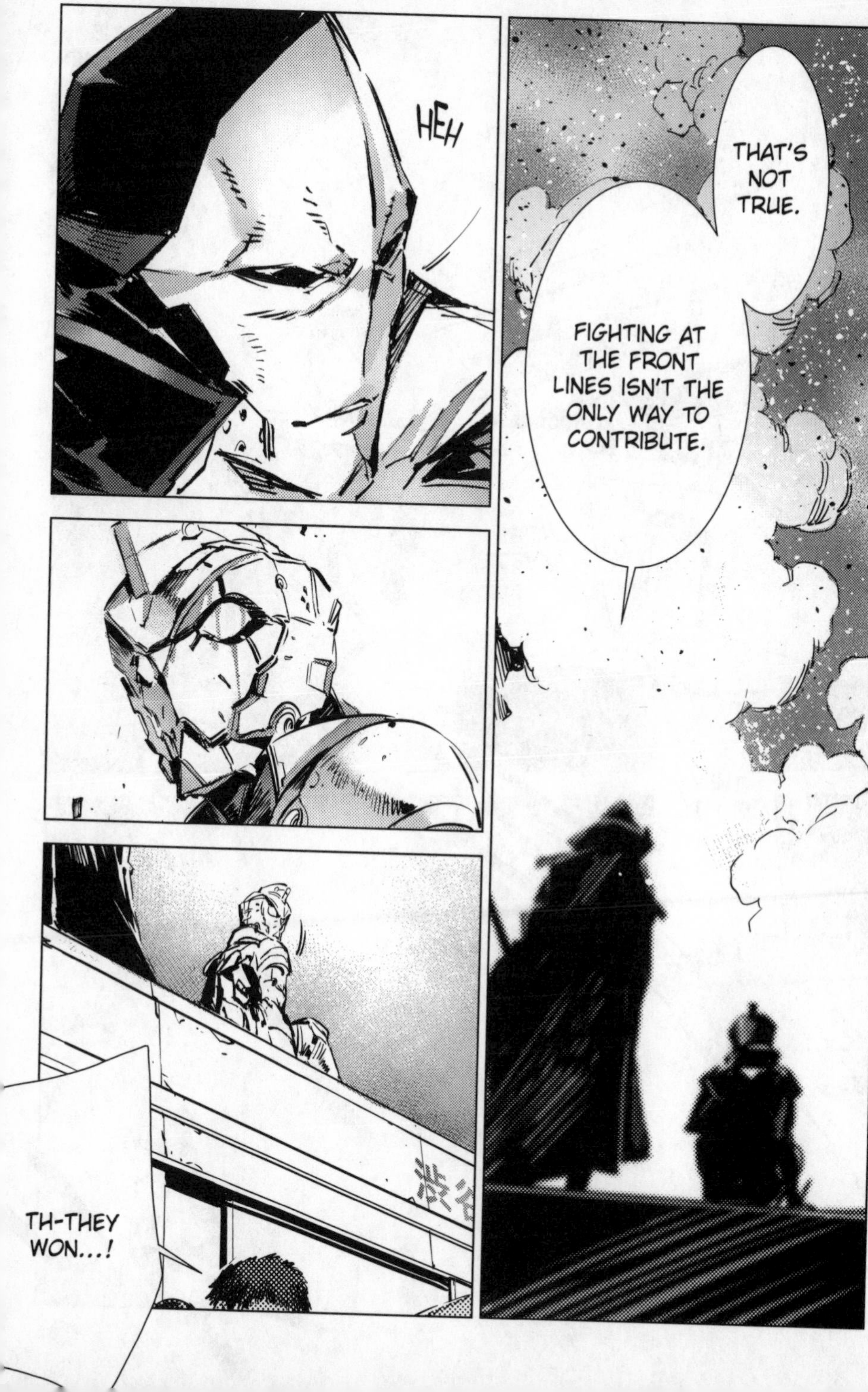
THAT'S NOT TRUE.
FIGHTING AT THE FRONT LINES ISN'T THE ONLY WAY TO CONTRIBUTE.
HEH
TH-THEY WON...!

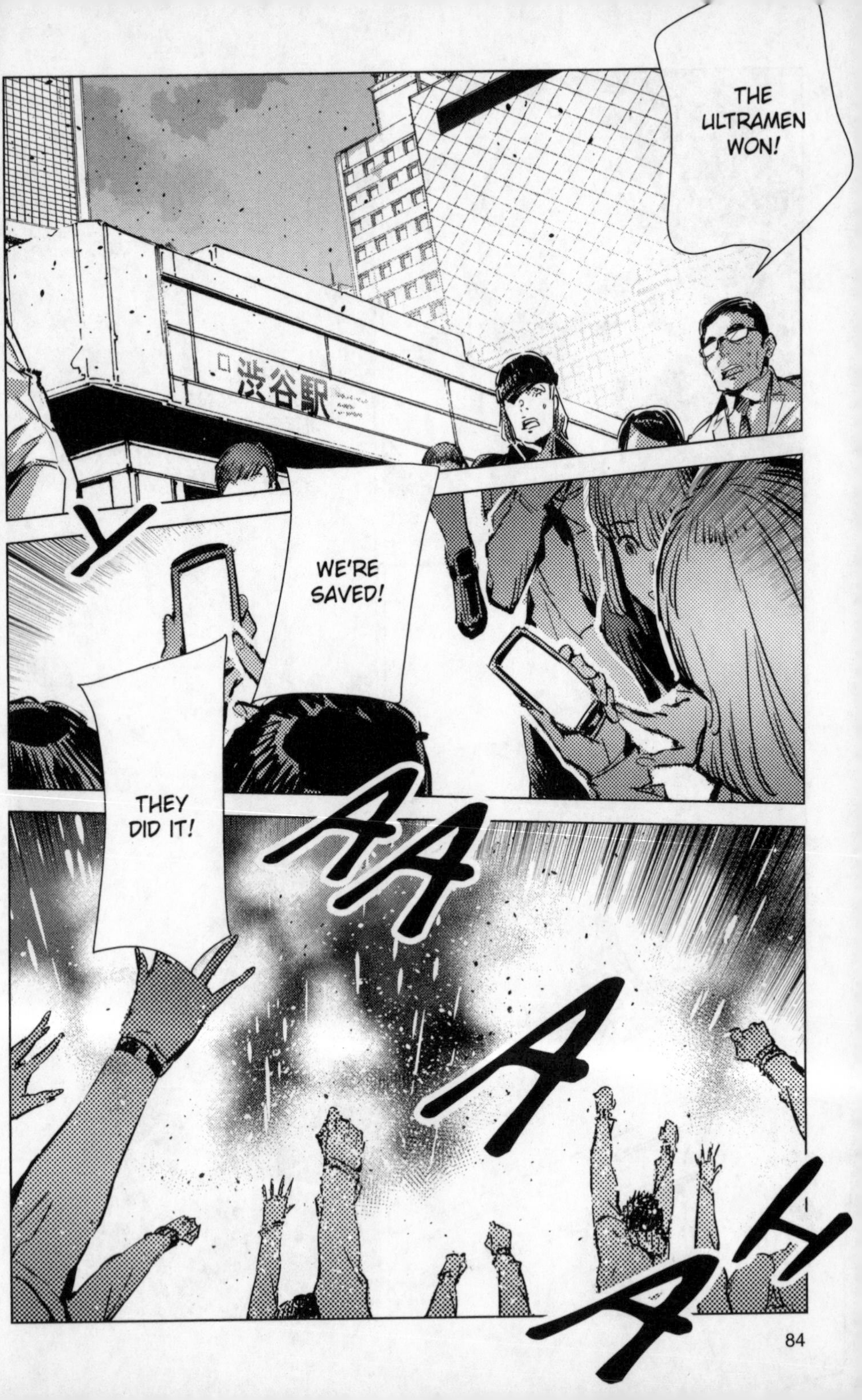
THE ULTRAMEN WON!
渋谷駅
WE'RE SAVED!
THEY DID IT!
YAAAAAH

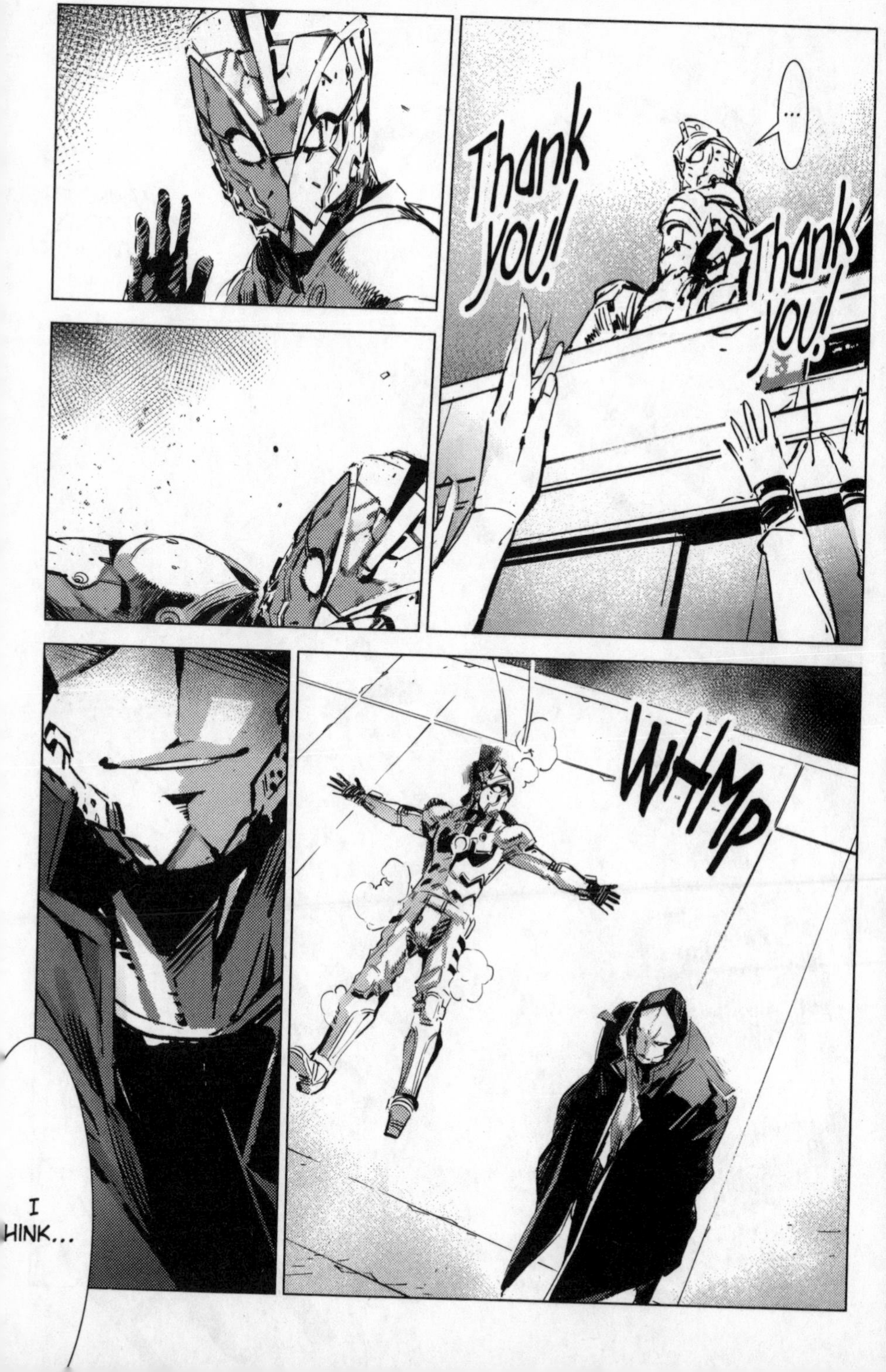
…
Thank you!
Thank you!
WHMP
I HINK...

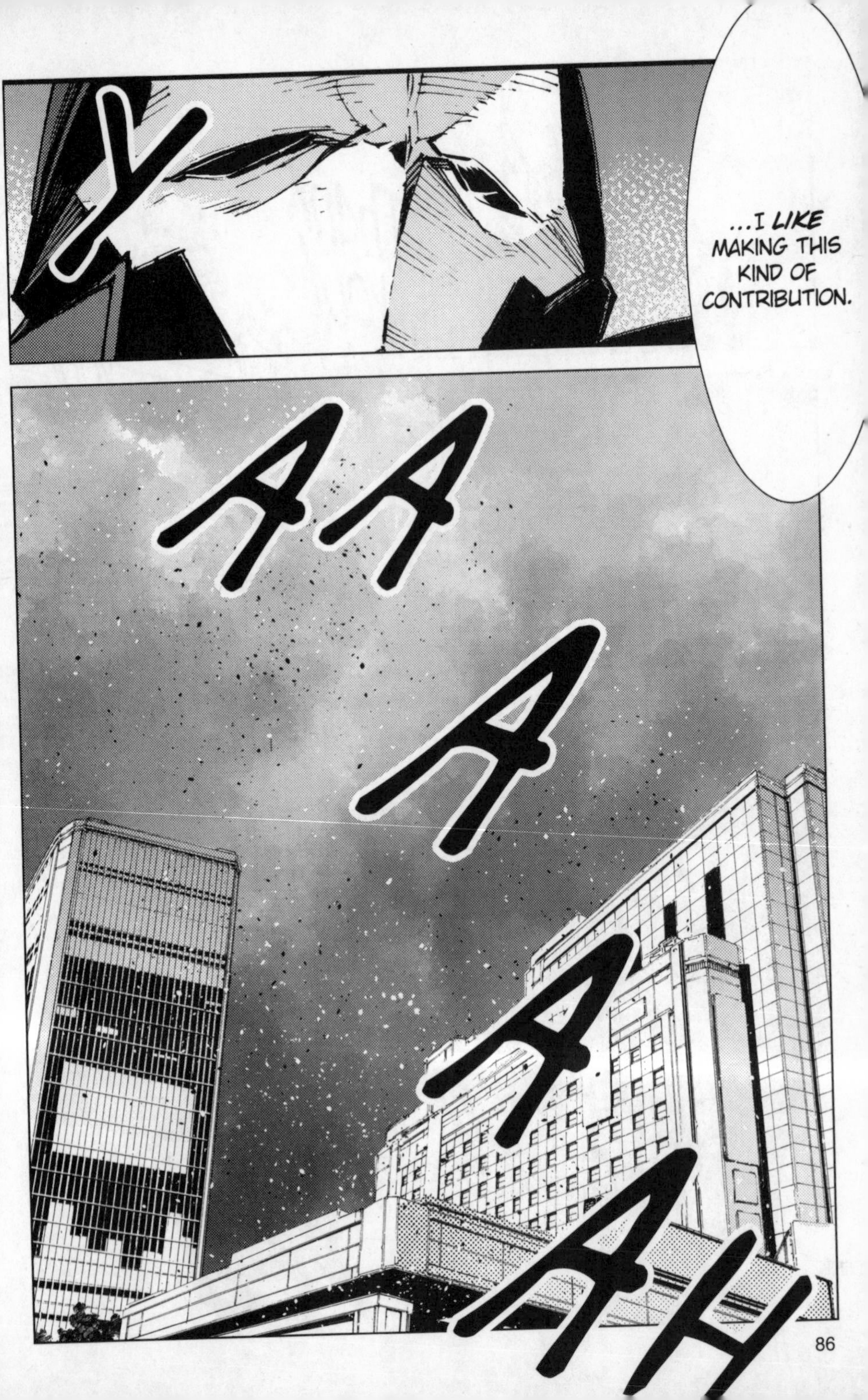
...I LIKE MAKING THIS KIND OF CONTRIBUTION.
Y
AAAAAH

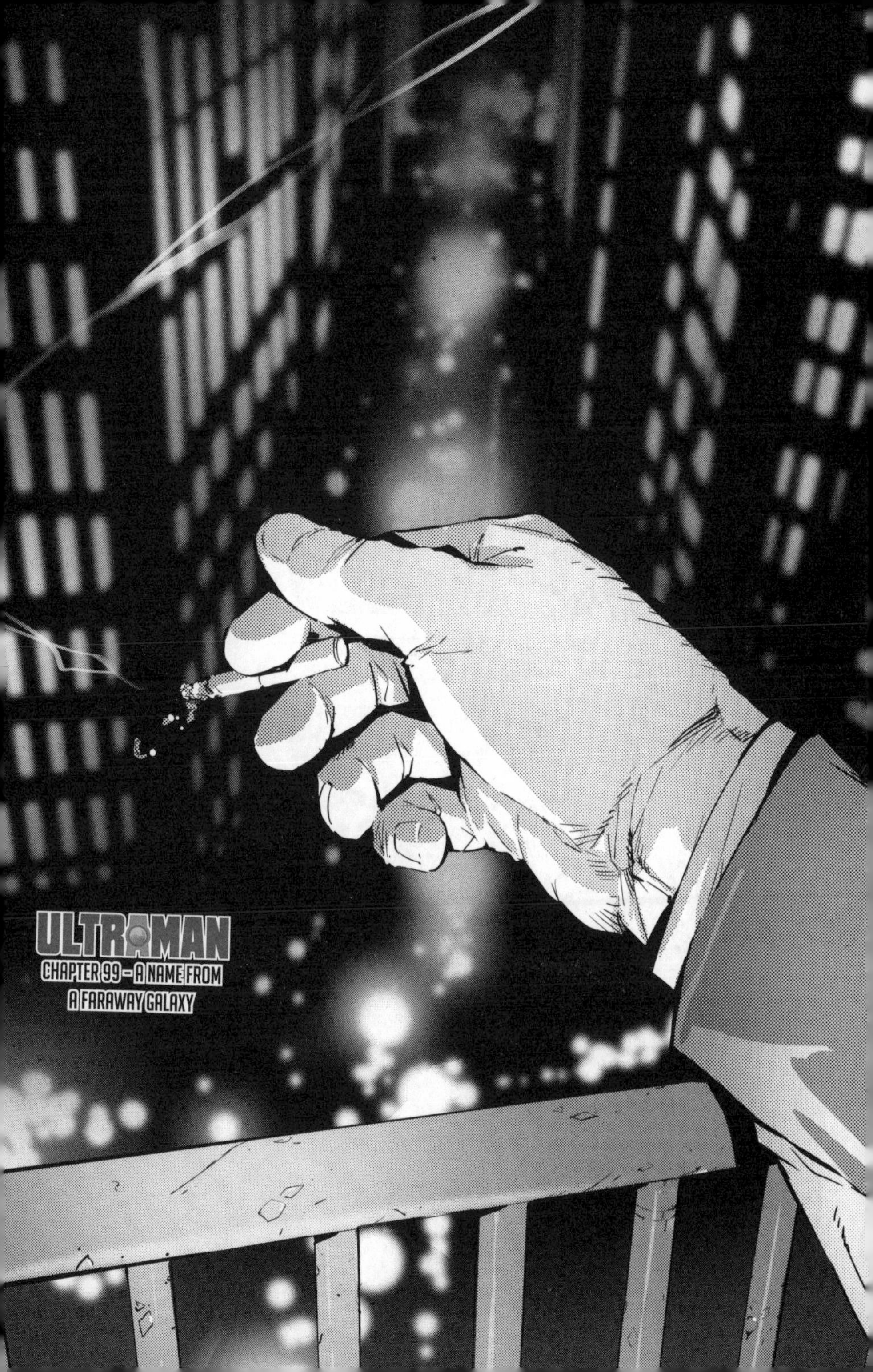
ULTRAMAN
CHAPTER 99 – A NAME FROM
A FARAWAY GALAXY

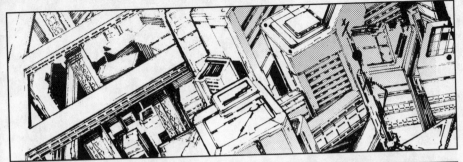

SON OF A...!

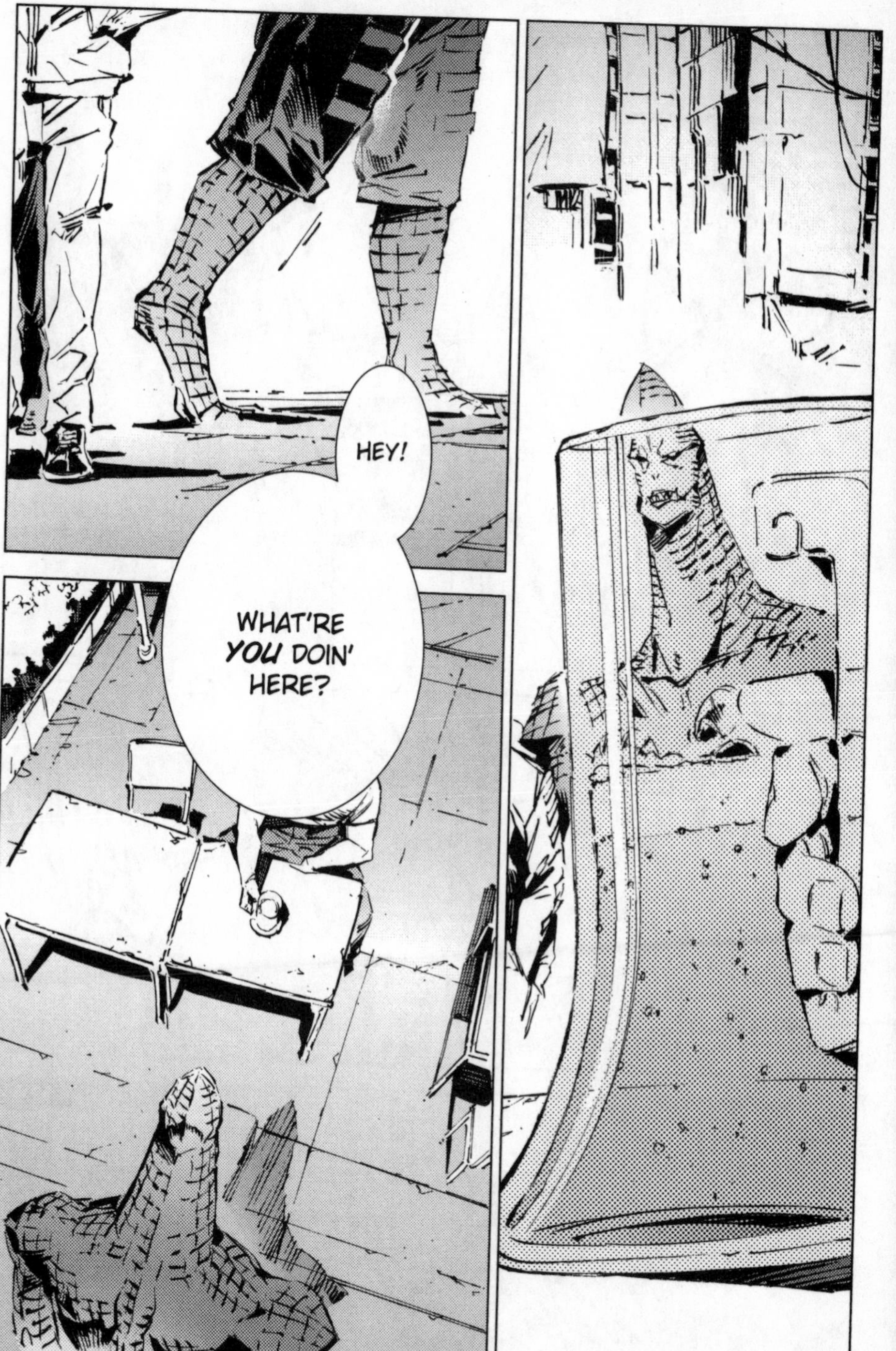
HEY!
WHAT'RE YOU DOIN' HERE?

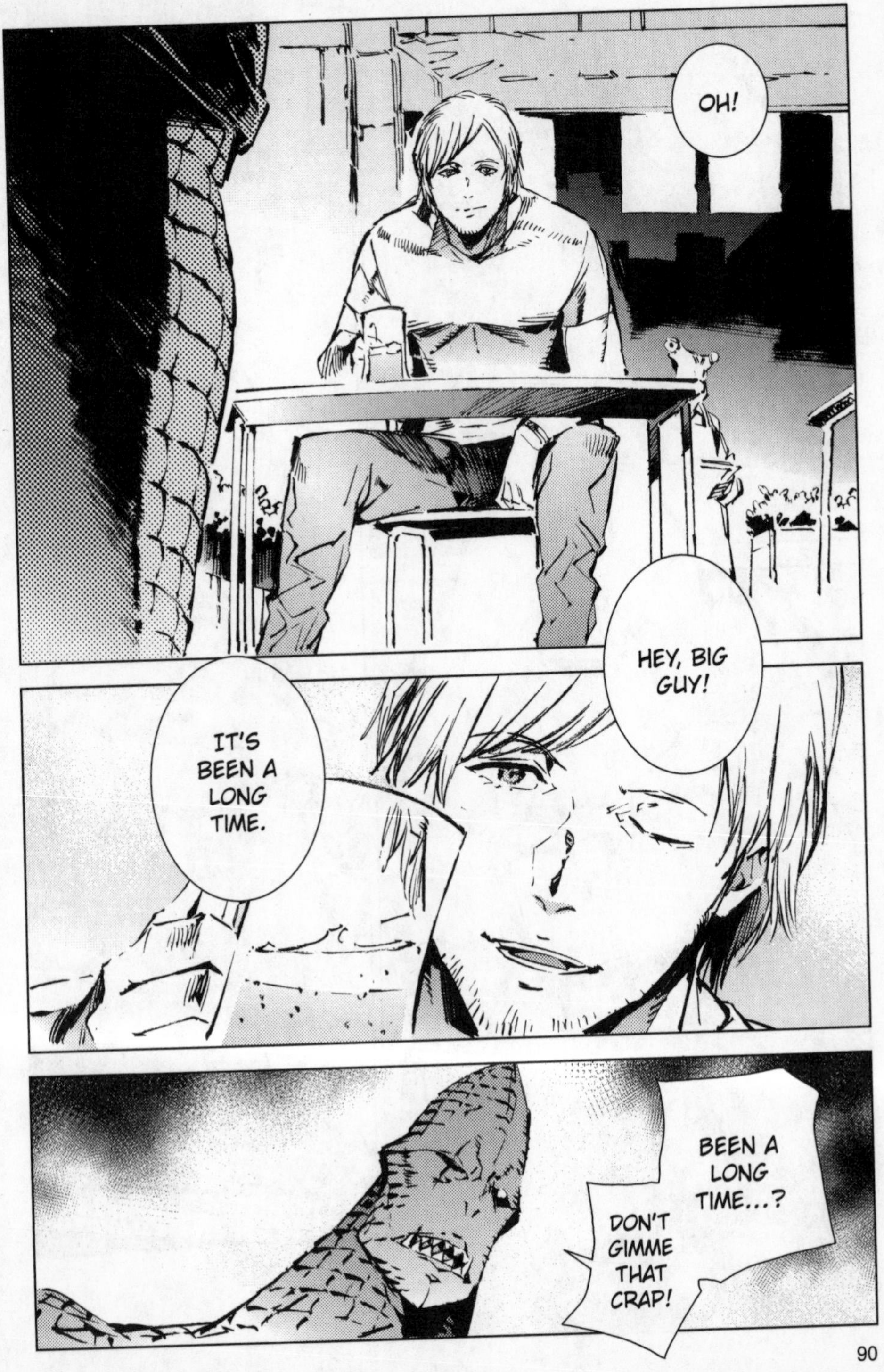
OH!
HEY, BIG GUY!
IT'S BEEN A LONG TIME.
BEEN A LONG TIME...?
DON'T GIMME THAT CRAP!

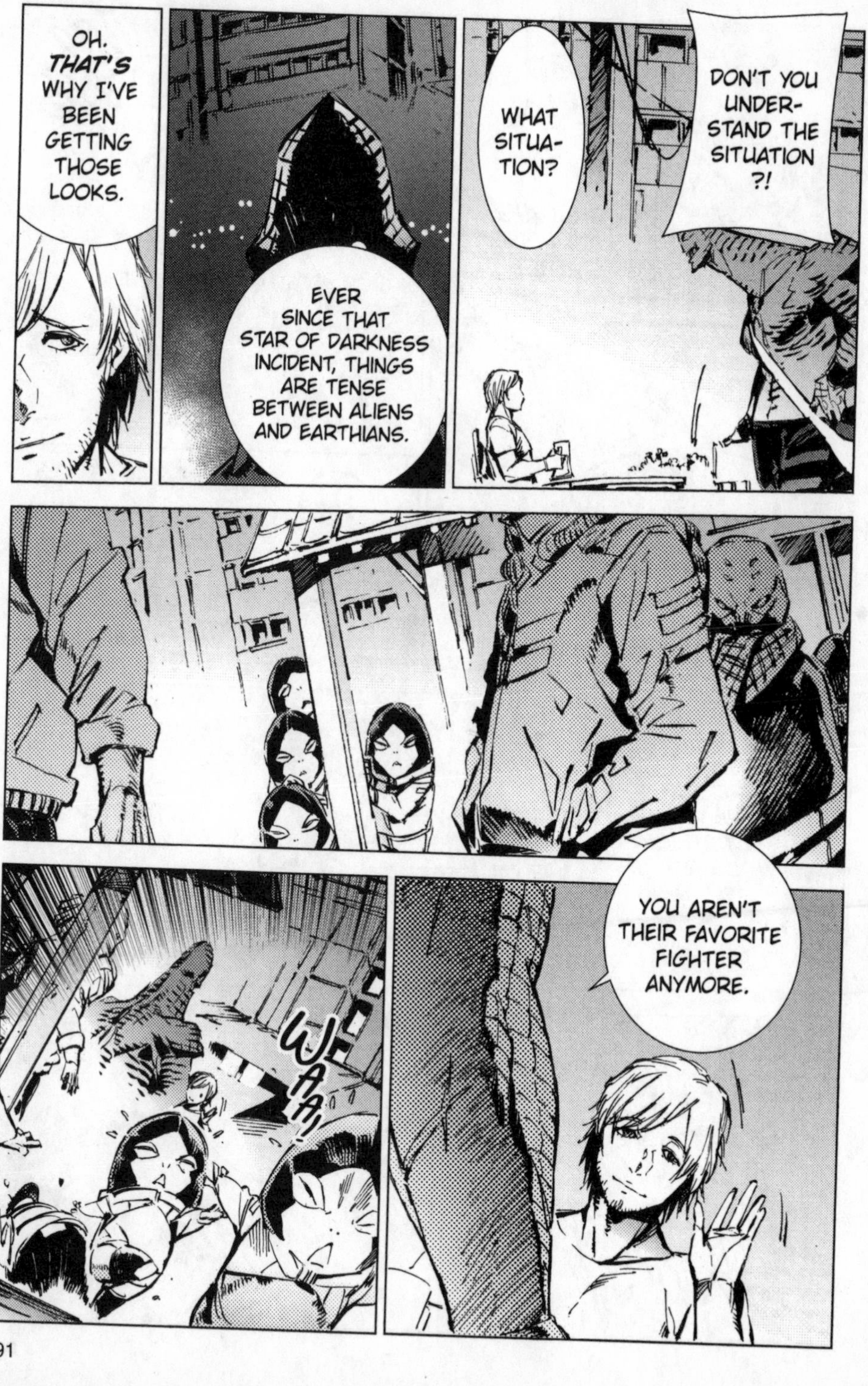
DON'T YOU UNDER-STAND THE SITUATION ?!
WHAT SITUATION?
EVER SINCE THAT STAR OF DARKNESS INCIDENT, THINGS ARE TENSE BETWEEN ALIENS AND EARTHIANS.
OH. *THAT'S* WHY I'VE BEEN GETTING THOSE LOOKS.
YOU AREN'T THEIR FAVORITE FIGHTER ANYMORE.
WAAA!

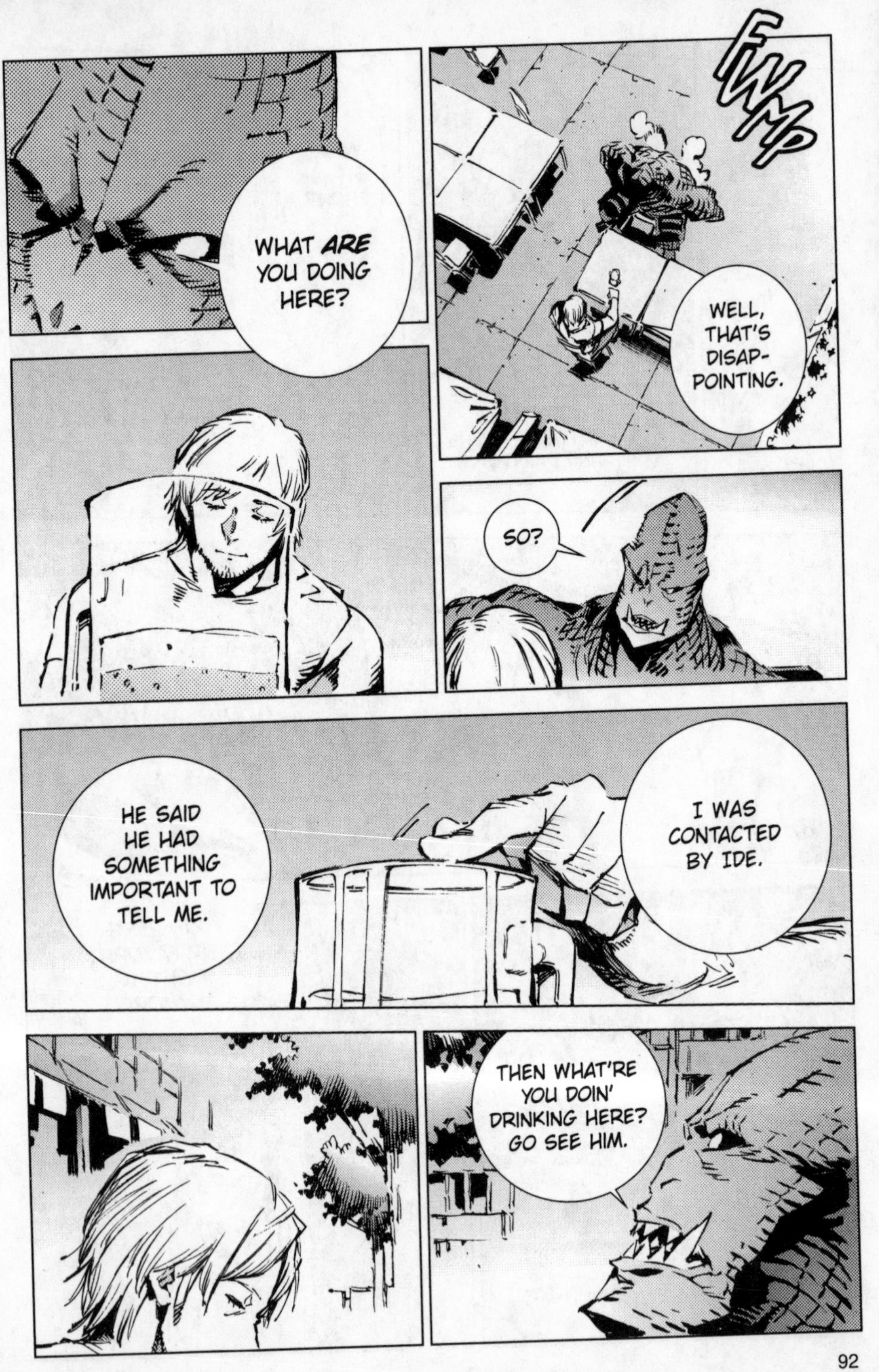
FWMP
WELL, THAT'S DISAP-POINTING.
WHAT *ARE* YOU DOING HERE?
SO?
I WAS CONTACTED BY IDE.
HE SAID HE HAD SOMETHING IMPORTANT TO TELL ME.
THEN WHAT'RE YOU DOIN' DRINKING HERE? GO SEE HIM.

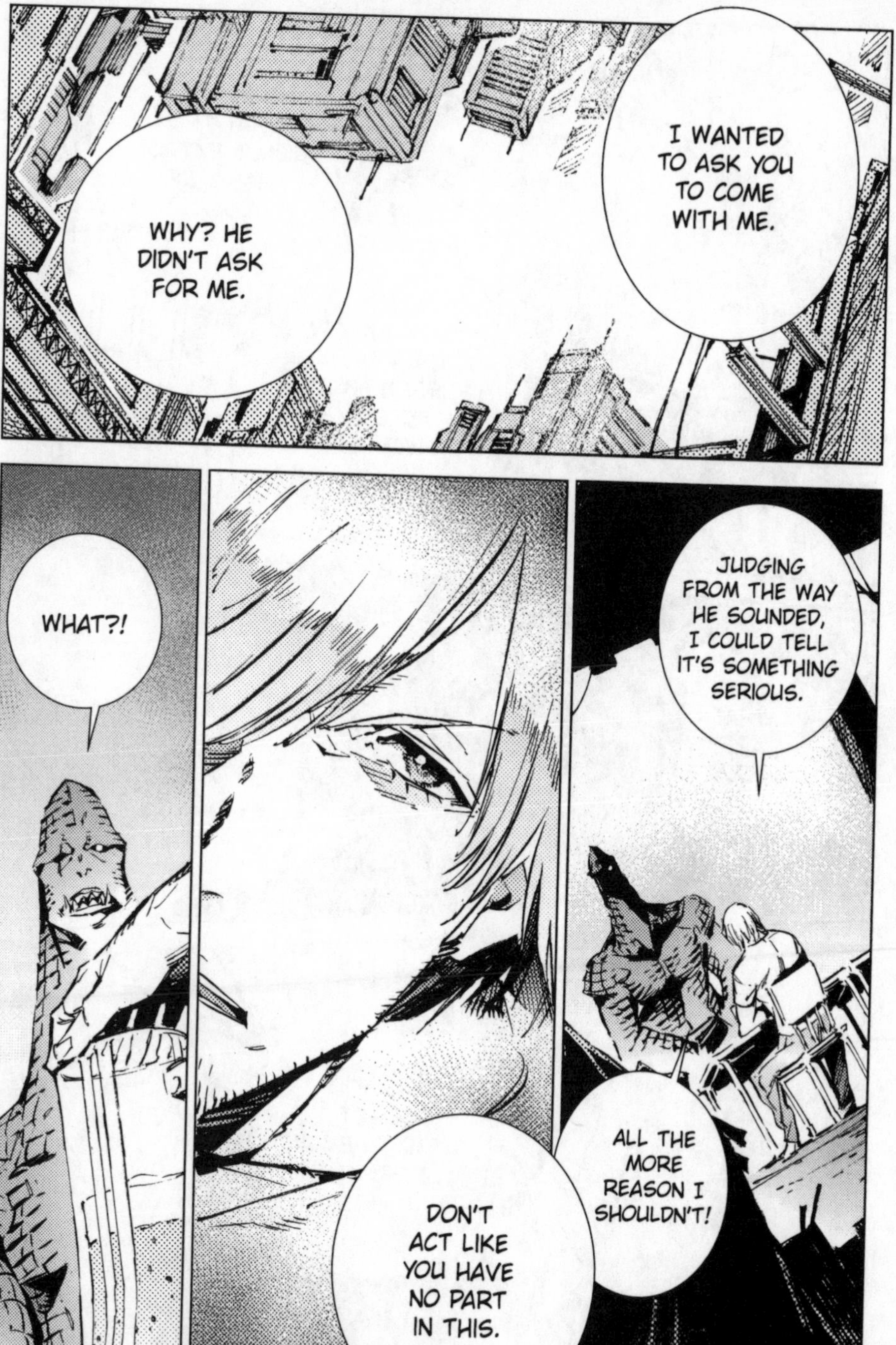
I WANTED TO ASK YOU TO COME WITH ME.
WHY? HE DIDN'T ASK FOR ME.
JUDGING FROM THE WAY HE SOUNDED, I COULD TELL IT'S SOMETHING SERIOUS.
ALL THE MORE REASON I SHOULDN'T!
DON'T ACT LIKE YOU HAVE NO PART IN THIS.
WHAT?!

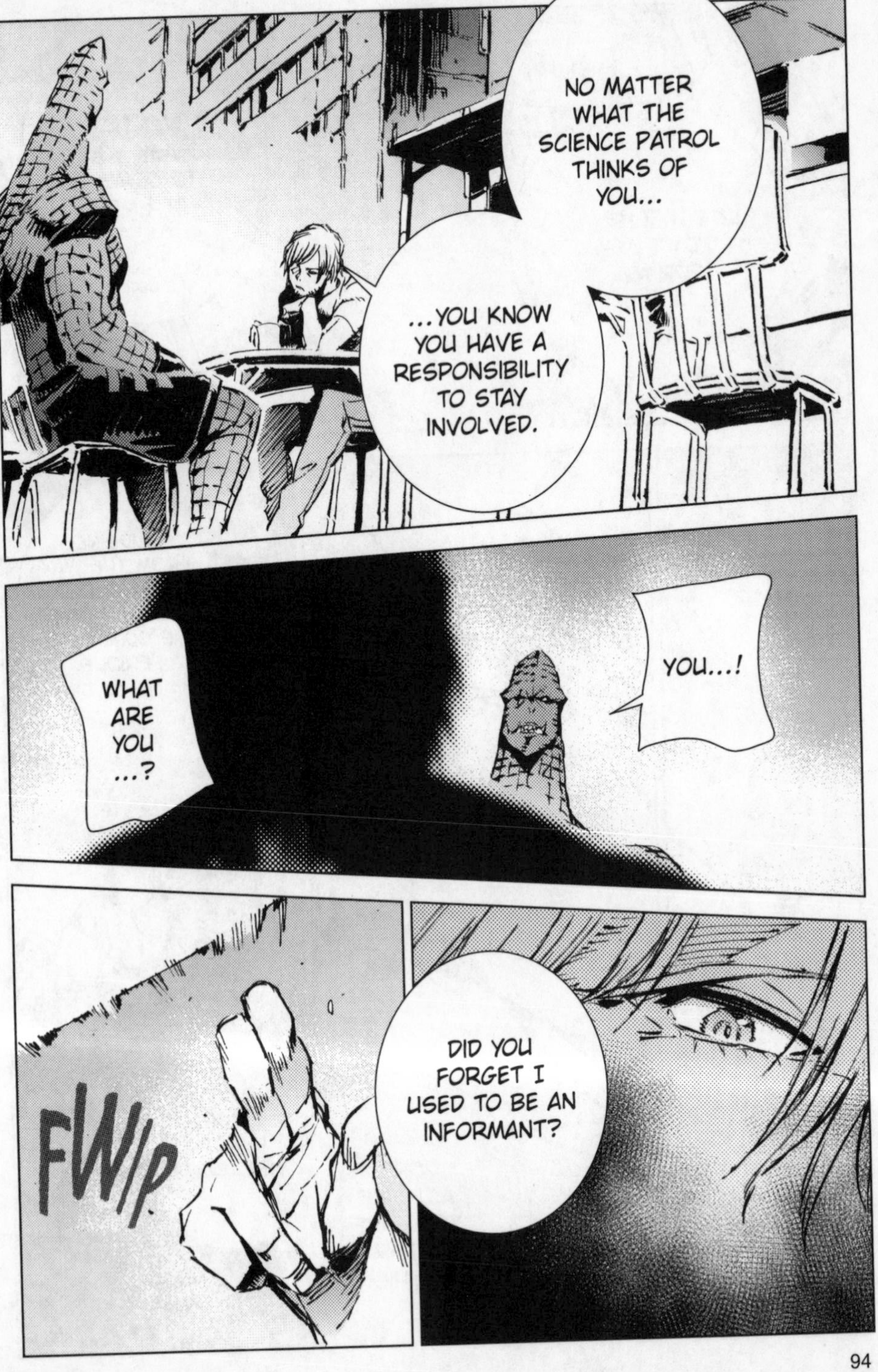
NO MATTER WHAT THE SCIENCE PATROL THINKS OF YOU...
...YOU KNOW YOU HAVE A RESPONSIBILITY TO STAY INVOLVED.
YOU...!
WHAT ARE YOU ...?
DID YOU FORGET I USED TO BE AN INFORMANT?
FWIP

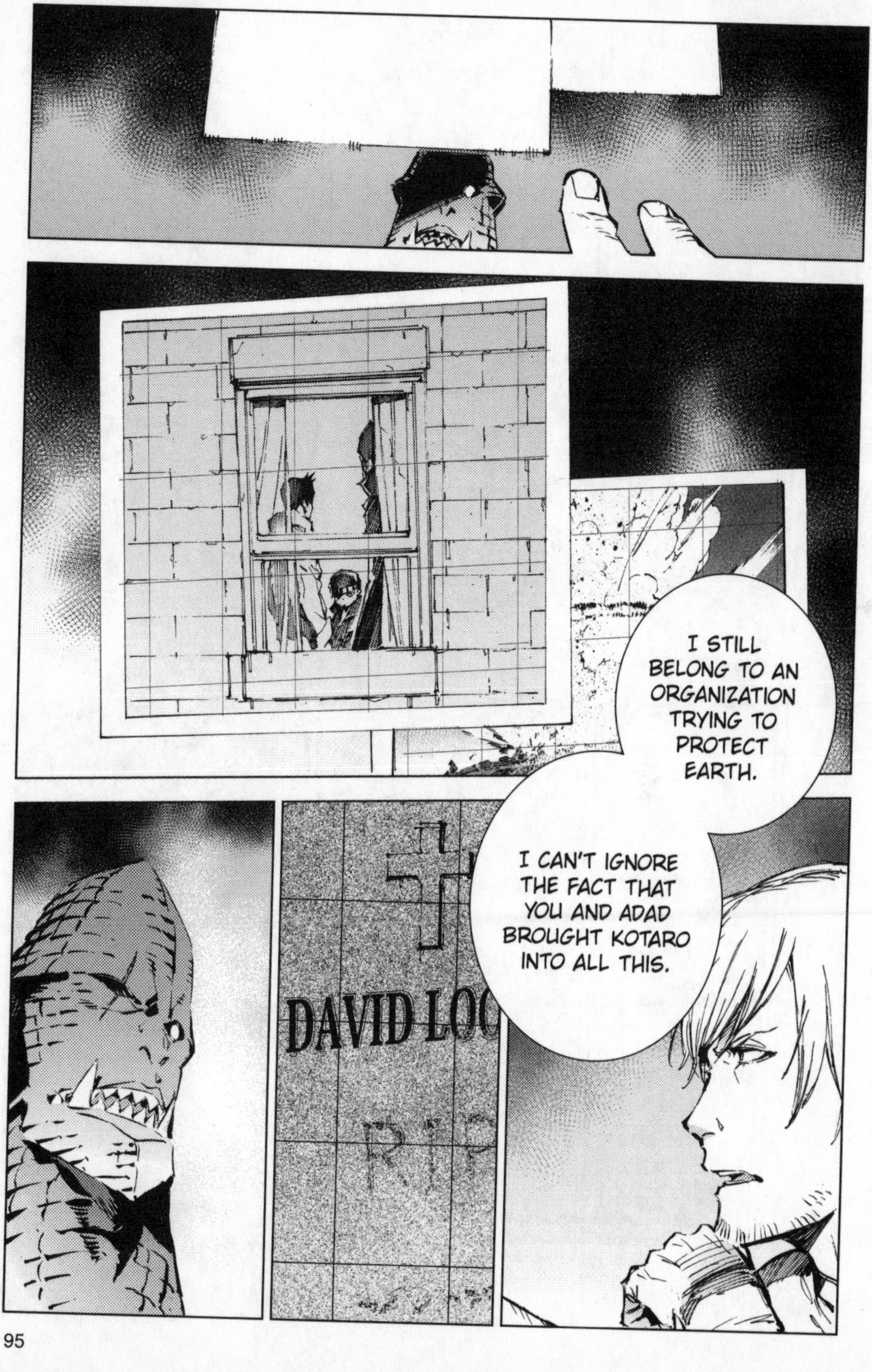
I STILL BELONG TO AN ORGANIZATION TRYING TO PROTECT EARTH.
I CAN'T IGNORE THE FACT THAT YOU AND ADAD BROUGHT KOTARO INTO ALL THIS.
DAVID LOC
RIP

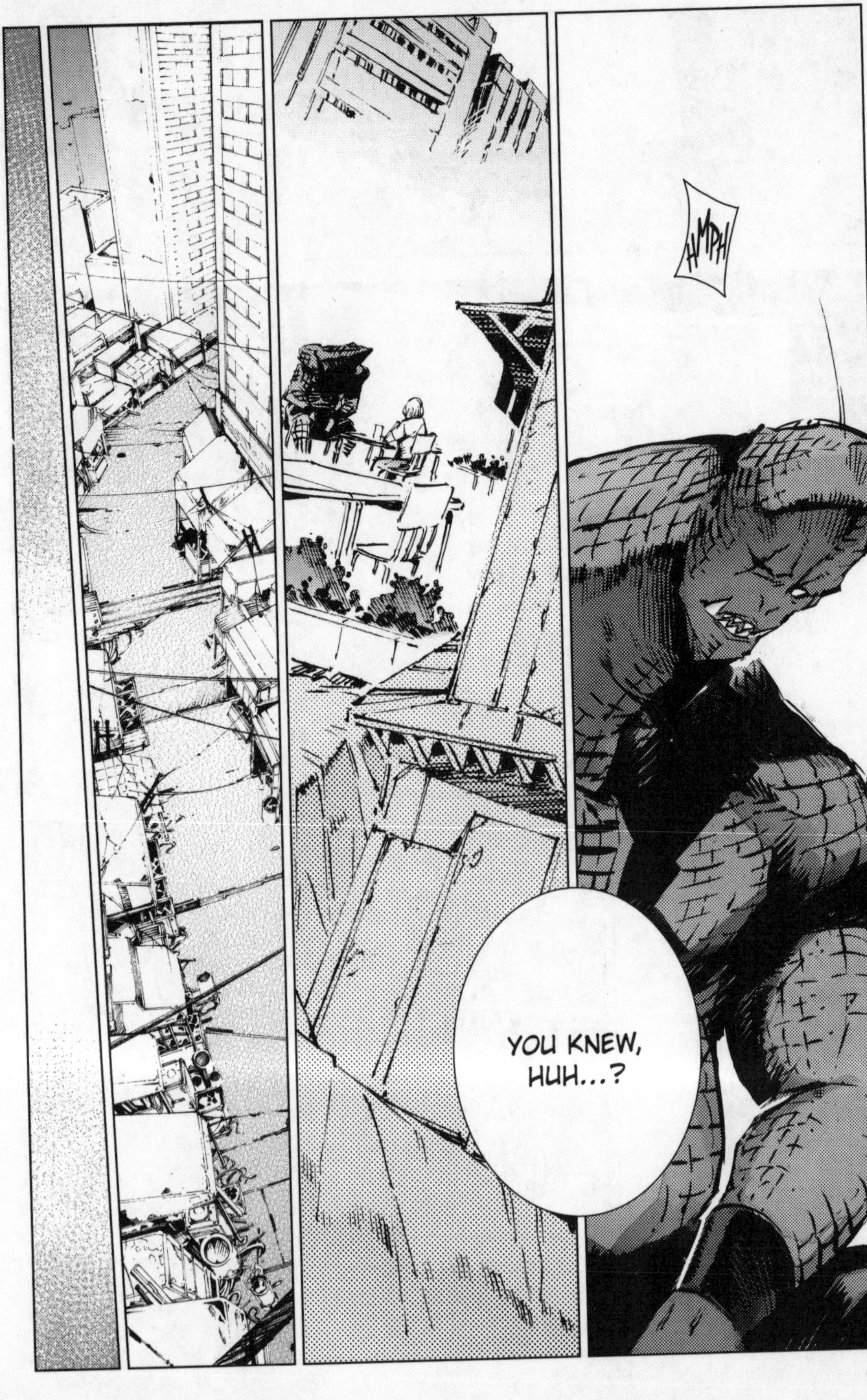
HMPH
YOU KNEW, HUH...?

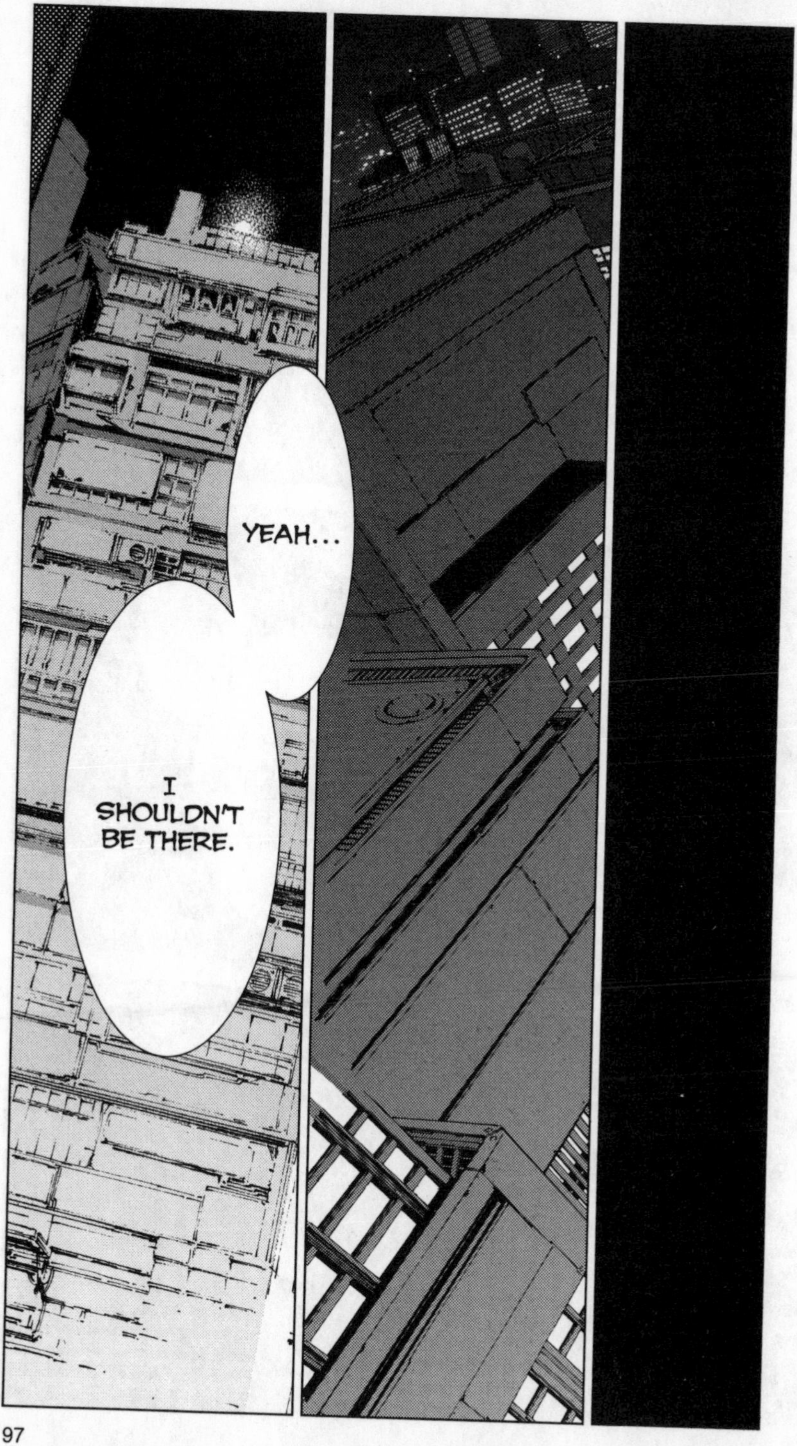
YEAH...
I SHOULDN'T BE THERE.

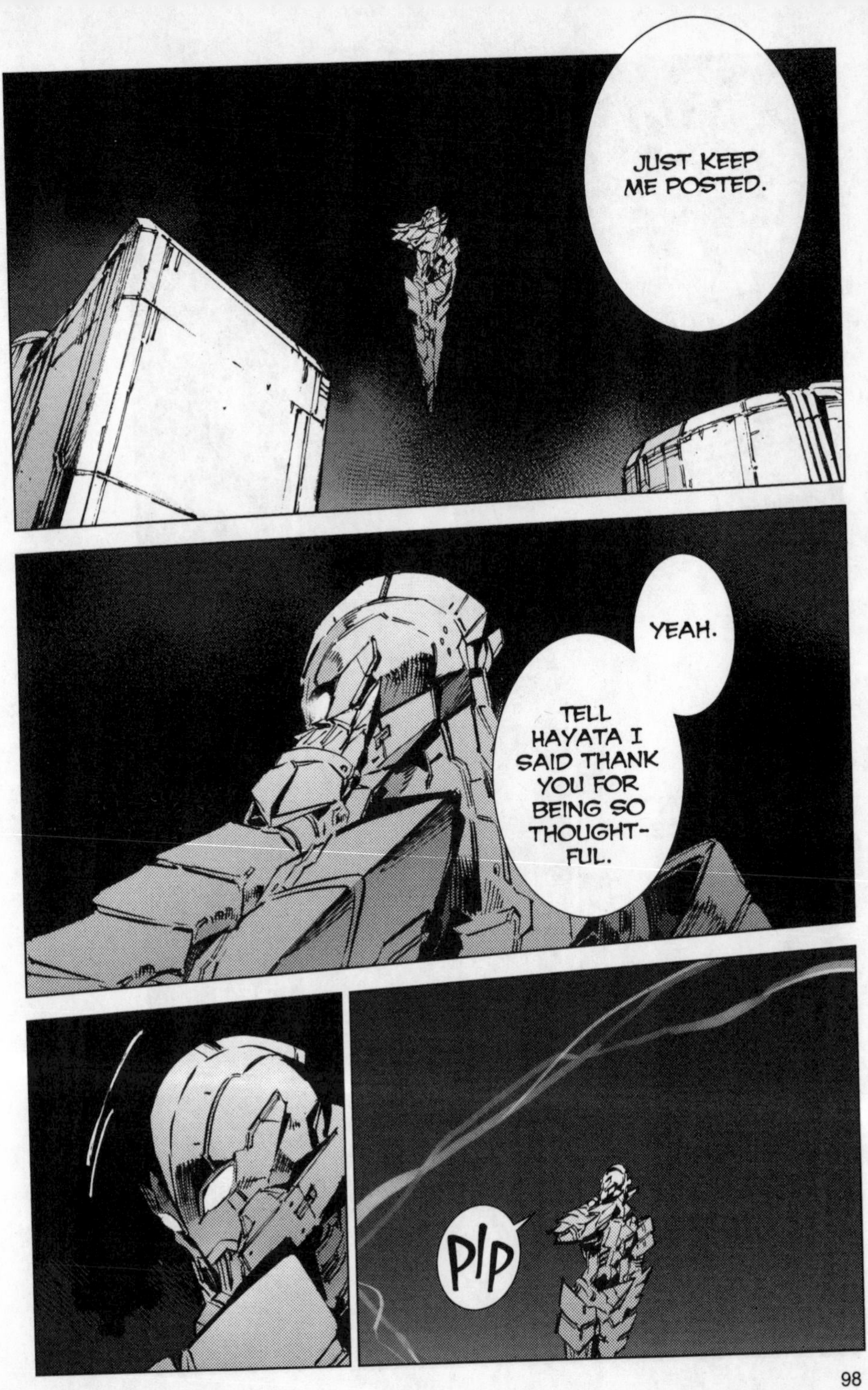
JUST KEEP ME POSTED.
YEAH.
TELL HAYATA I SAID THANK YOU FOR BEING SO THOUGHT-FUL.
PIP

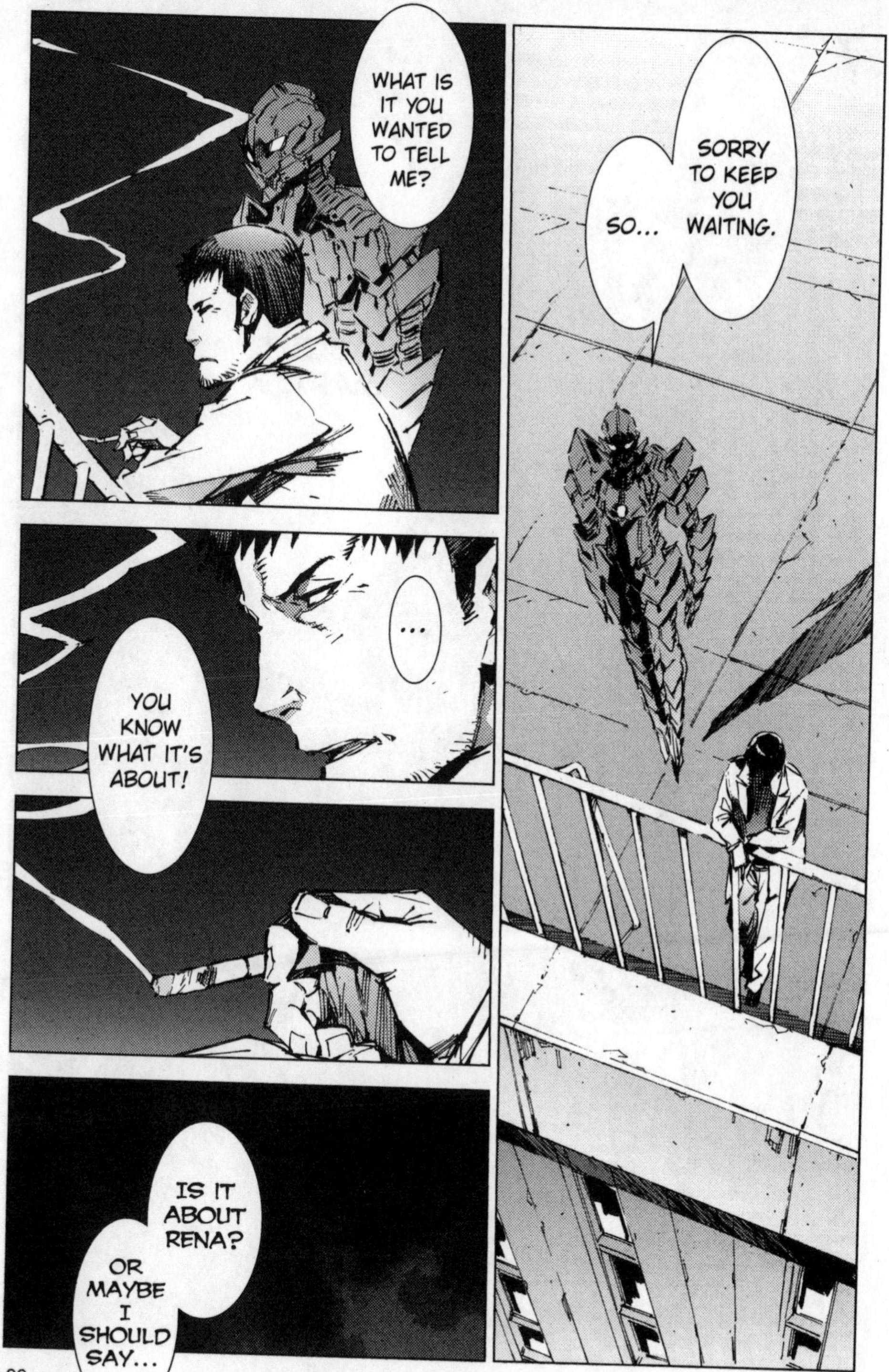
SORRY TO KEEP YOU WAITING.
SO...
WHAT IS IT YOU WANTED TO TELL ME?
...
YOU KNOW WHAT IT'S ABOUT!
IS IT ABOUT RENA?
OR MAYBE I SHOULD SAY...

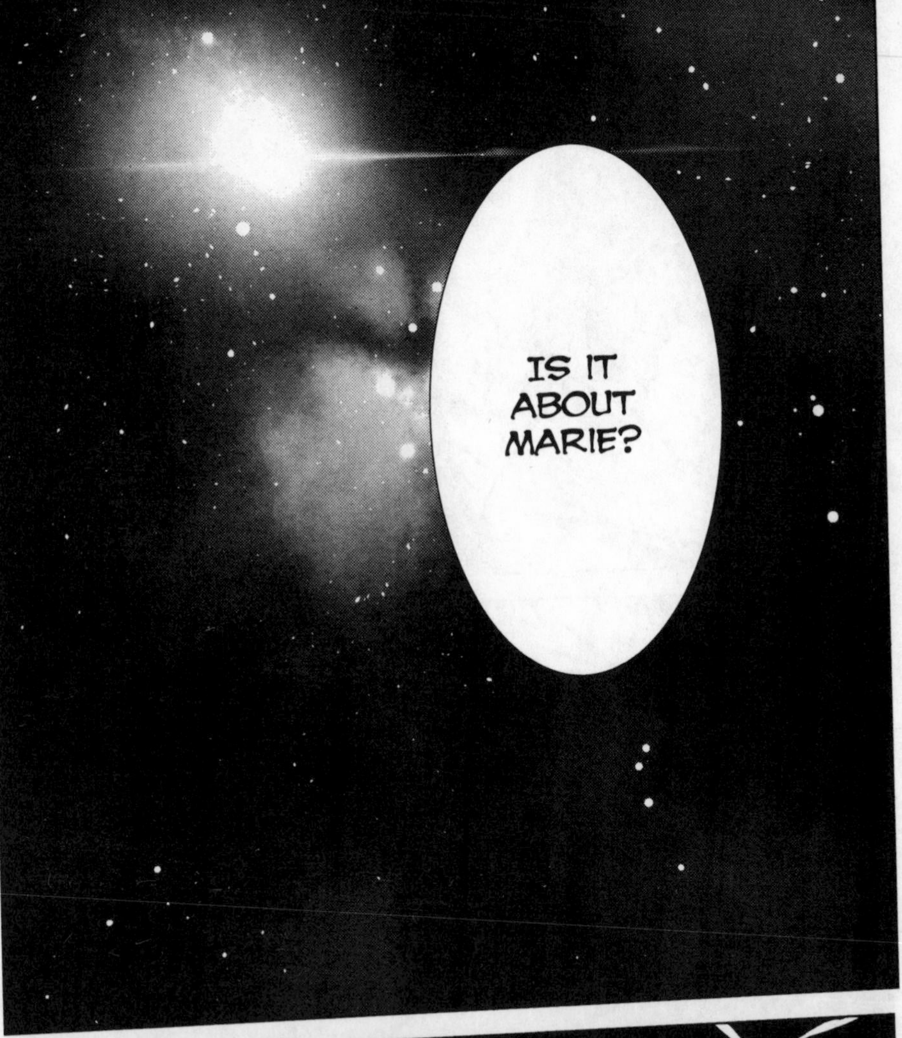
IS IT ABOUT MARIE?
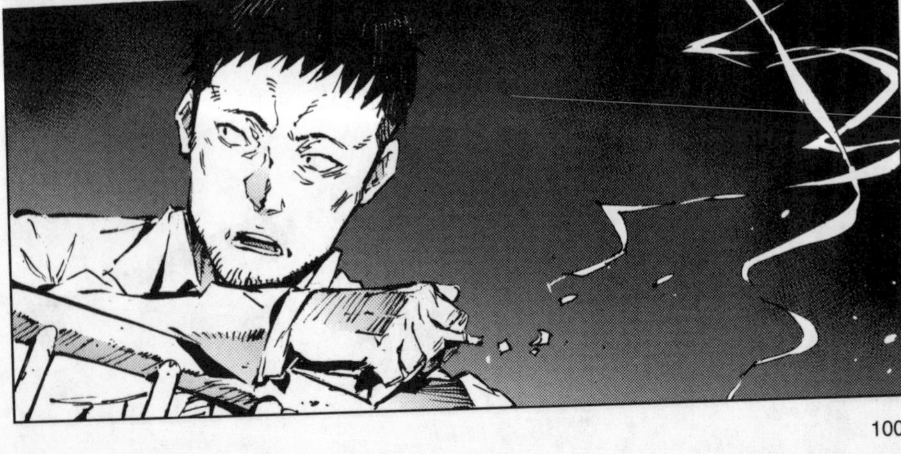

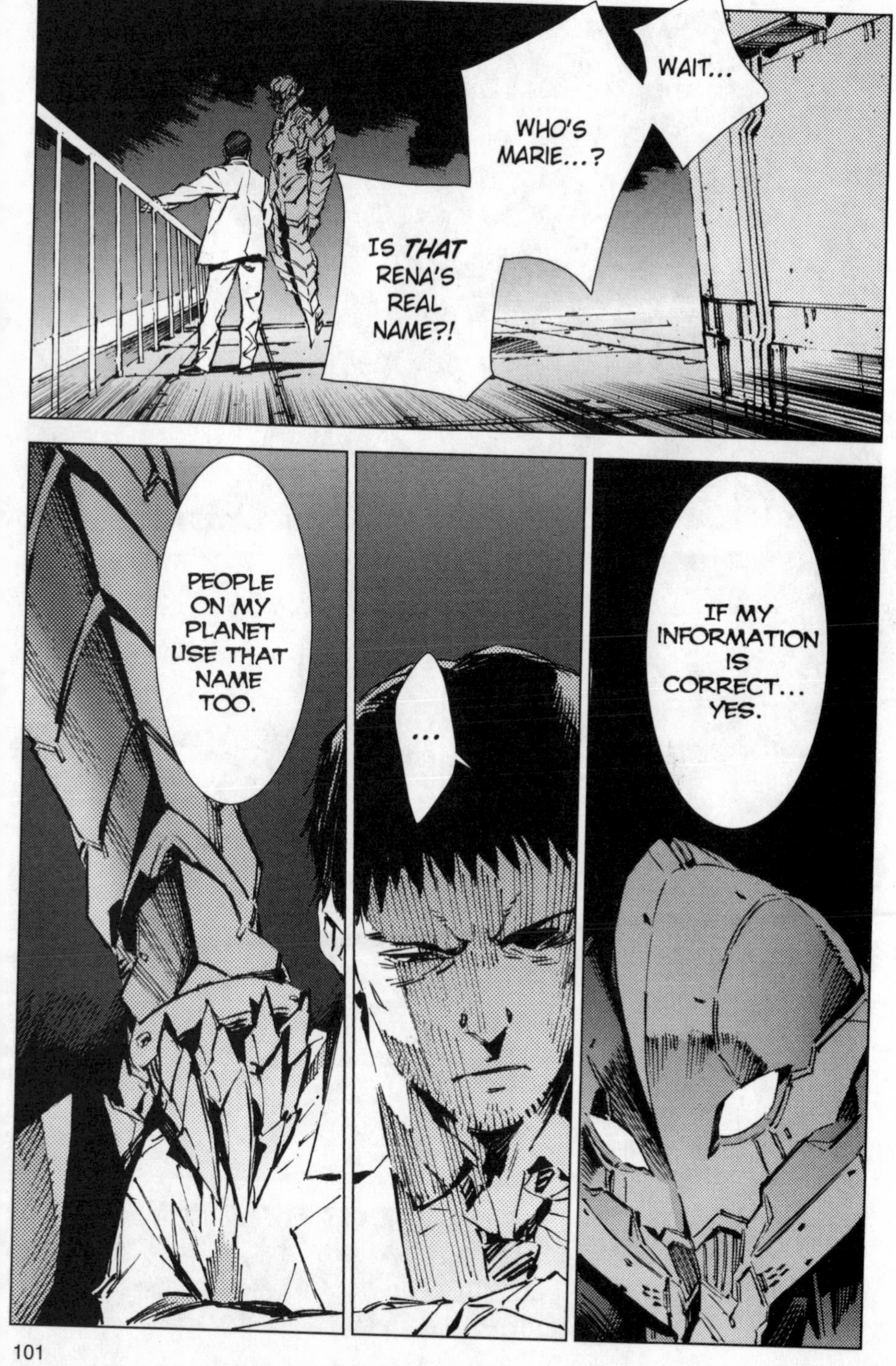
WAIT...
WHO'S MARIE...?
IS *THAT* RENA'S REAL NAME?!
IF MY INFORMATION IS CORRECT... YES.
...
PEOPLE ON MY PLANET USE THAT NAME TOO.

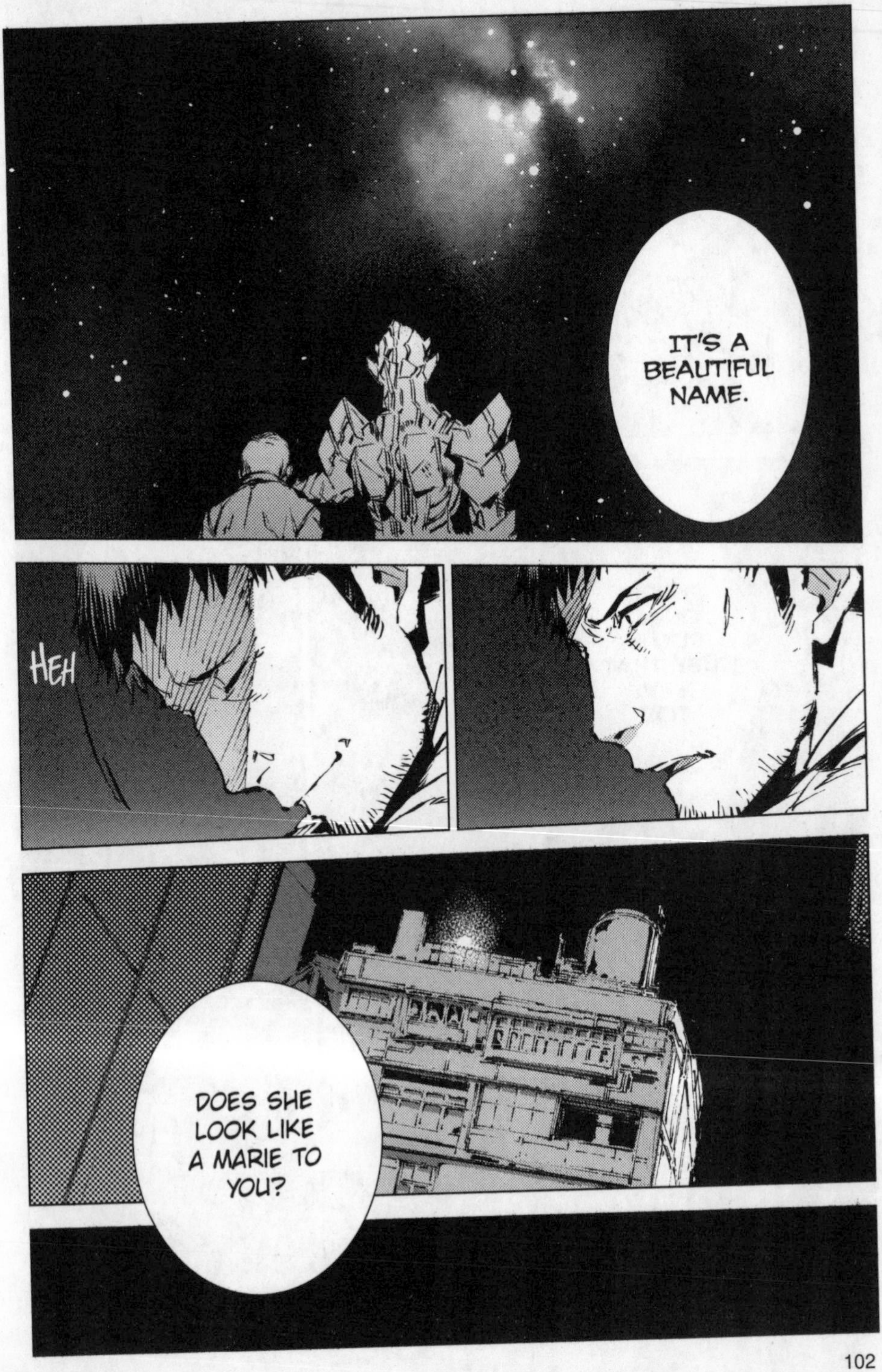
IT'S A BEAUTIFUL NAME.
HEH
DOES SHE LOOK LIKE A MARIE TO YOU?

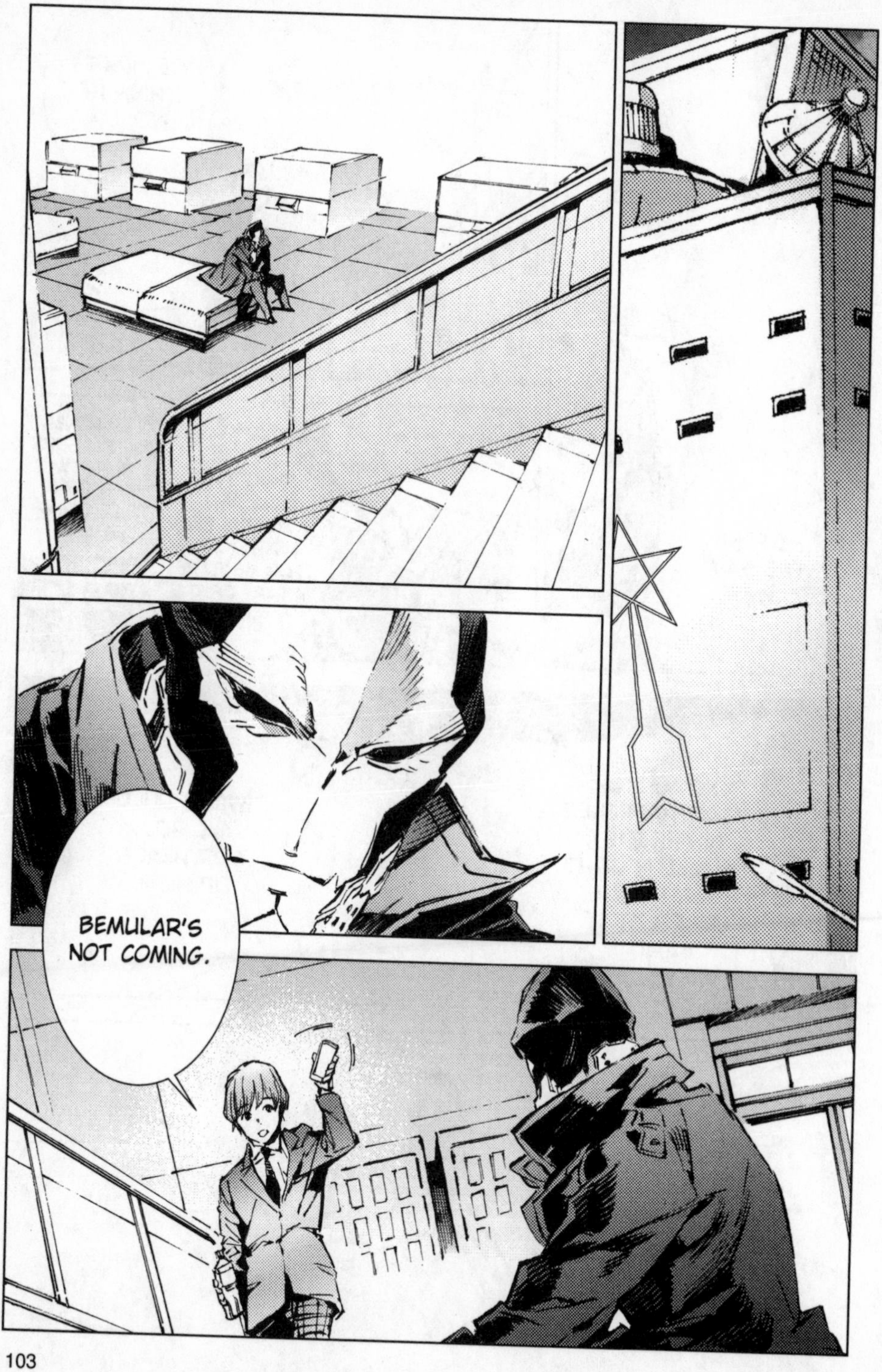
BEMULAR'S NOT COMING.

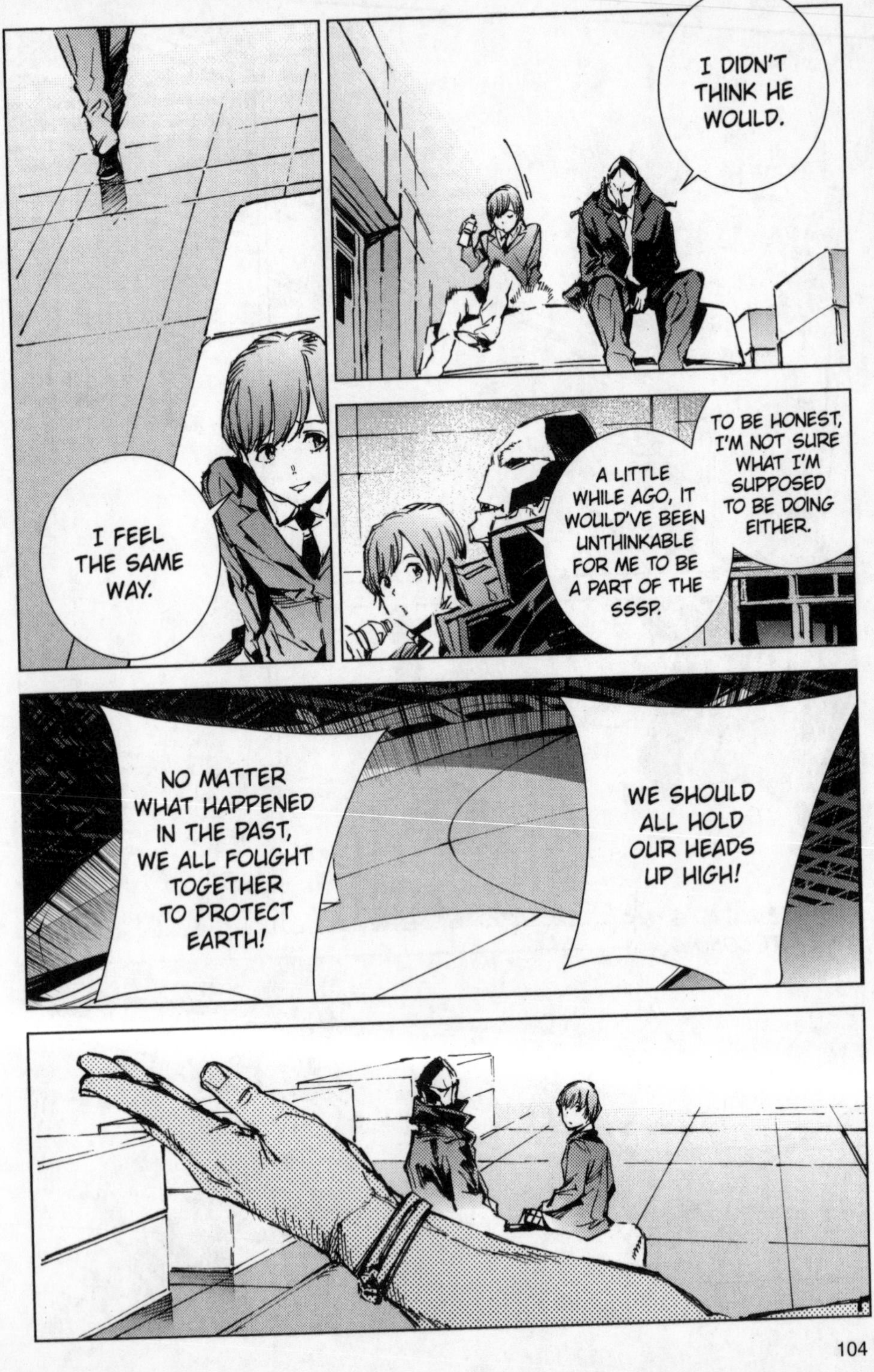
I DIDN'T THINK HE WOULD.
TO BE HONEST, I'M NOT SURE WHAT I'M SUPPOSED TO BE DOING EITHER.
A LITTLE WHILE AGO, IT WOULD'VE BEEN UNTHINKABLE FOR ME TO BE A PART OF THE SSSP.
I FEEL THE SAME WAY.
NO MATTER WHAT HAPPENED IN THE PAST, WE ALL FOUGHT TOGETHER TO PROTECT EARTH!
WE SHOULD ALL HOLD OUR HEADS UP HIGH!

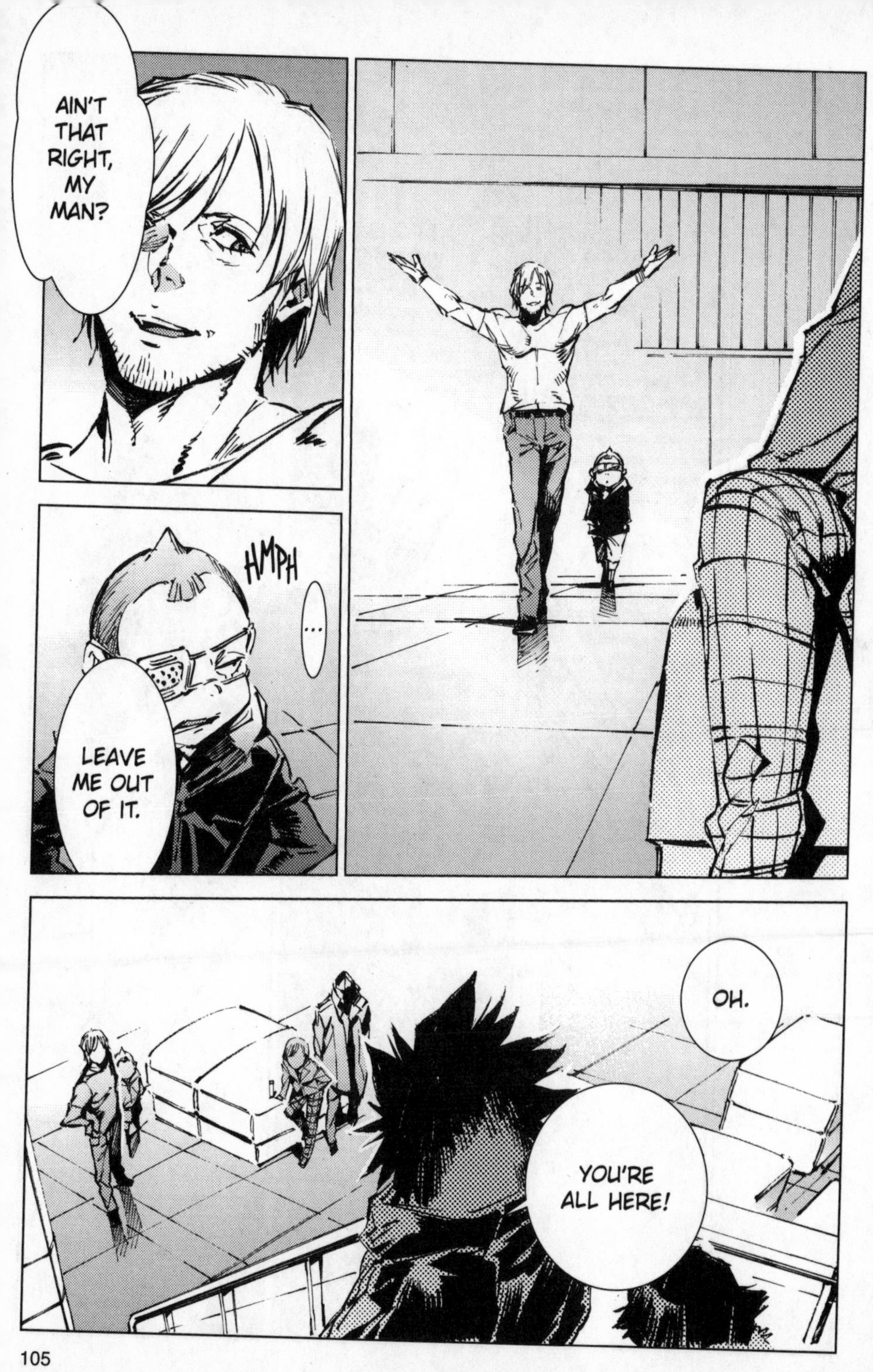
AIN'T THAT RIGHT, MY MAN?
HMPH
...
LEAVE ME OUT OF IT.
OH.
YOU'RE ALL HERE!

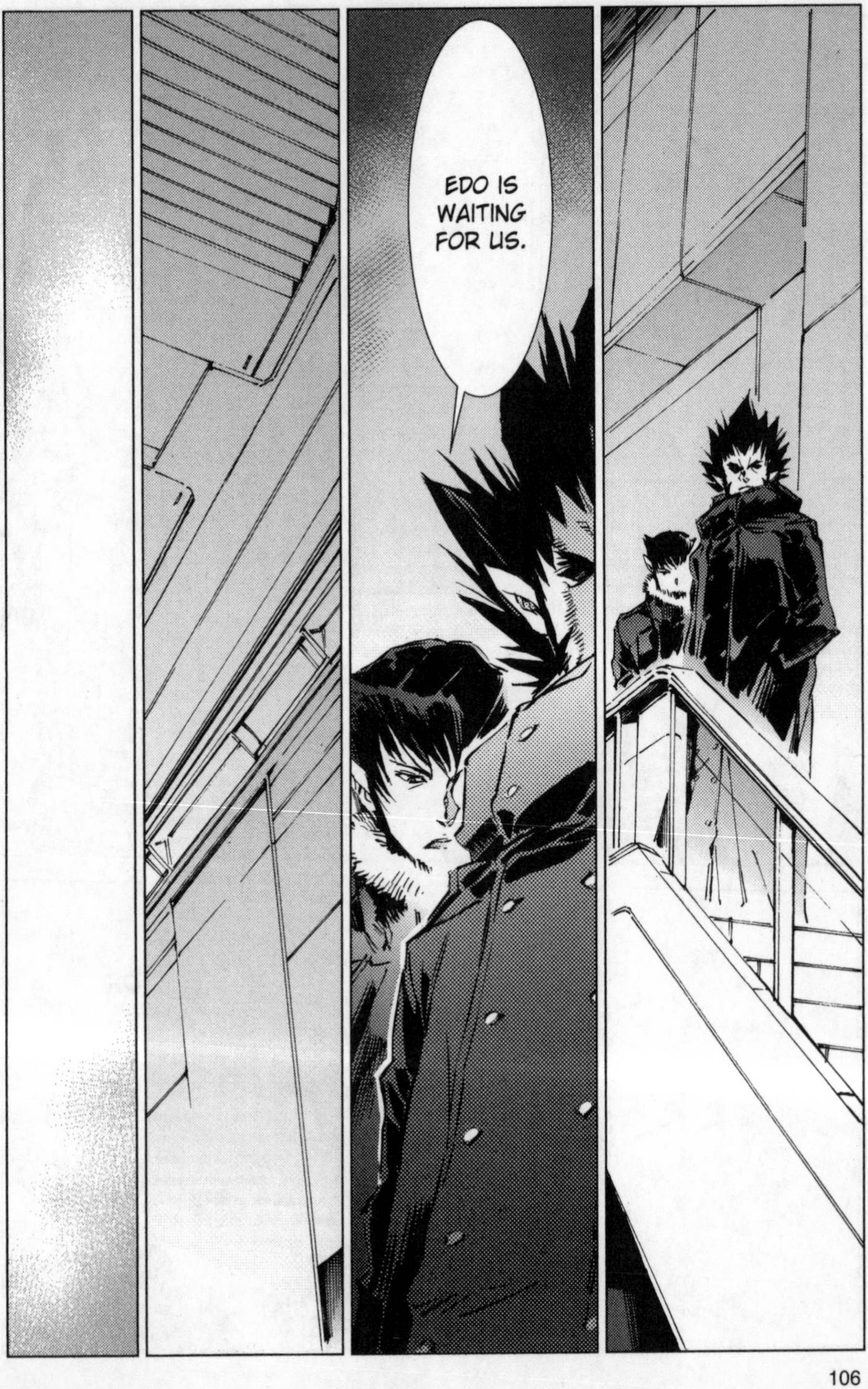
EDO IS WAITING FOR US.

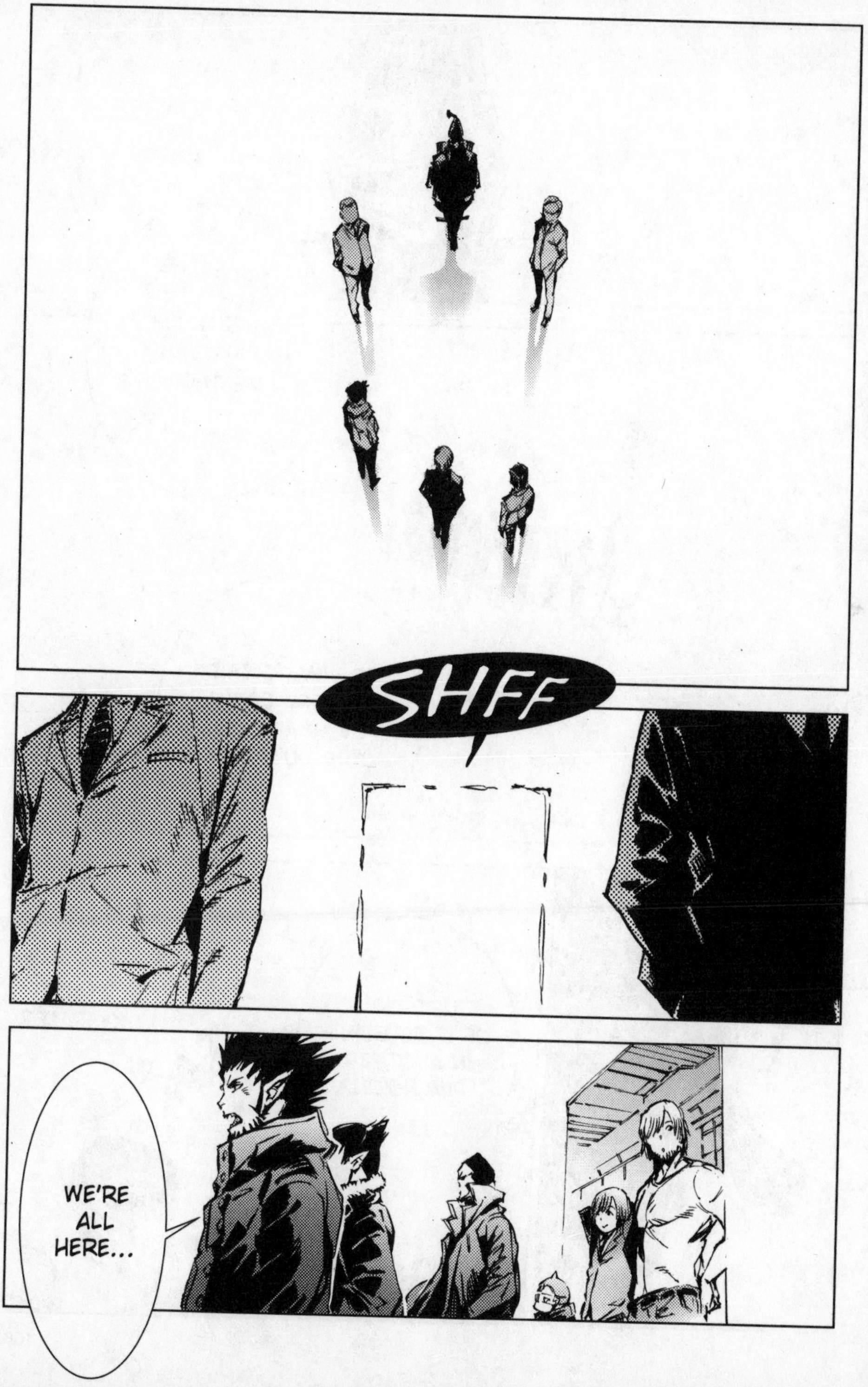
SHFF
WE'RE ALL HERE...

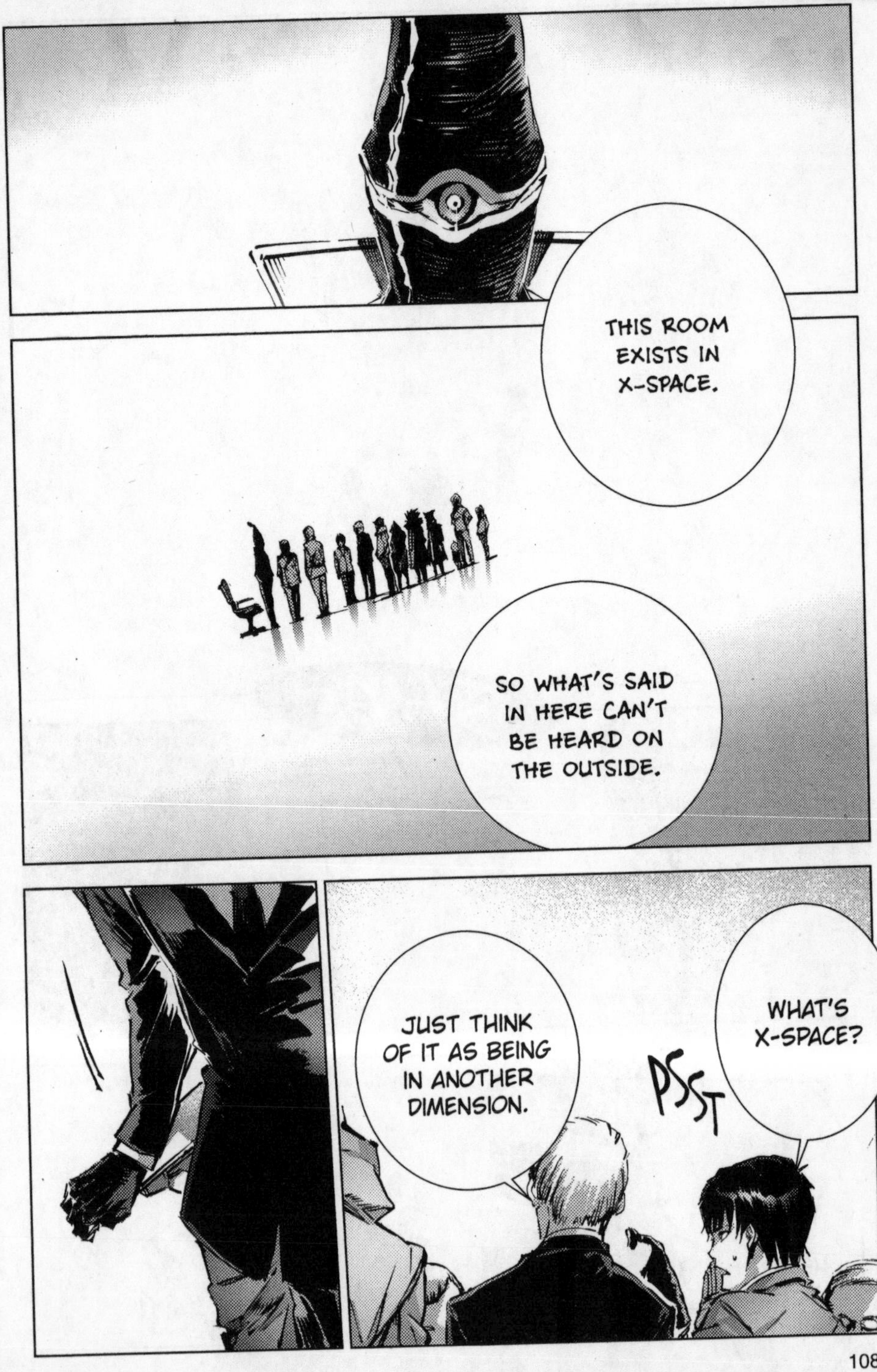
THIS ROOM EXISTS IN X-SPACE.
SO WHAT'S SAID IN HERE CAN'T BE HEARD ON THE OUTSIDE.
WHAT'S X-SPACE?
PSSST
JUST THINK OF IT AS BEING IN ANOTHER DIMENSION.

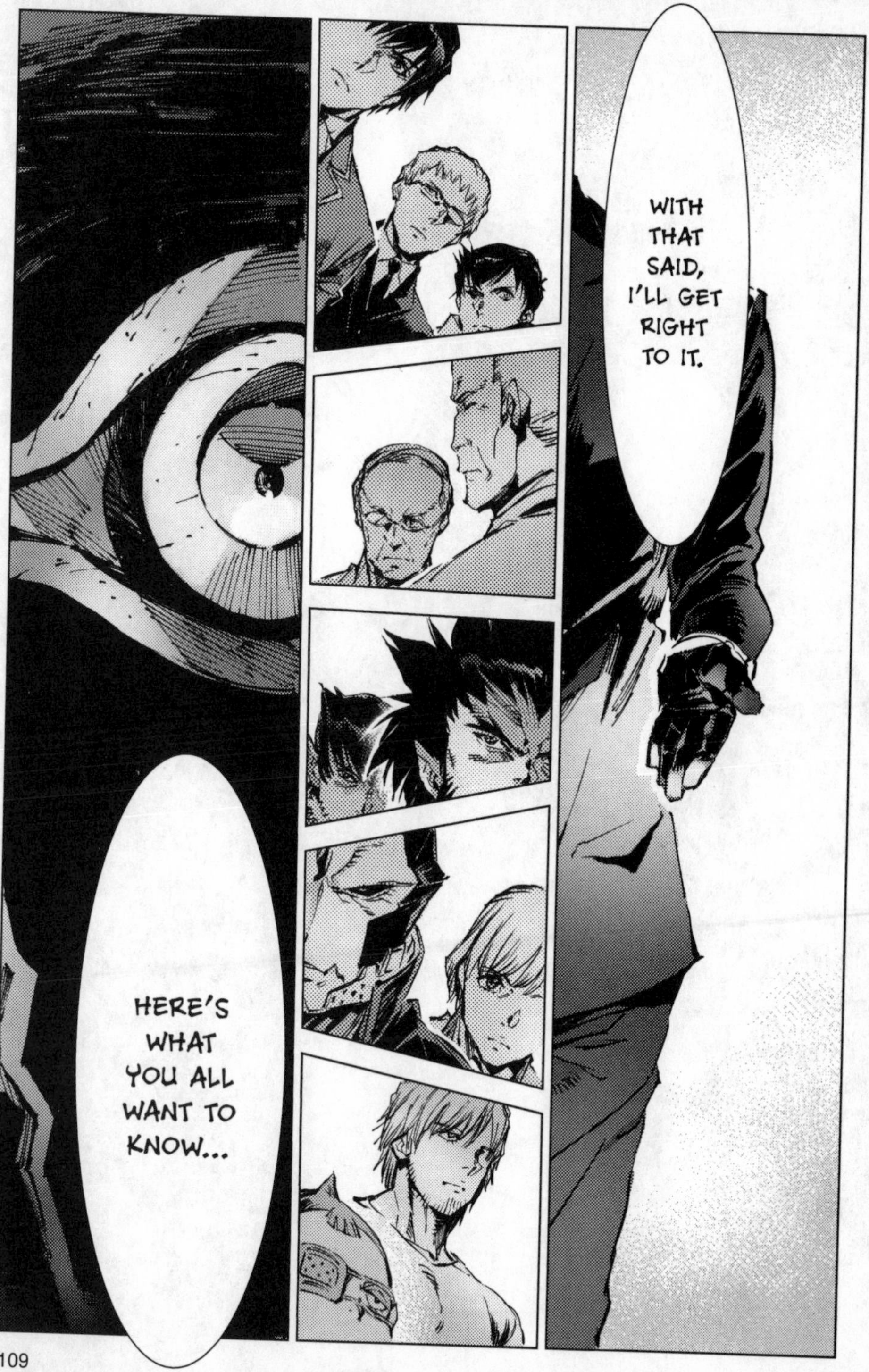
WITH THAT SAID, I'LL GET RIGHT TO IT.
HERE'S WHAT YOU ALL WANT TO KNOW...

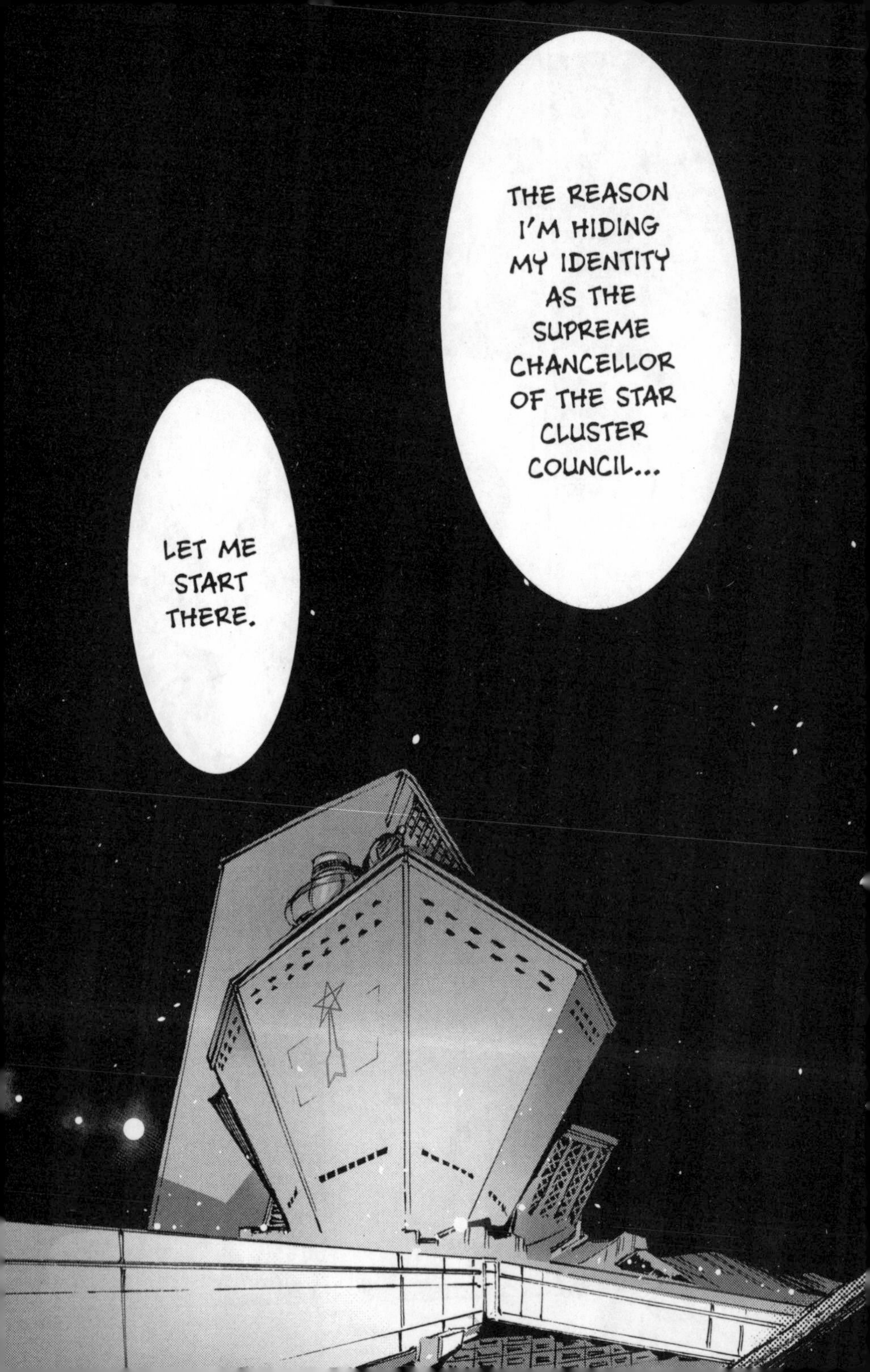
THE REASON I'M HIDING MY IDENTITY AS THE SUPREME CHANCELLOR OF THE STAR CLUSTER COUNCIL...
LET ME START THERE.

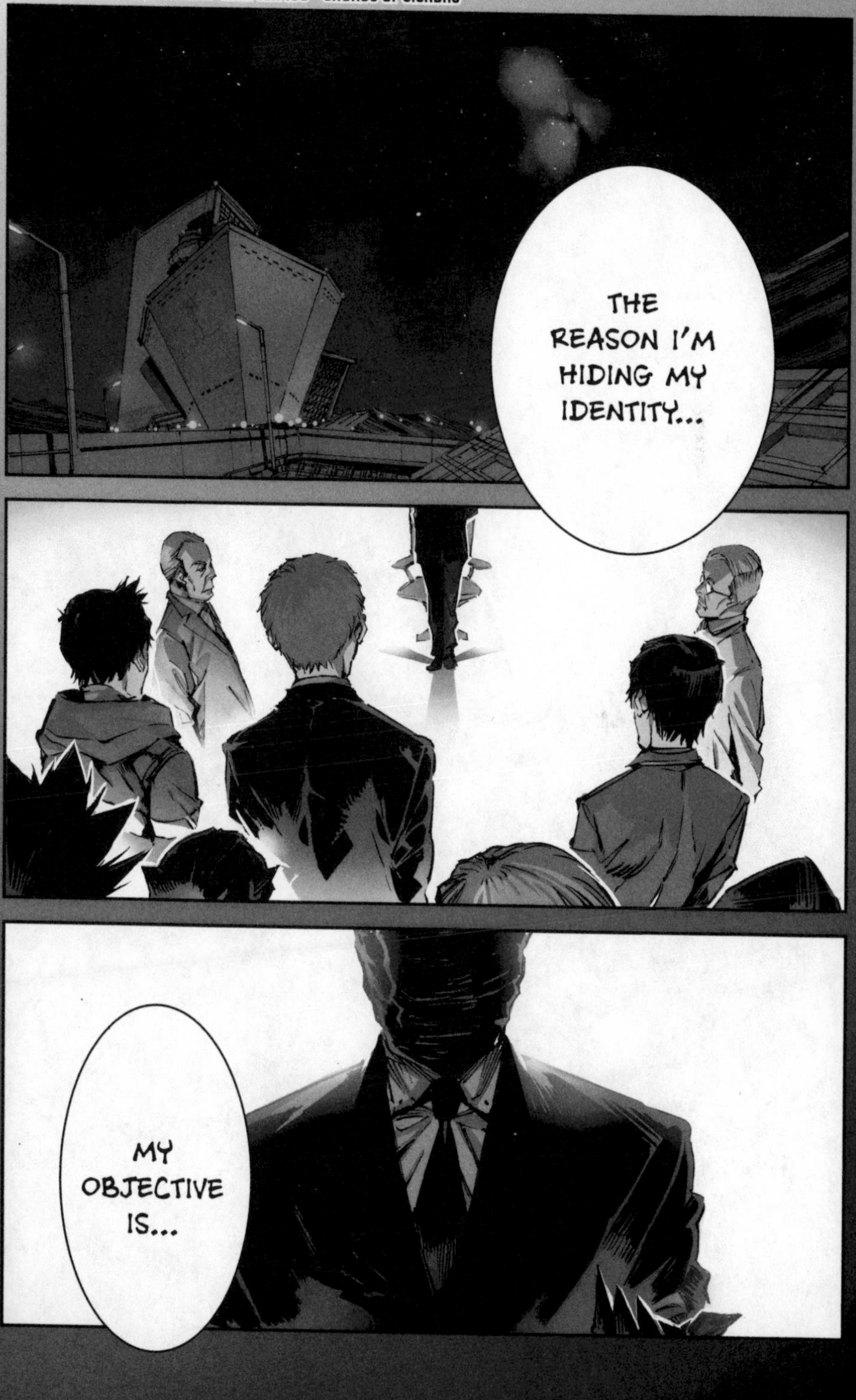
THE REASON I'M HIDING MY IDENTITY...
MY OBJECTIVE IS...

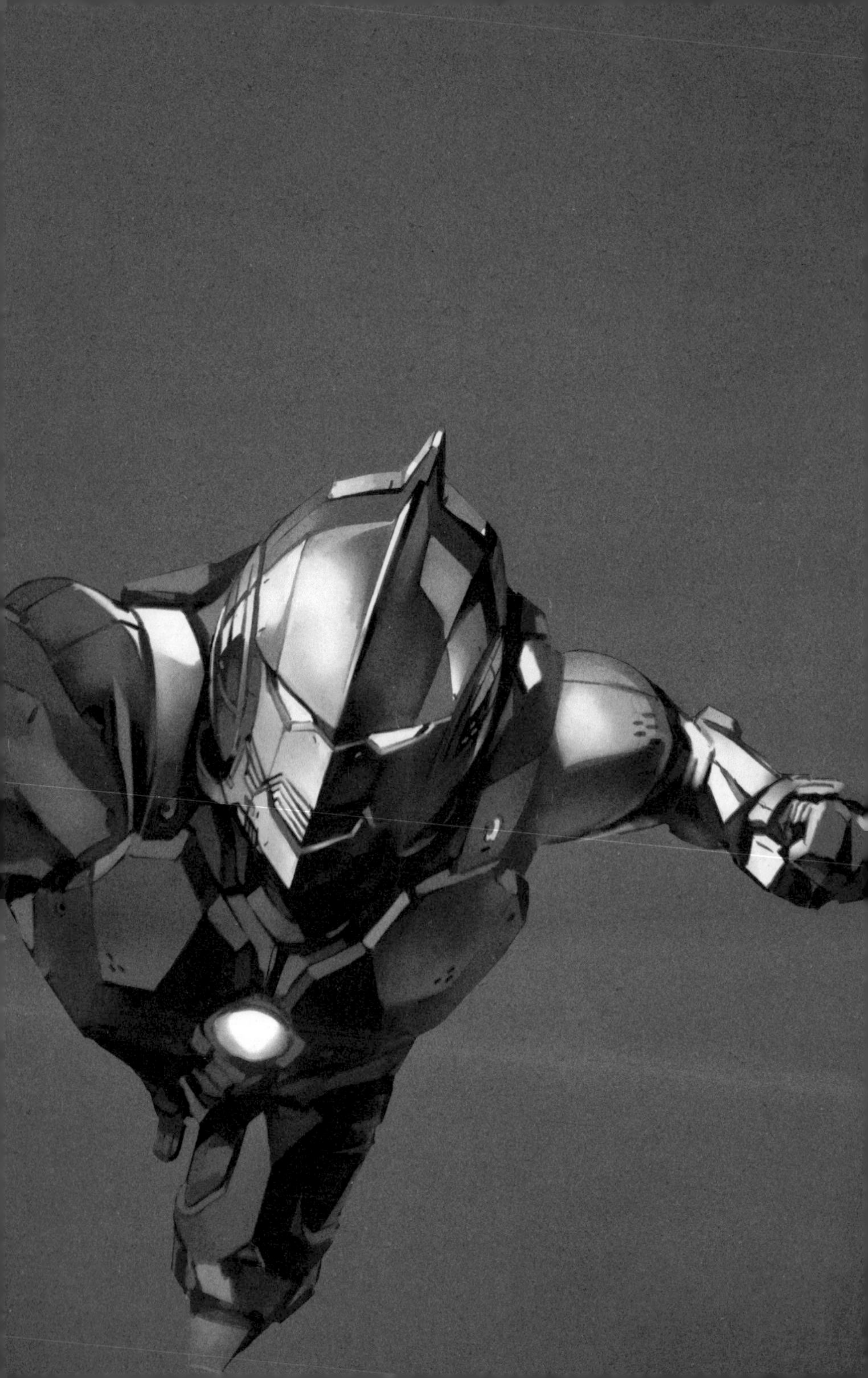

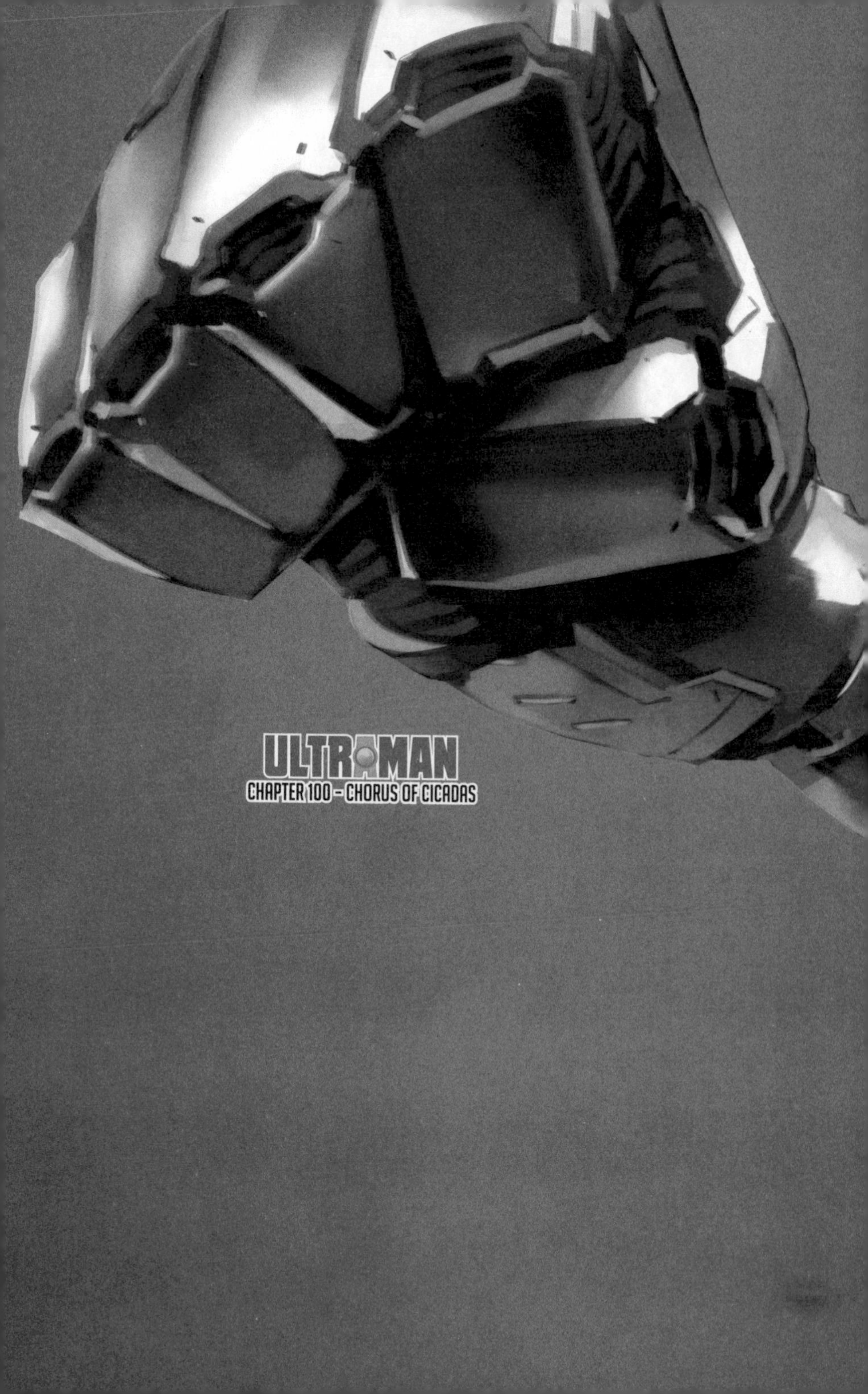
ULTRAMAN
CHAPTER 100 - CHORUS OF CICADAS

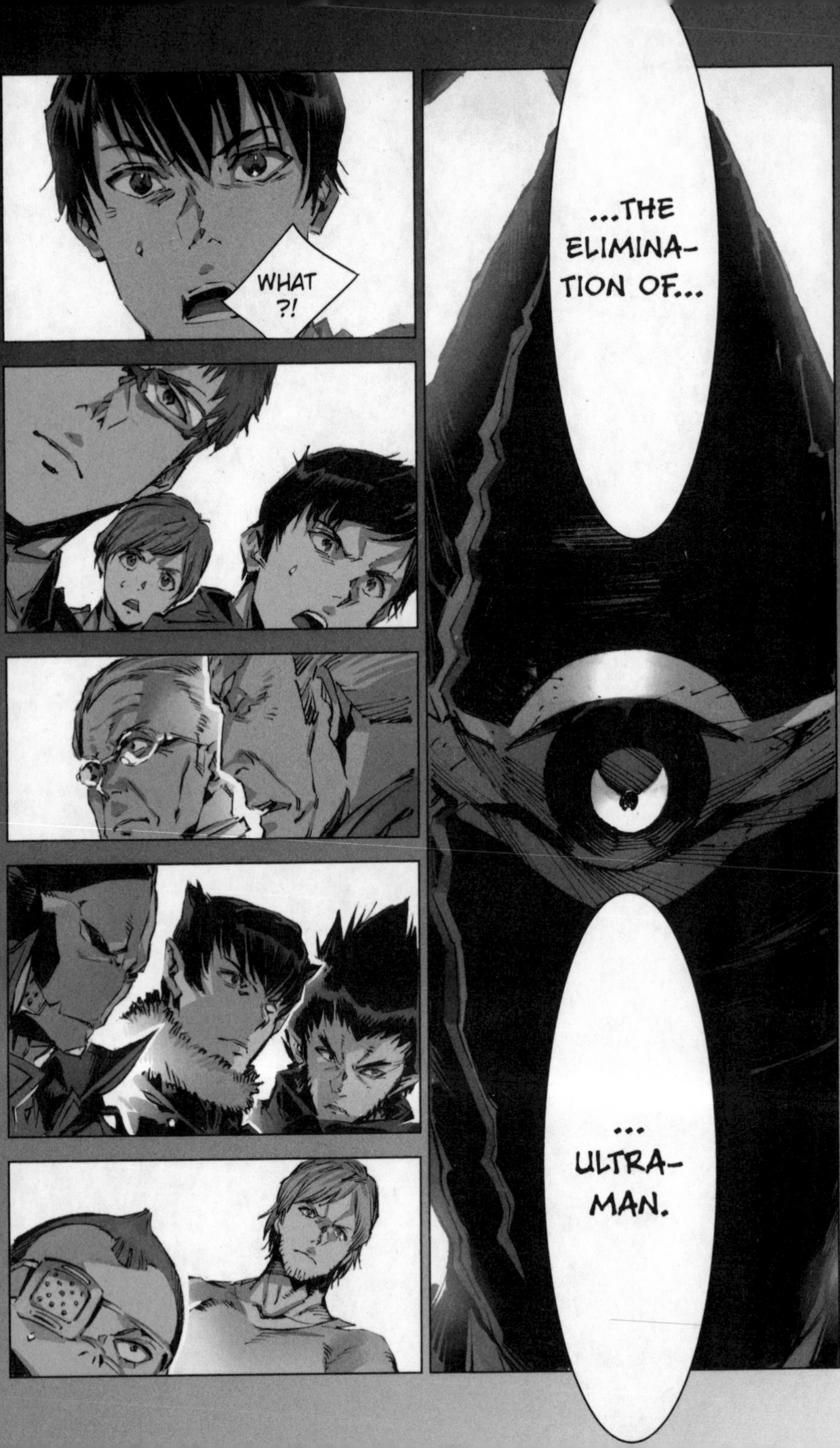
...THE ELIMINA-TION OF...
...ULTRA-MAN.
WHAT ?!

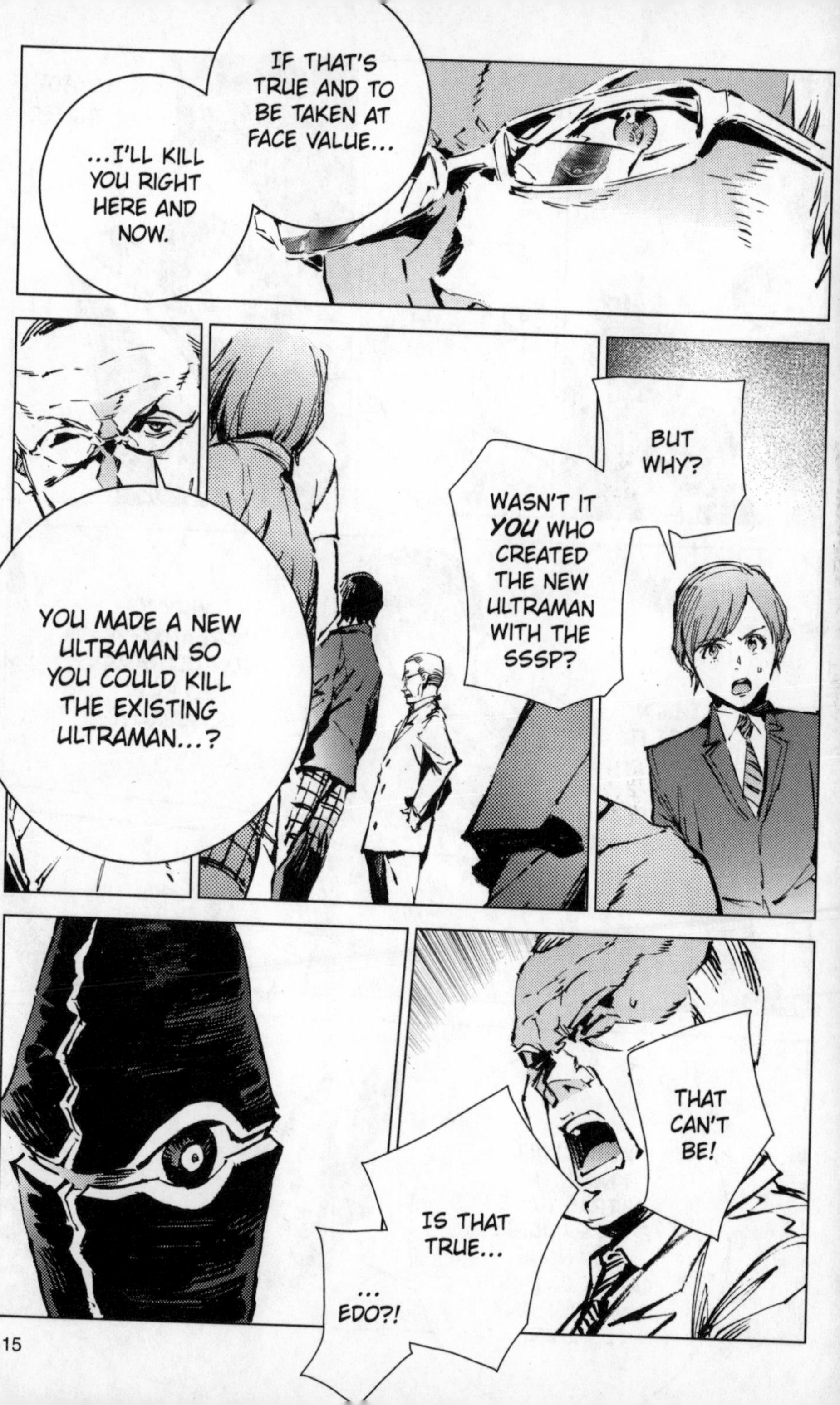
IF THAT'S TRUE AND TO BE TAKEN AT FACE VALUE...
...I'LL KILL YOU RIGHT HERE AND NOW.
BUT WHY?
WASN'T IT *YOU* WHO CREATED THE NEW ULTRAMAN WITH THE SSSP?
YOU MADE A NEW ULTRAMAN SO YOU COULD KILL THE EXISTING ULTRAMAN...?
THAT CAN'T BE!
IS THAT TRUE...
...EDO?!

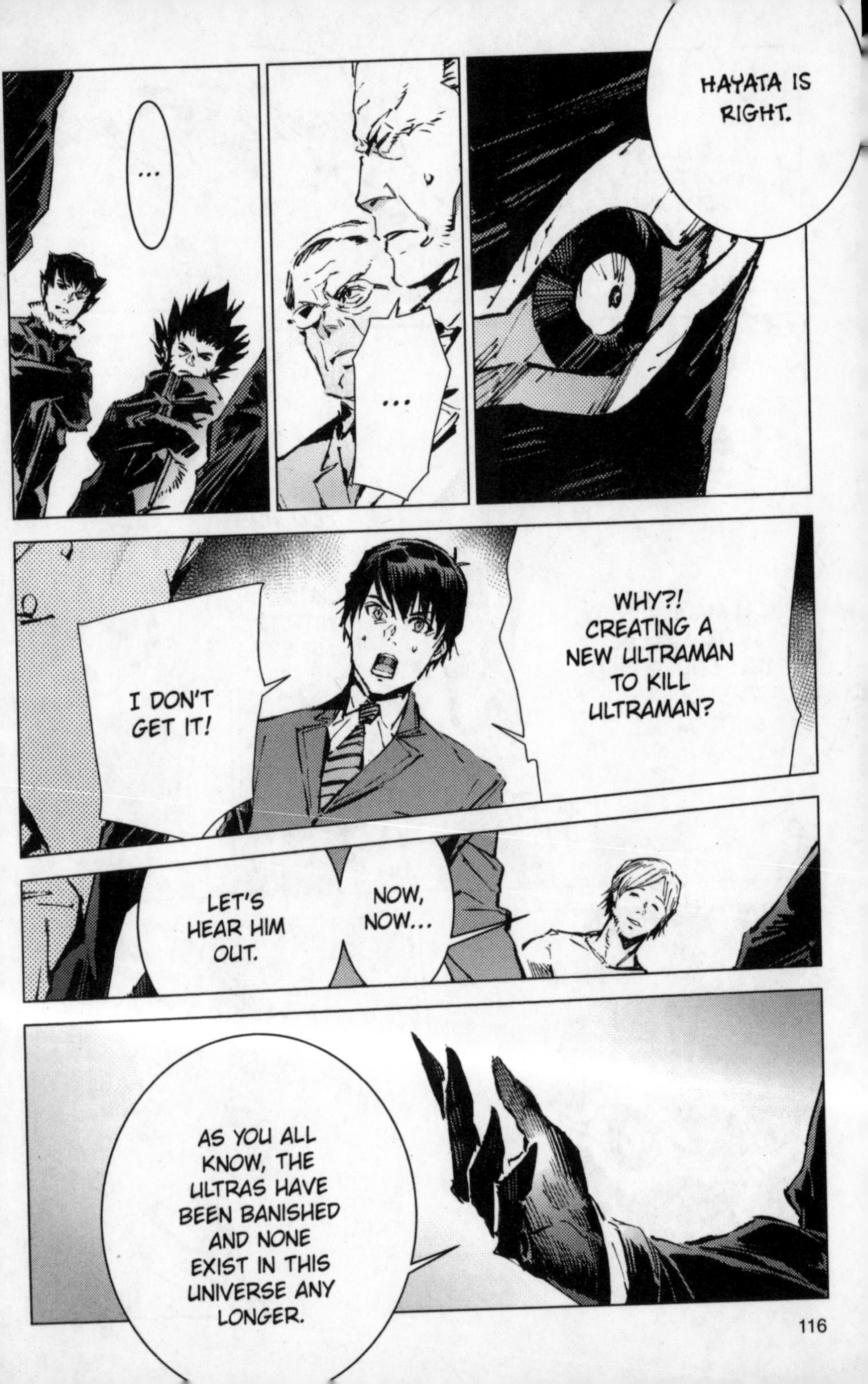
HAYATA IS RIGHT.
...
...
WHY?! CREATING A NEW ULTRAMAN TO KILL ULTRAMAN?
I DON'T GET IT!
NOW, NOW...
LET'S HEAR HIM OUT.
AS YOU ALL KNOW, THE ULTRAS HAVE BEEN BANISHED AND NONE EXIST IN THIS UNIVERSE ANY LONGER.

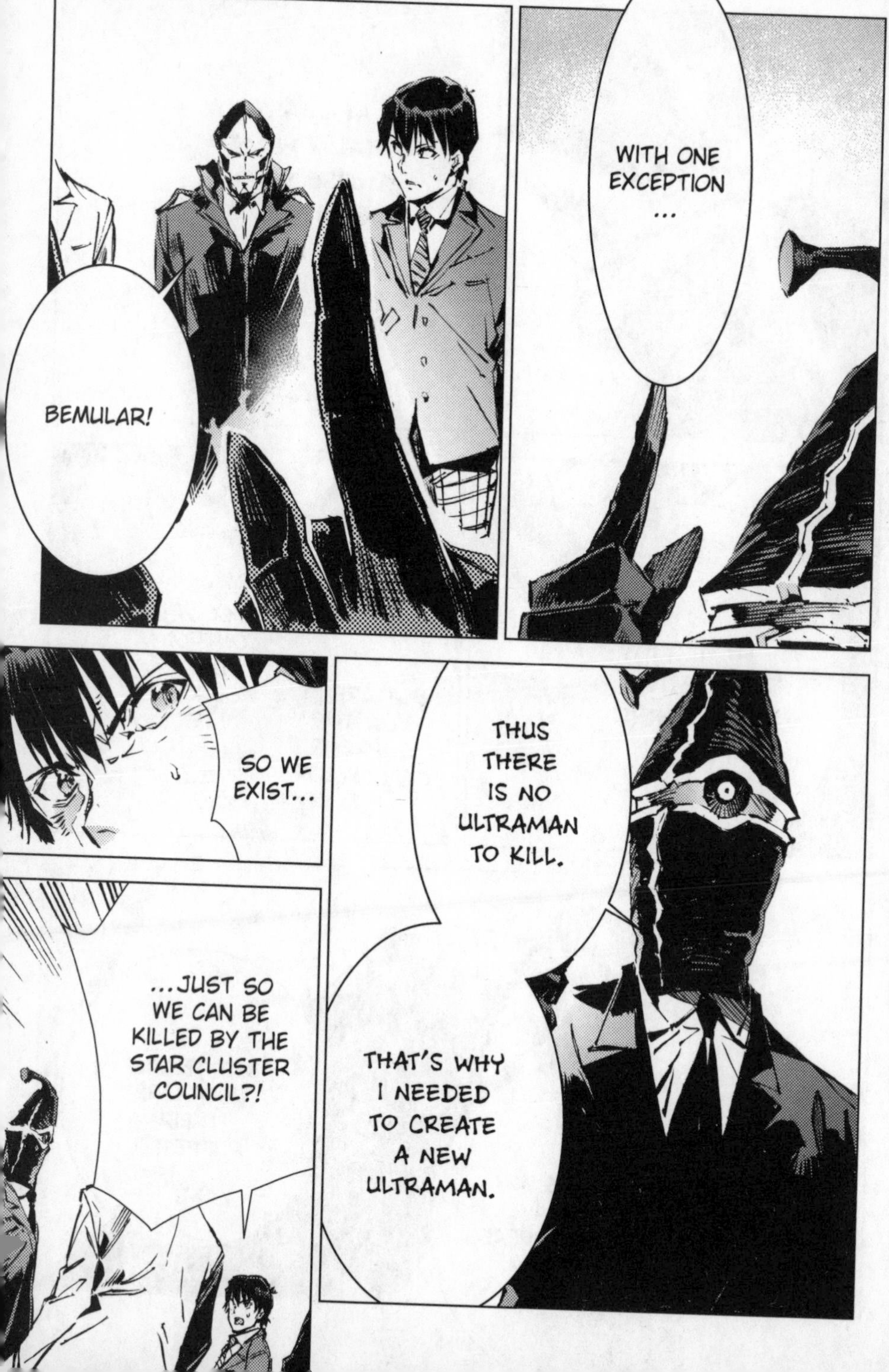
WITH ONE EXCEPTION ...
BEMULAR!
THUS THERE IS NO ULTRAMAN TO KILL.
THAT'S WHY I NEEDED TO CREATE A NEW ULTRAMAN.
SO WE EXIST...
...JUST SO WE CAN BE KILLED BY THE STAR CLUSTER COUNCIL?!

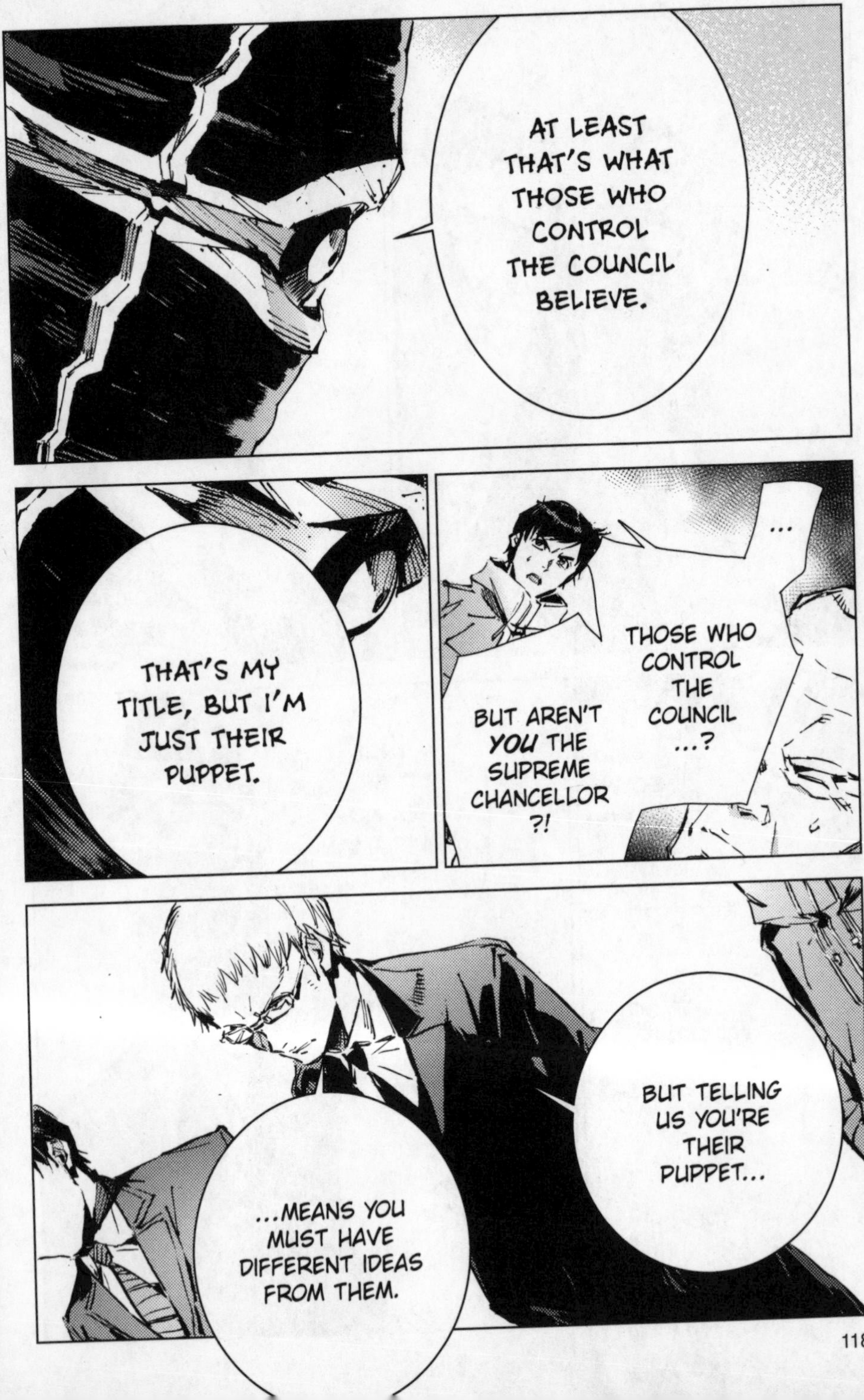
AT LEAST THAT'S WHAT THOSE WHO CONTROL THE COUNCIL BELIEVE.
...
THOSE WHO CONTROL THE COUNCIL ...?
BUT AREN'T *YOU* THE SUPREME CHANCELLOR ?!
THAT'S MY TITLE, BUT I'M JUST THEIR PUPPET.
BUT TELLING US YOU'RE THEIR PUPPET...
...MEANS YOU MUST HAVE DIFFERENT IDEAS FROM THEM.

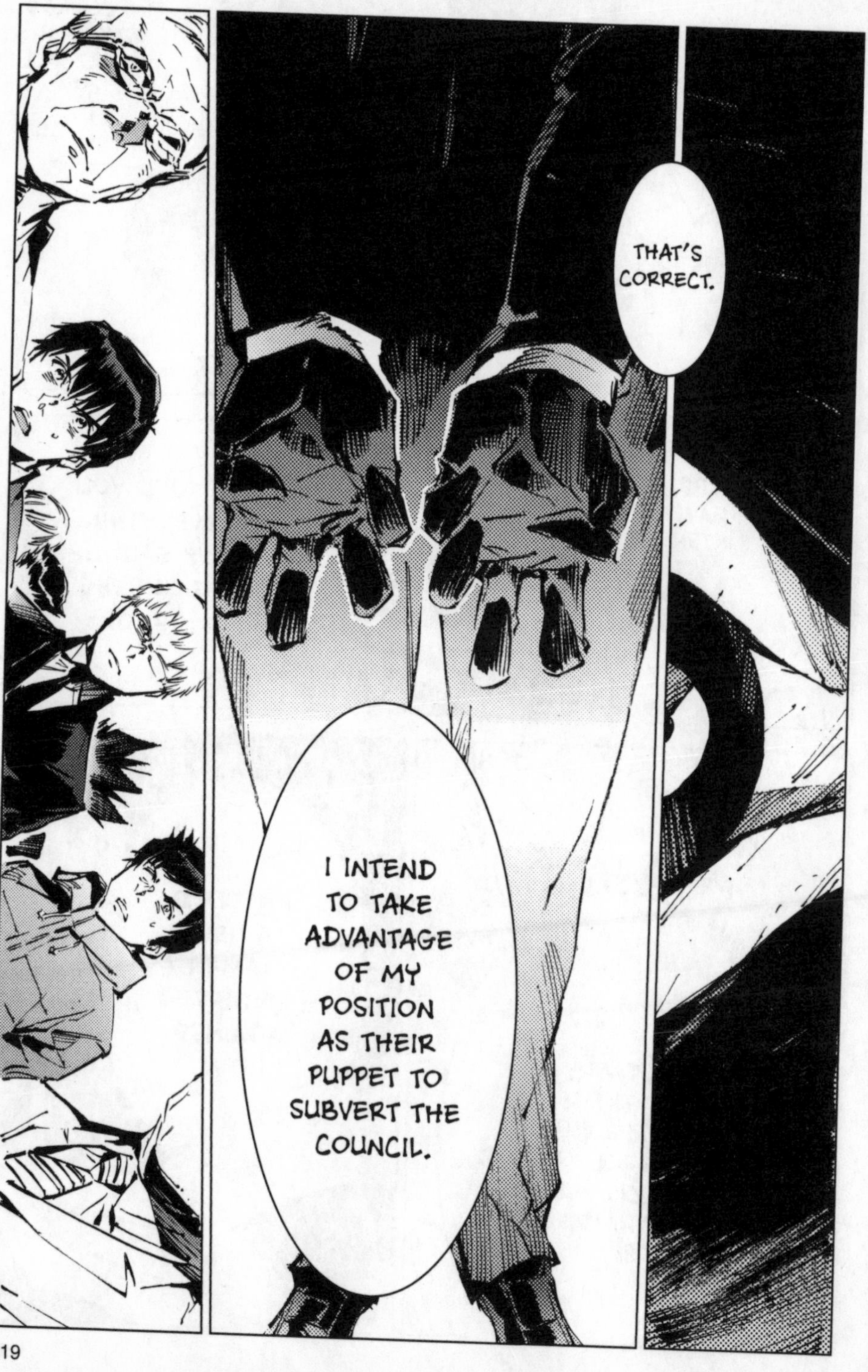
THAT'S CORRECT.
I INTEND TO TAKE ADVANTAGE OF MY POSITION AS THEIR PUPPET TO SUBVERT THE COUNCIL.

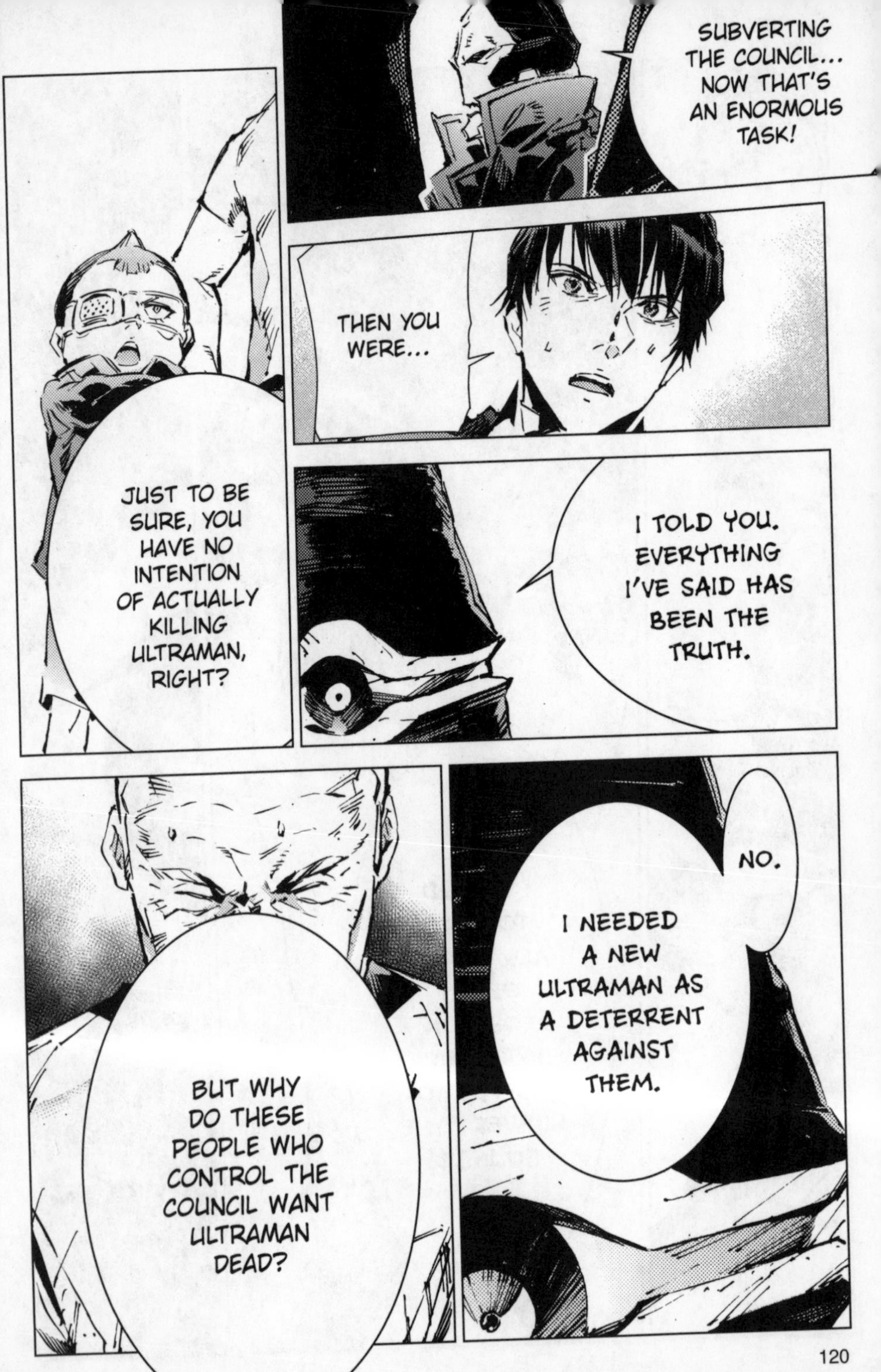
SUBVERTING THE COUNCIL... NOW THAT'S AN ENORMOUS TASK!
THEN YOU WERE...
I TOLD YOU. EVERYTHING I'VE SAID HAS BEEN THE TRUTH.
JUST TO BE SURE, YOU HAVE NO INTENTION OF ACTUALLY KILLING ULTRAMAN, RIGHT?
NO.
I NEEDED A NEW ULTRAMAN AS A DETERRENT AGAINST THEM.
BUT WHY DO THESE PEOPLE WHO CONTROL THE COUNCIL WANT ULTRAMAN DEAD?

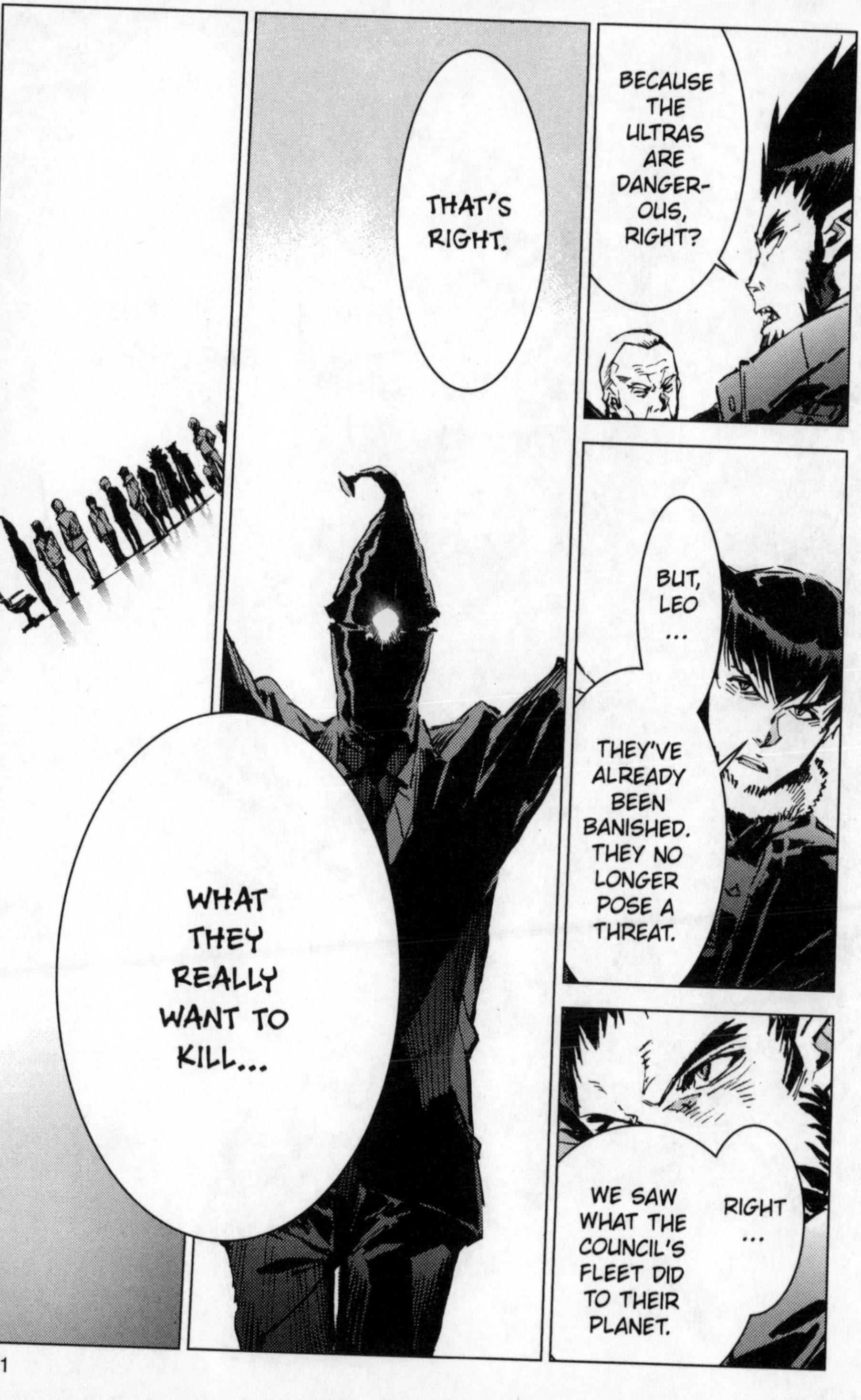
BECAUSE THE ULTRAS ARE DANGER-OUS, RIGHT?
BUT, LEO...
THEY'VE ALREADY BEEN BANISHED. THEY NO LONGER POSE A THREAT.
RIGHT...
WE SAW WHAT THE COUNCIL'S FLEET DID TO THEIR PLANET.
THAT'S RIGHT.
WHAT THEY REALLY WANT TO KILL...

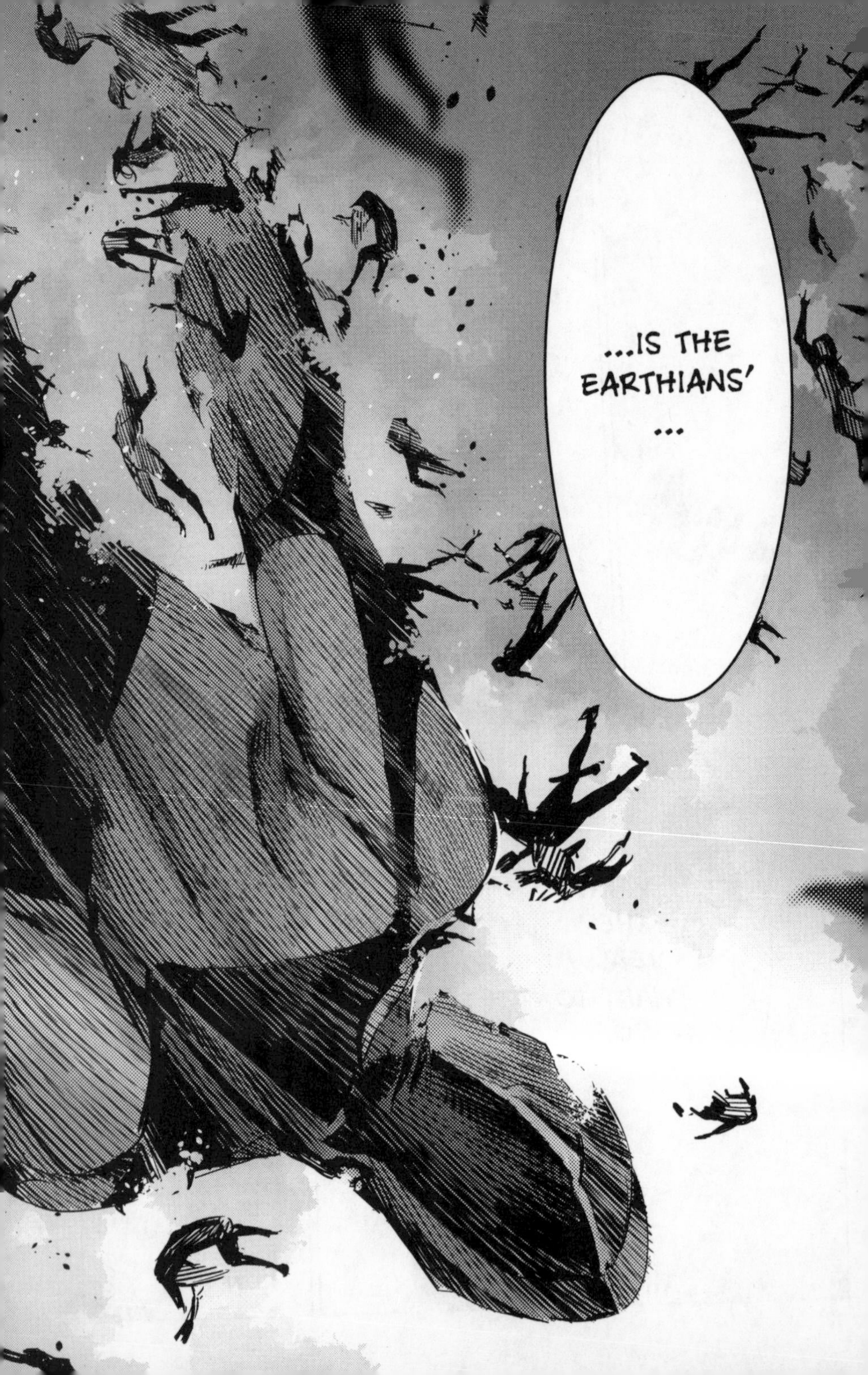
...IS THE EARTHIANS' ...

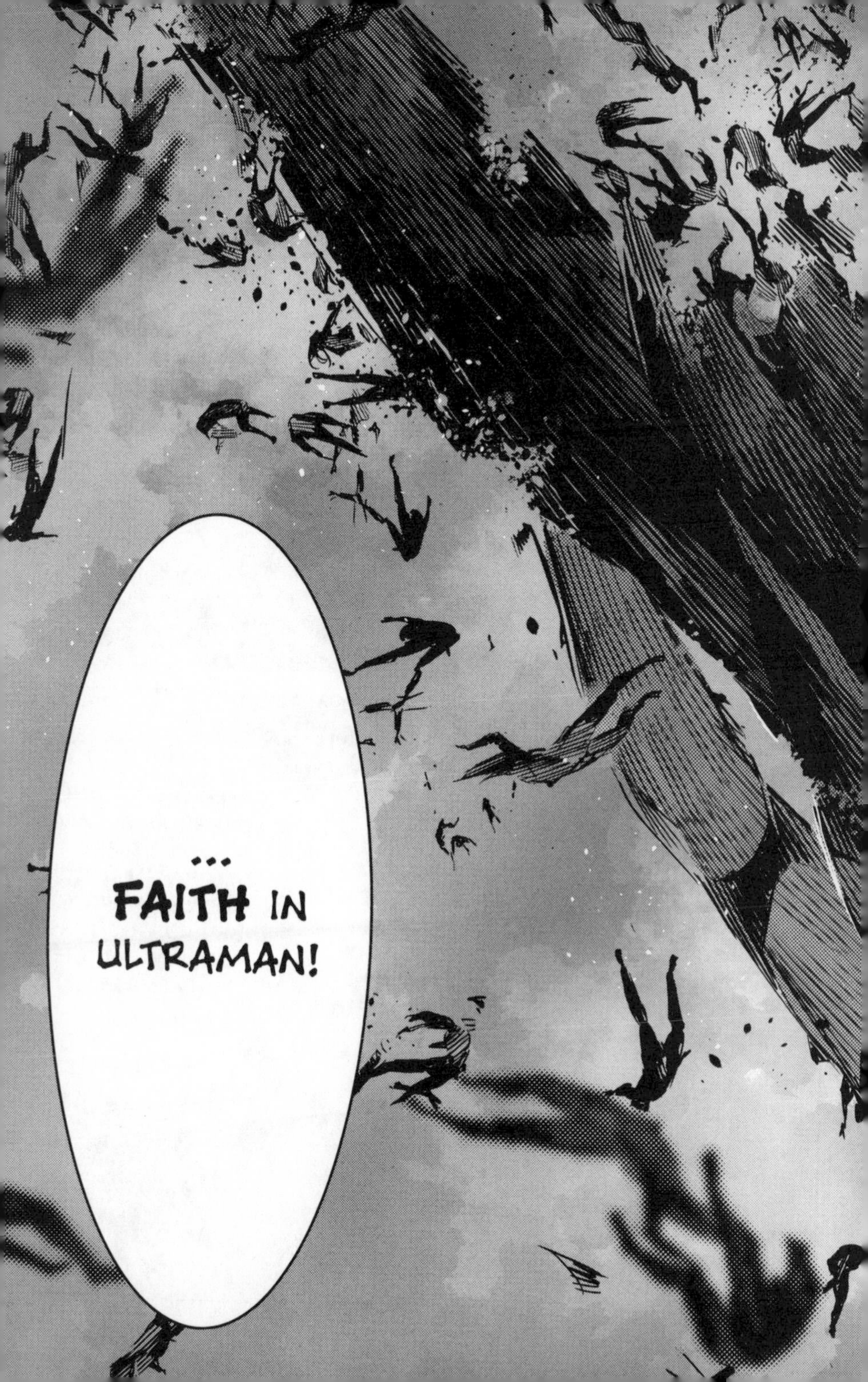
... FAITH IN ULTRAMAN!

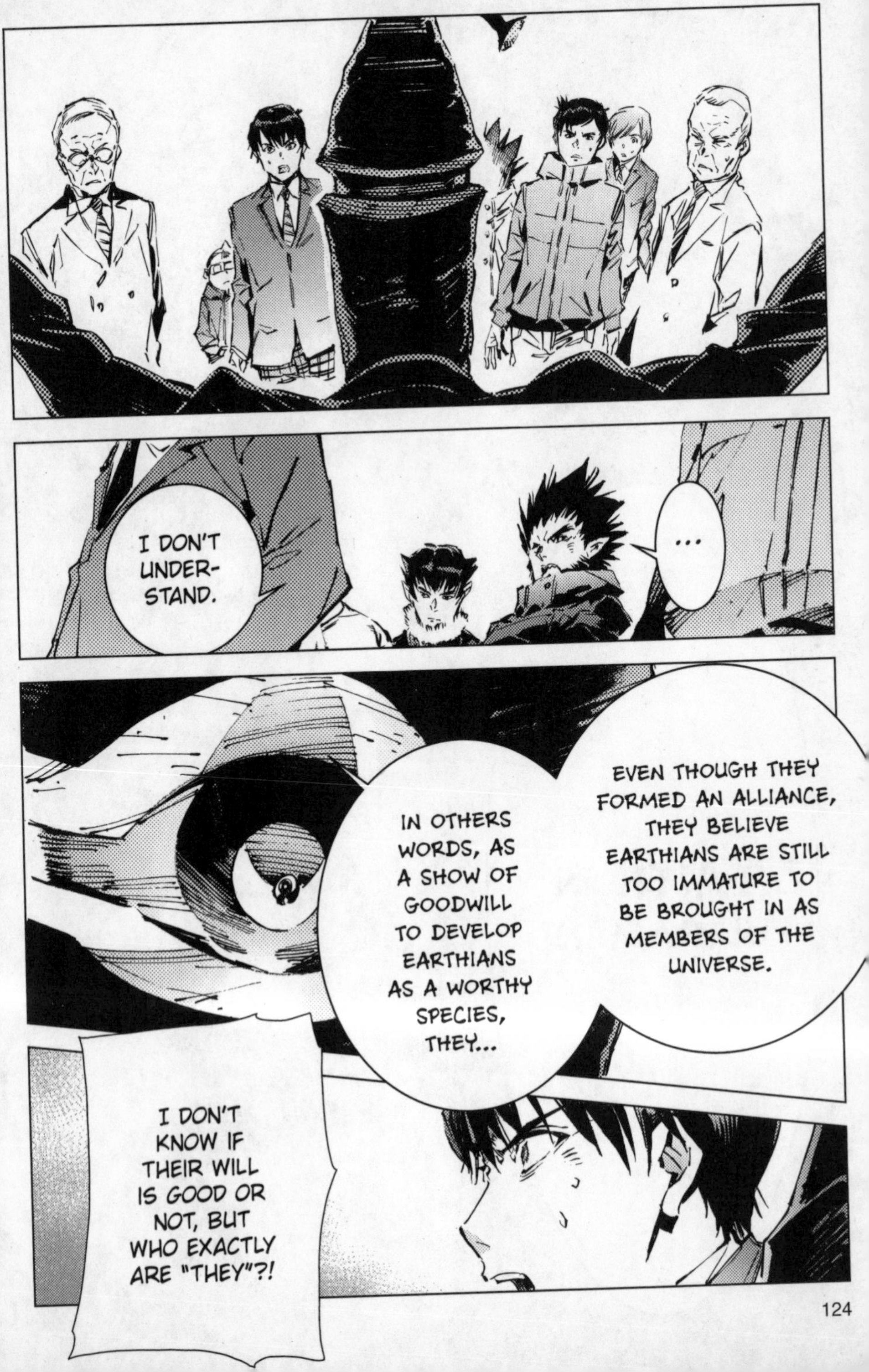
...
I DON'T UNDERSTAND.
EVEN THOUGH THEY FORMED AN ALLIANCE, THEY BELIEVE EARTHIANS ARE STILL TOO IMMATURE TO BE BROUGHT IN AS MEMBERS OF THE UNIVERSE.
IN OTHERS WORDS, AS A SHOW OF GOODWILL TO DEVELOP EARTHIANS AS A WORTHY SPECIES, THEY...
I DON'T KNOW IF THEIR WILL IS GOOD OR NOT, BUT WHO EXACTLY ARE "THEY"?!

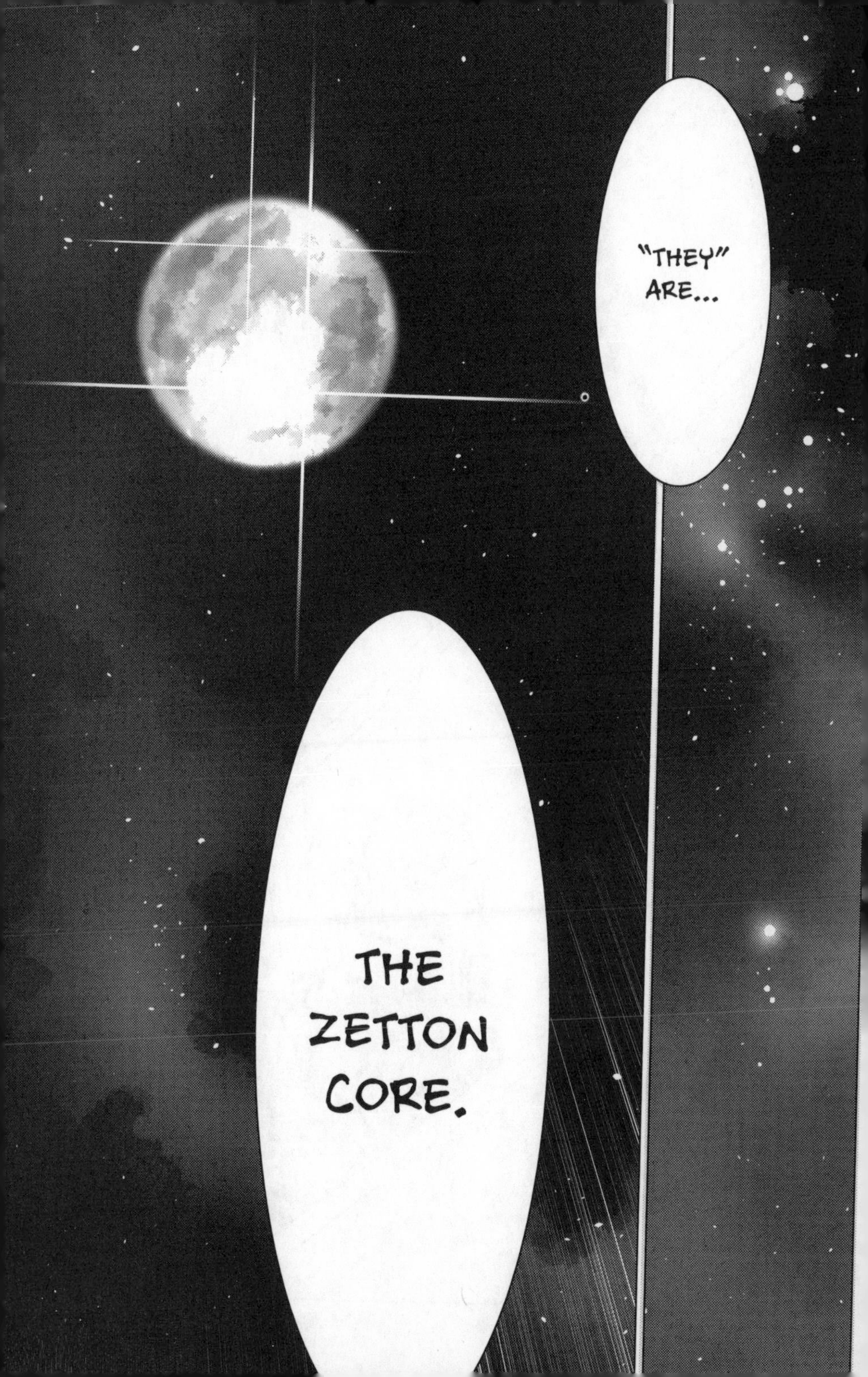
"THEY" ARE...
THE ZETTON CORE.

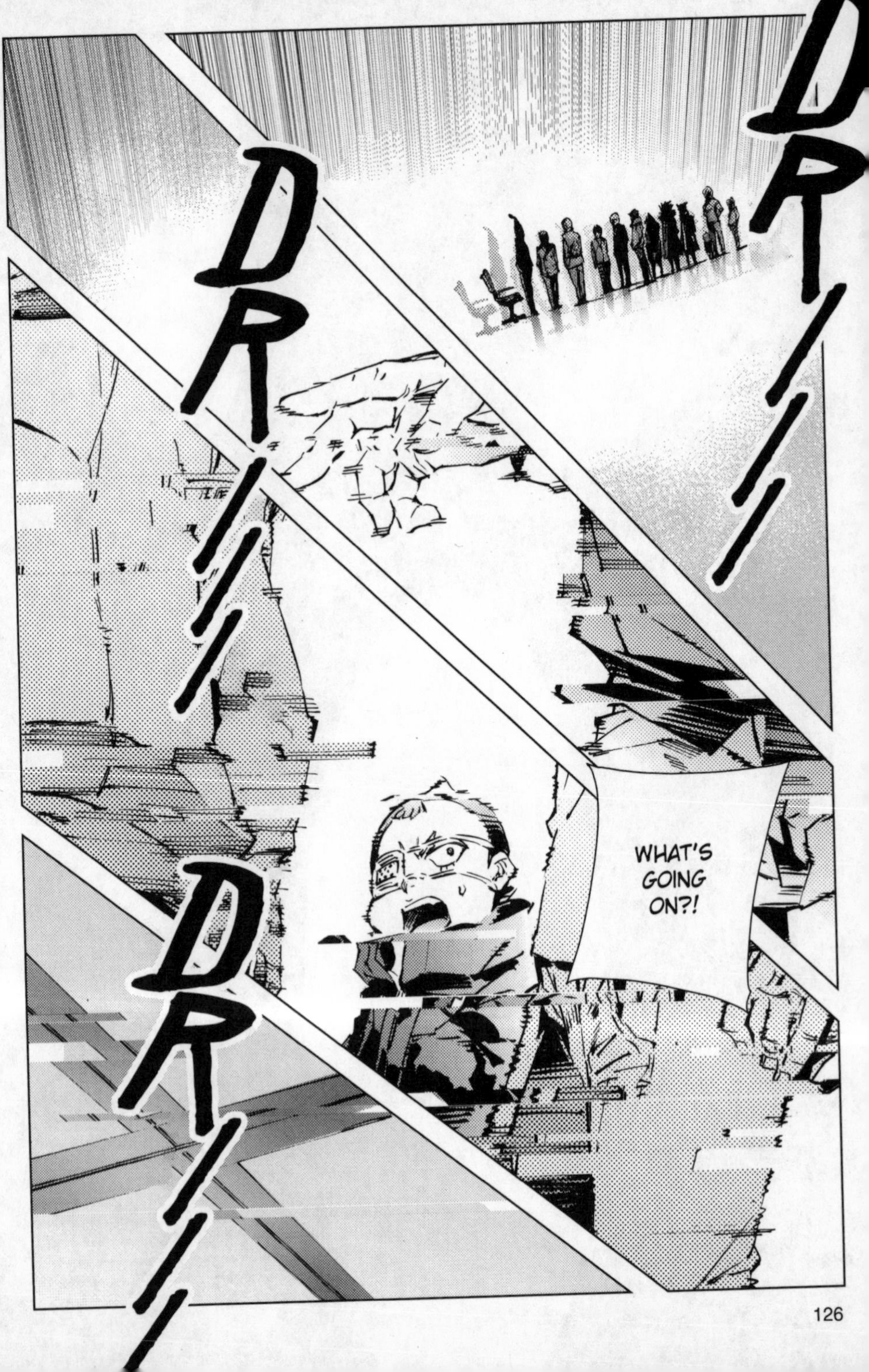
DRIIII
DRIIII
WHAT'S GOING ON?!
DRIII

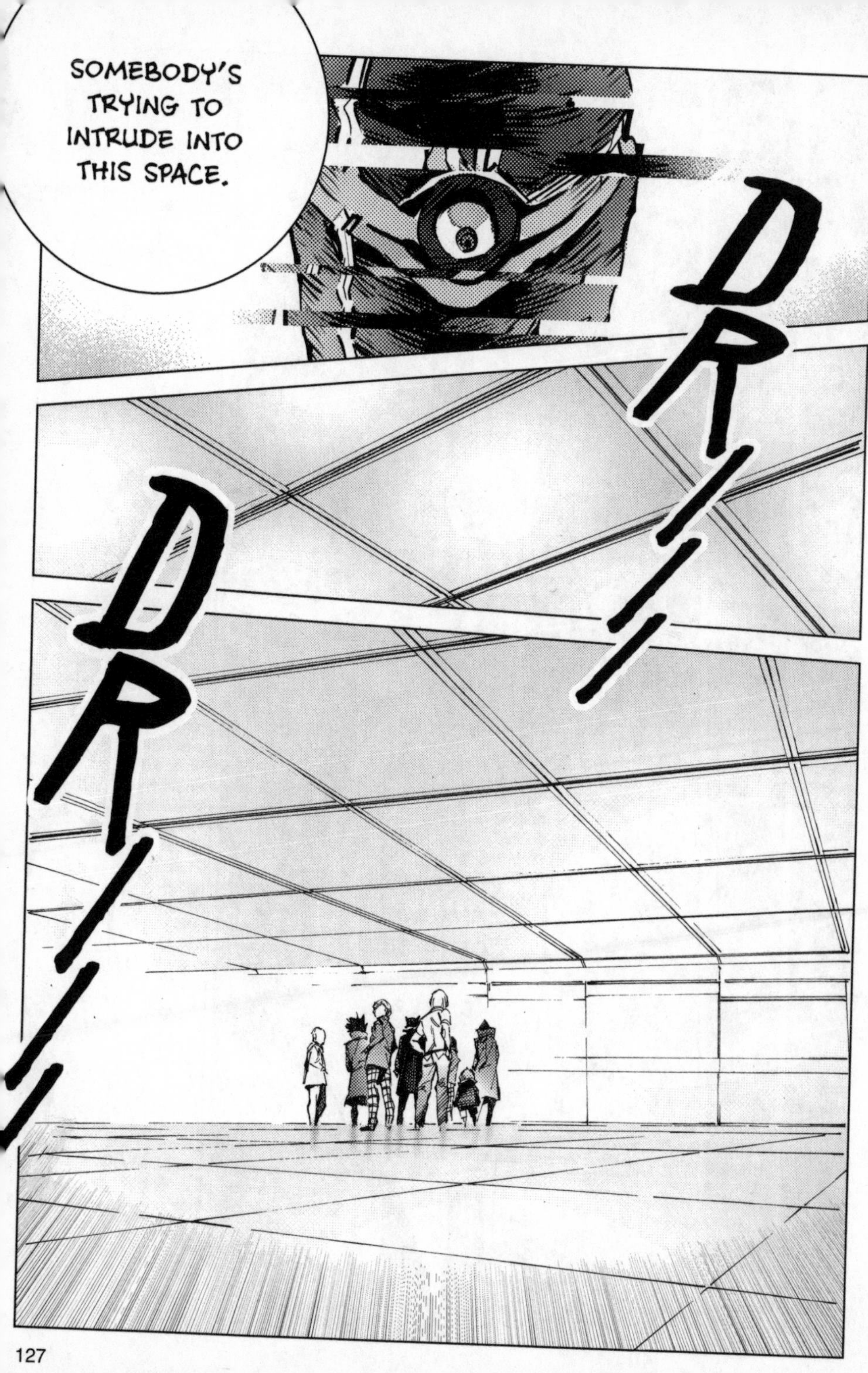
SOMEBODY'S TRYING TO INTRUDE INTO THIS SPACE.
DR—
DR—

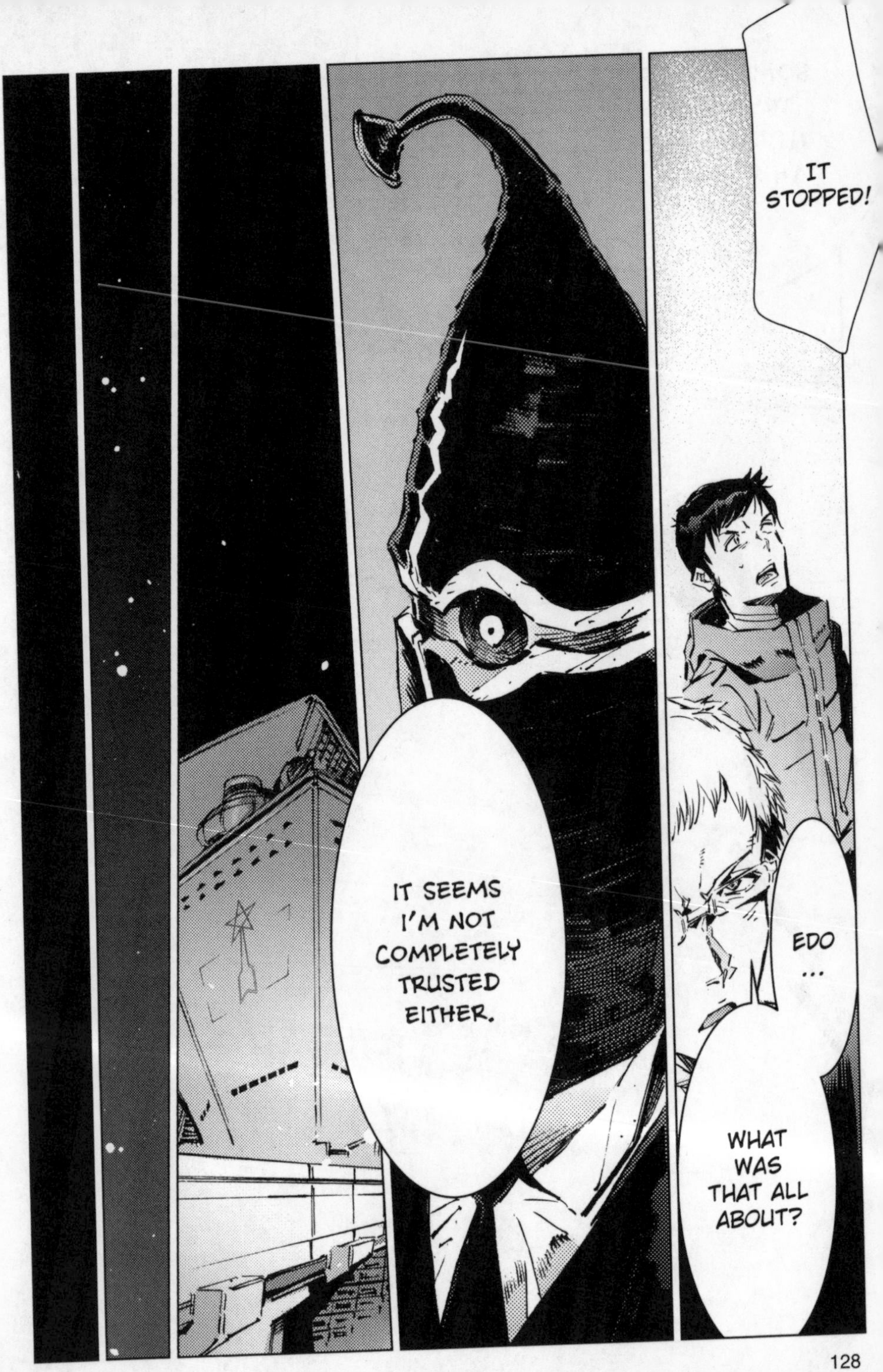
IT STOPPED!
EDO ...
WHAT WAS THAT ALL ABOUT?
IT SEEMS I'M NOT COMPLETELY TRUSTED EITHER.

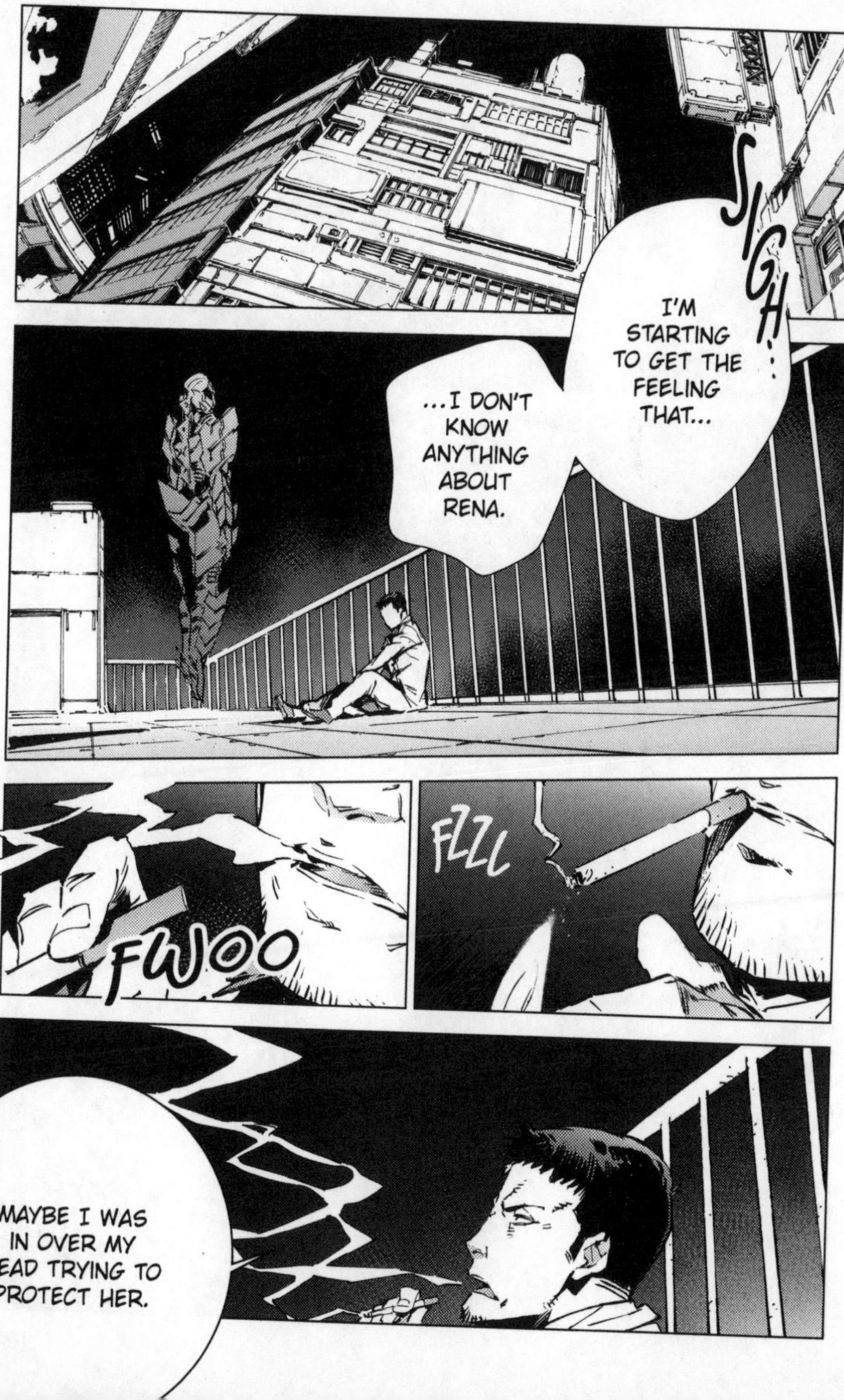
SIGH...
I'M STARTING TO GET THE FEELING THAT...
...I DON'T KNOW ANYTHING ABOUT RENA.
FZZL
FWOO
MAYBE I WAS IN OVER MY HEAD TRYING TO PROTECT HER.

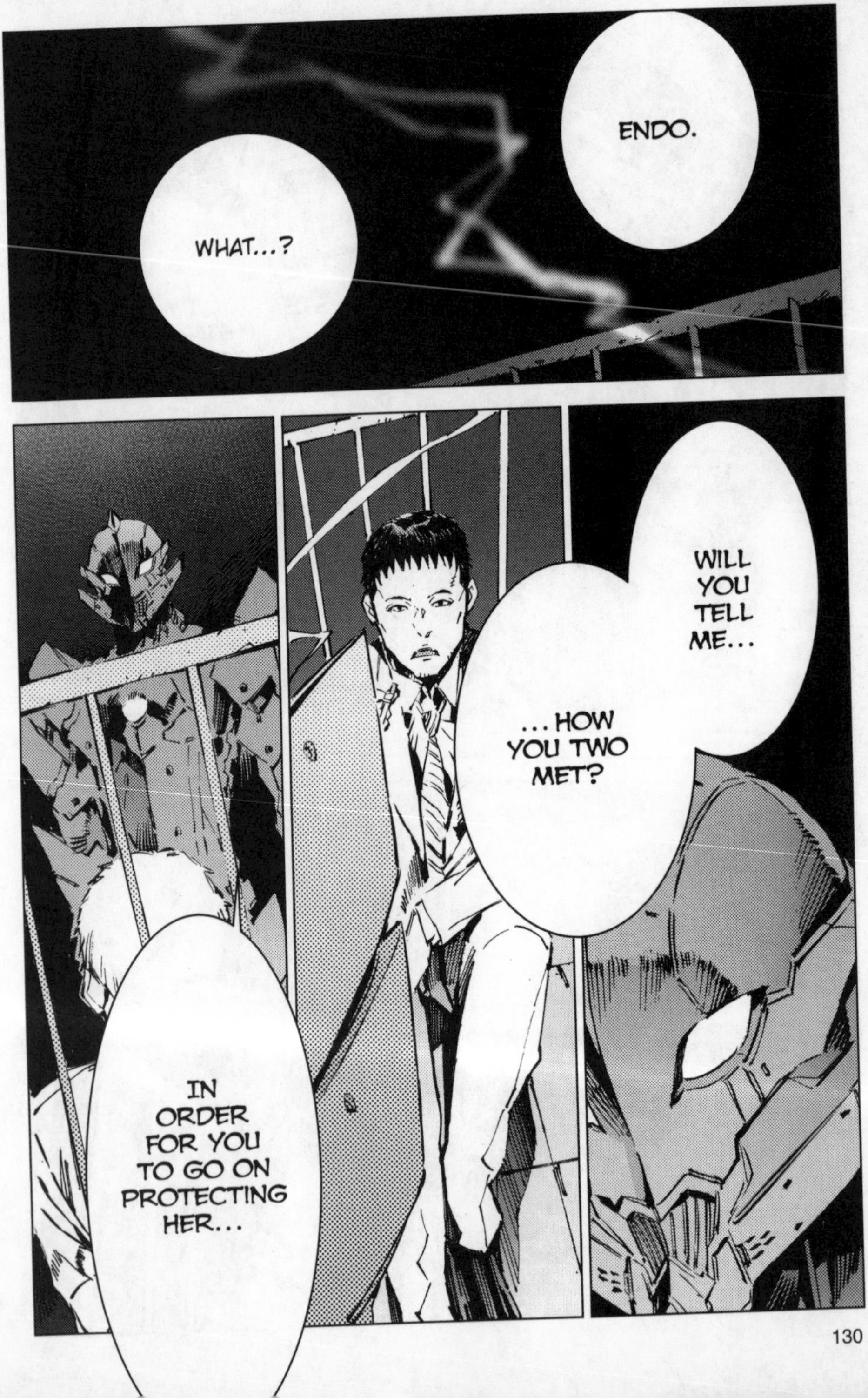
ENDO.
WHAT...?
WILL YOU TELL ME...
...HOW YOU TWO MET?
IN ORDER FOR YOU TO GO ON PROTECTING HER...

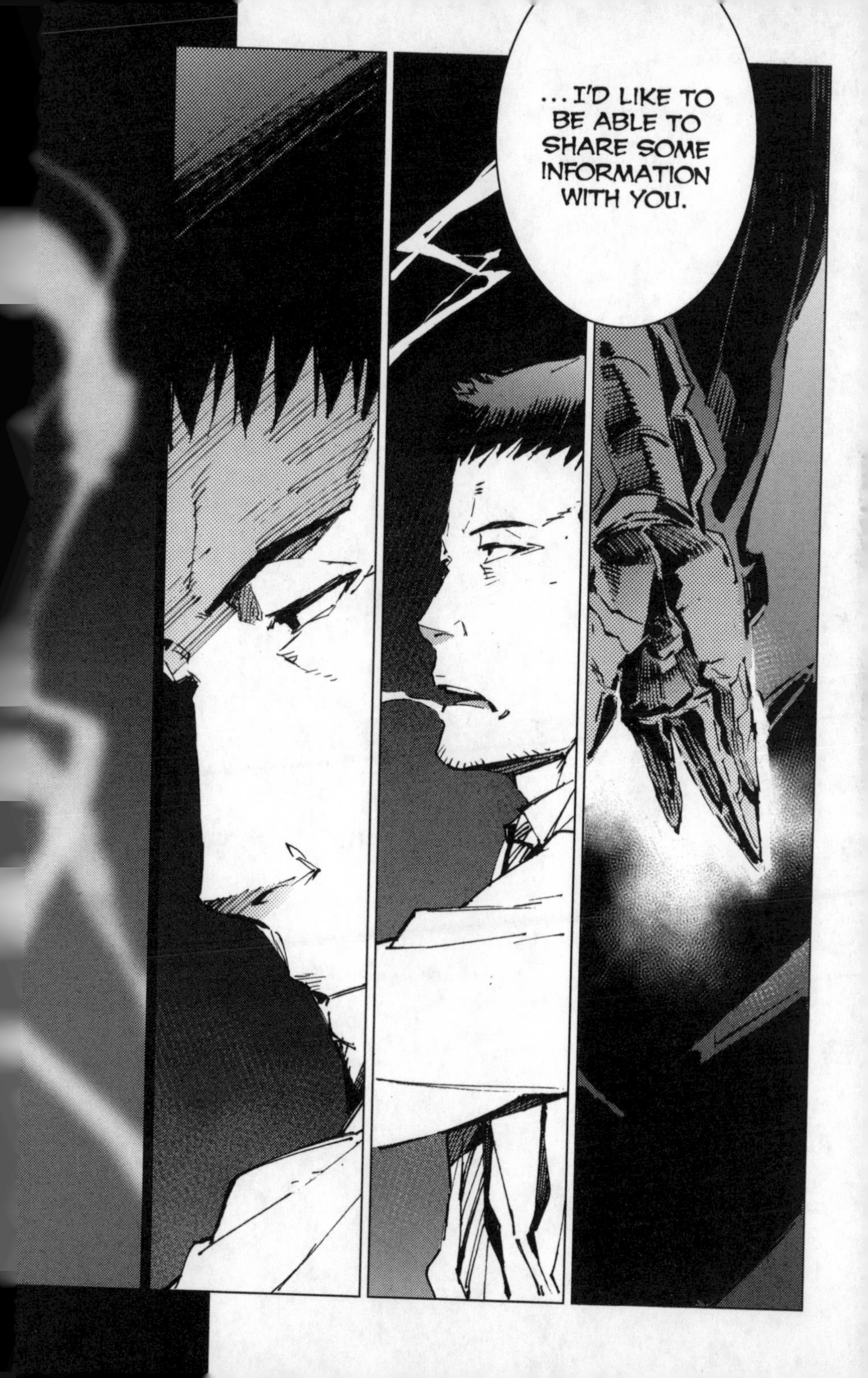
...I'D LIKE TO BE ABLE TO SHARE SOME INFORMATION WITH YOU.

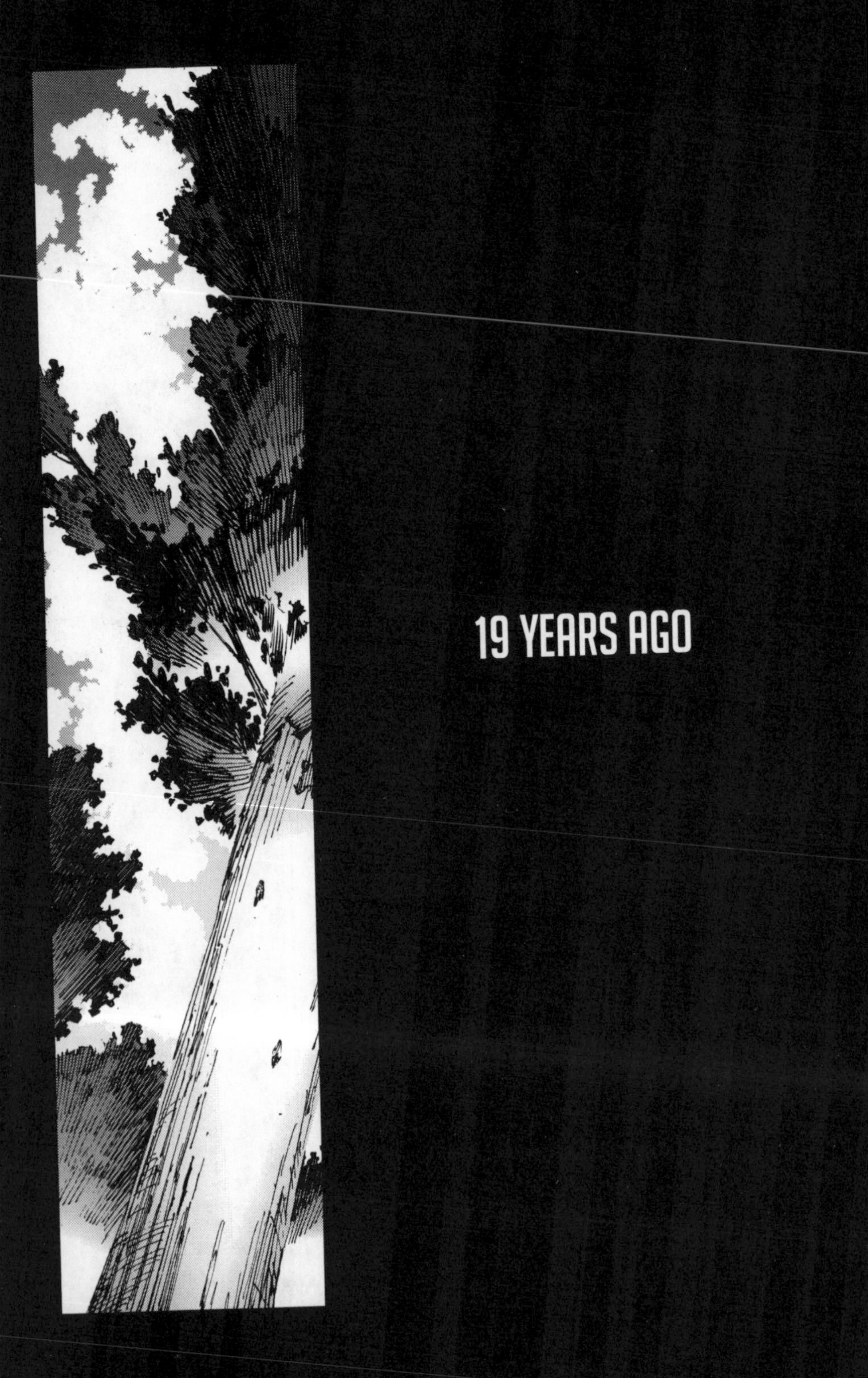
19 YEARS AGO

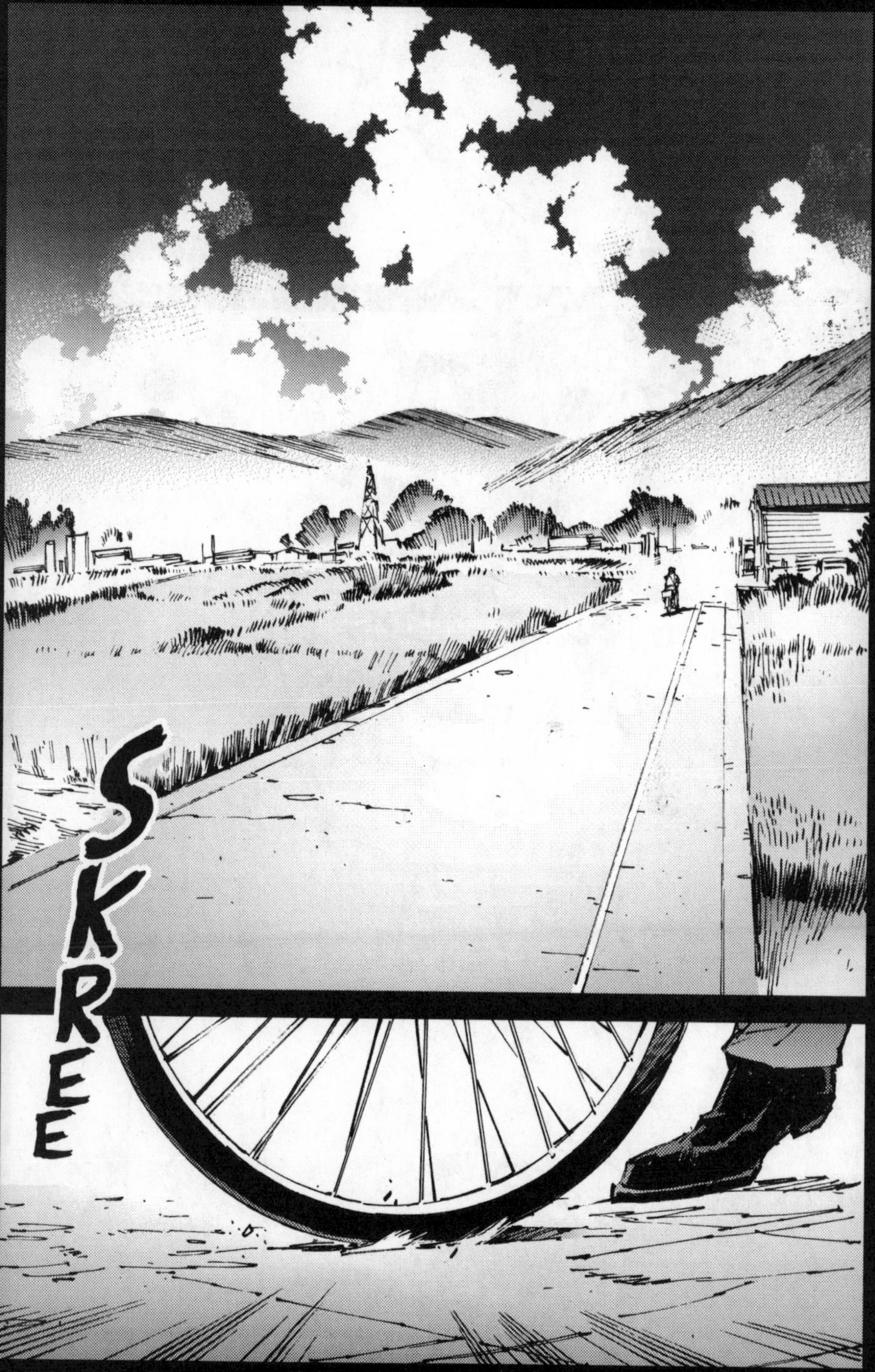
SKREE

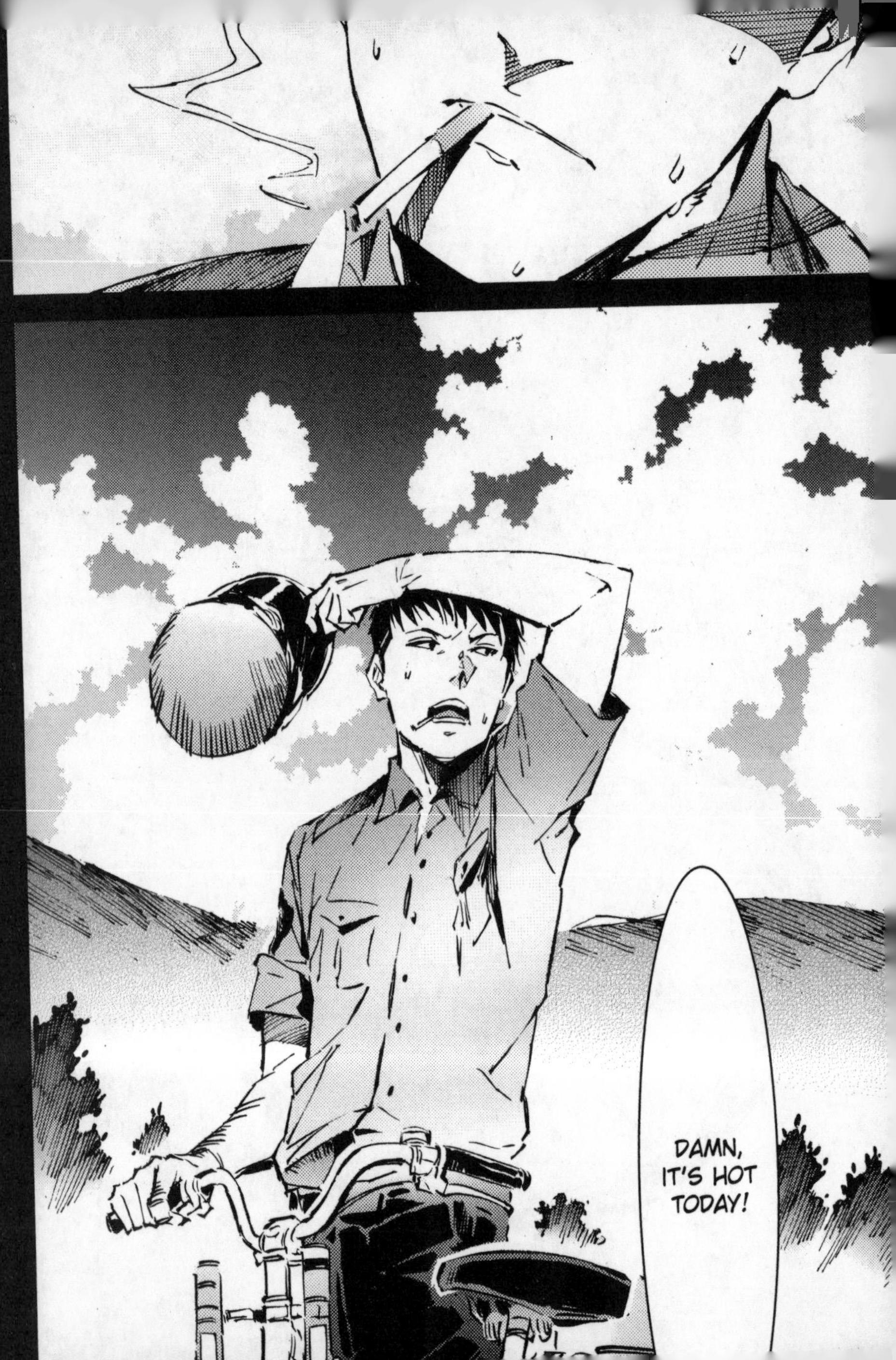
DAMN, IT'S HOT TODAY!

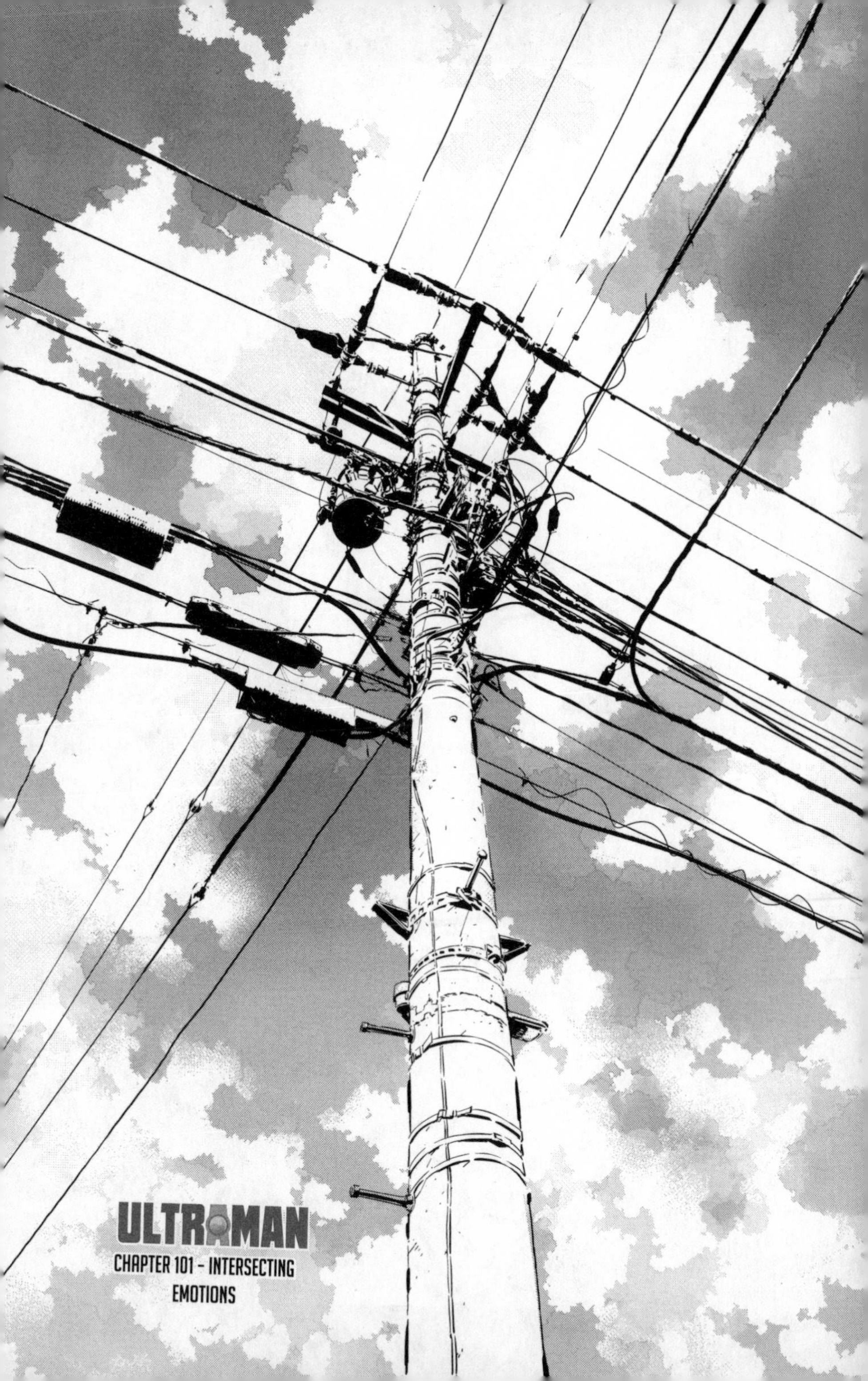
ULTRAMAN
CHAPTER 101 - INTERSECTING EMOTIONS

SUMMER

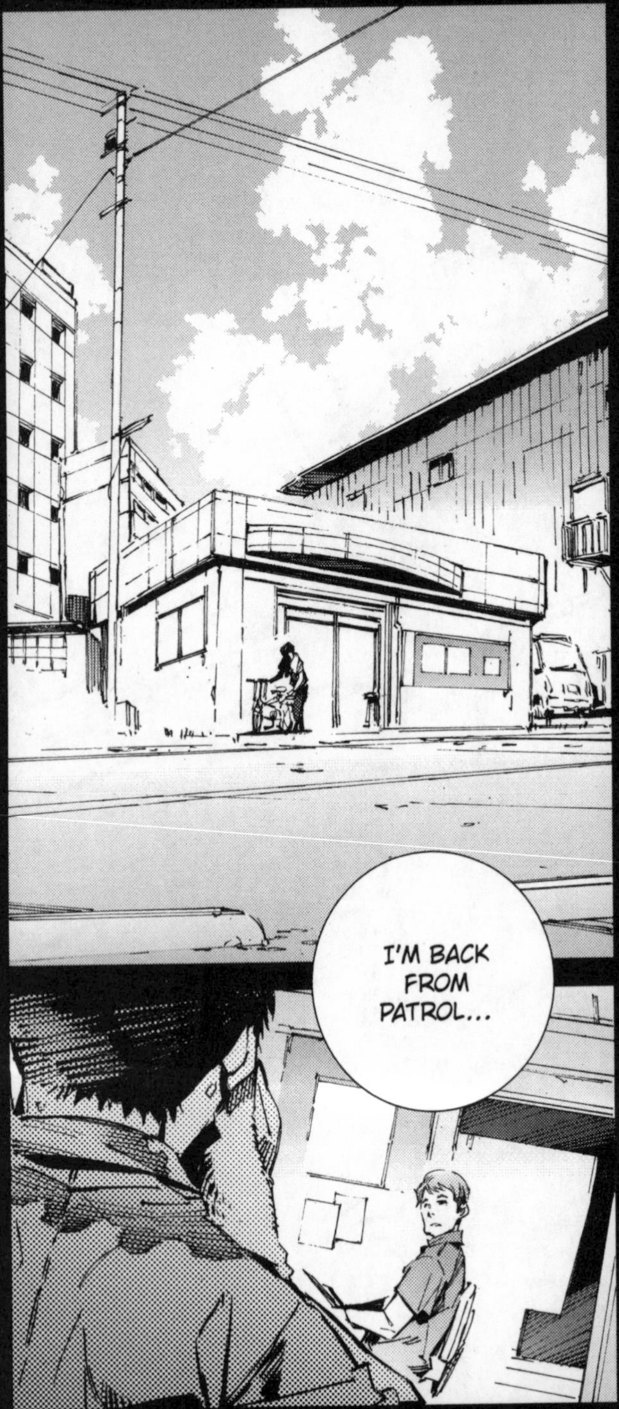
I'M BACK FROM PATROL...

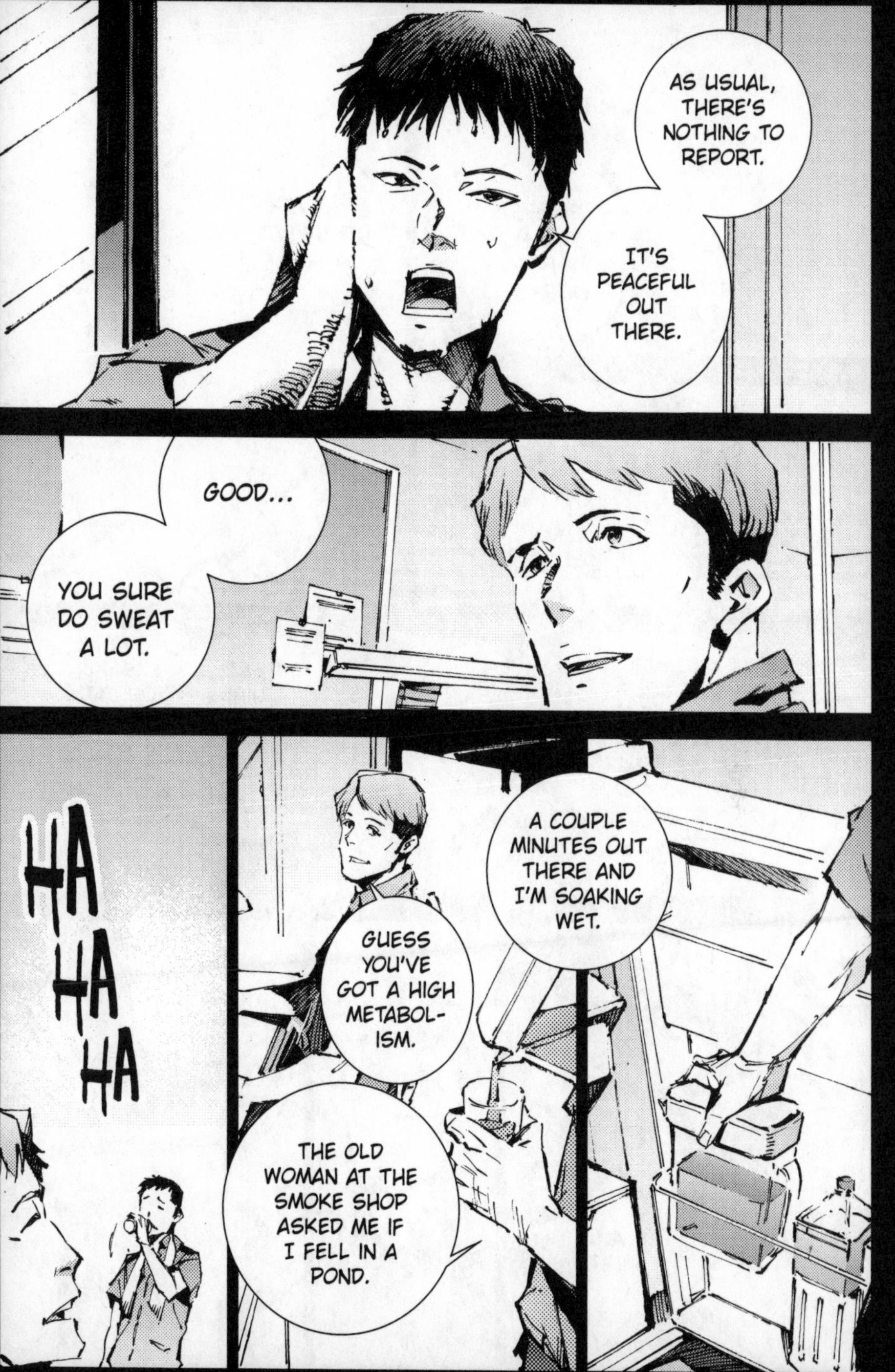
AS USUAL, THERE'S NOTHING TO REPORT.
IT'S PEACEFUL OUT THERE.
GOOD...
YOU SURE DO SWEAT A LOT.
A COUPLE MINUTES OUT THERE AND I'M SOAKING WET.
GUESS YOU'VE GOT A HIGH METABOL-ISM.
THE OLD WOMAN AT THE SMOKE SHOP ASKED ME IF I FELL IN A POND.
HA HA HA

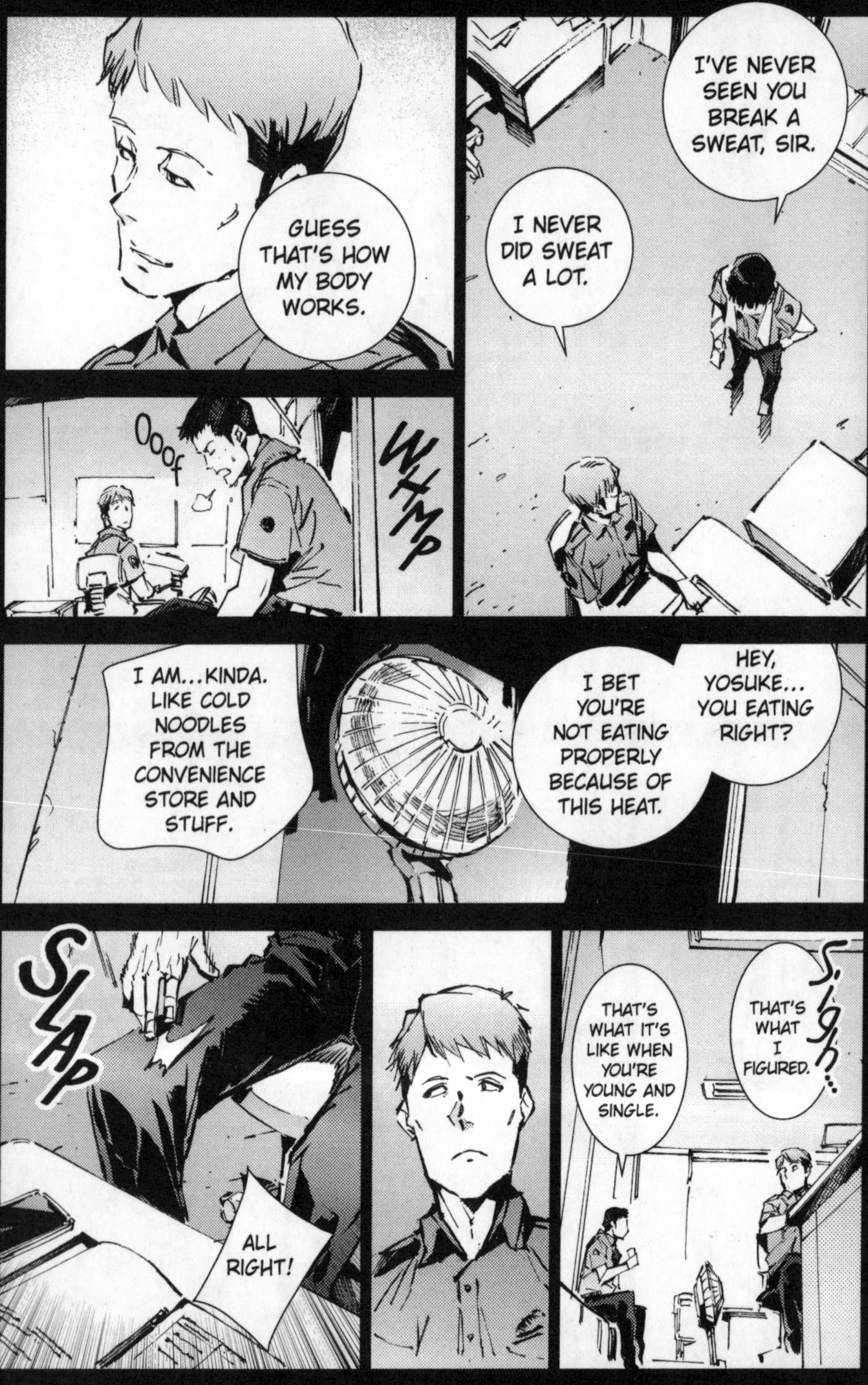
I'VE NEVER SEEN YOU BREAK A SWEAT, SIR.
I NEVER DID SWEAT A LOT.
GUESS THAT'S HOW MY BODY WORKS.
WHMP
Ooof
HEY, YOSUKE... YOU EATING RIGHT?
I BET YOU'RE NOT EATING PROPERLY BECAUSE OF THIS HEAT.
I AM...KINDA. LIKE COLD NOODLES FROM THE CONVENIENCE STORE AND STUFF.
Sigh...
THAT'S WHAT I FIGURED.
THAT'S WHAT IT'S LIKE WHEN YOU'RE YOUNG AND SINGLE.
SLAP
ALL RIGHT!

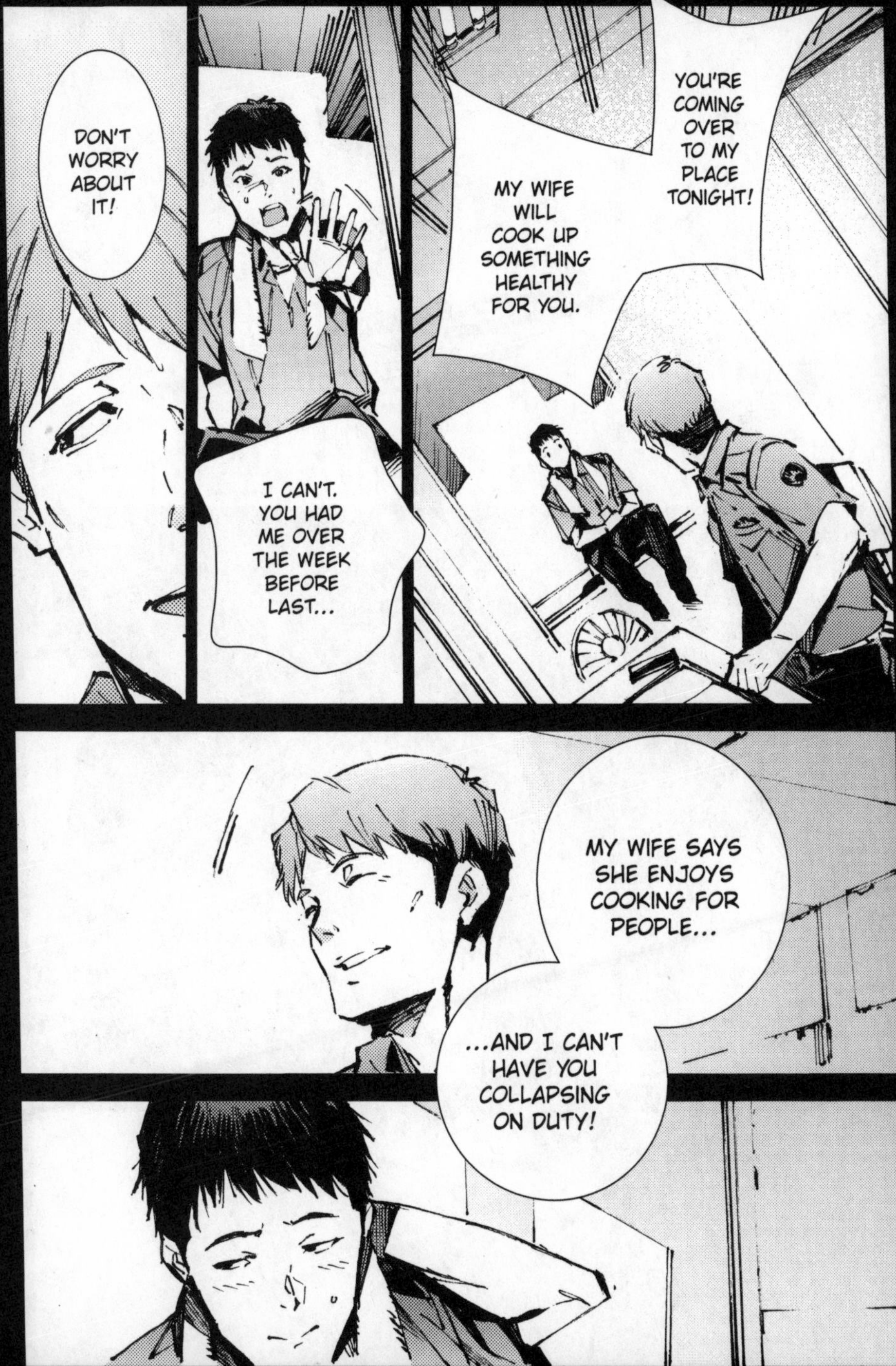
YOU'RE COMING OVER TO MY PLACE TONIGHT!
MY WIFE WILL COOK UP SOMETHING HEALTHY FOR YOU.
I CAN'T. YOU HAD ME OVER THE WEEK BEFORE LAST...
DON'T WORRY ABOUT IT!
MY WIFE SAYS SHE ENJOYS COOKING FOR PEOPLE...
...AND I CAN'T HAVE YOU COLLAPSING ON DUTY!

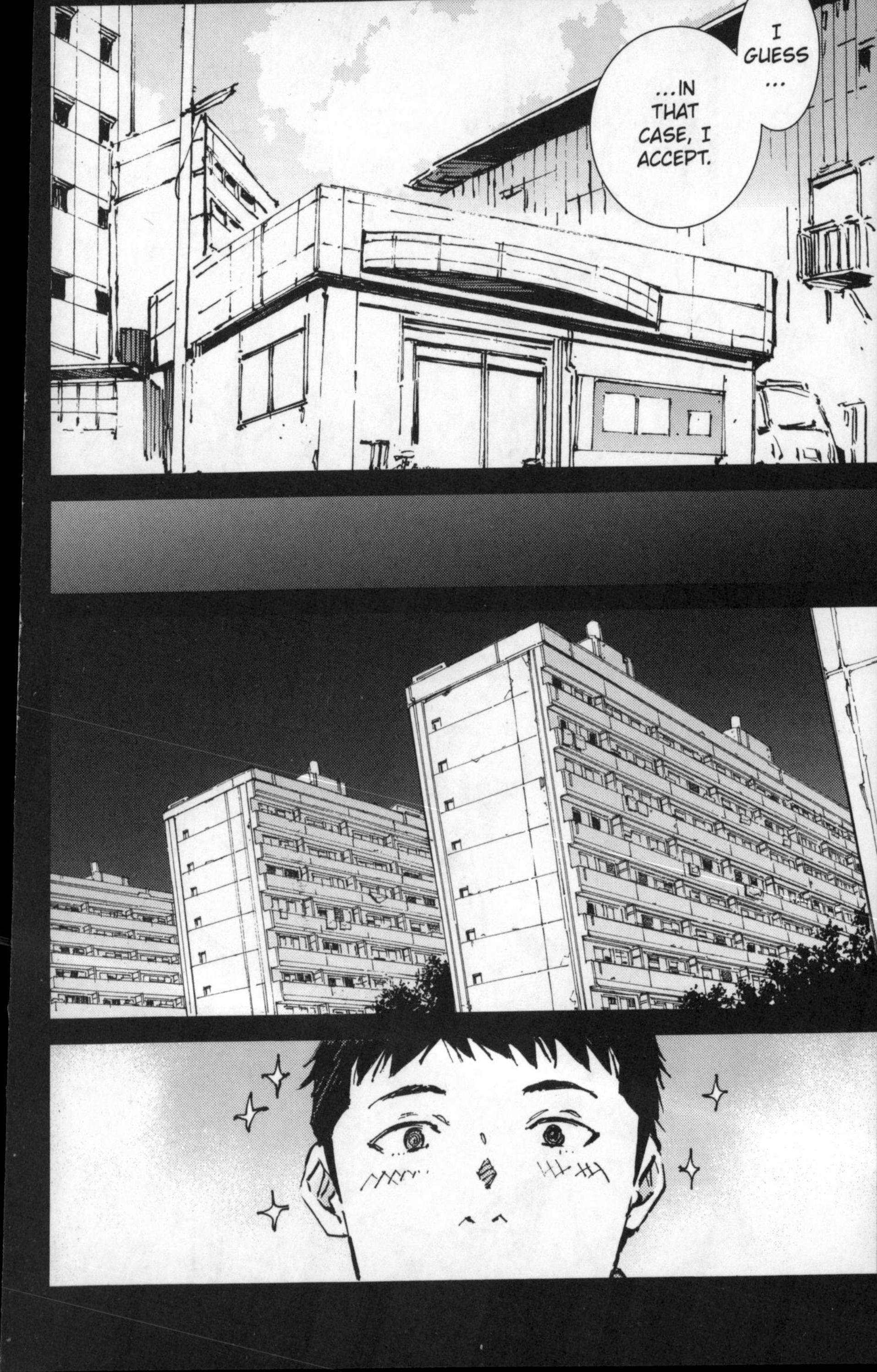
I GUESS ...
...IN THAT CASE, I ACCEPT.

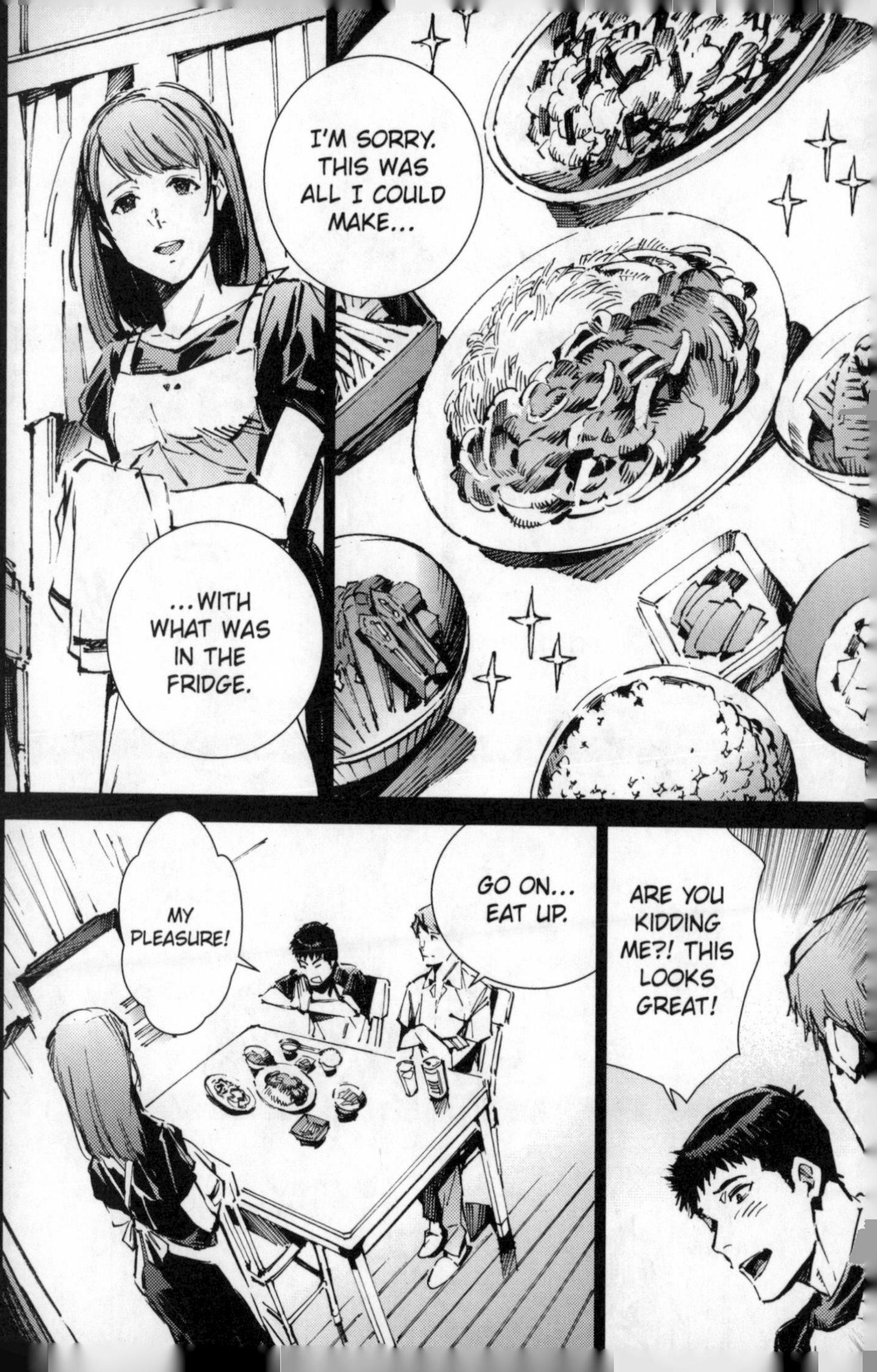
I'M SORRY. THIS WAS ALL I COULD MAKE...
...WITH WHAT WAS IN THE FRIDGE.
ARE YOU KIDDING ME?! THIS LOOKS GREAT!
GO ON... EAT UP.
MY PLEASURE!

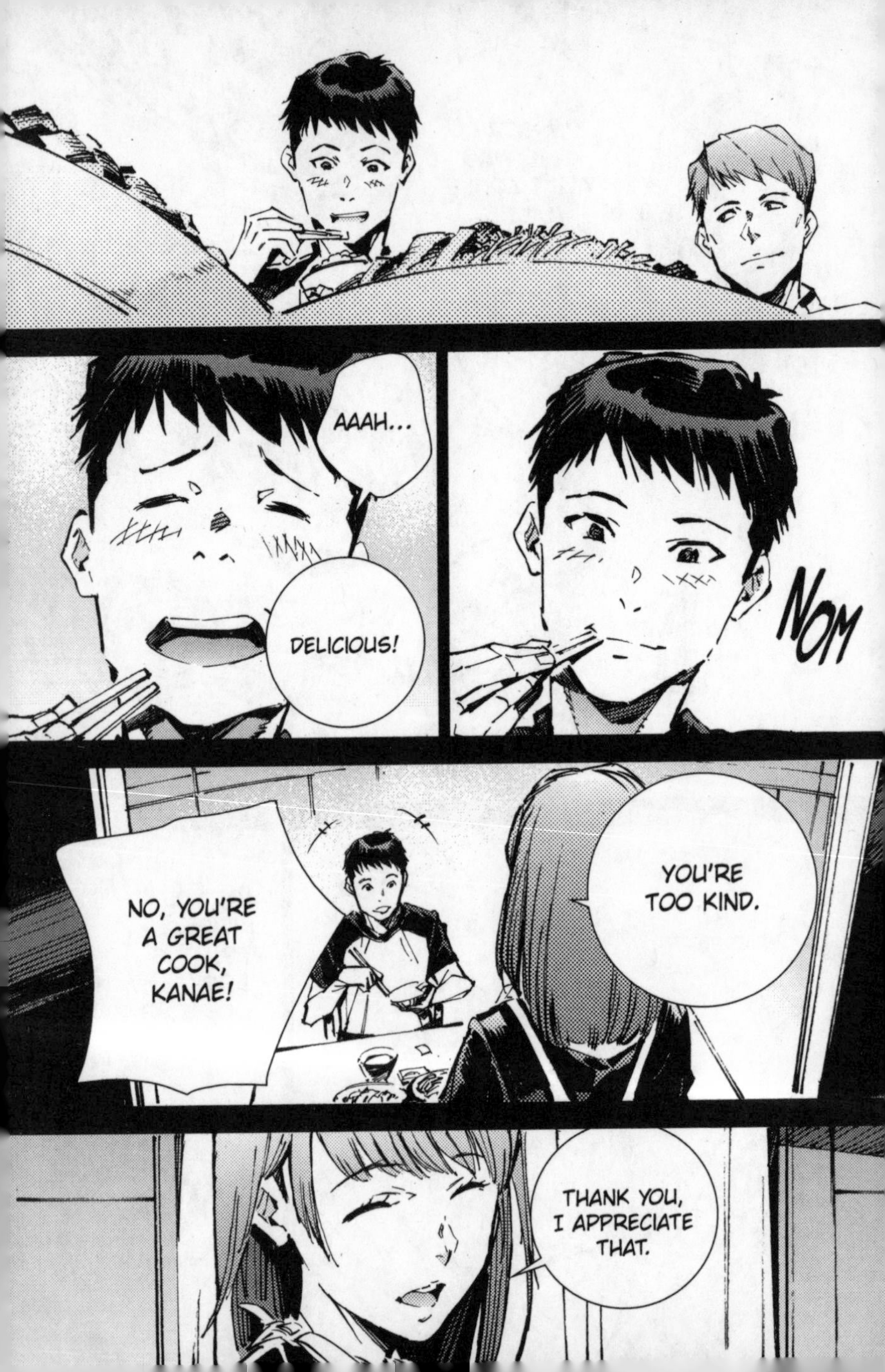
NOM
AAAH...
DELICIOUS!
YOU'RE TOO KIND.
NO, YOU'RE A GREAT COOK, KANAE!
THANK YOU, I APPRECIATE THAT.

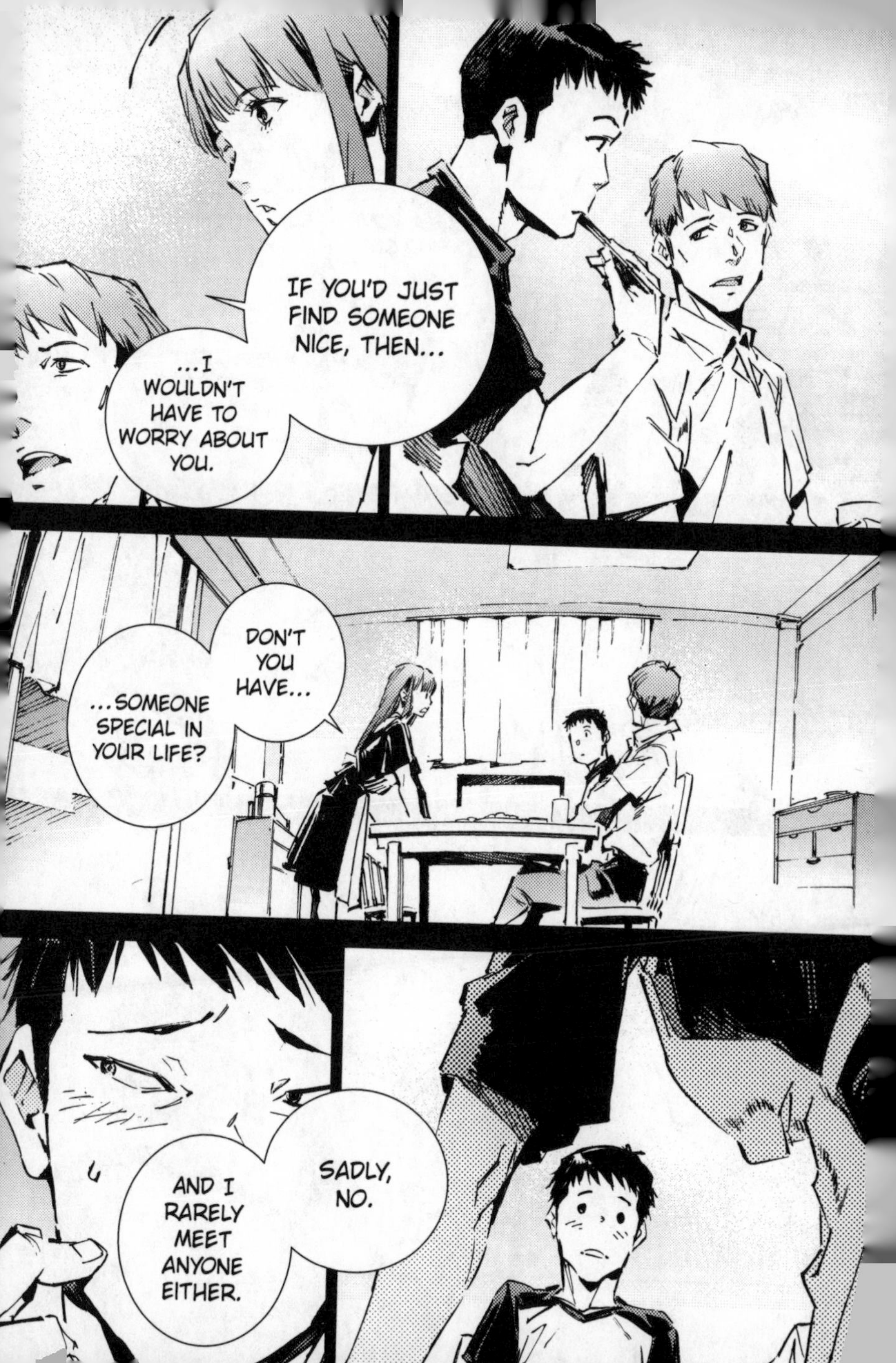
IF YOU'D JUST FIND SOMEONE NICE, THEN...
...I WOULDN'T HAVE TO WORRY ABOUT YOU.
DON'T YOU HAVE...
...SOMEONE SPECIAL IN YOUR LIFE?
SADLY, NO.
AND I RARELY MEET ANYONE EITHER.

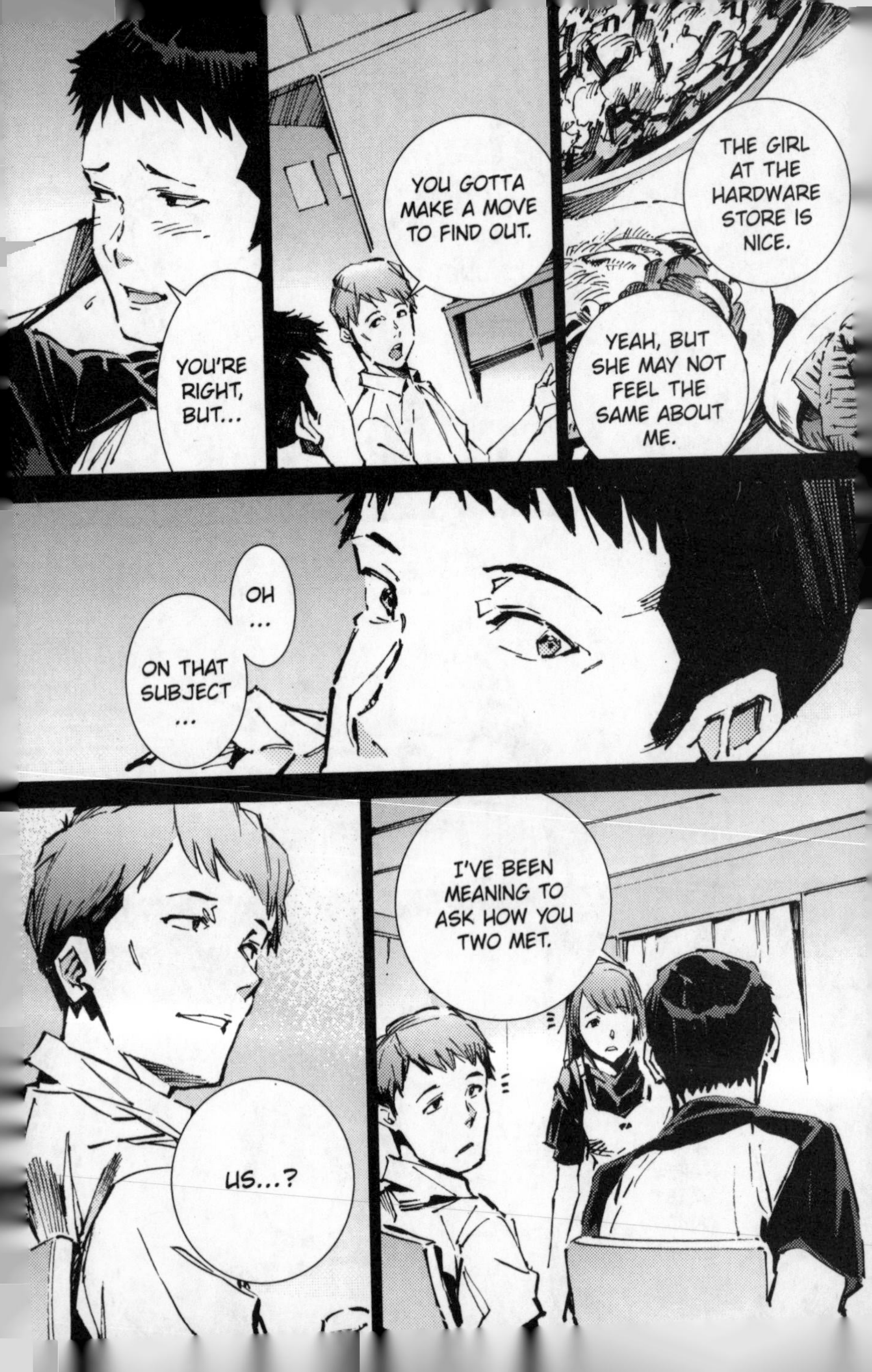
THE GIRL AT THE HARDWARE STORE IS NICE.
YEAH, BUT SHE MAY NOT FEEL THE SAME ABOUT ME.
YOU GOTTA MAKE A MOVE TO FIND OUT.
YOU'RE RIGHT, BUT...
OH ...
ON THAT SUBJECT ...
I'VE BEEN MEANING TO ASK HOW YOU TWO MET.
US...?

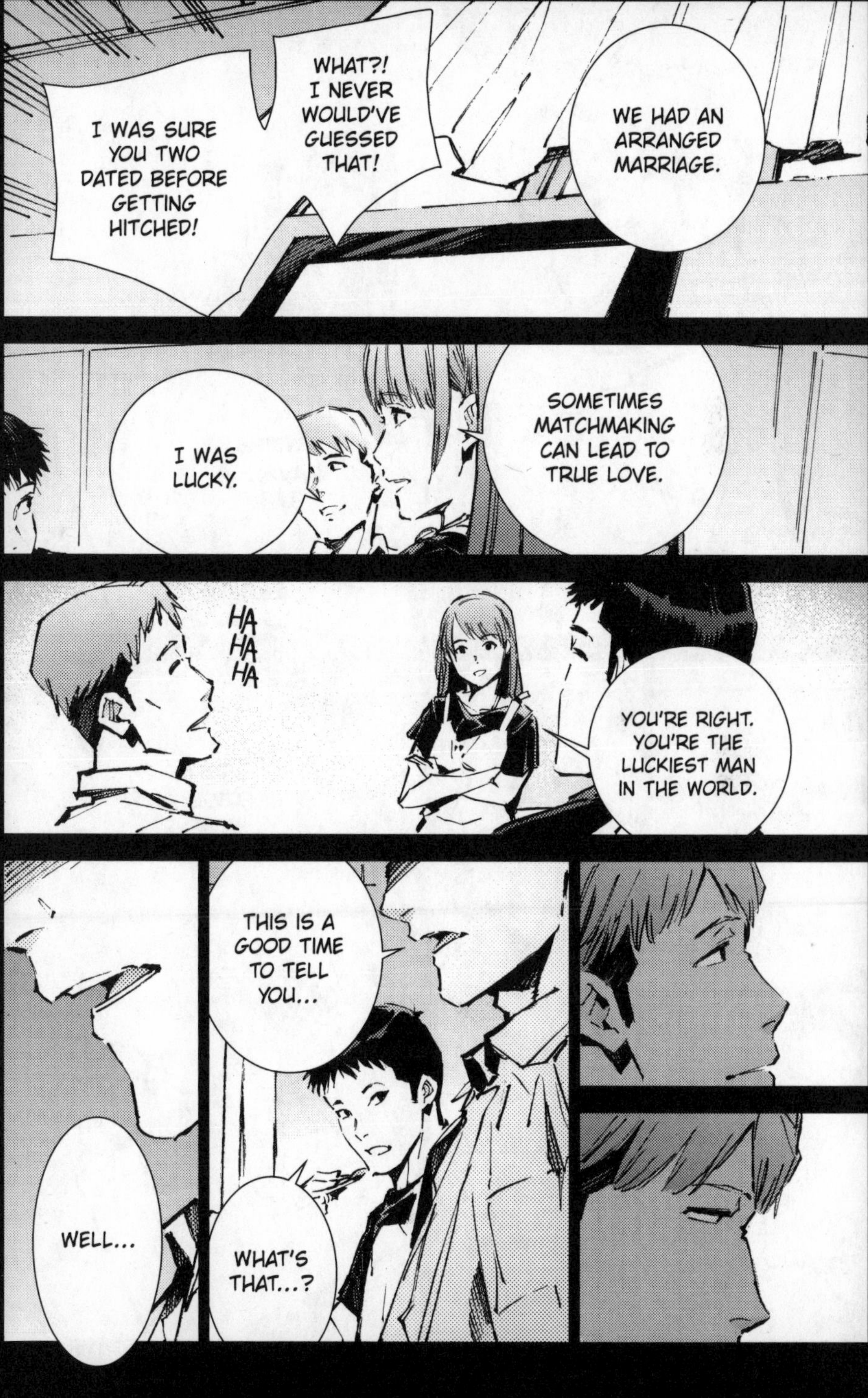
WE HAD AN ARRANGED MARRIAGE.
WHAT?! I NEVER WOULD'VE GUESSED THAT!
I WAS SURE YOU TWO DATED BEFORE GETTING HITCHED!
SOMETIMES MATCHMAKING CAN LEAD TO TRUE LOVE.
I WAS LUCKY.
YOU'RE RIGHT. YOU'RE THE LUCKIEST MAN IN THE WORLD.
HA HA HA
THIS IS A GOOD TIME TO TELL YOU...
WHAT'S THAT...?
WELL...

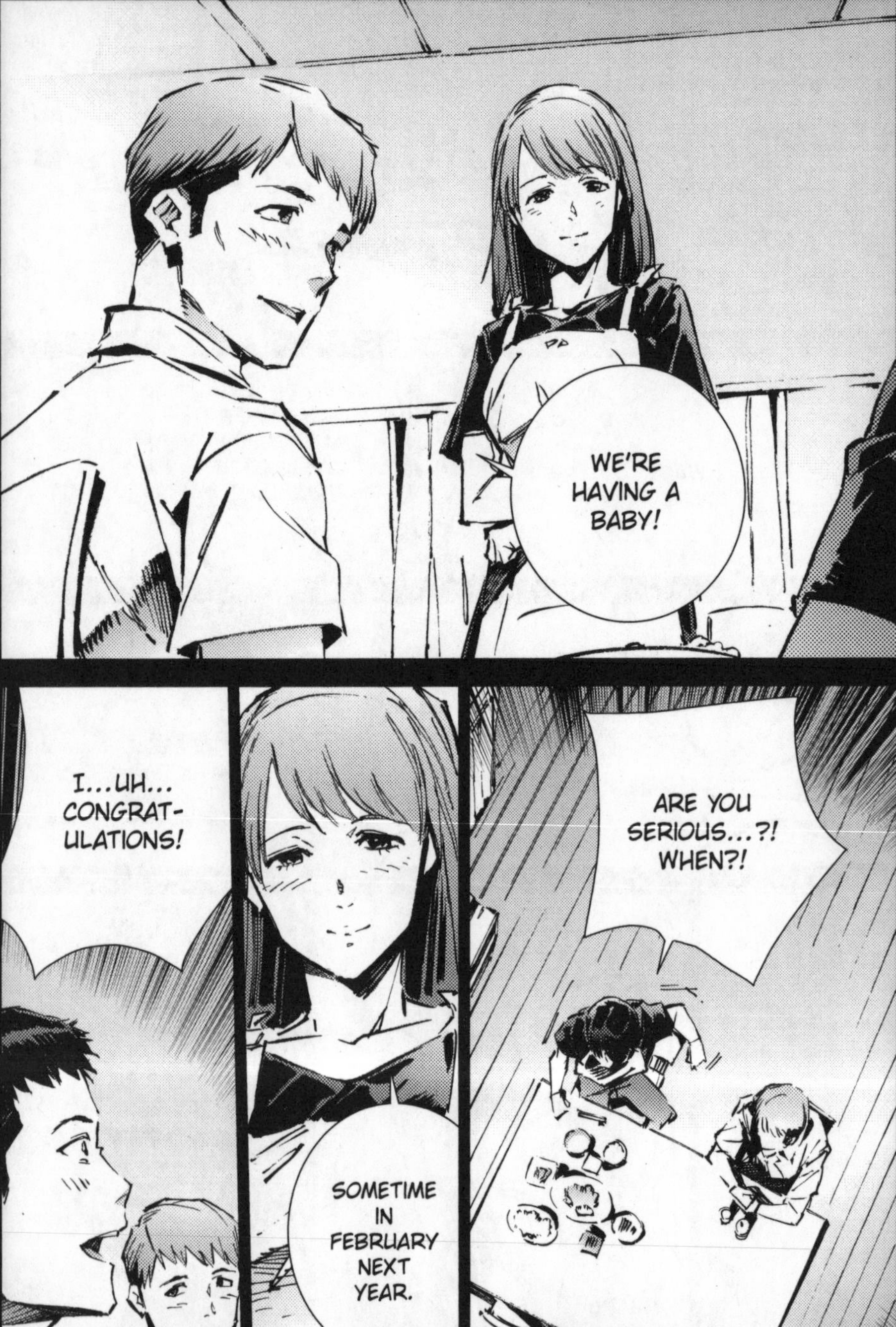
WE'RE HAVING A BABY!
ARE YOU SERIOUS...?! WHEN?!
SOMETIME IN FEBRUARY NEXT YEAR.
I...UH... CONGRAT-ULATIONS!

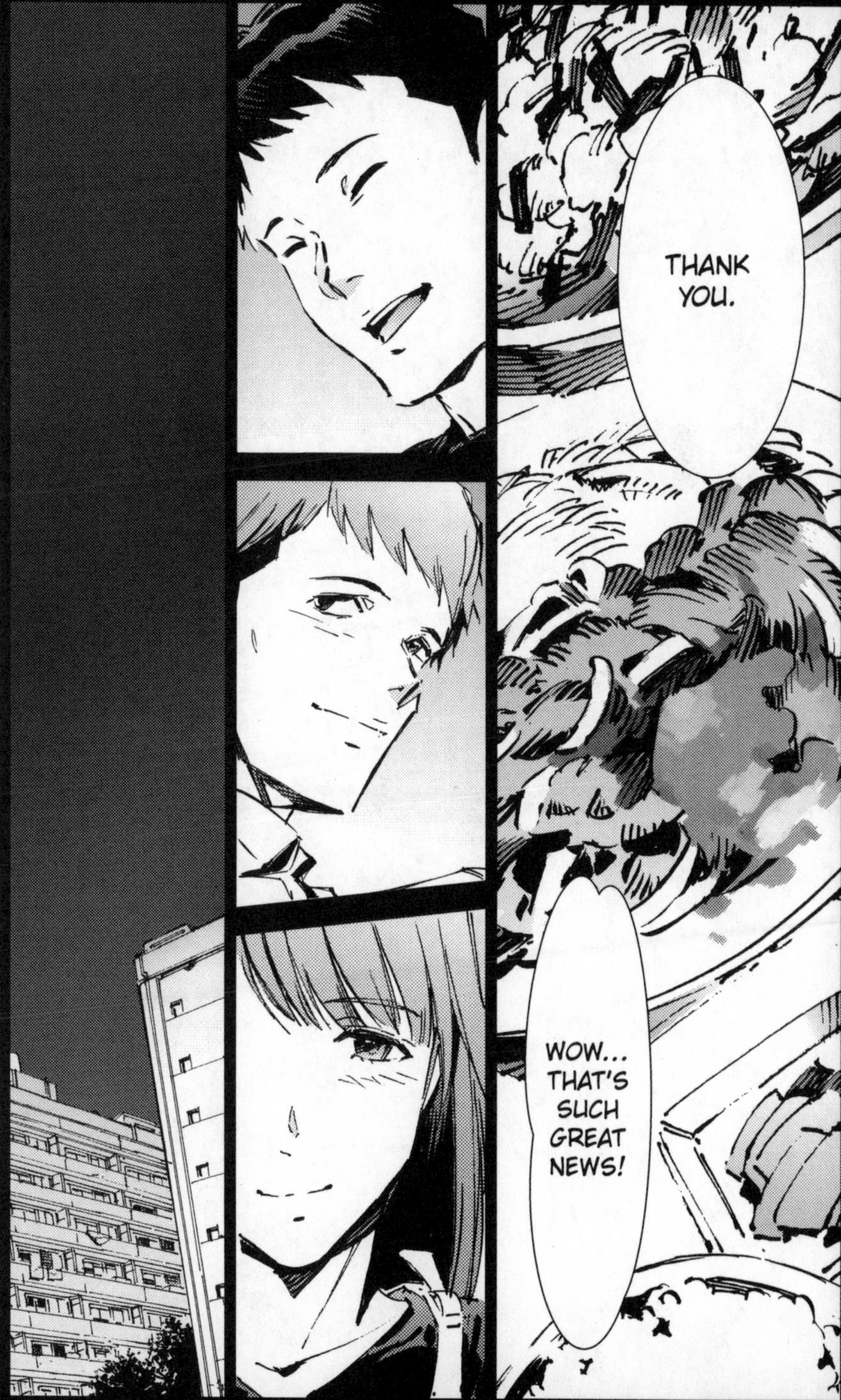
THANK YOU.
WOW... THAT'S SUCH GREAT NEWS!

FALL

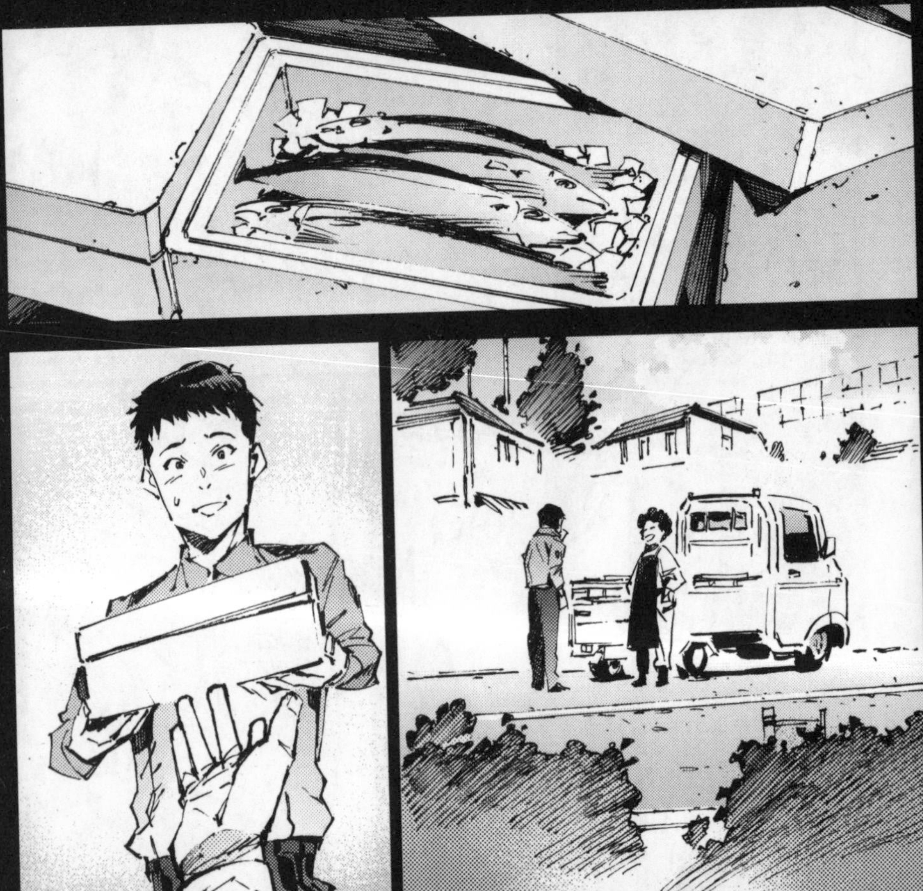

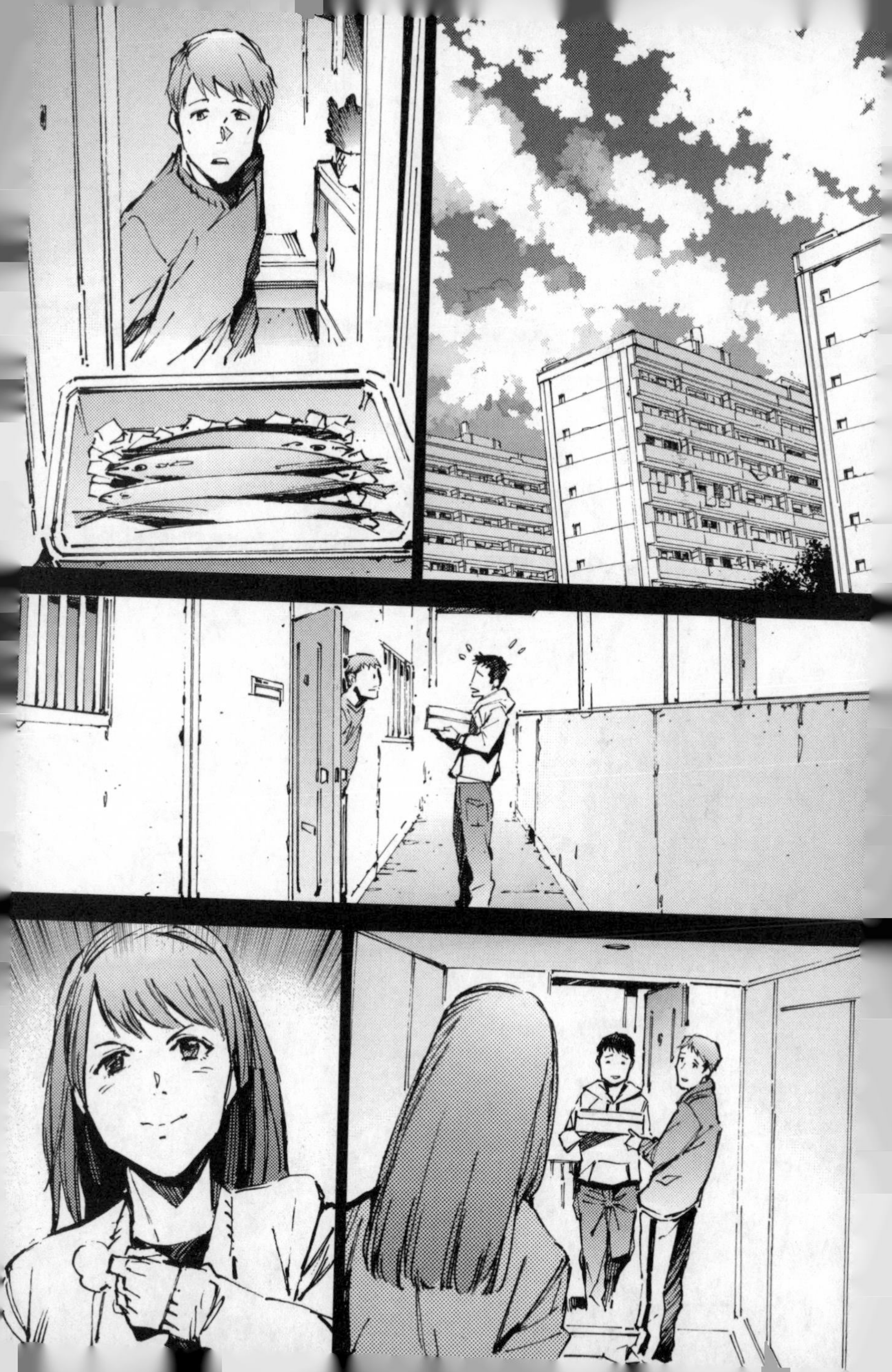

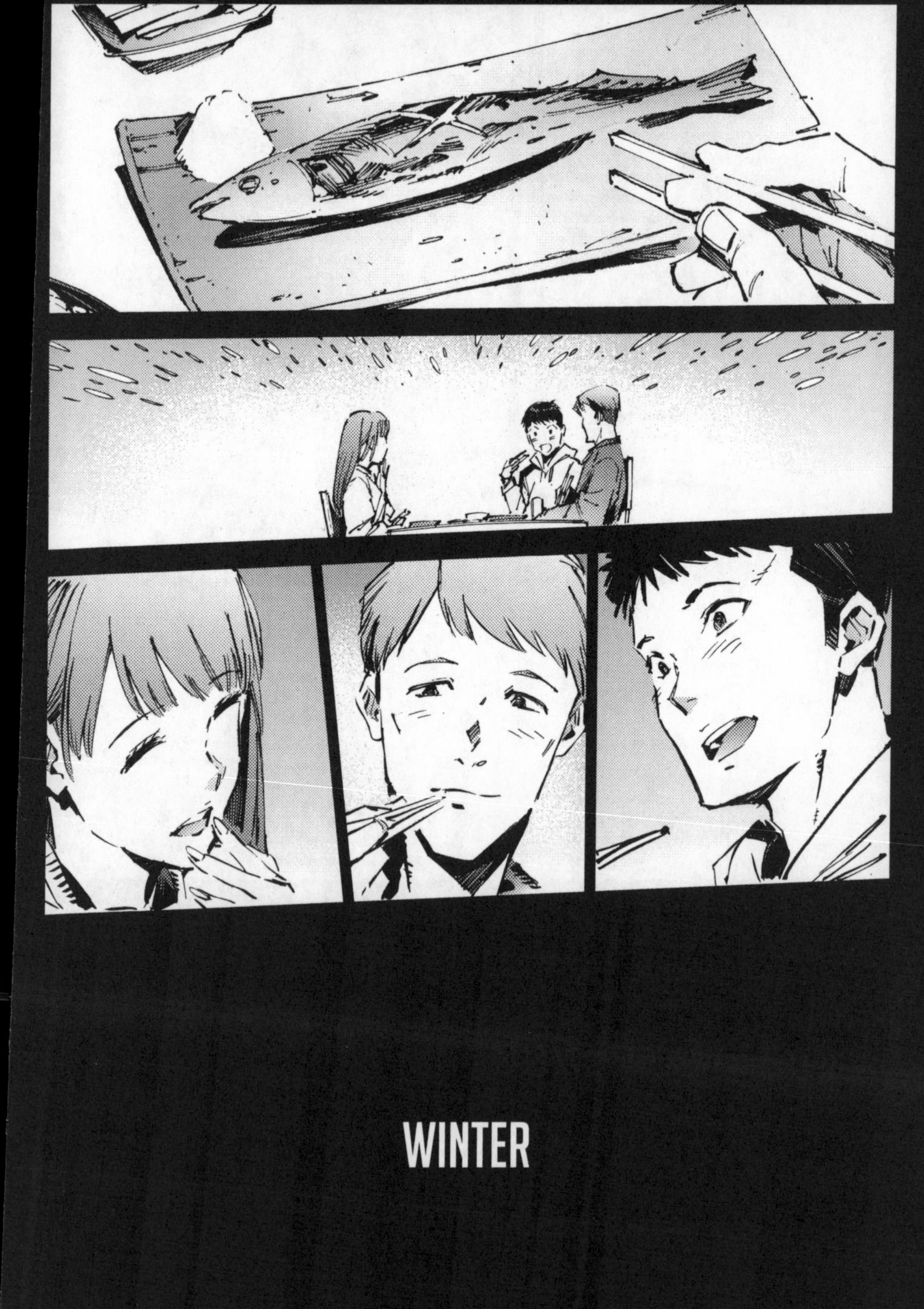

WINTER

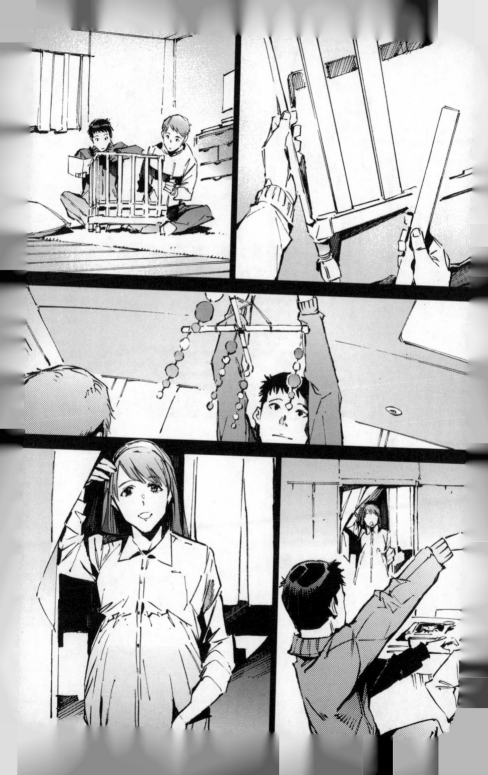

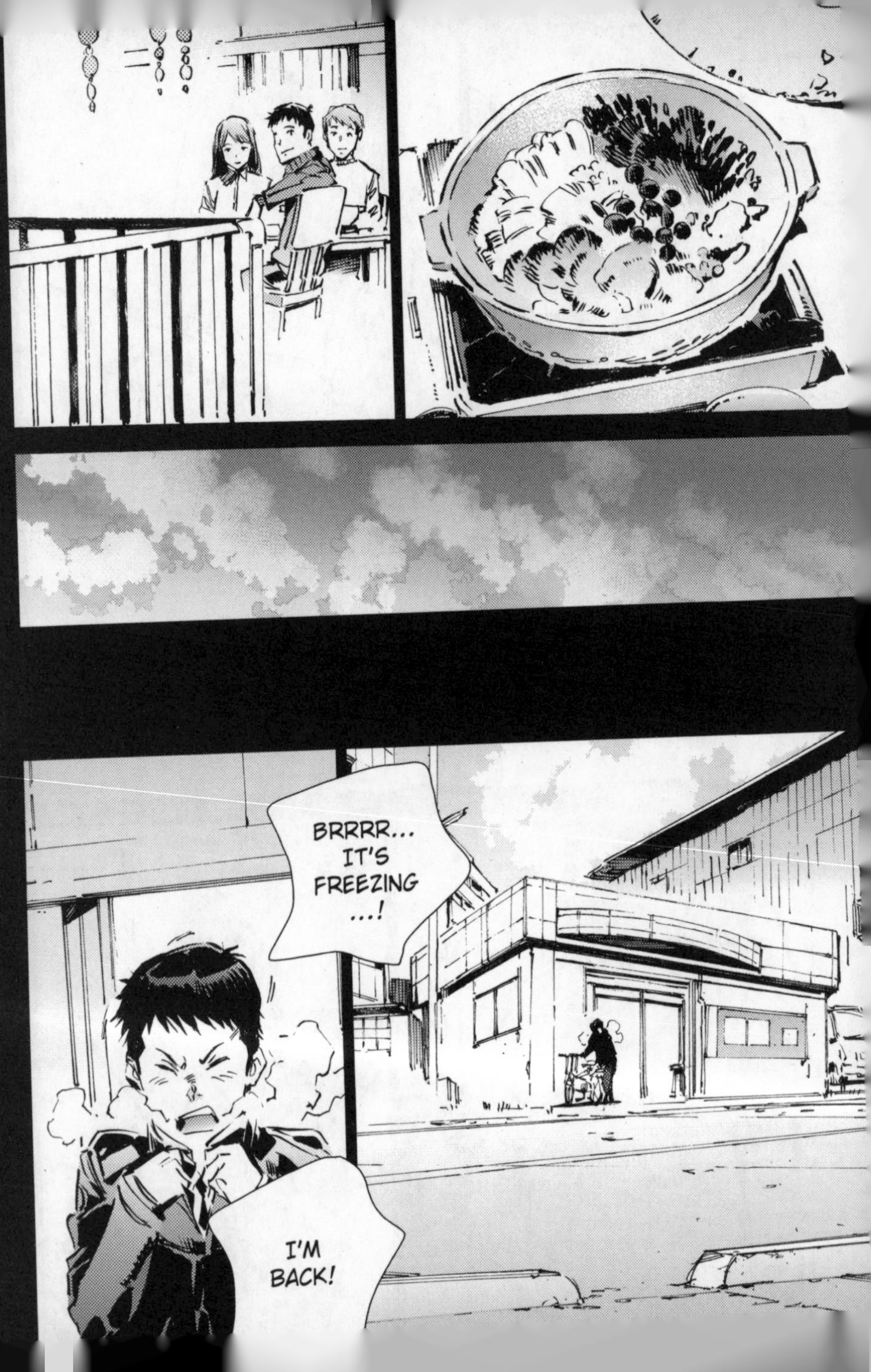
BRRRR... IT'S FREEZING ...!
I'M BACK!

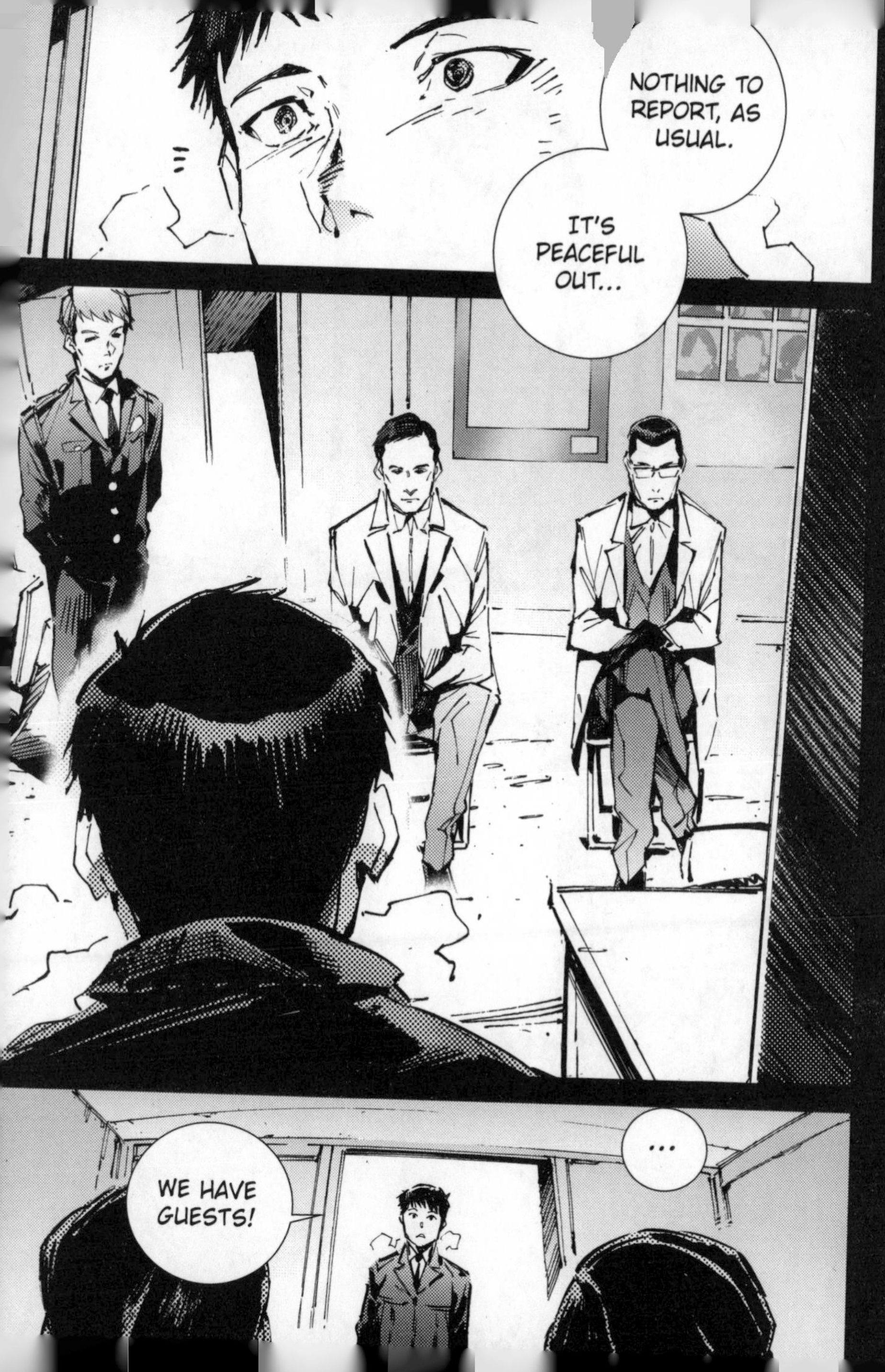
NOTHING TO REPORT, AS USUAL.
IT'S PEACEFUL OUT...
...
WE HAVE GUESTS!

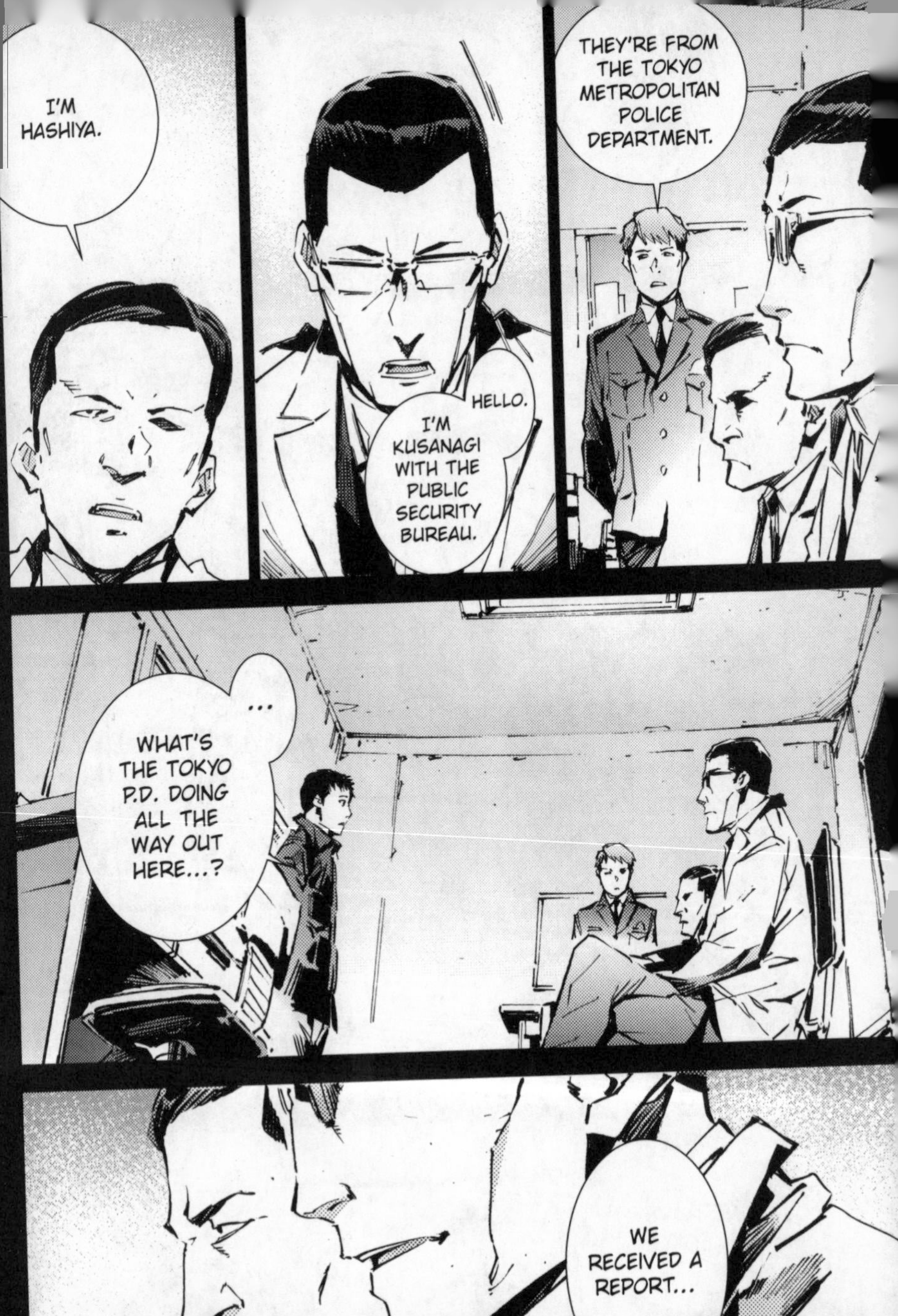
THEY'RE FROM THE TOKYO METROPOLITAN POLICE DEPARTMENT.
HELLO.
I'M KUSANAGI WITH THE PUBLIC SECURITY BUREAU.
I'M HASHIYA.
...
WHAT'S THE TOKYO P.D. DOING ALL THE WAY OUT HERE...?
WE RECEIVED A REPORT...

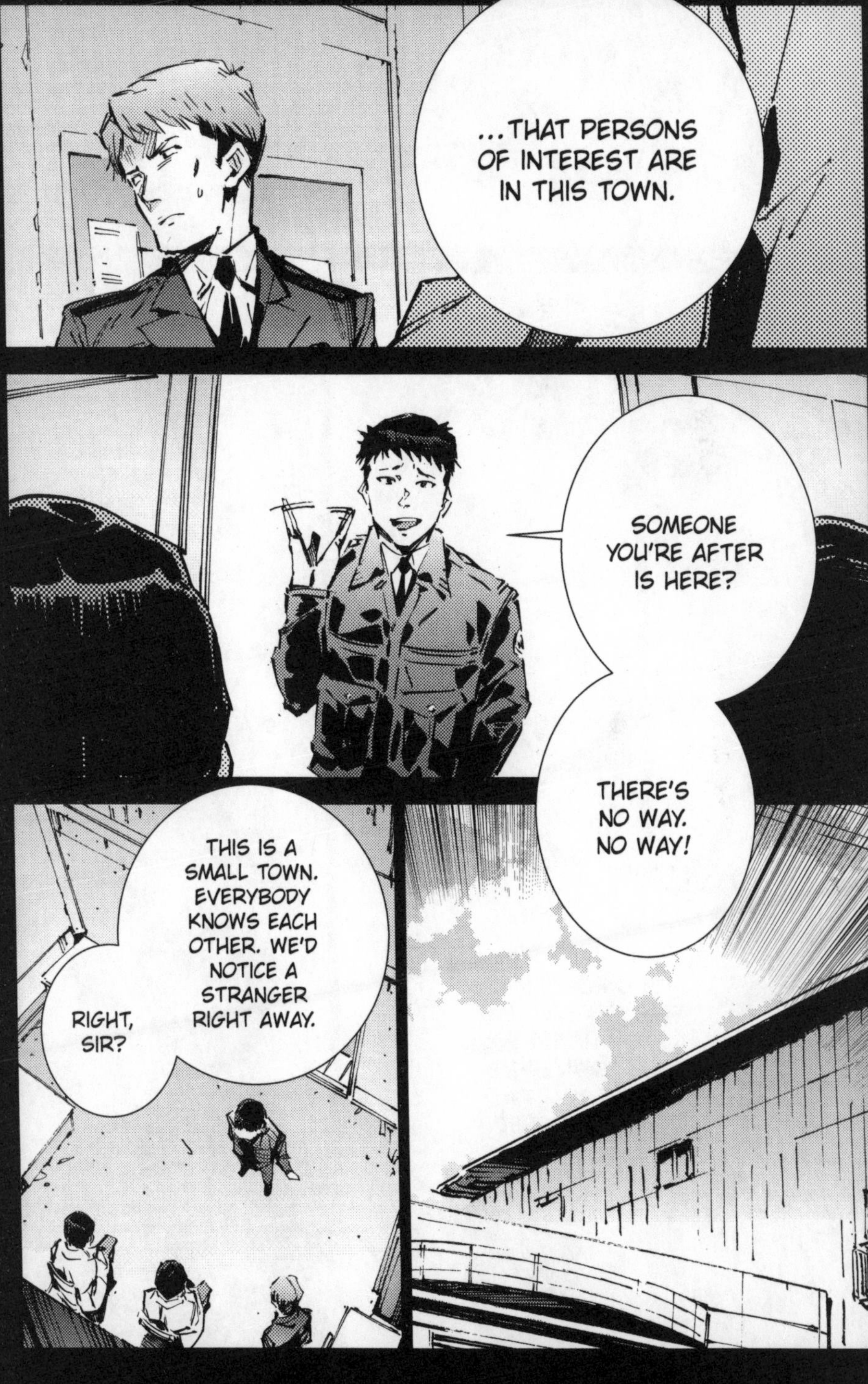
...THAT PERSONS OF INTEREST ARE IN THIS TOWN.
SOMEONE YOU'RE AFTER IS HERE?
THERE'S NO WAY. NO WAY!
THIS IS A SMALL TOWN. EVERYBODY KNOWS EACH OTHER. WE'D NOTICE A STRANGER RIGHT AWAY.
RIGHT, SIR?

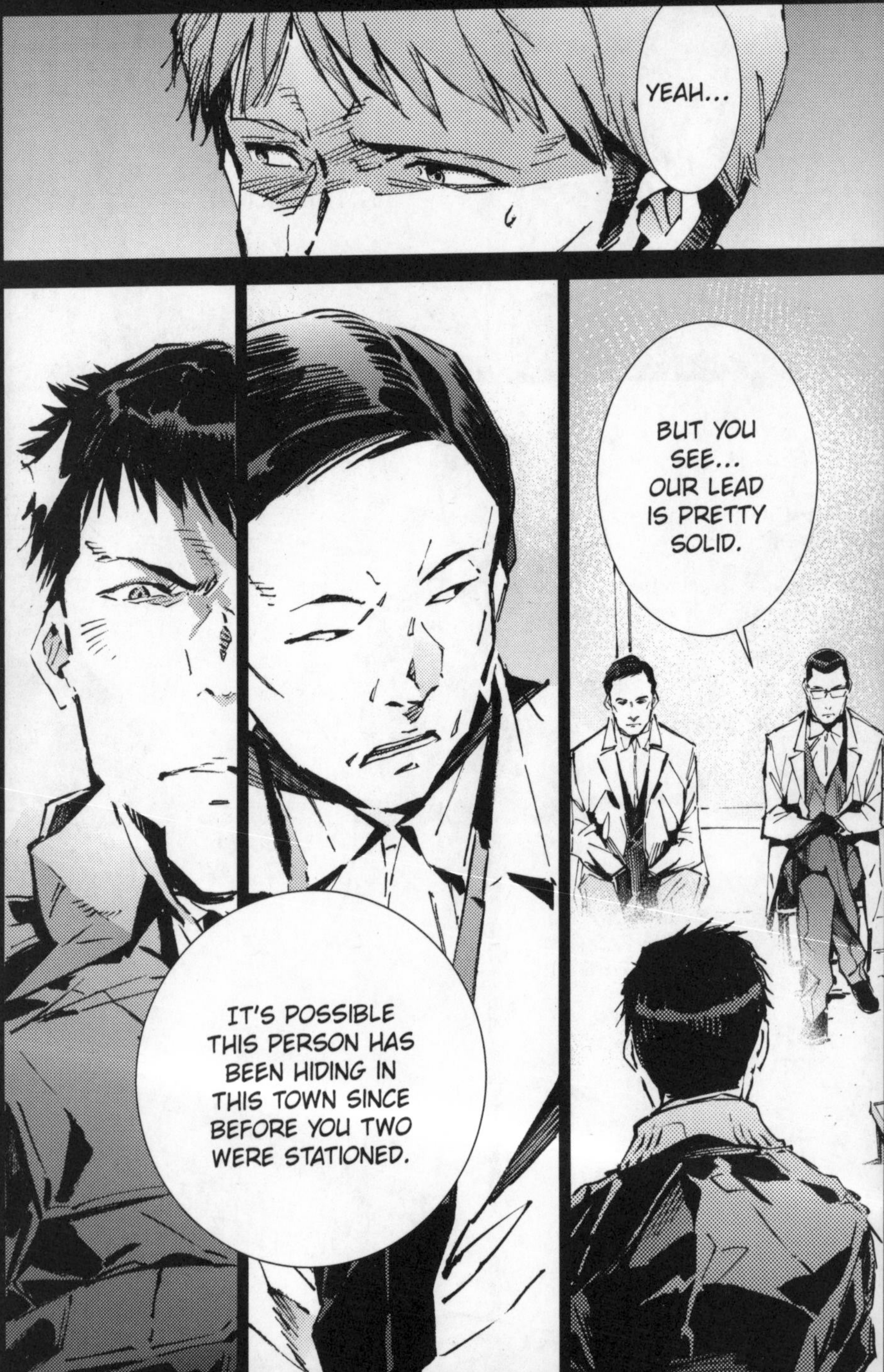
YEAH...
BUT YOU SEE... OUR LEAD IS PRETTY SOLID.
IT'S POSSIBLE THIS PERSON HAS BEEN HIDING IN THIS TOWN SINCE BEFORE YOU TWO WERE STATIONED.

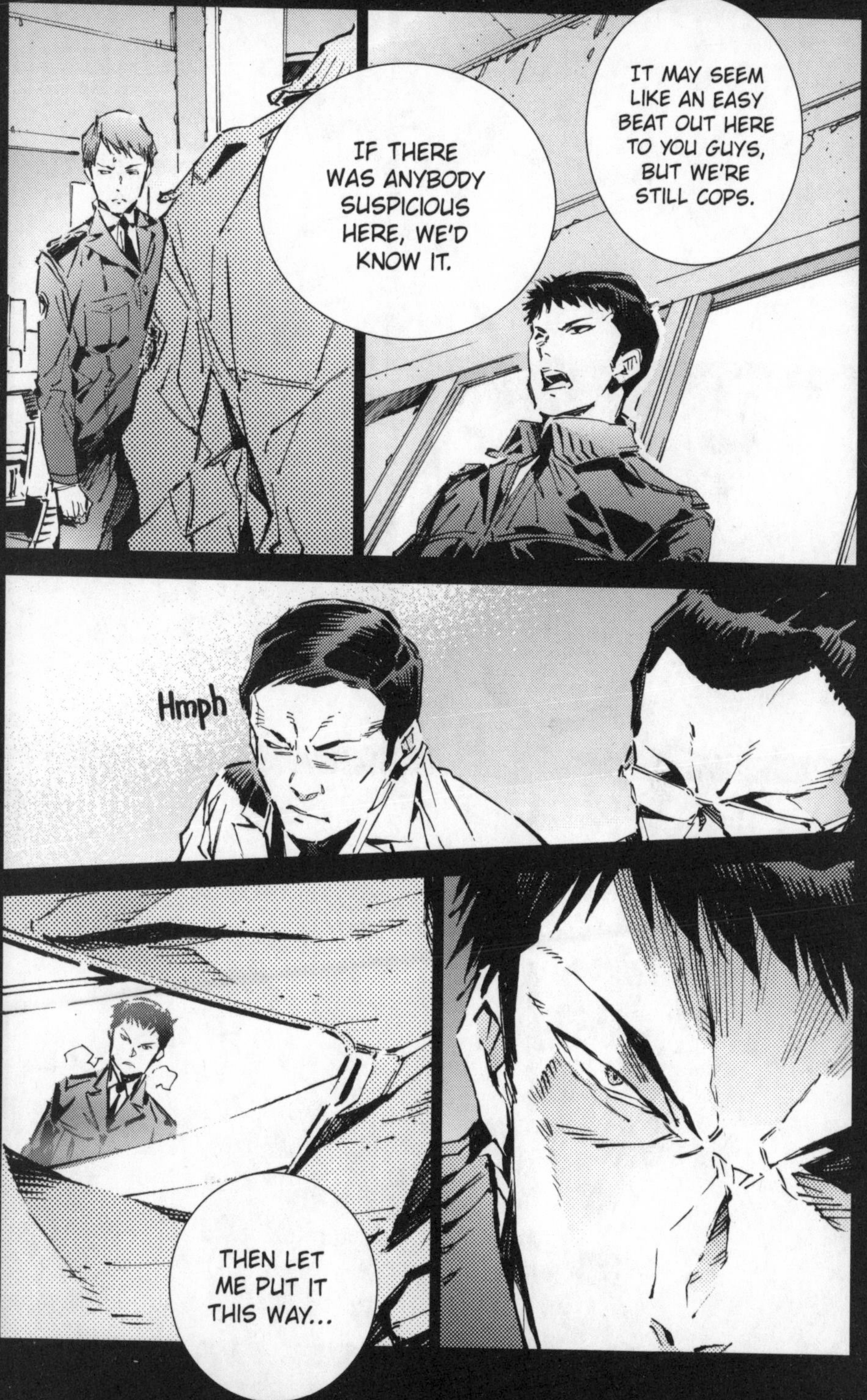
IT MAY SEEM LIKE AN EASY BEAT OUT HERE TO YOU GUYS, BUT WE'RE STILL COPS.
IF THERE WAS ANYBODY SUSPICIOUS HERE, WE'D KNOW IT.
Hmph
THEN LET ME PUT IT THIS WAY...

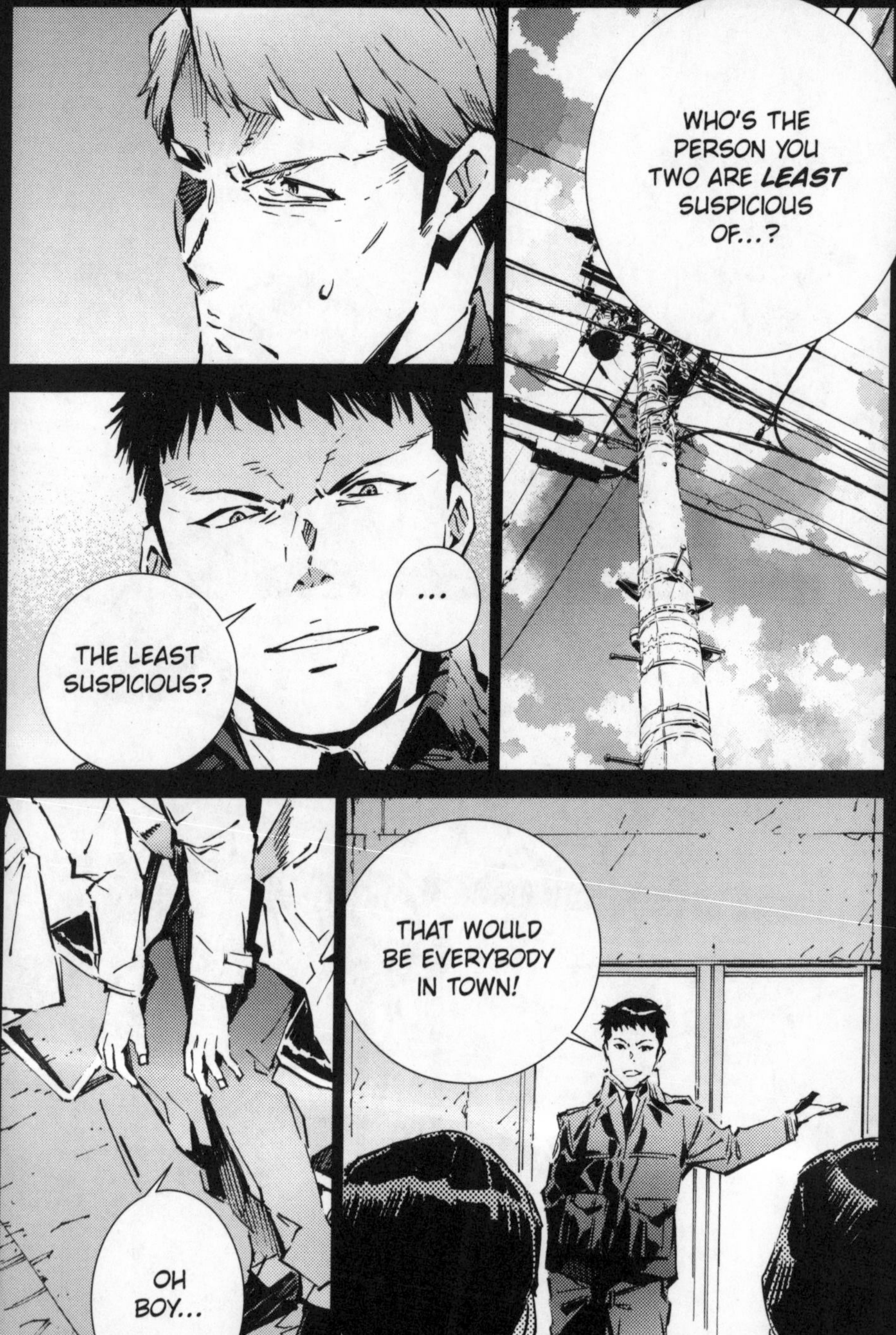
WHO'S THE PERSON YOU TWO ARE ***LEAST*** SUSPICIOUS OF...?
...
THE LEAST SUSPICIOUS?
THAT WOULD BE EVERYBODY IN TOWN!
OH BOY...

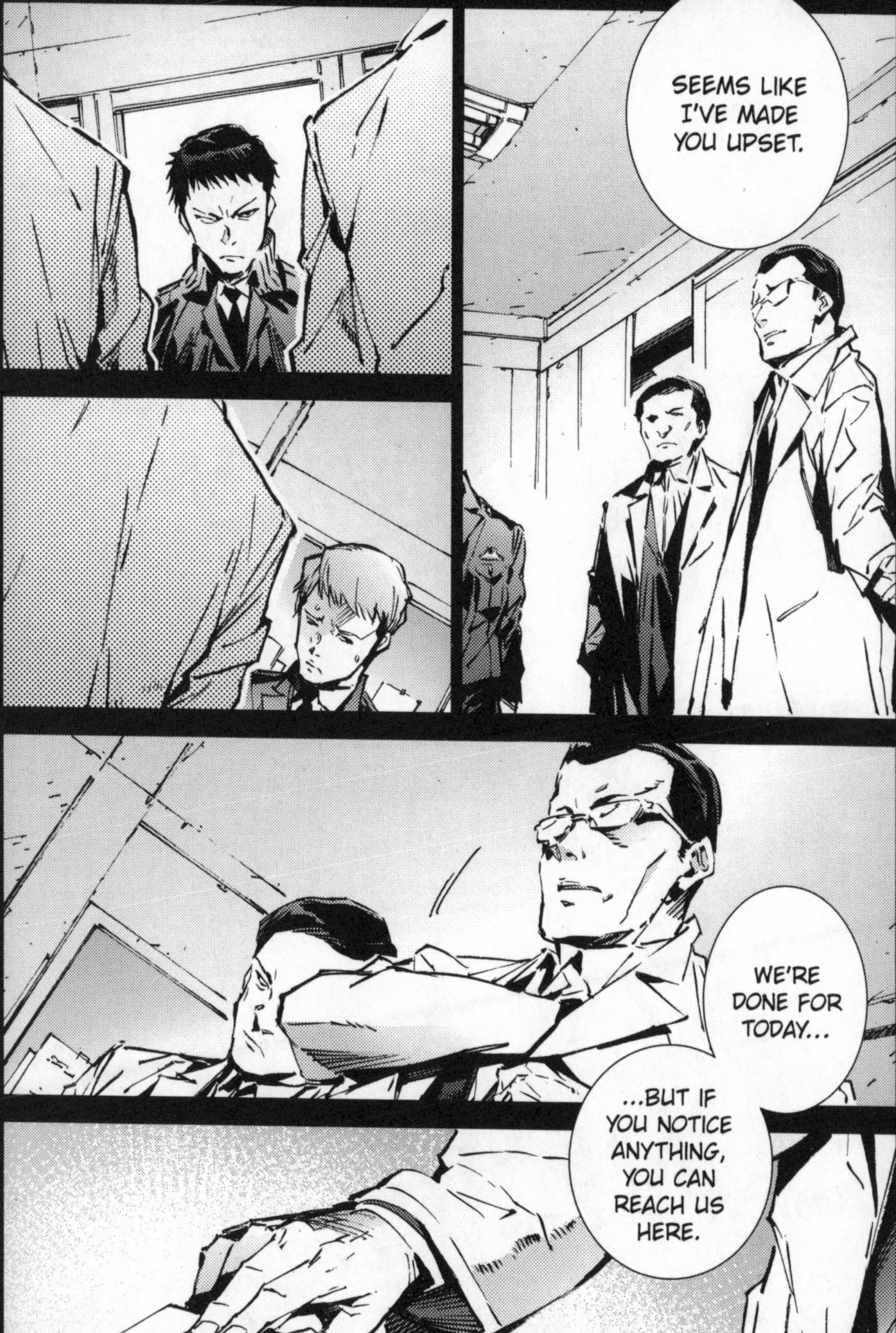
SEEMS LIKE I'VE MADE YOU UPSET.
WE'RE DONE FOR TODAY...
...BUT IF YOU NOTICE ANYTHING, YOU CAN REACH US HERE.

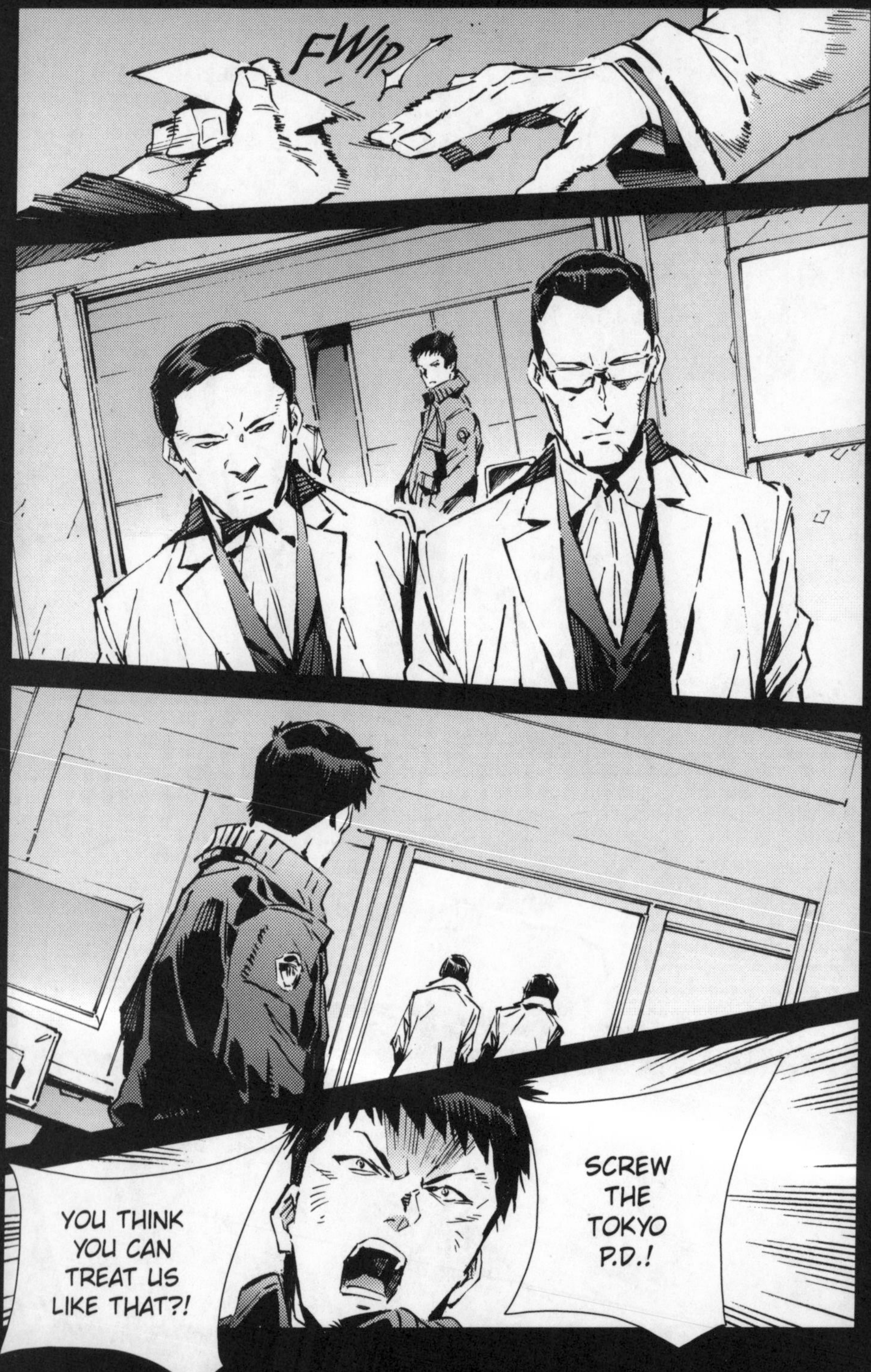
FWIP
SCREW THE TOKYO P.D.!
YOU THINK YOU CAN TREAT US LIKE THAT?!

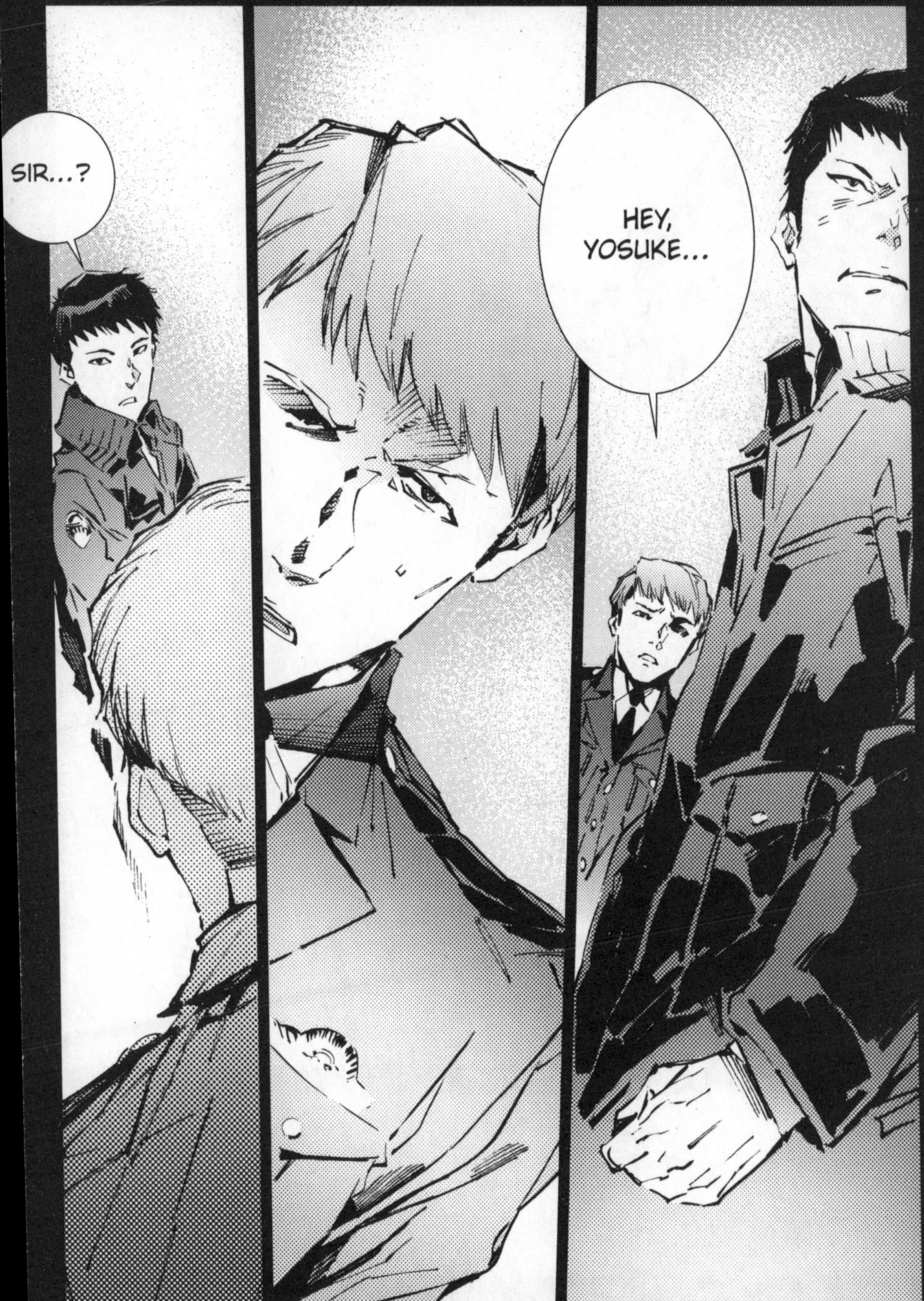
HEY, YOSUKE...
SIR...?

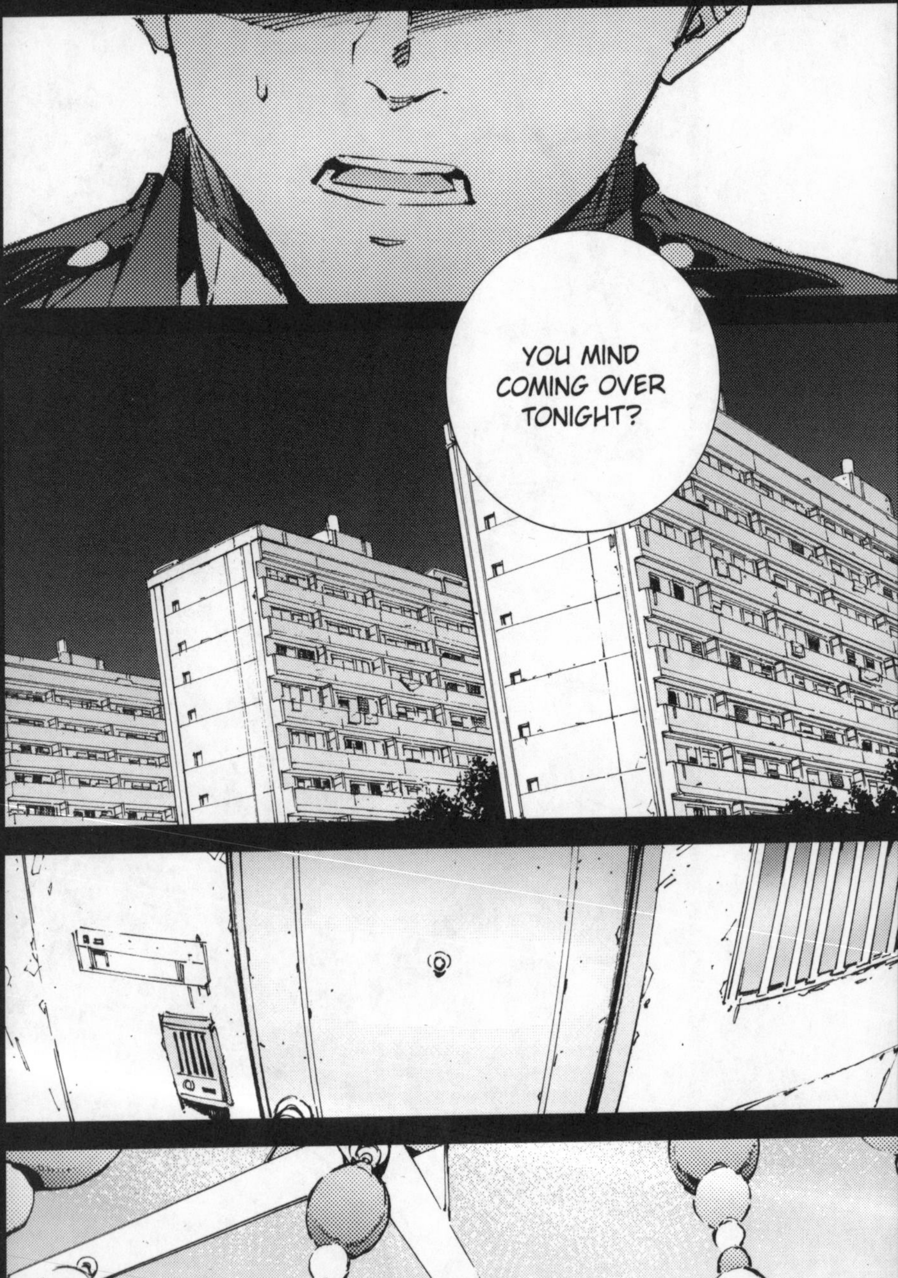
YOU MIND COMING OVER TONIGHT?

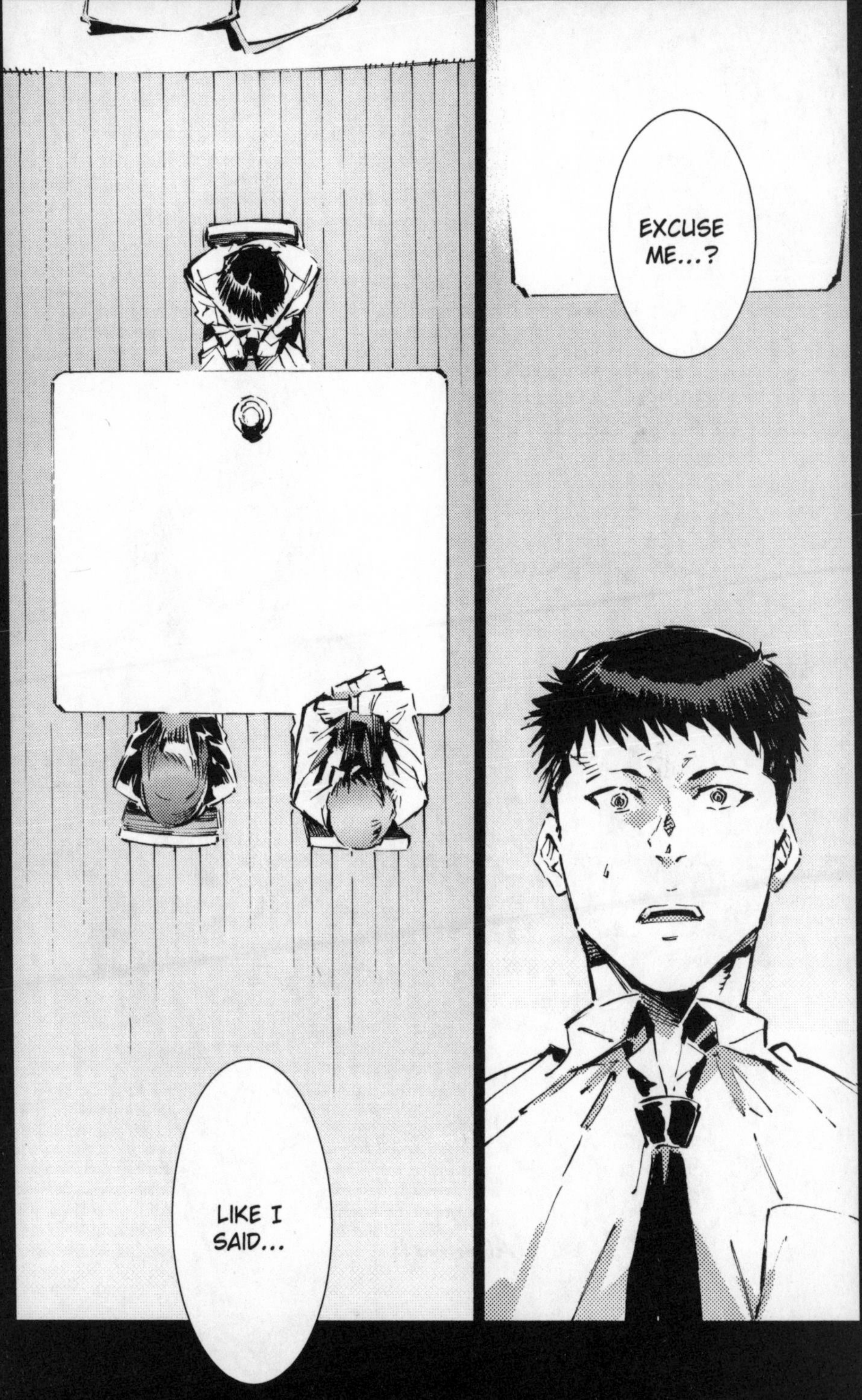
EXCUSE ME...?
LIKE I SAID...

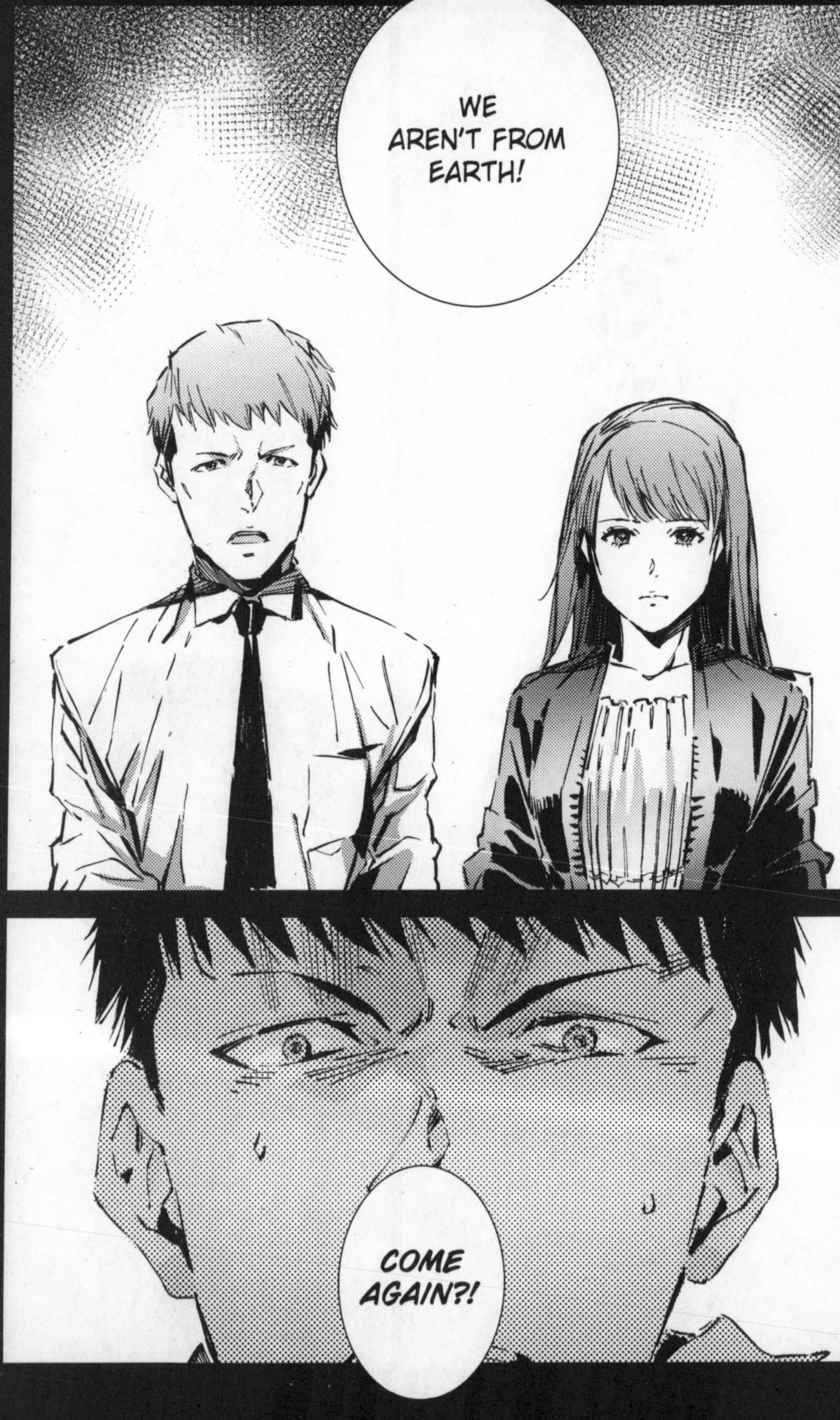
WE AREN'T FROM EARTH!
COME AGAIN?!

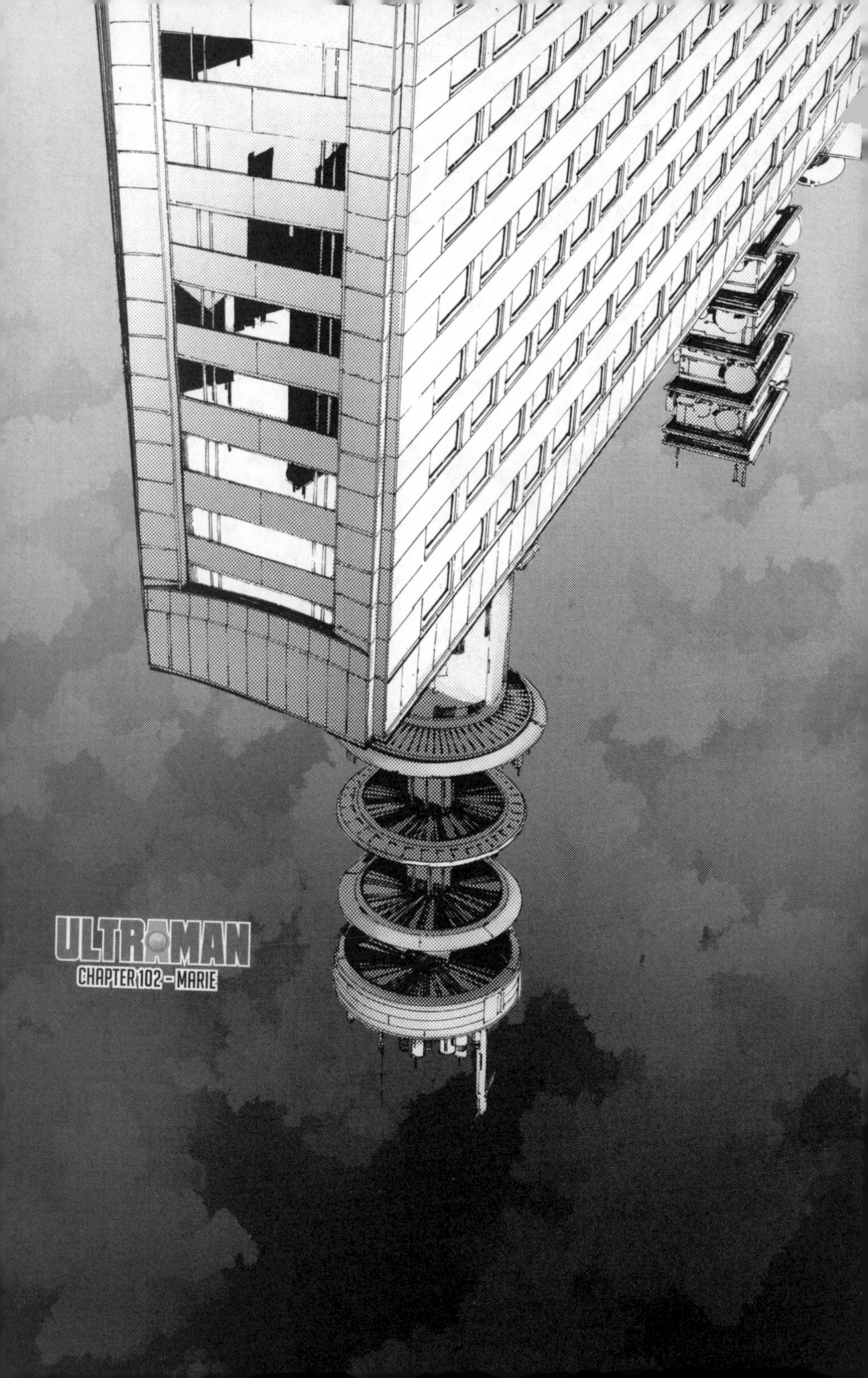
ULTRAMAN
CHAPTER 102 – MARIE

SPRING

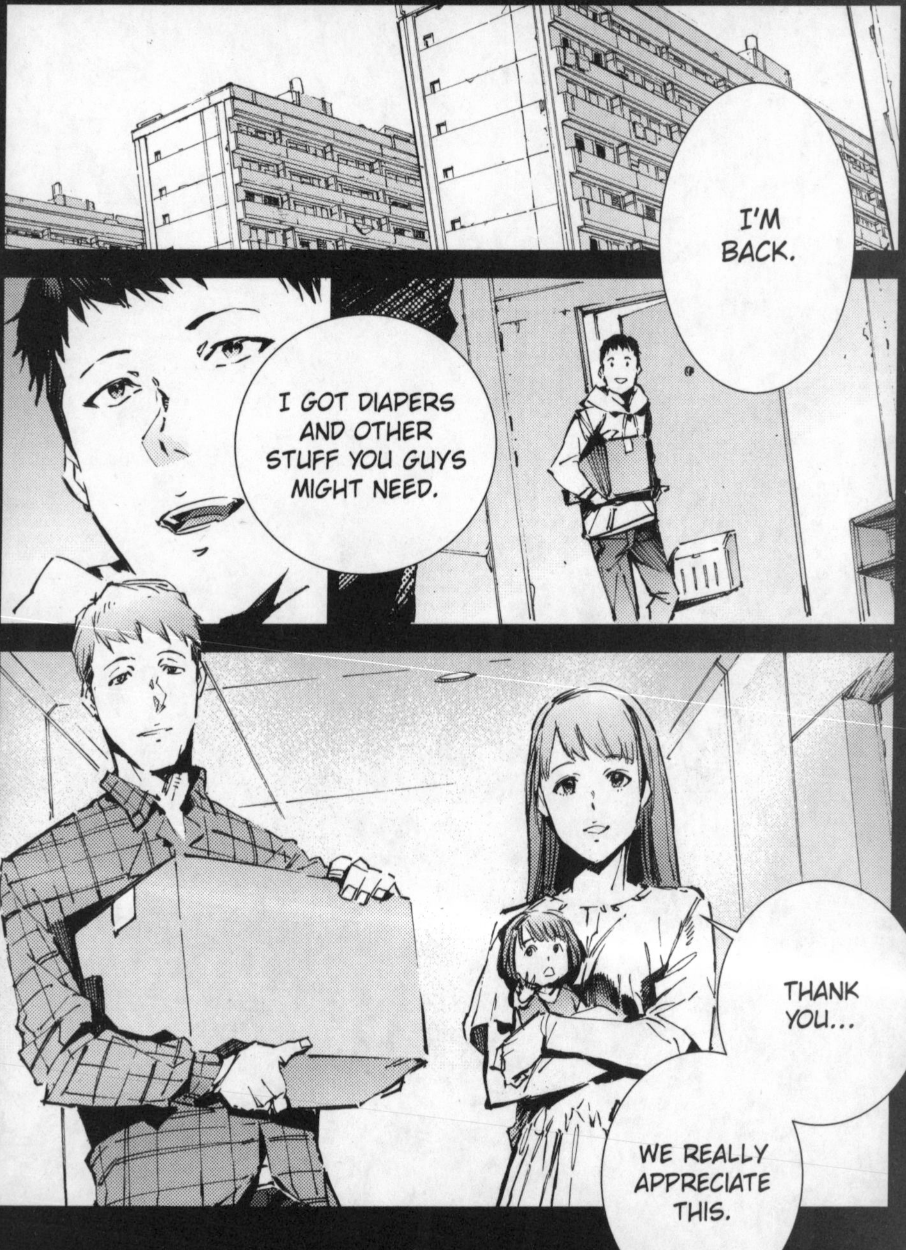
I'M BACK.
I GOT DIAPERS AND OTHER STUFF YOU GUYS MIGHT NEED.
THANK YOU...
WE REALLY APPRECIATE THIS.

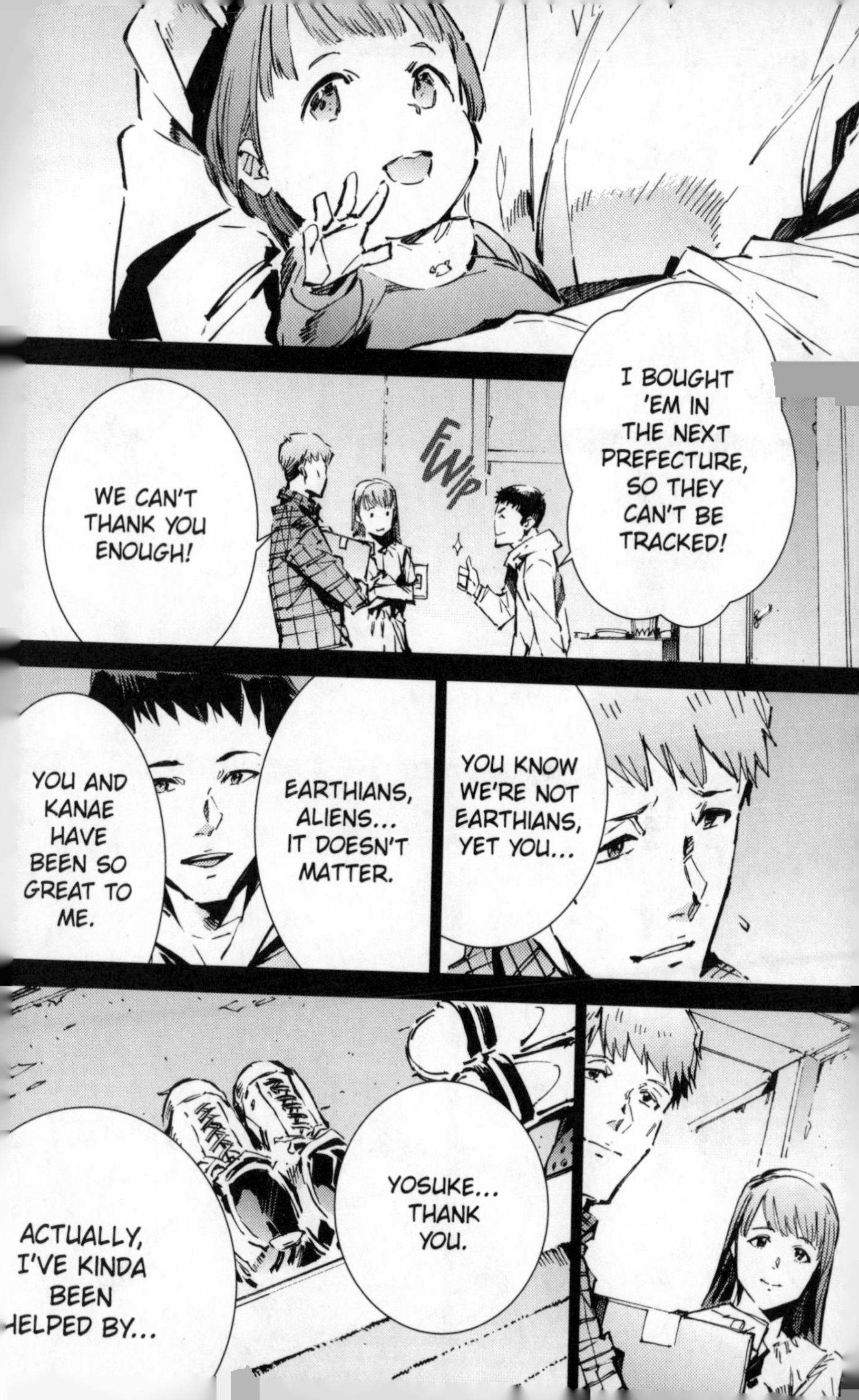
I BOUGHT 'EM IN THE NEXT PREFECTURE, SO THEY CAN'T BE TRACKED!
FWIP
WE CAN'T THANK YOU ENOUGH!
YOU KNOW WE'RE NOT EARTHIANS, YET YOU...
EARTHIANS, ALIENS... IT DOESN'T MATTER.
YOU AND KANAE HAVE BEEN SO GREAT TO ME.
YOSUKE... THANK YOU.
ACTUALLY, I'VE KINDA BEEN HELPED BY...

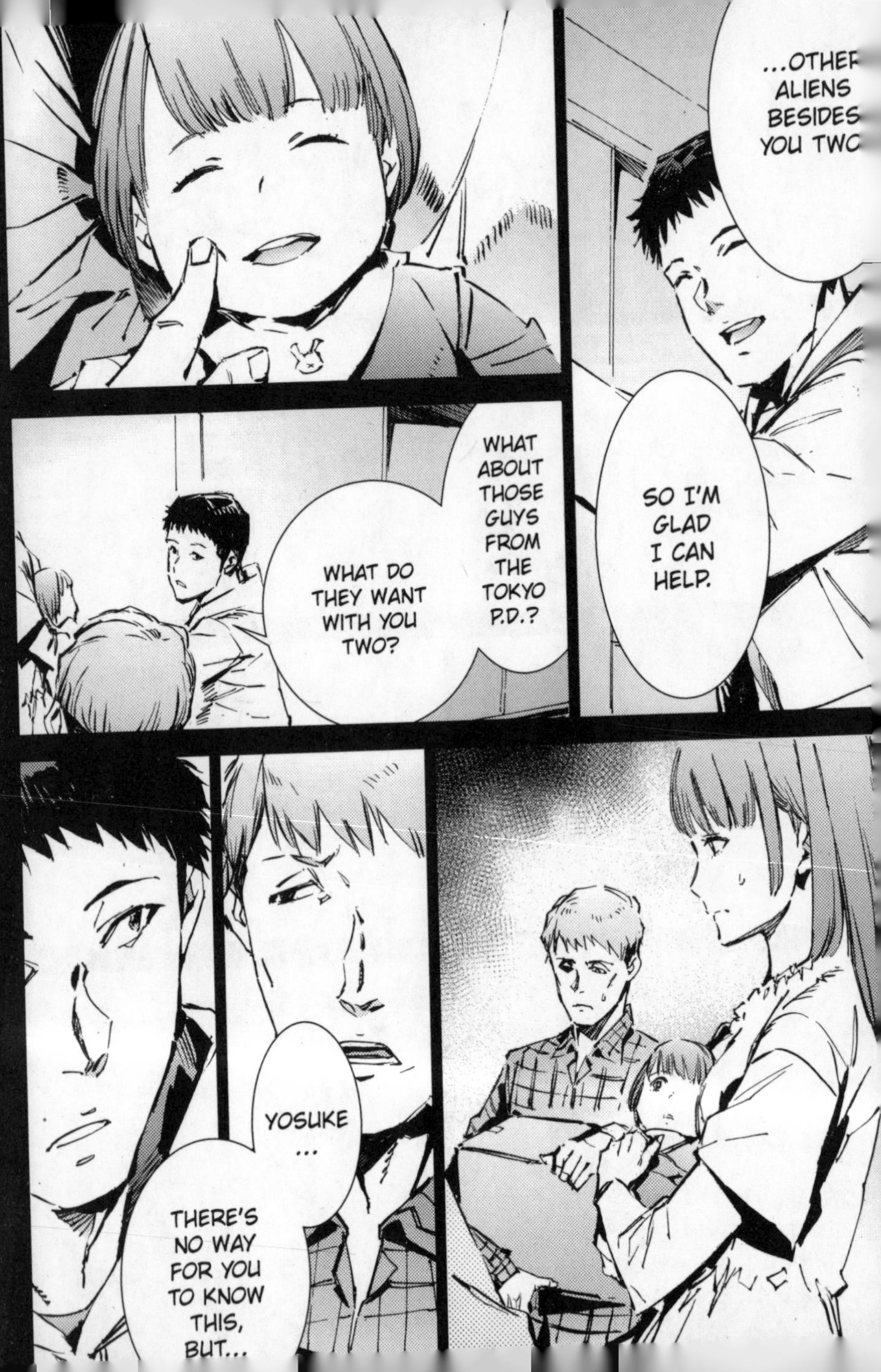
...OTHER ALIENS BESIDES YOU TWO
SO I'M GLAD I CAN HELP.
WHAT ABOUT THOSE GUYS FROM THE TOKYO P.D.?
WHAT DO THEY WANT WITH YOU TWO?
YOSUKE ...
THERE'S NO WAY FOR YOU TO KNOW THIS, BUT...

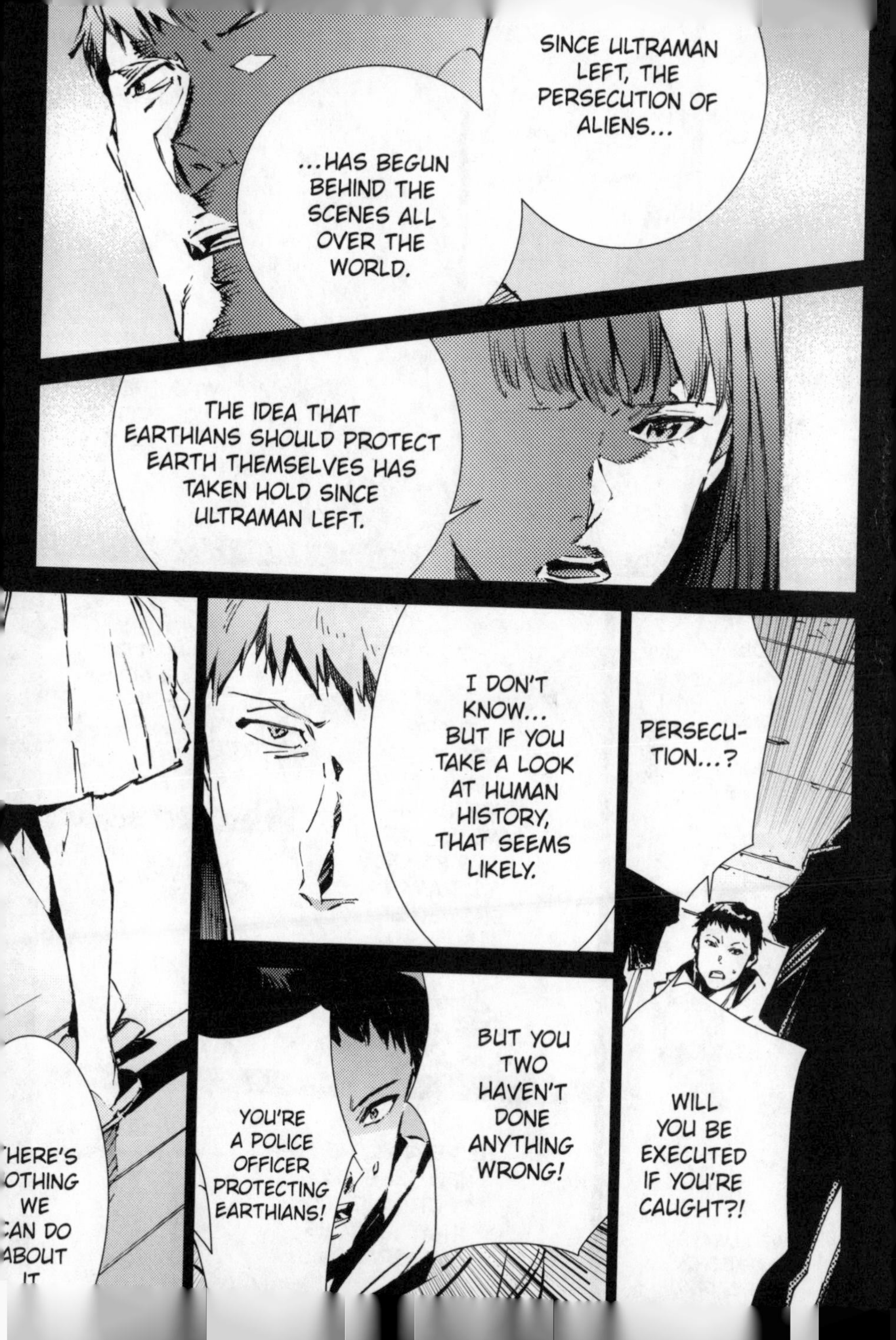
SINCE ULTRAMAN LEFT, THE PERSECUTION OF ALIENS...
...HAS BEGUN BEHIND THE SCENES ALL OVER THE WORLD.
THE IDEA THAT EARTHIANS SHOULD PROTECT EARTH THEMSELVES HAS TAKEN HOLD SINCE ULTRAMAN LEFT.
PERSECU-TION...?
WILL YOU BE EXECUTED IF YOU'RE CAUGHT?!
I DON'T KNOW... BUT IF YOU TAKE A LOOK AT HUMAN HISTORY, THAT SEEMS LIKELY.
BUT YOU TWO HAVEN'T DONE ANYTHING WRONG!
YOU'RE A POLICE OFFICER PROTECTING EARTHIANS!
HERE'S OTHING WE CAN DO ABOUT IT

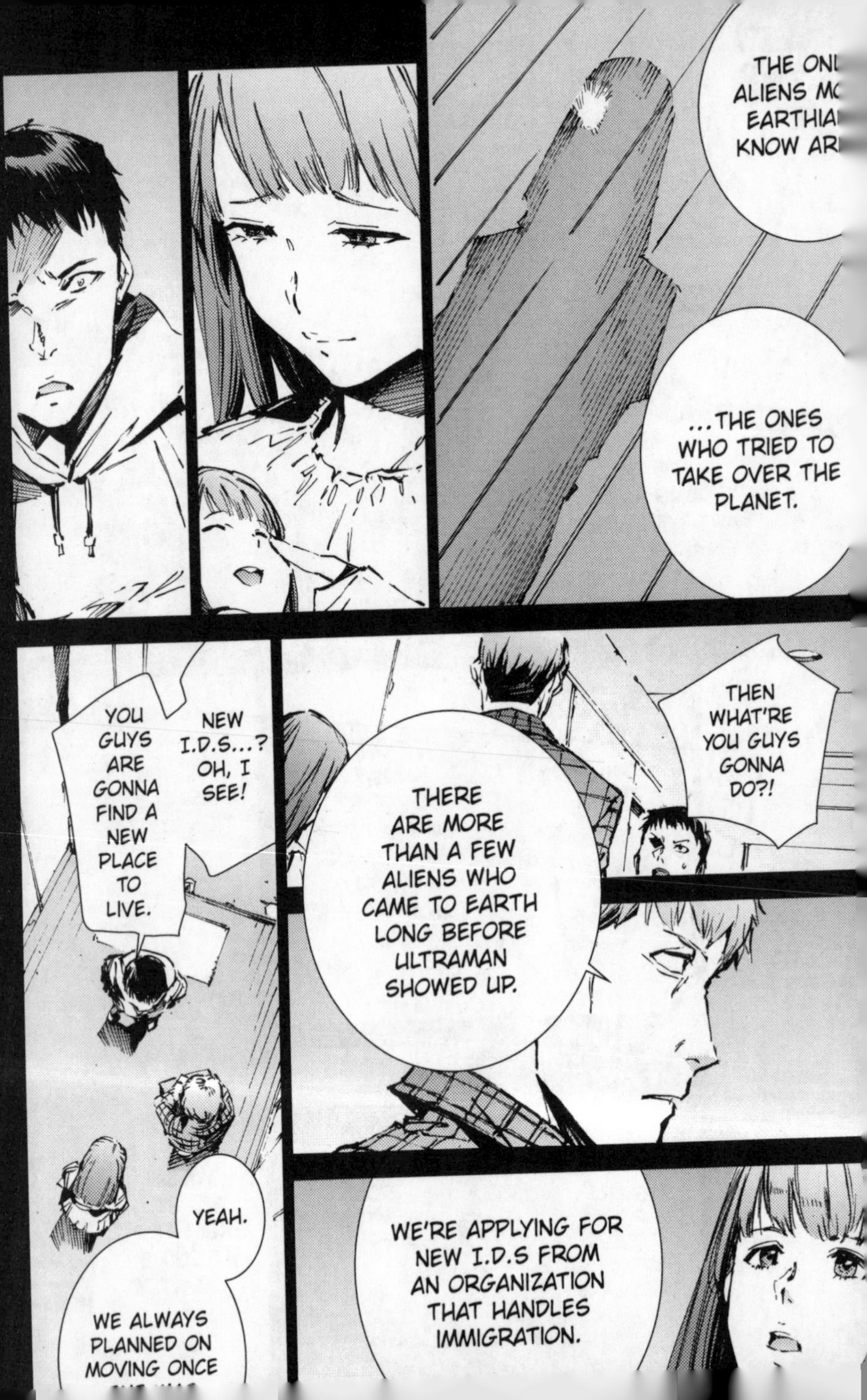
THE ONL ALIENS MO EARTHIA KNOW AR
...THE ONES WHO TRIED TO TAKE OVER THE PLANET.
THEN WHAT'RE YOU GUYS GONNA DO?!
THERE ARE MORE THAN A FEW ALIENS WHO CAME TO EARTH LONG BEFORE ULTRAMAN SHOWED UP.
WE'RE APPLYING FOR NEW I.D.S FROM AN ORGANIZATION THAT HANDLES IMMIGRATION.
NEW I.D.S...? OH, I SEE!
YOU GUYS ARE GONNA FIND A NEW PLACE TO LIVE.
YEAH.
WE ALWAYS PLANNED ON MOVING ONCE

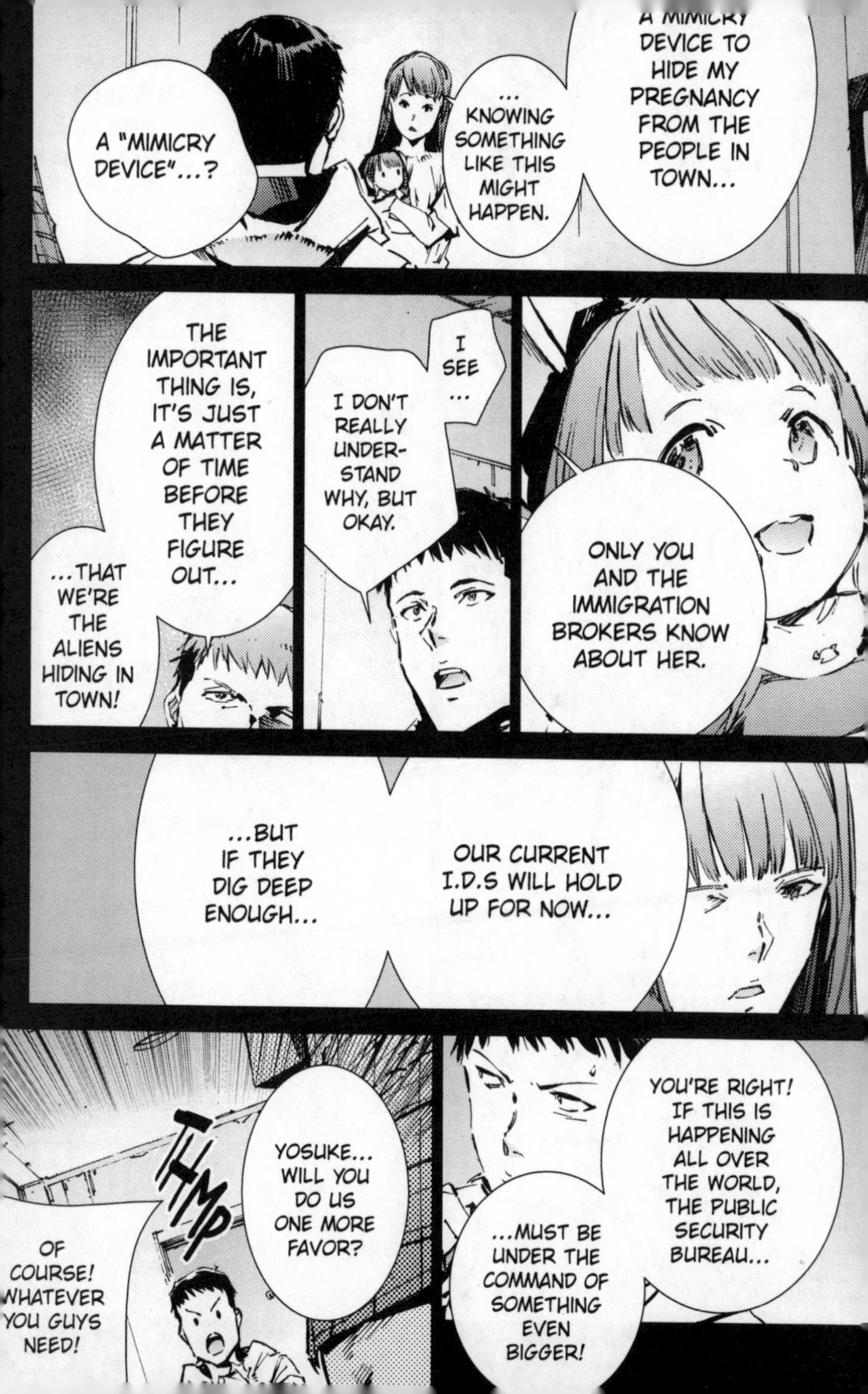
A MIMICRY DEVICE TO HIDE MY PREGNANCY FROM THE PEOPLE IN TOWN...
... KNOWING SOMETHING LIKE THIS MIGHT HAPPEN.
A "MIMICRY DEVICE"...?
ONLY YOU AND THE IMMIGRATION BROKERS KNOW ABOUT HER.
I SEE...
I DON'T REALLY UNDER-STAND WHY, BUT OKAY.
THE IMPORTANT THING IS, IT'S JUST A MATTER OF TIME BEFORE THEY FIGURE OUT...
...THAT WE'RE THE ALIENS HIDING IN TOWN!
OUR CURRENT I.D.S WILL HOLD UP FOR NOW...
...BUT IF THEY DIG DEEP ENOUGH...
YOU'RE RIGHT! IF THIS IS HAPPENING ALL OVER THE WORLD, THE PUBLIC SECURITY BUREAU...
...MUST BE UNDER THE COMMAND OF SOMETHING EVEN BIGGER!
YOSUKE... WILL YOU DO US ONE MORE FAVOR?
THMP
OF COURSE! WHATEVER YOU GUYS NEED!

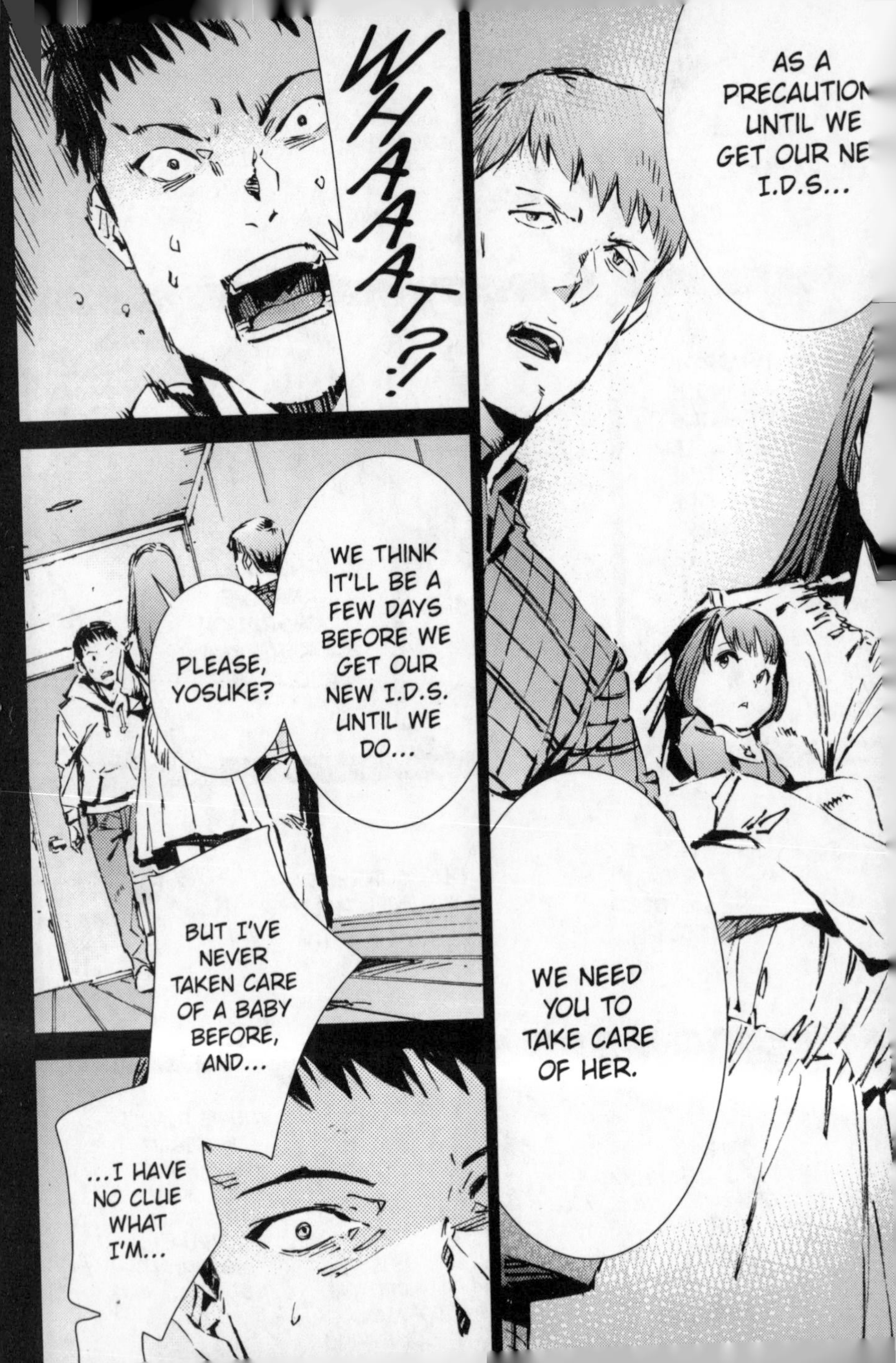
AS A PRECAUTION UNTIL WE GET OUR NE I.D.S...
WE NEED YOU TO TAKE CARE OF HER.
WHAAAT?!
WE THINK IT'LL BE A FEW DAYS BEFORE WE GET OUR NEW I.D.S. UNTIL WE DO...
PLEASE, YOSUKE?
BUT I'VE NEVER TAKEN CARE OF A BABY BEFORE, AND...
...I HAVE NO CLUE WHAT I'M...

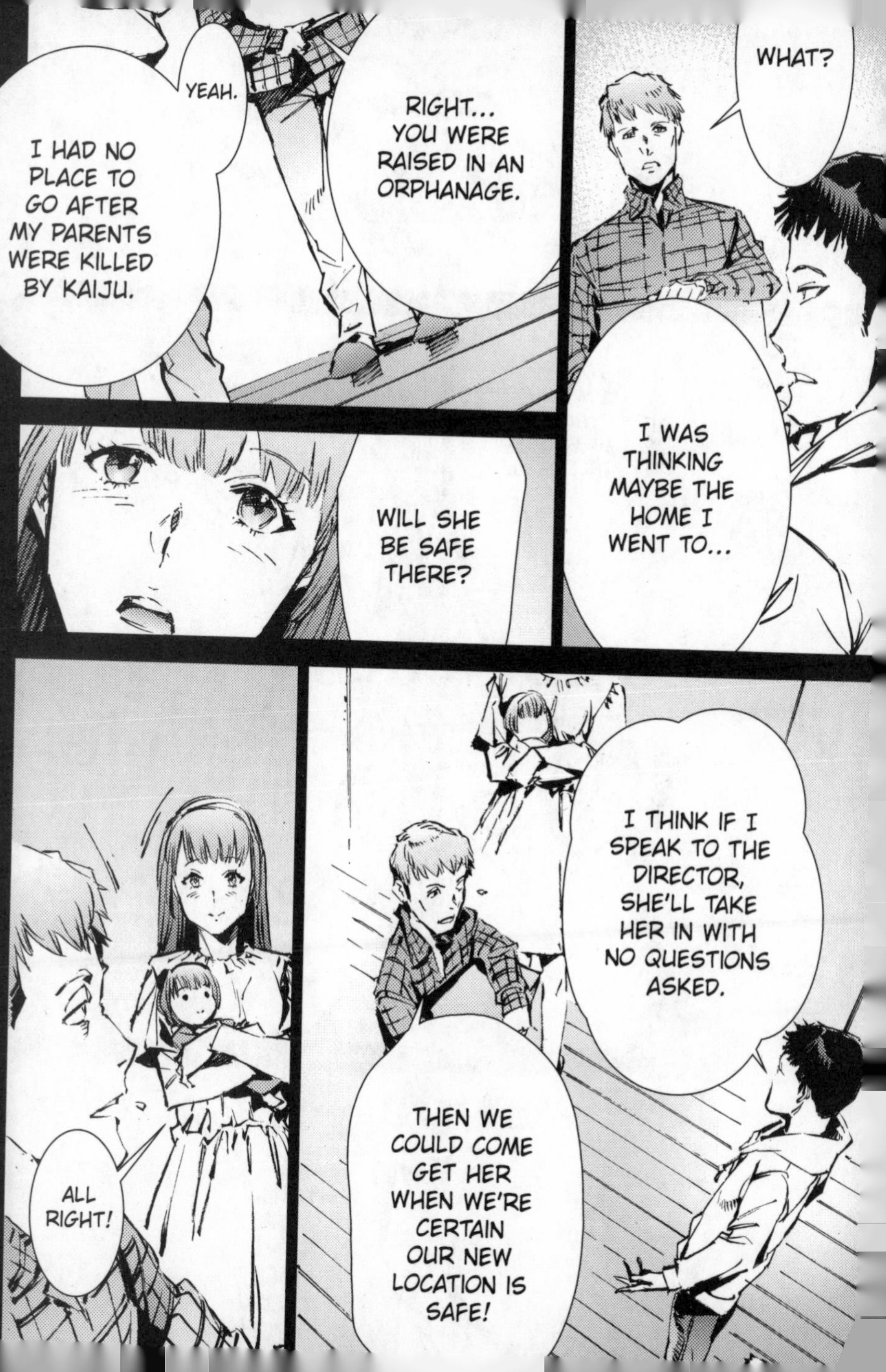
WHAT?
I WAS THINKING MAYBE THE HOME I WENT TO...
RIGHT... YOU WERE RAISED IN AN ORPHANAGE.
YEAH.
I HAD NO PLACE TO GO AFTER MY PARENTS WERE KILLED BY KAIJU.
WILL SHE BE SAFE THERE?
I THINK IF I SPEAK TO THE DIRECTOR, SHE'LL TAKE HER IN WITH NO QUESTIONS ASKED.
THEN WE COULD COME GET HER WHEN WE'RE CERTAIN OUR NEW LOCATION IS SAFE!
ALL RIGHT!

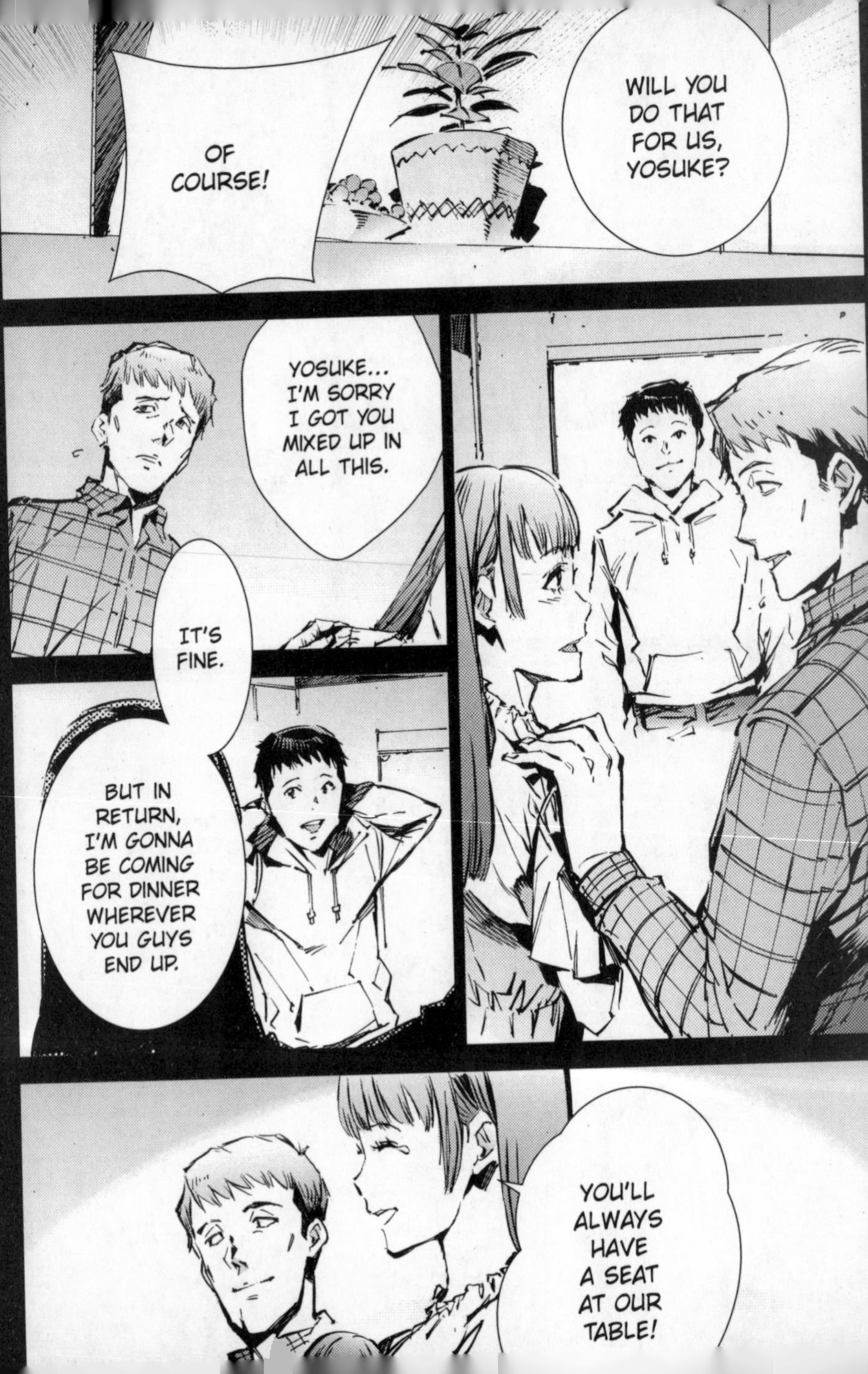
WILL YOU DO THAT FOR US, YOSUKE?
OF COURSE!
YOSUKE... I'M SORRY I GOT YOU MIXED UP IN ALL THIS.
IT'S FINE.
BUT IN RETURN, I'M GONNA BE COMING FOR DINNER WHEREVER YOU GUYS END UP.
YOU'LL ALWAYS HAVE A SEAT AT OUR TABLE!

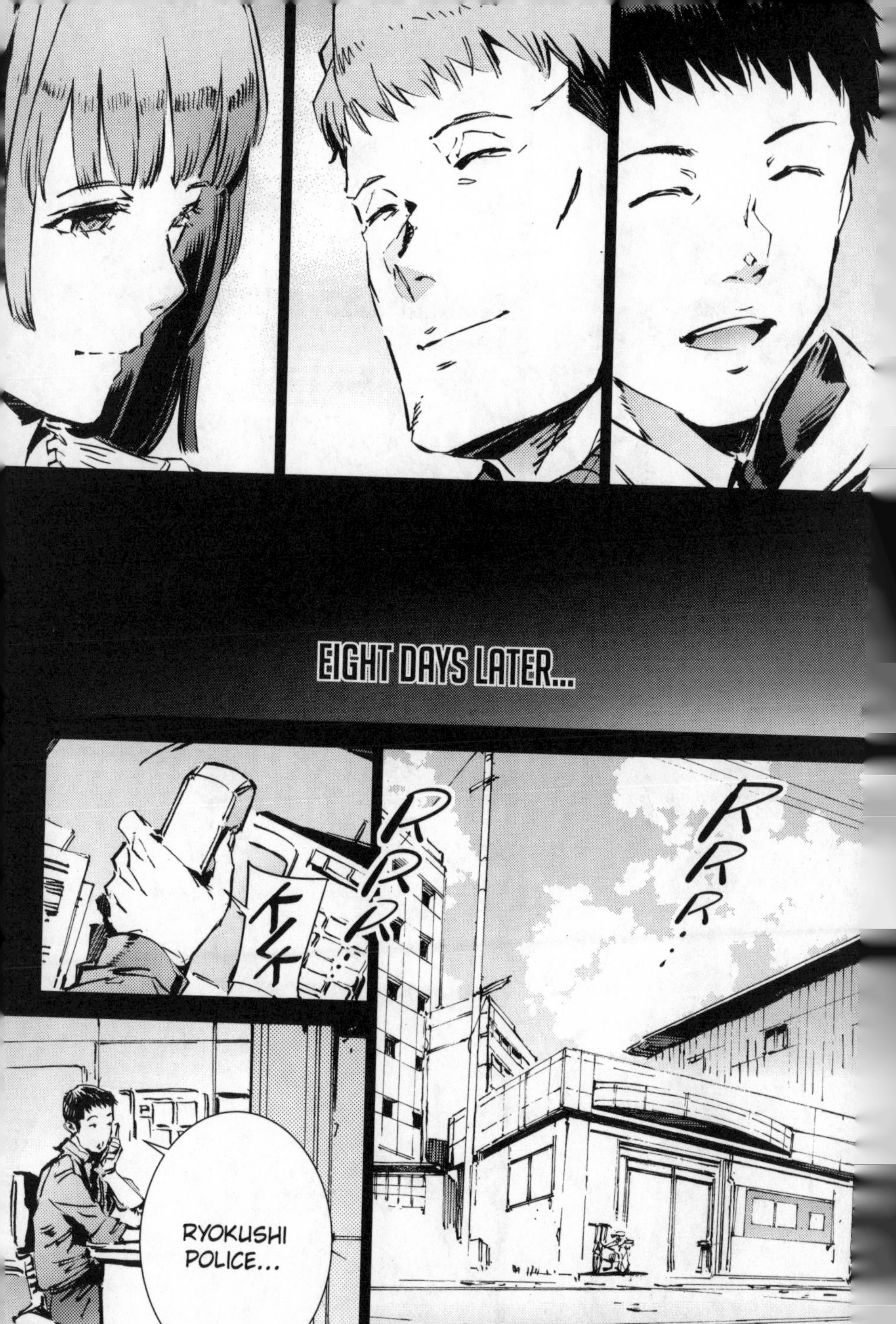
EIGHT DAYS LATER...
RRR...
RRR...
KA
RYOKUSHI POLICE...

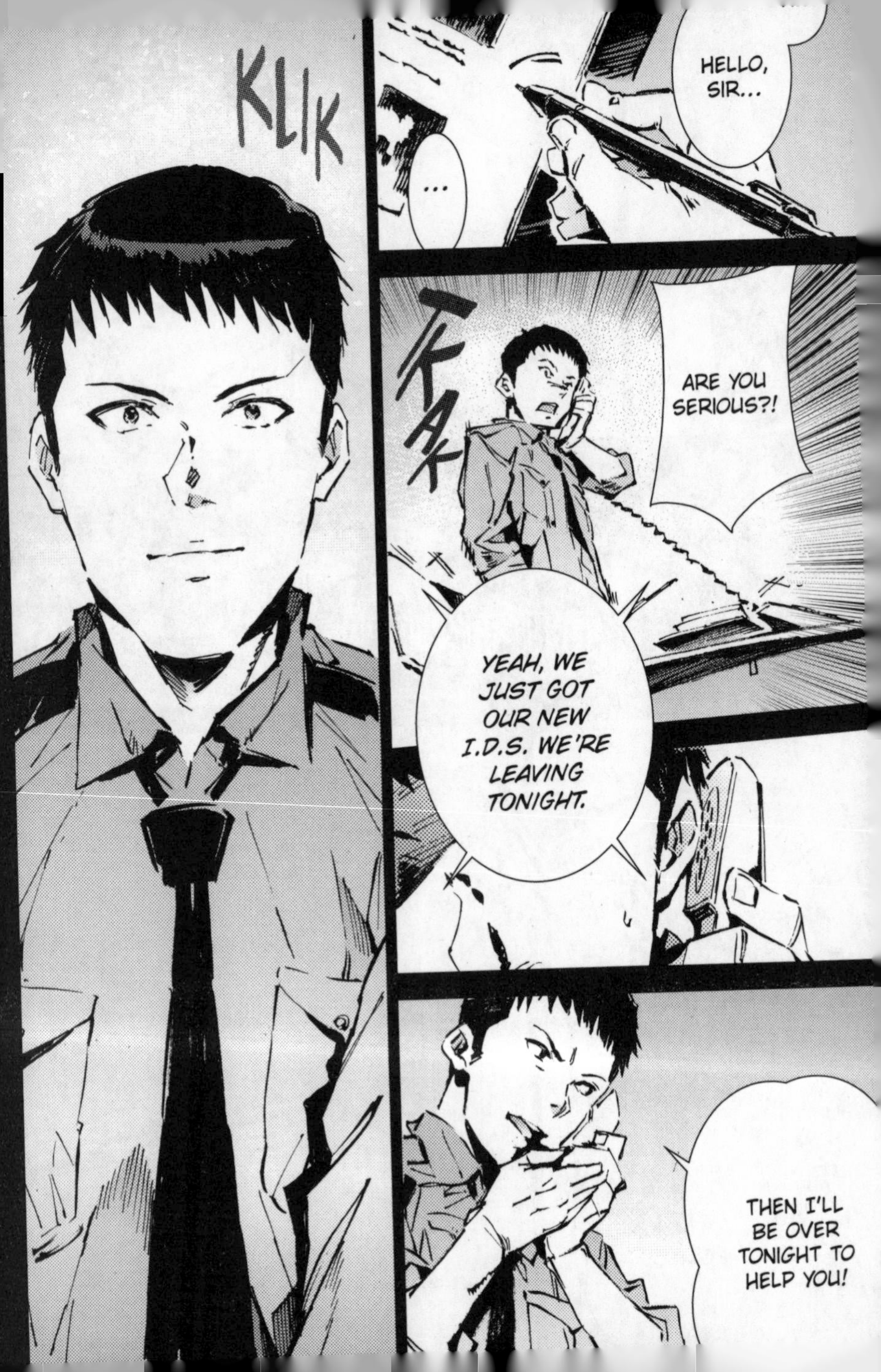
HELLO, SIR...
...
ARE YOU SERIOUS?!
TAK
YEAH, WE JUST GOT OUR NEW I.D.S. WE'RE LEAVING TONIGHT.
THEN I'LL BE OVER TONIGHT TO HELP YOU!
KLIK

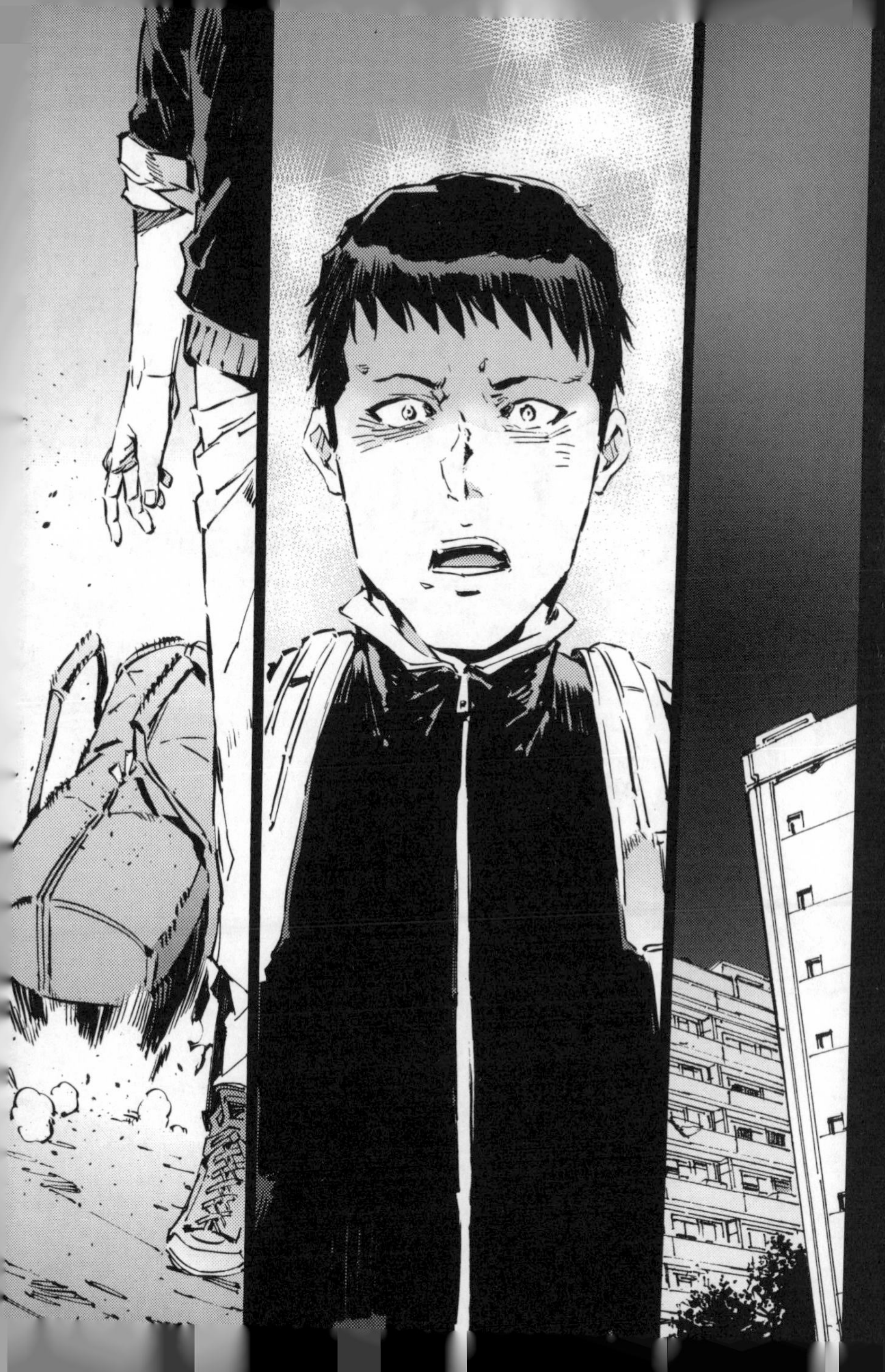

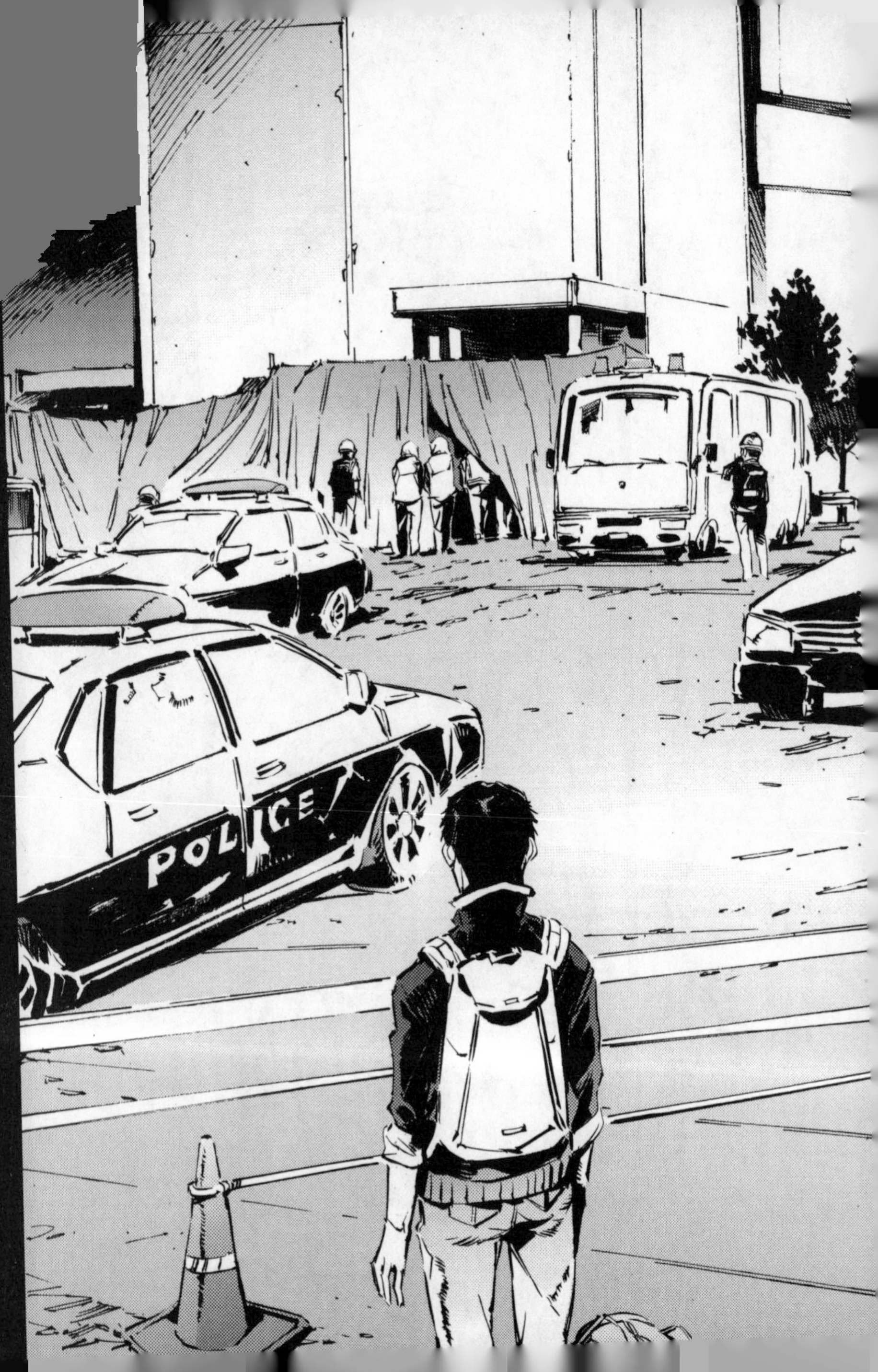
POLICE

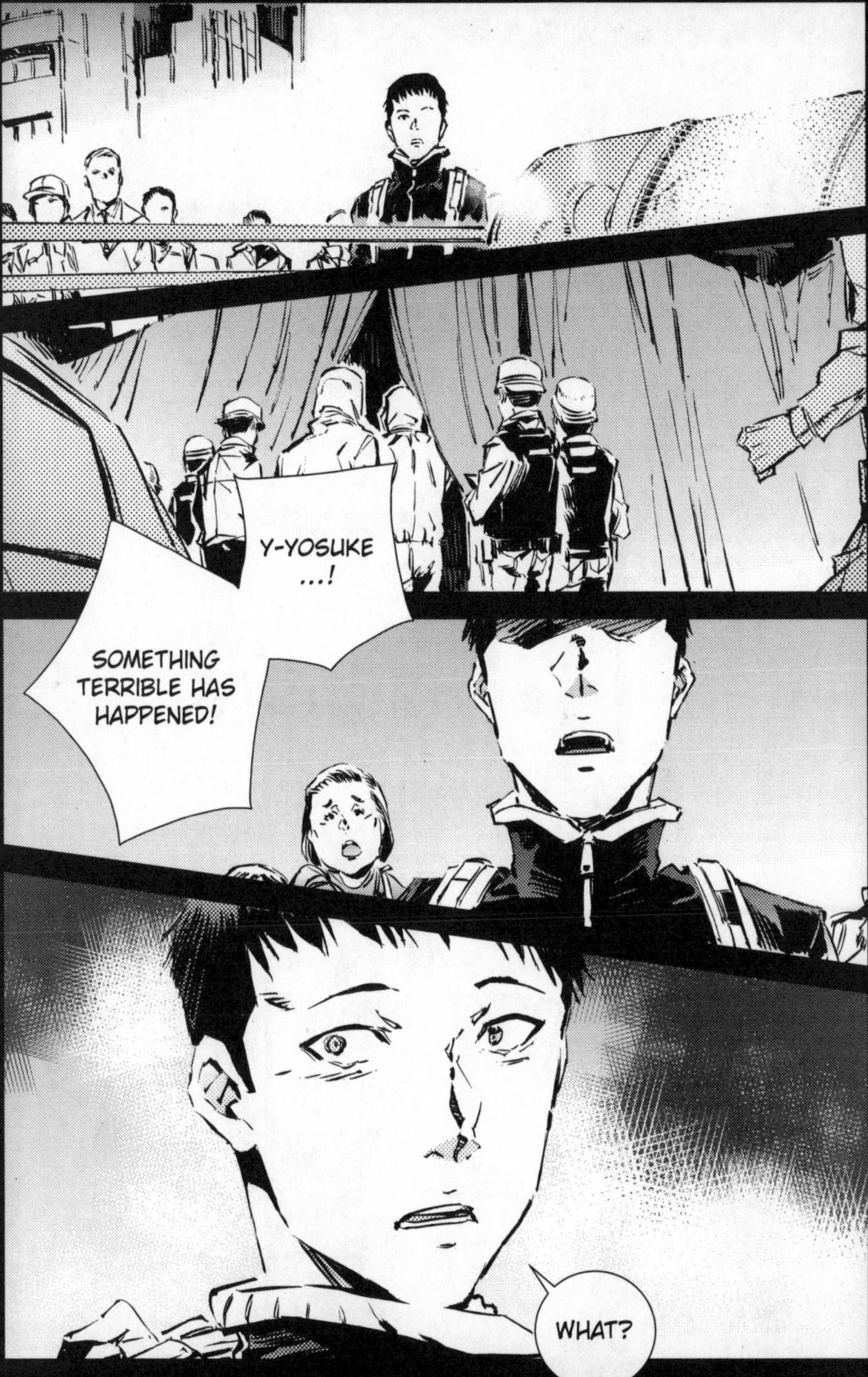
Y-YOSUKE ...!
SOMETHING TERRIBLE HAS HAPPENED!
WHAT?

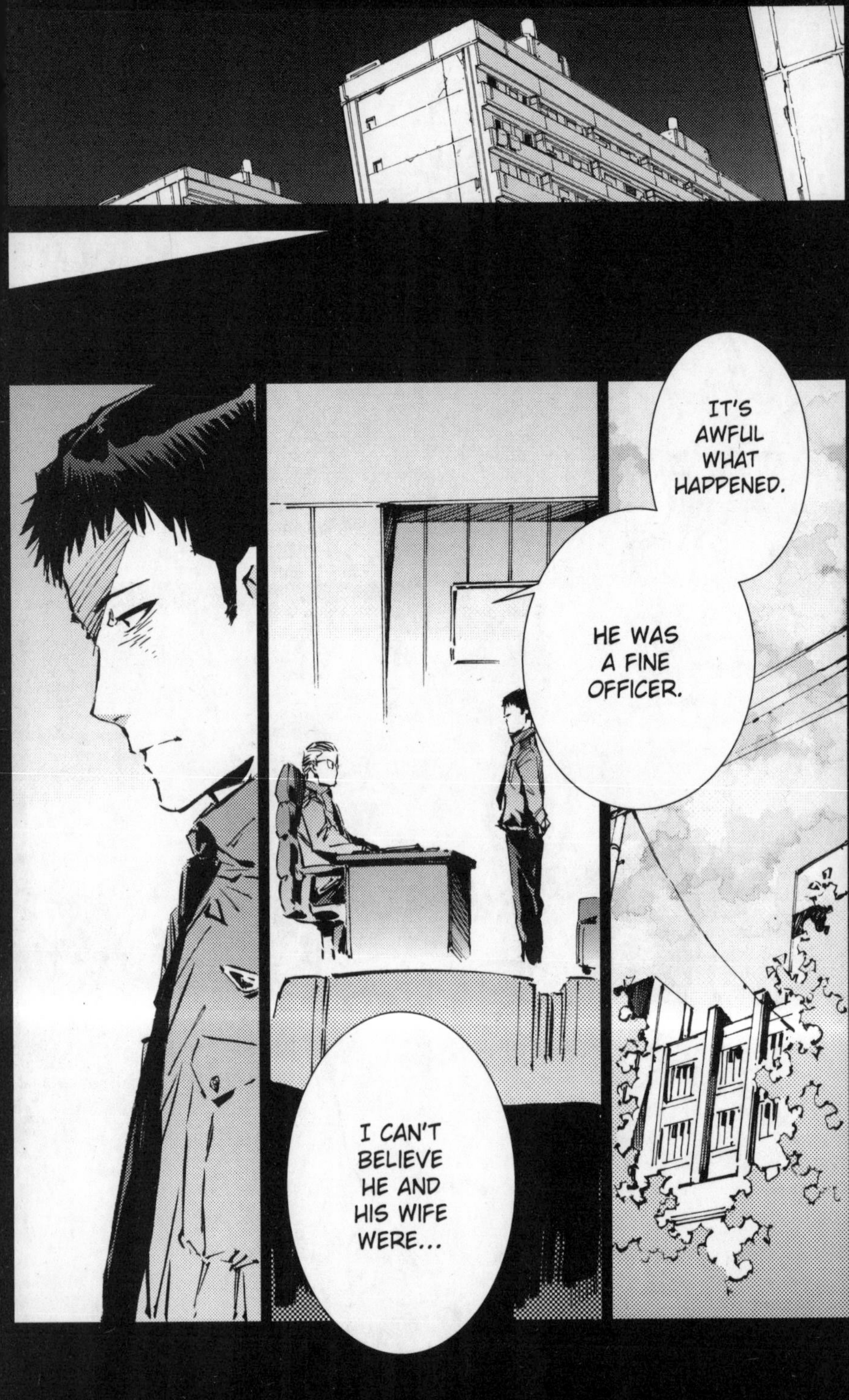
IT'S AWFUL WHAT HAPPENED.
HE WAS A FINE OFFICER.
I CAN'T BELIEVE HE AND HIS WIFE WERE...

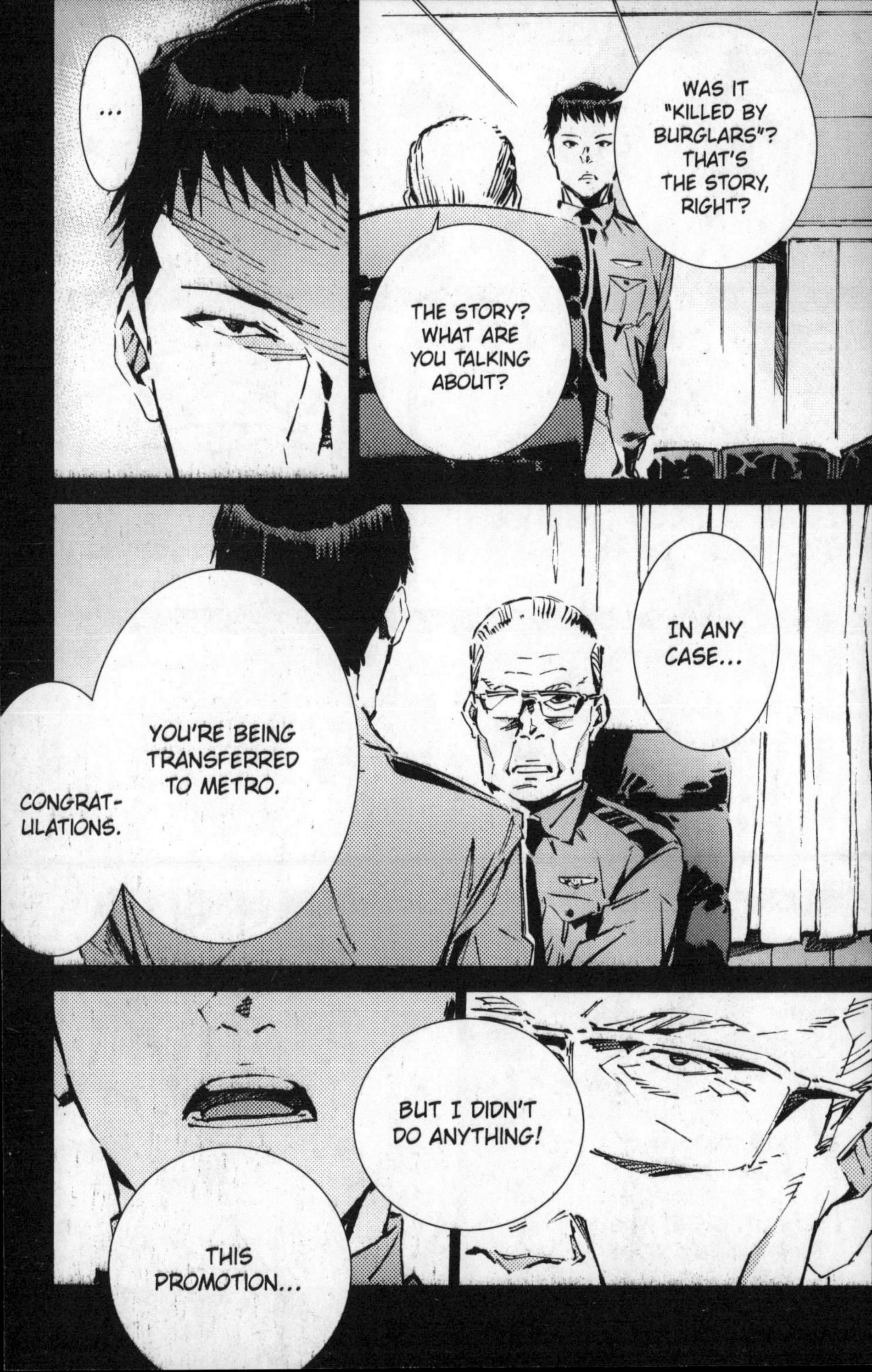
WAS IT "KILLED BY BURGLARS"? THAT'S THE STORY, RIGHT?
THE STORY? WHAT ARE YOU TALKING ABOUT?
...
IN ANY CASE...
YOU'RE BEING TRANSFERRED TO METRO.
CONGRAT-ULATIONS.
BUT I DIDN'T DO ANYTHING!
THIS PROMOTION...

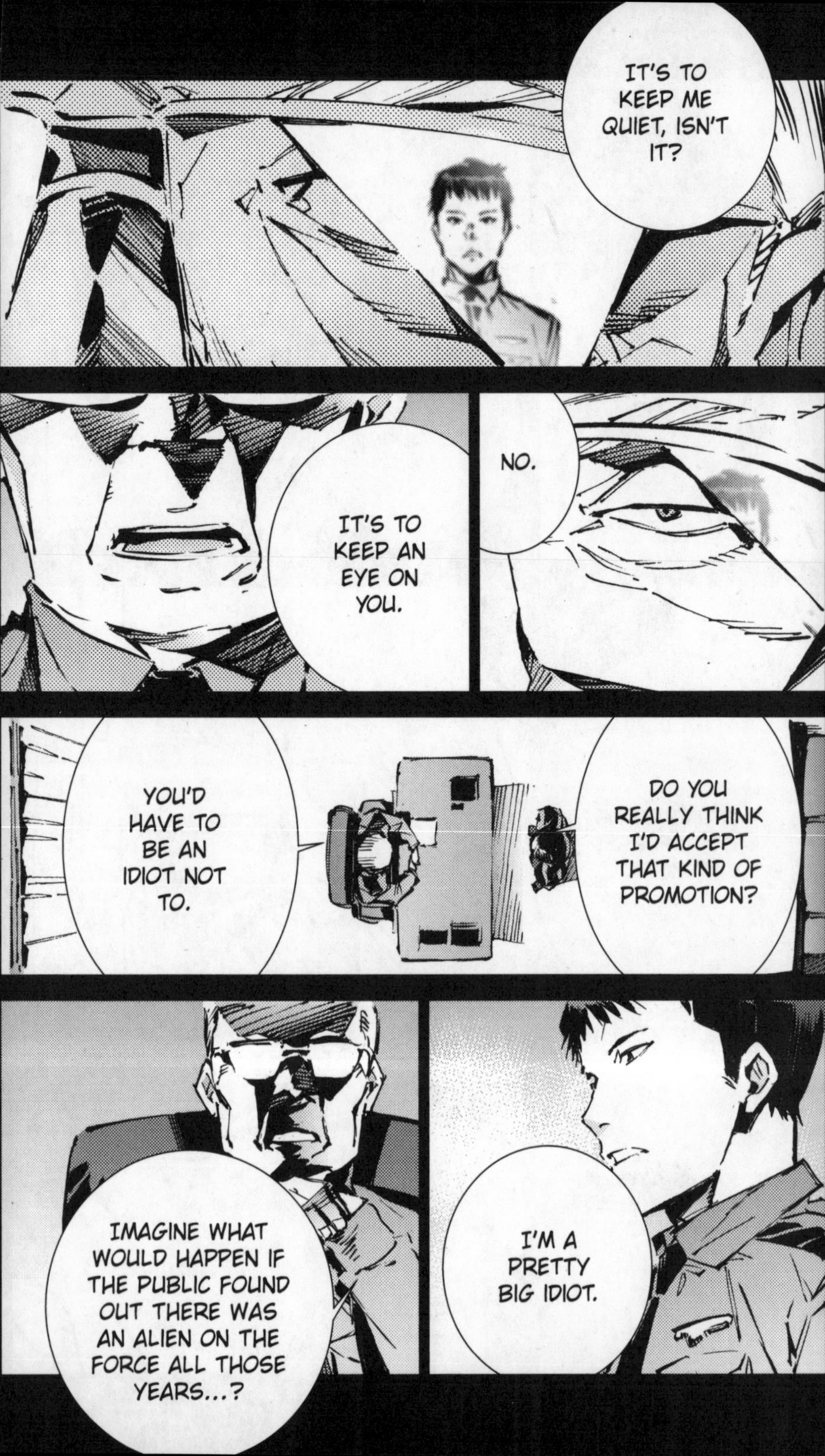
IT'S TO KEEP ME QUIET, ISN'T IT?
NO.
IT'S TO KEEP AN EYE ON YOU.
DO YOU REALLY THINK I'D ACCEPT THAT KIND OF PROMOTION?
YOU'D HAVE TO BE AN IDIOT NOT TO.
I'M A PRETTY BIG IDIOT.
IMAGINE WHAT WOULD HAPPEN IF THE PUBLIC FOUND OUT THERE WAS AN ALIEN ON THE FORCE ALL THOSE YEARS...?

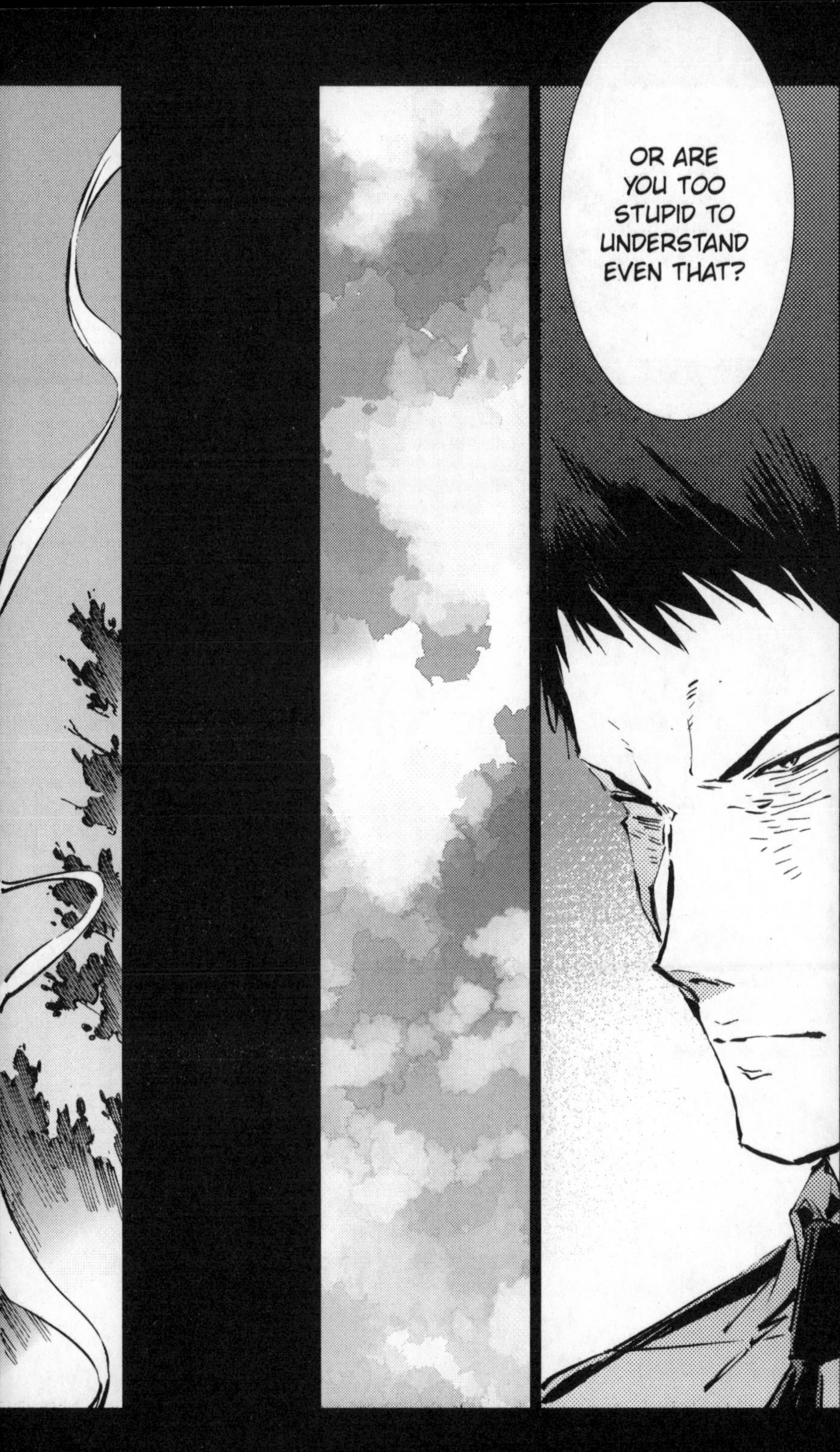
OR ARE YOU TOO STUPID TO UNDERSTAND EVEN THAT?

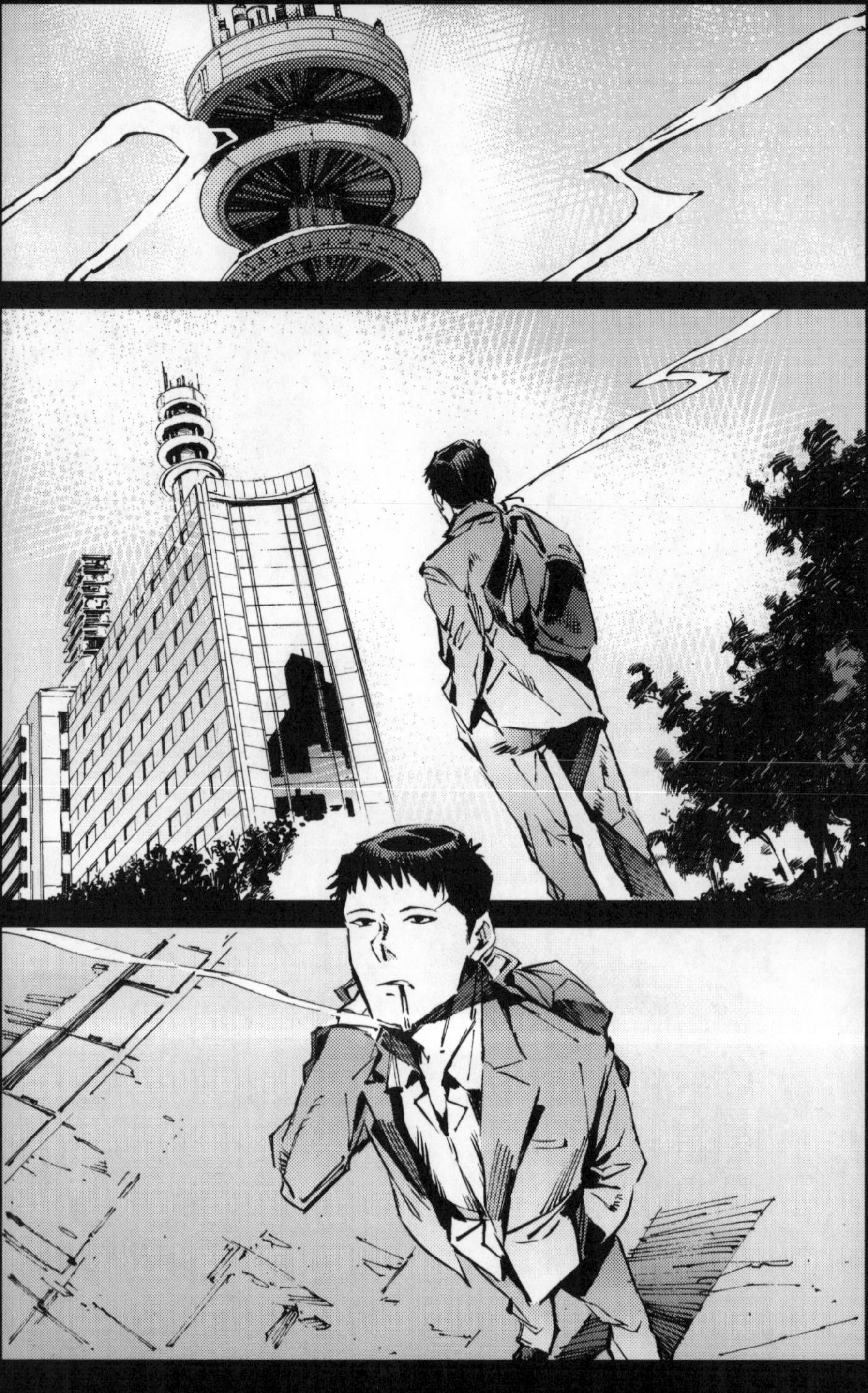

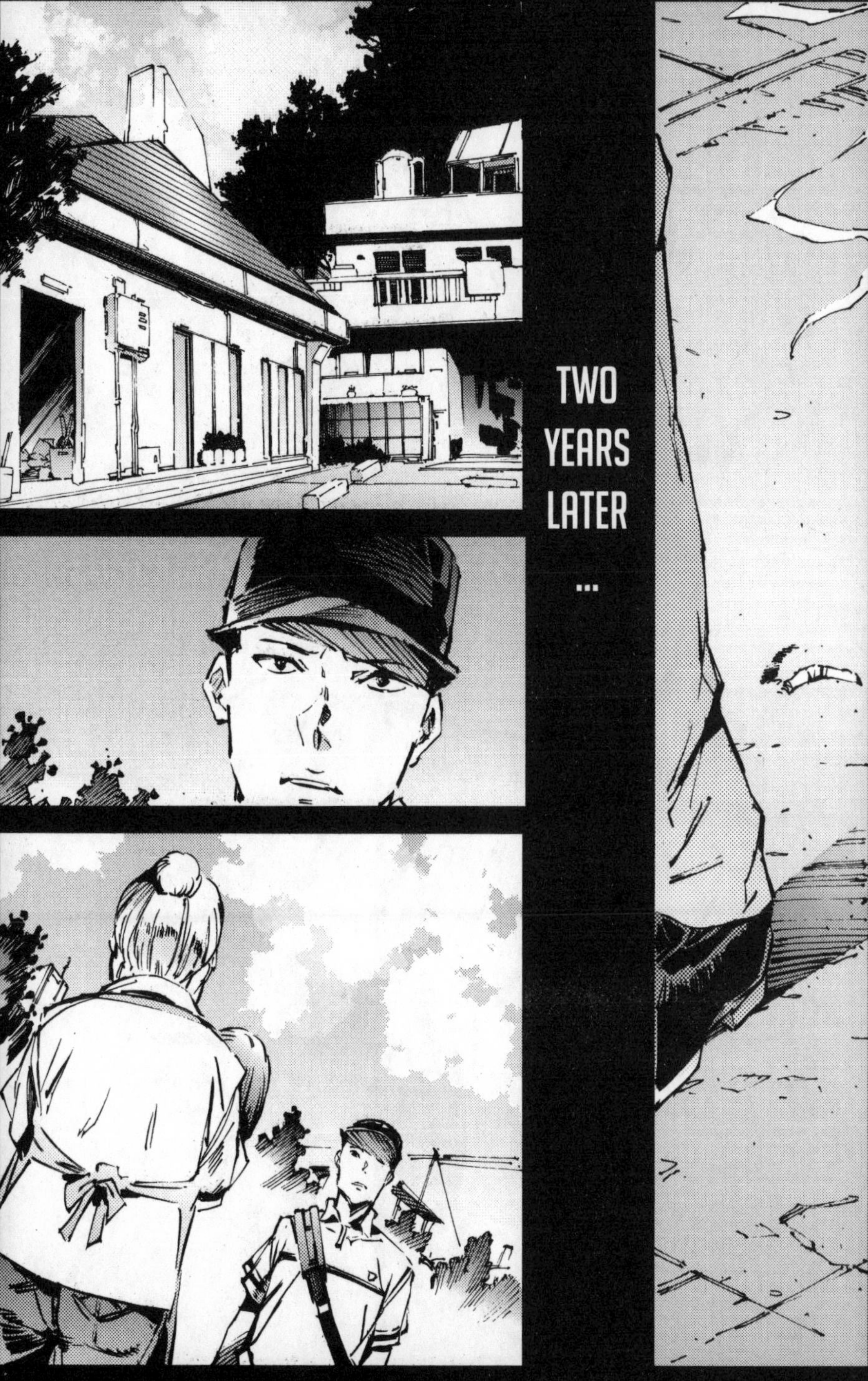
TWO YEARS LATER ...

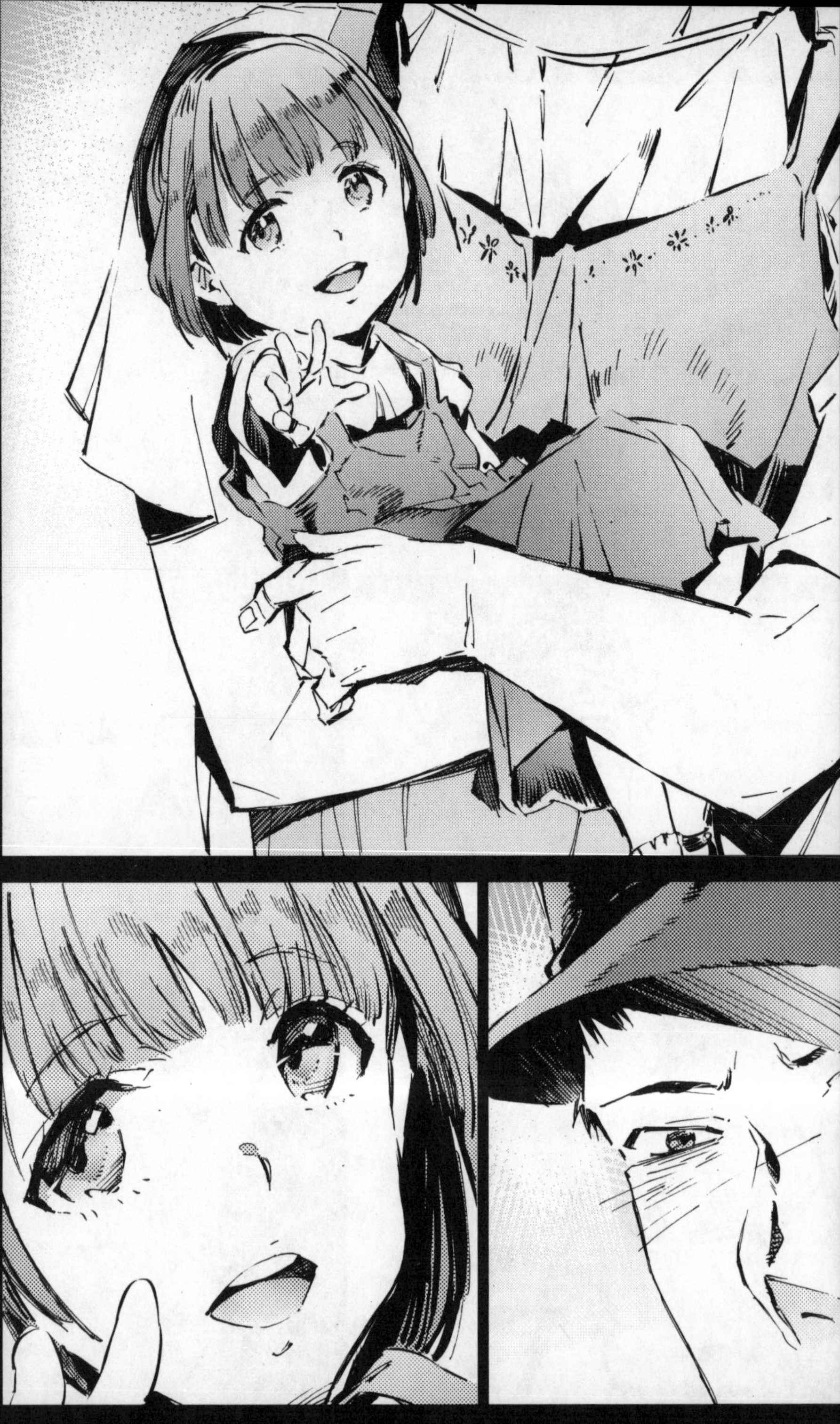

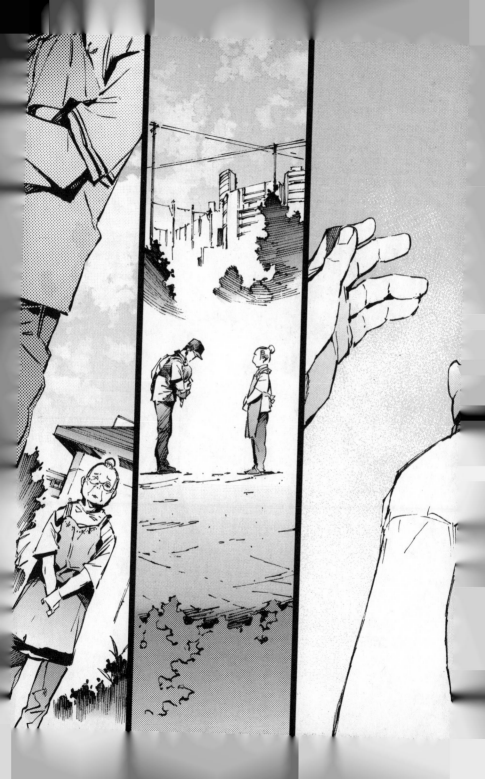

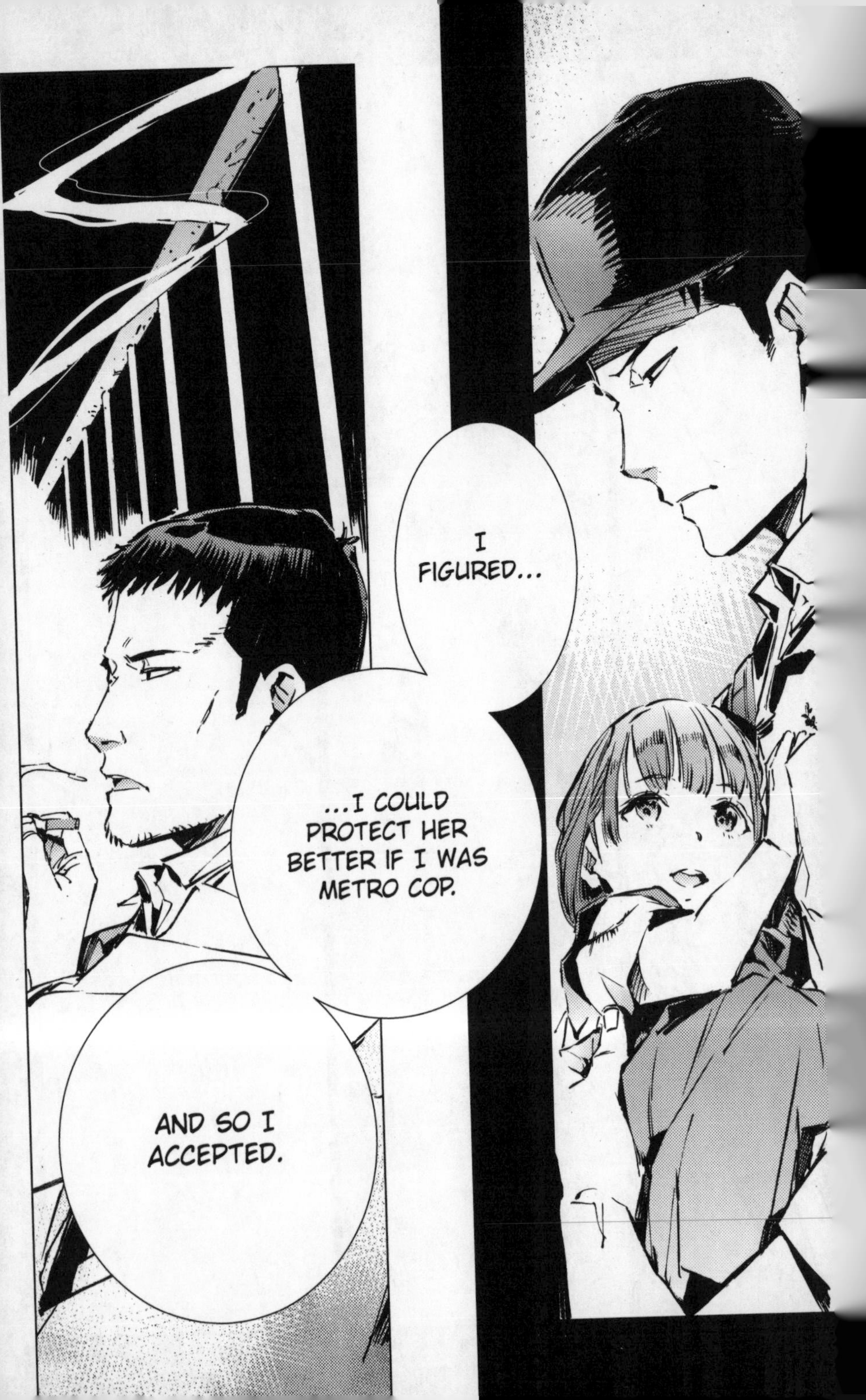
I FIGURED...
...I COULD PROTECT HER BETTER IF I WAS METRO COP.
AND SO I ACCEPTED.

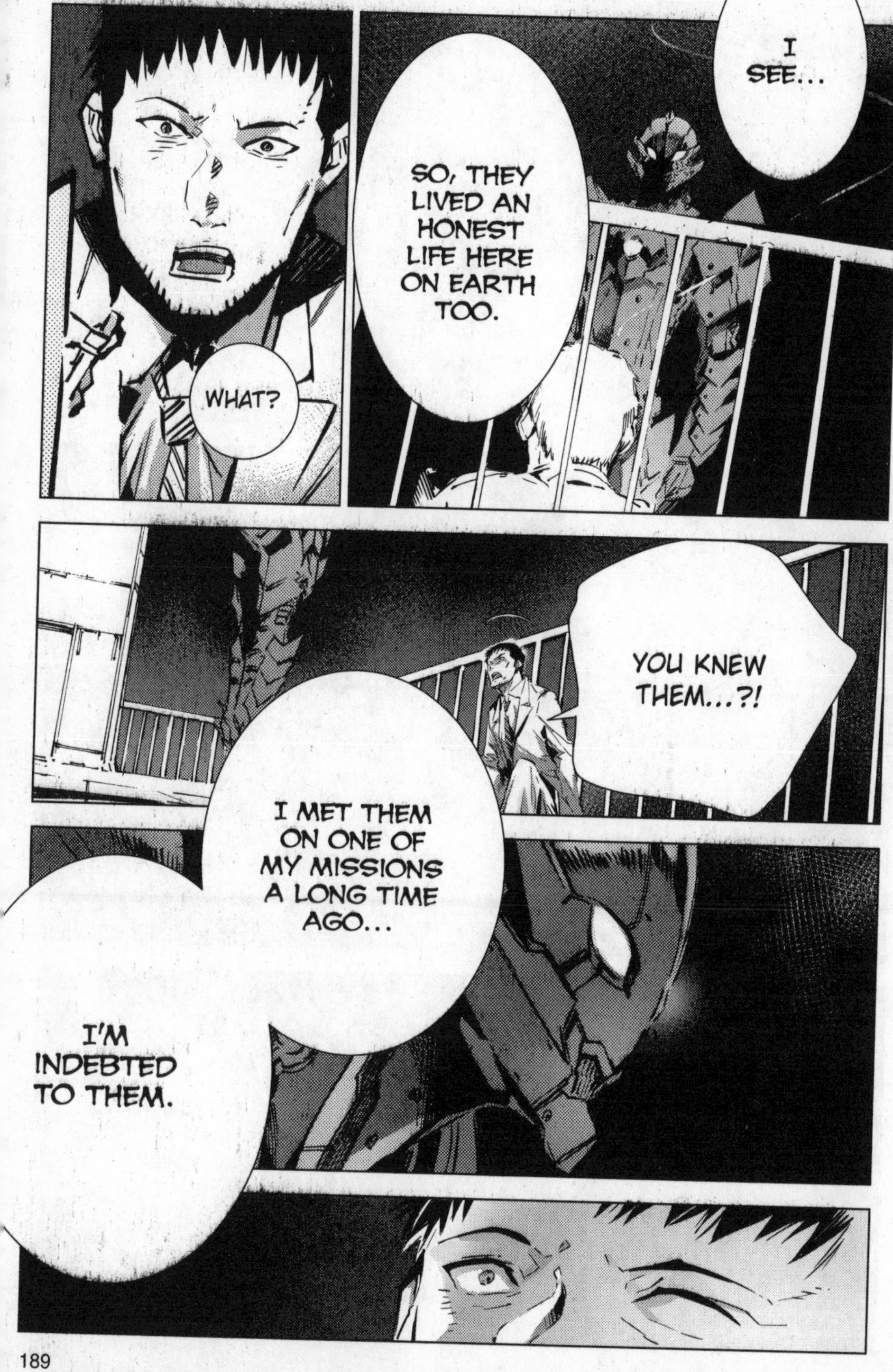
I SEE...
SO, THEY LIVED AN HONEST LIFE HERE ON EARTH TOO.
WHAT?
YOU KNEW THEM...?!
I MET THEM ON ONE OF MY MISSIONS A LONG TIME AGO...
I'M INDEBTED TO THEM.

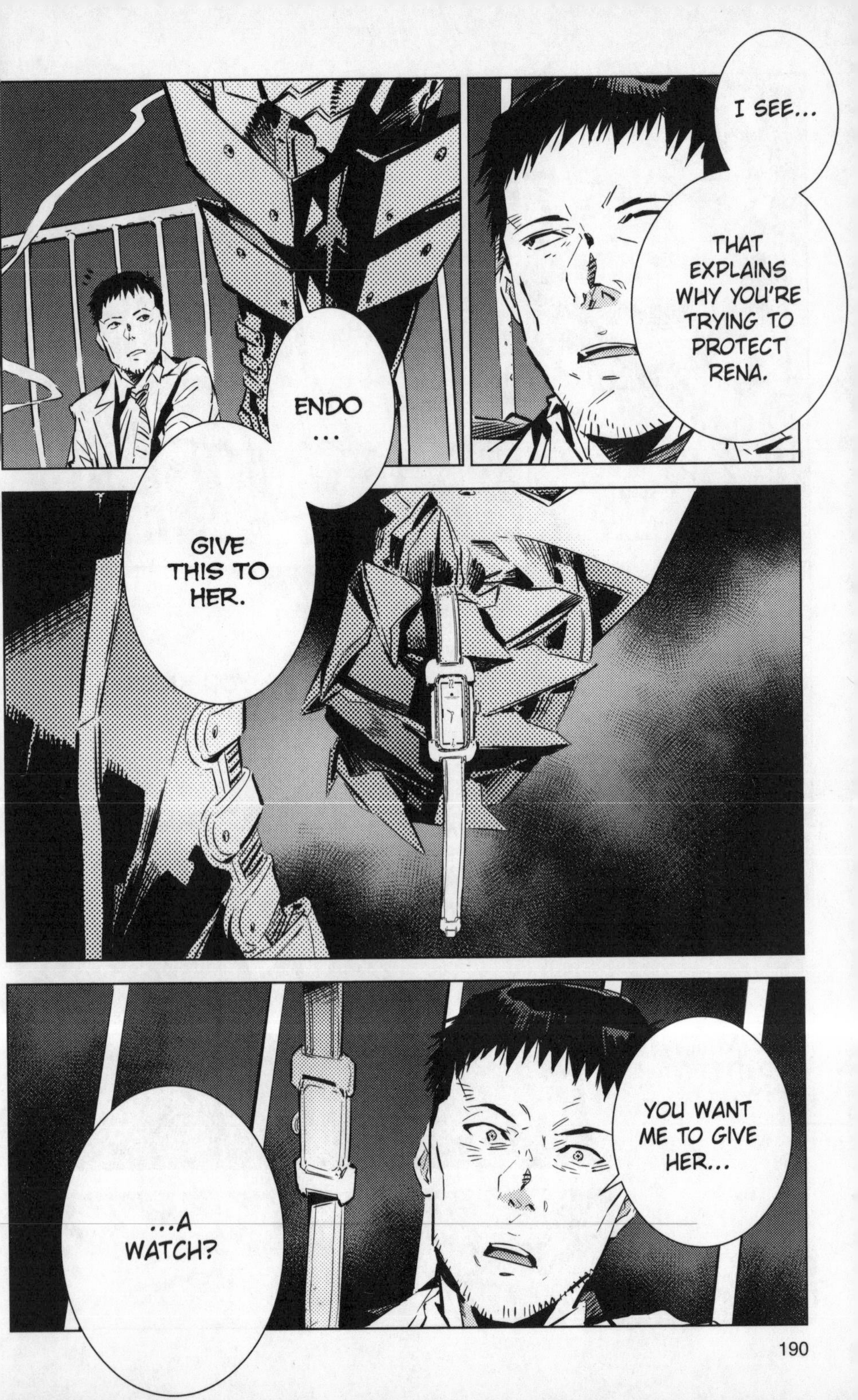
I SEE...
THAT EXPLAINS WHY YOU'RE TRYING TO PROTECT RENA.
ENDO...
GIVE THIS TO HER.
YOU WANT ME TO GIVE HER...
...A WATCH?

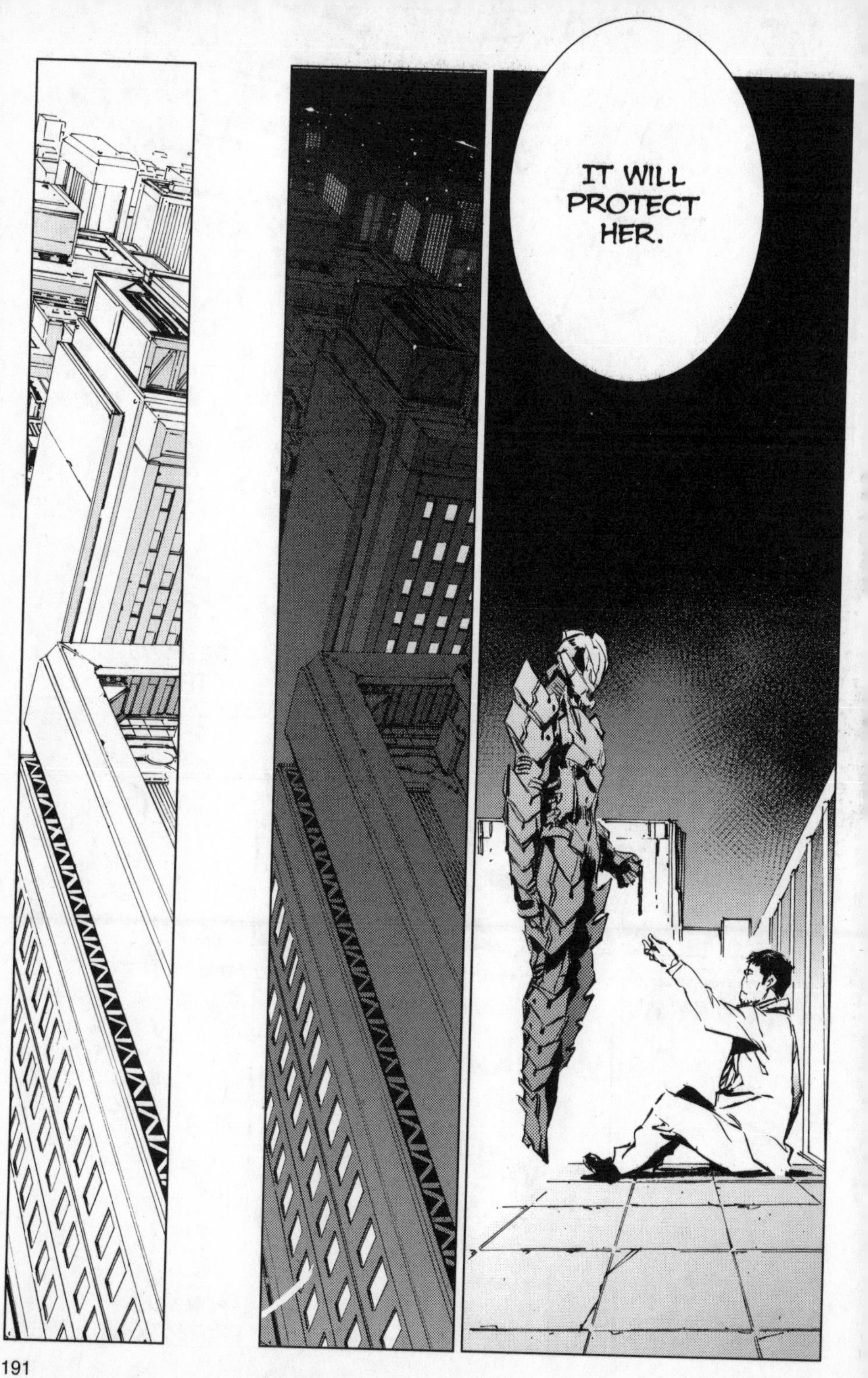
IT WILL PROTECT HER.

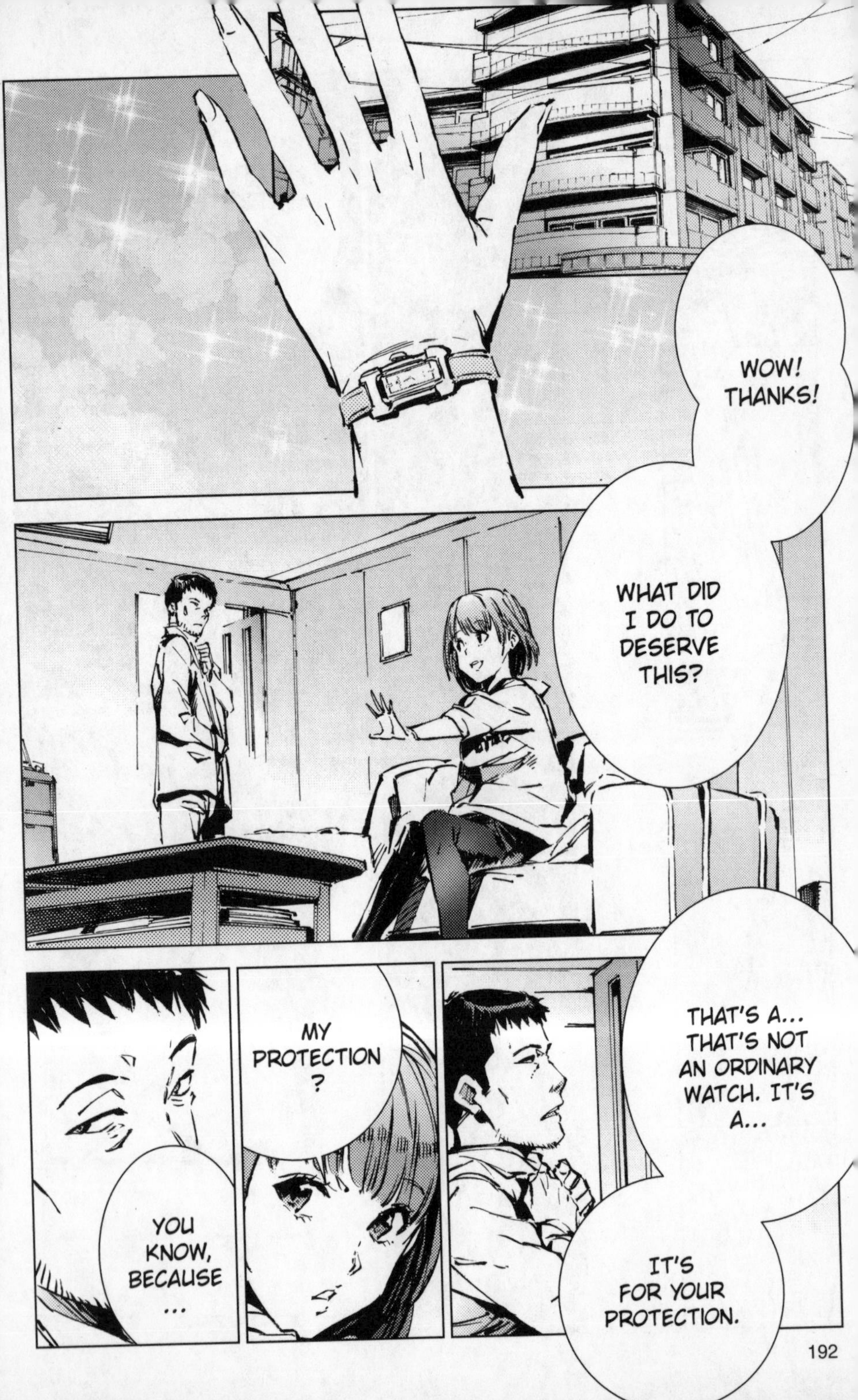
WOW! THANKS!
WHAT DID I DO TO DESERVE THIS?
THAT'S A... THAT'S NOT AN ORDINARY WATCH. IT'S A...
IT'S FOR YOUR PROTECTION.
MY PROTECTION ?
YOU KNOW, BECAUSE ...

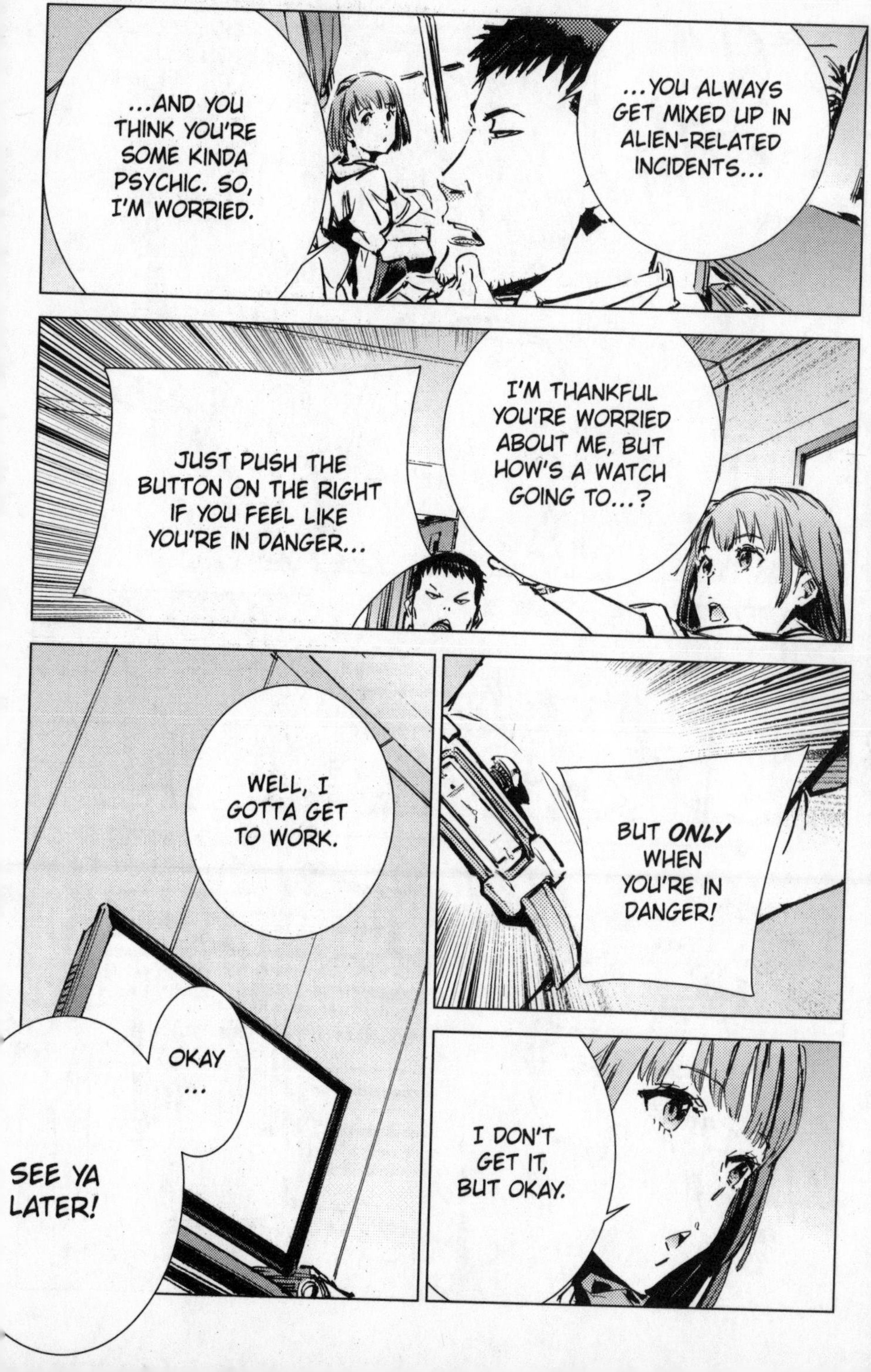
...YOU ALWAYS GET MIXED UP IN ALIEN-RELATED INCIDENTS...
...AND YOU THINK YOU'RE SOME KINDA PSYCHIC. SO, I'M WORRIED.
I'M THANKFUL YOU'RE WORRIED ABOUT ME, BUT HOW'S A WATCH GOING TO...?
JUST PUSH THE BUTTON ON THE RIGHT IF YOU FEEL LIKE YOU'RE IN DANGER...
BUT *ONLY* WHEN YOU'RE IN DANGER!
I DON'T GET IT, BUT OKAY.
WELL, I GOTTA GET TO WORK.
OKAY ...
SEE YA LATER!

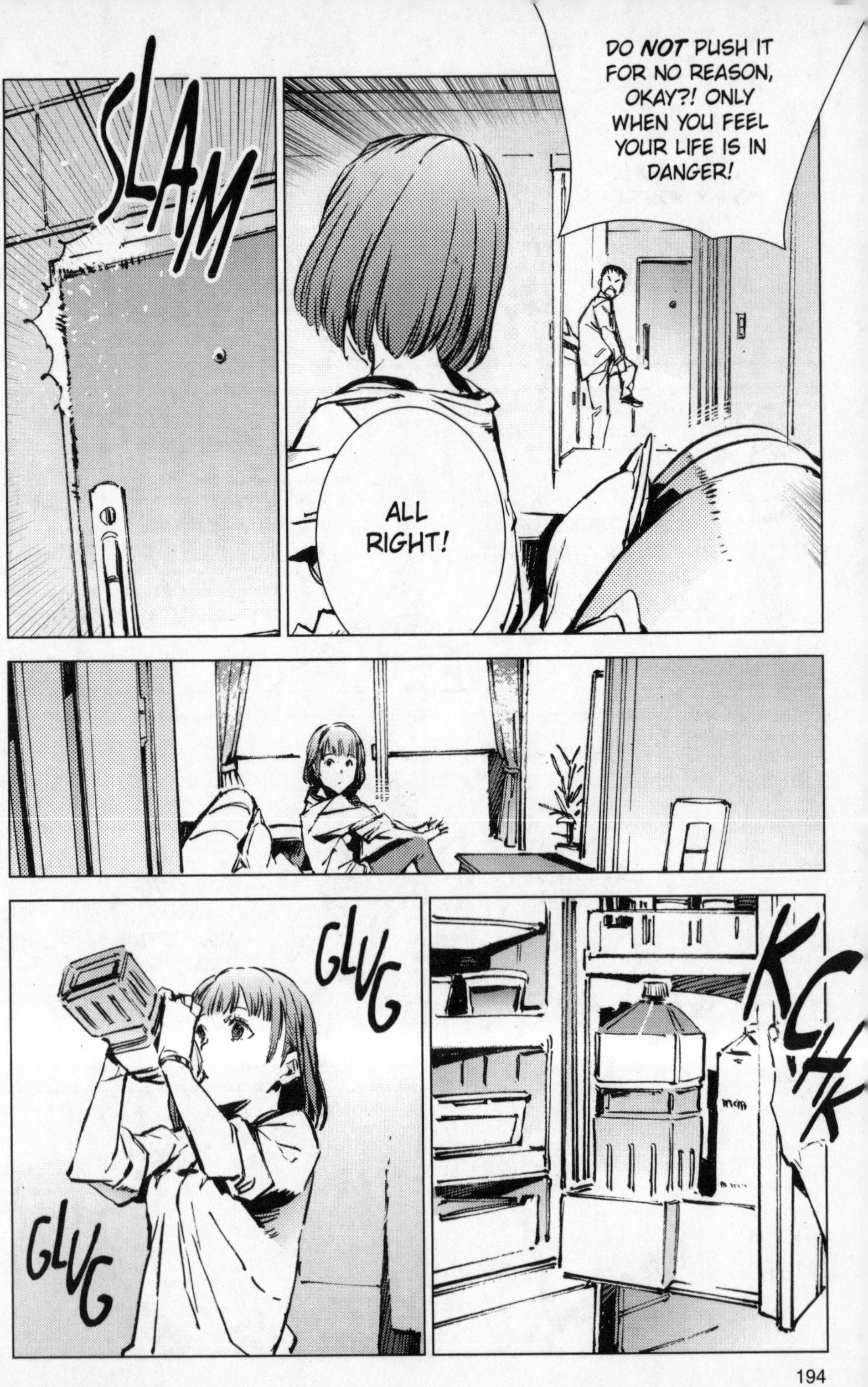
DO NOT PUSH IT FOR NO REASON, OKAY?! ONLY WHEN YOU FEEL YOUR LIFE IS IN DANGER!
ALL RIGHT!
SLAM
KCHK
GLUG
GLUG

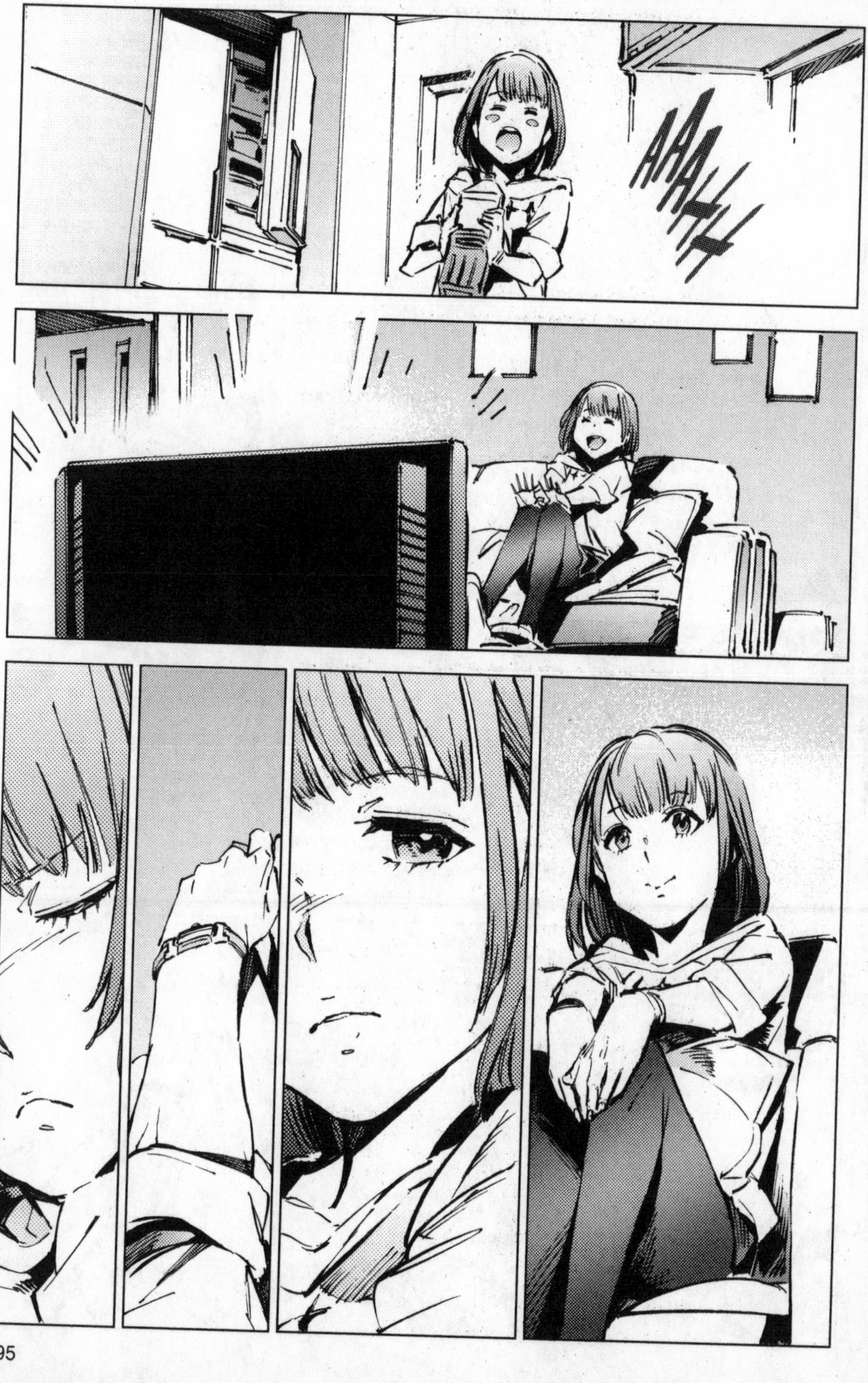
AHAHH

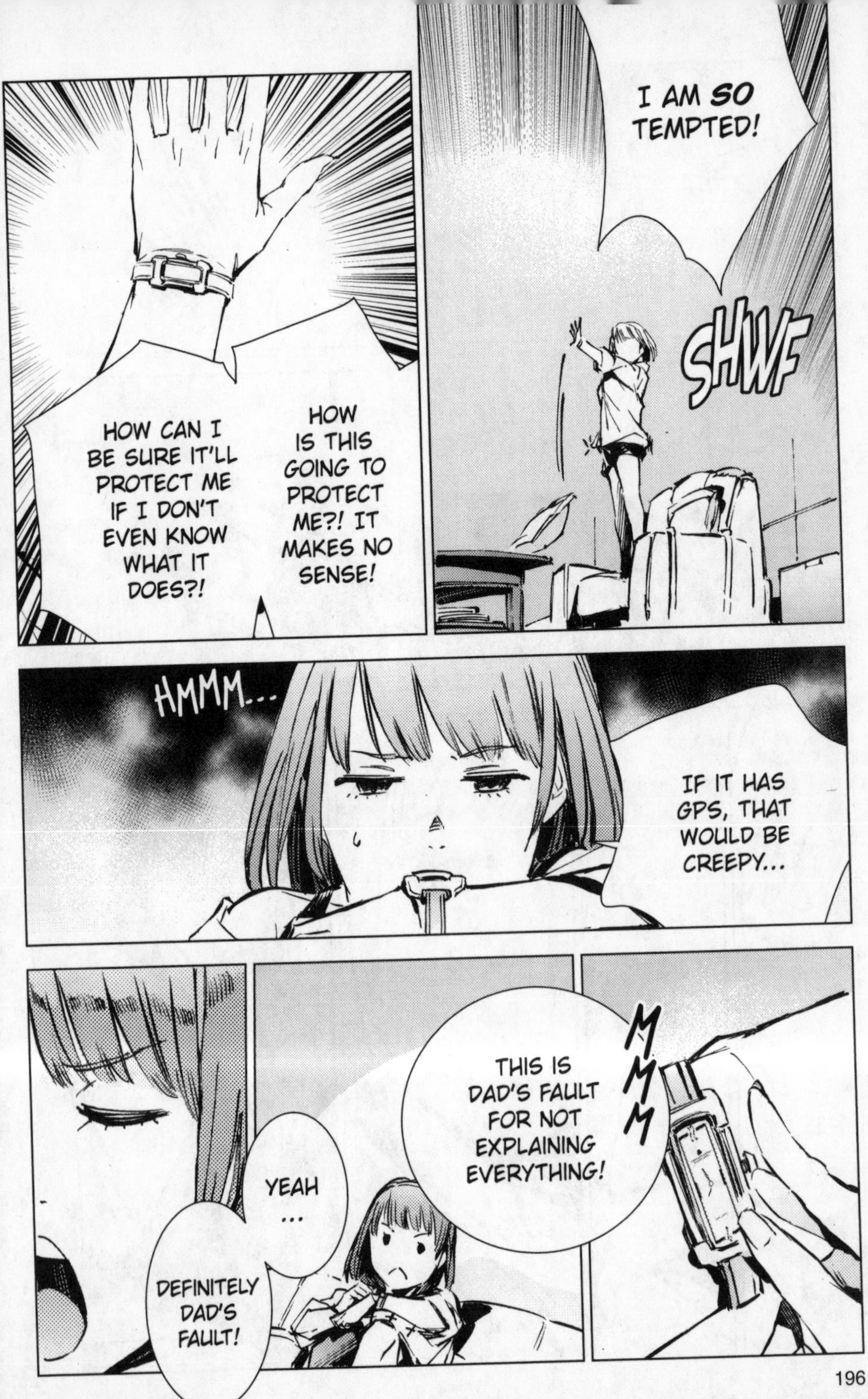
I AM SO TEMPTED!
SHWF
HOW IS THIS GOING TO PROTECT ME?! IT MAKES NO SENSE!
HOW CAN I BE SURE IT'LL PROTECT ME IF I DON'T EVEN KNOW WHAT IT DOES?!
HMMM...
IF IT HAS GPS, THAT WOULD BE CREEPY...
MMMM
THIS IS DAD'S FAULT FOR NOT EXPLAINING EVERYTHING!
YEAH...
DEFINITELY DAD'S FAULT!

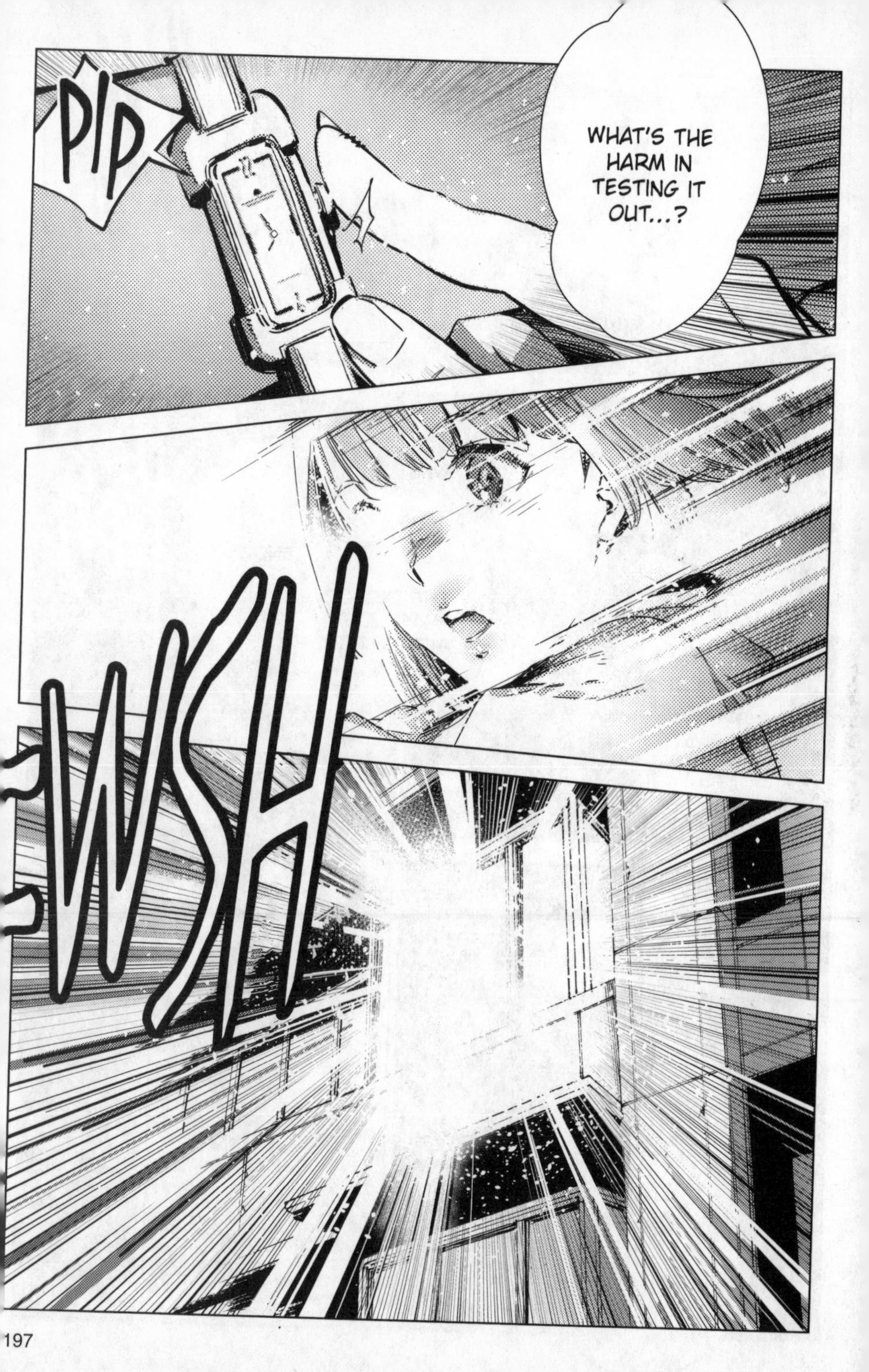
WHAT'S THE HARM IN TESTING IT OUT...?
PIP
WSH

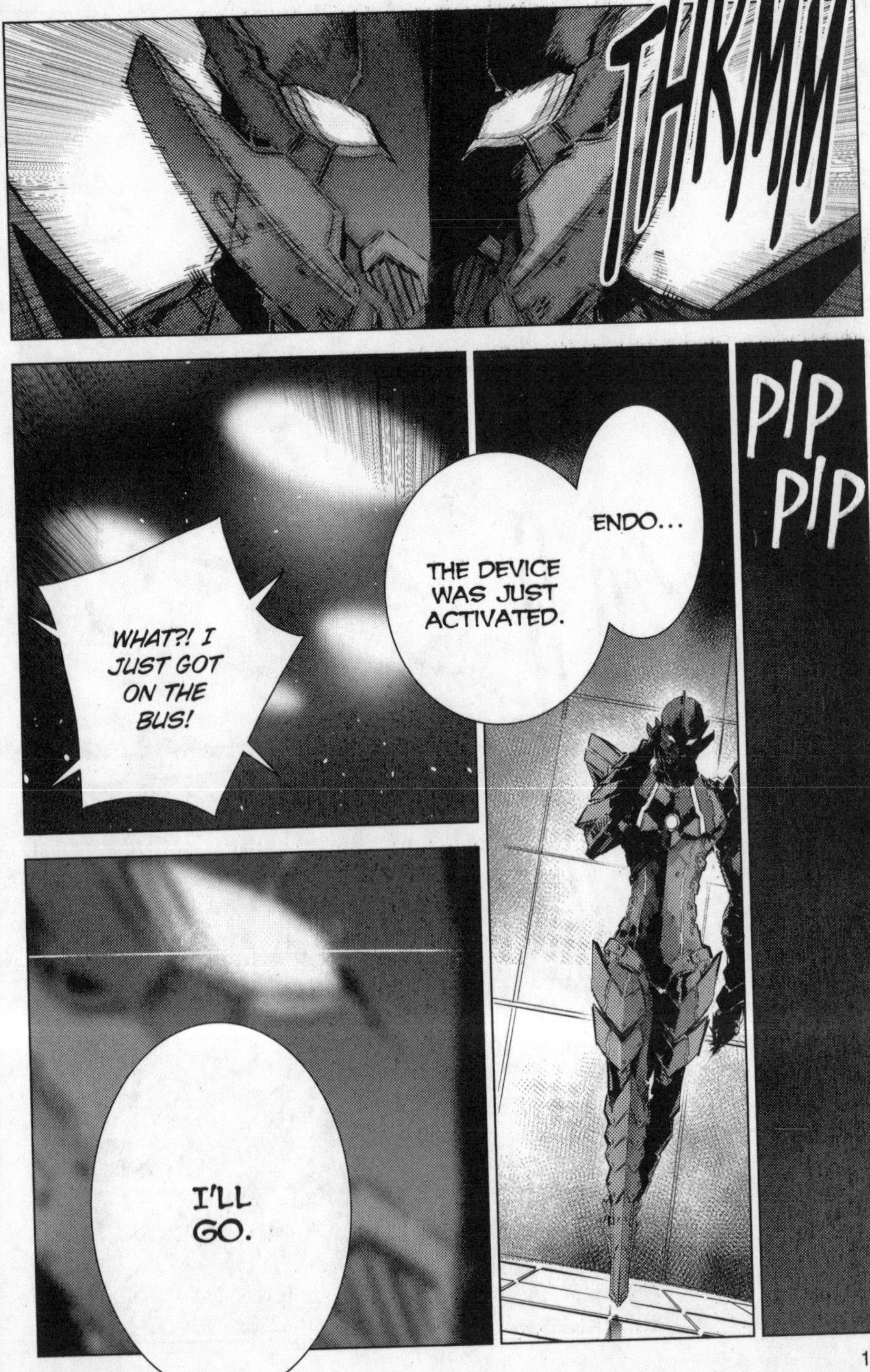
THRMM
PIP PIP
ENDO...
THE DEVICE WAS JUST ACTIVATED.
WHAT?! I JUST GOT ON THE BUS!
I'LL GO.

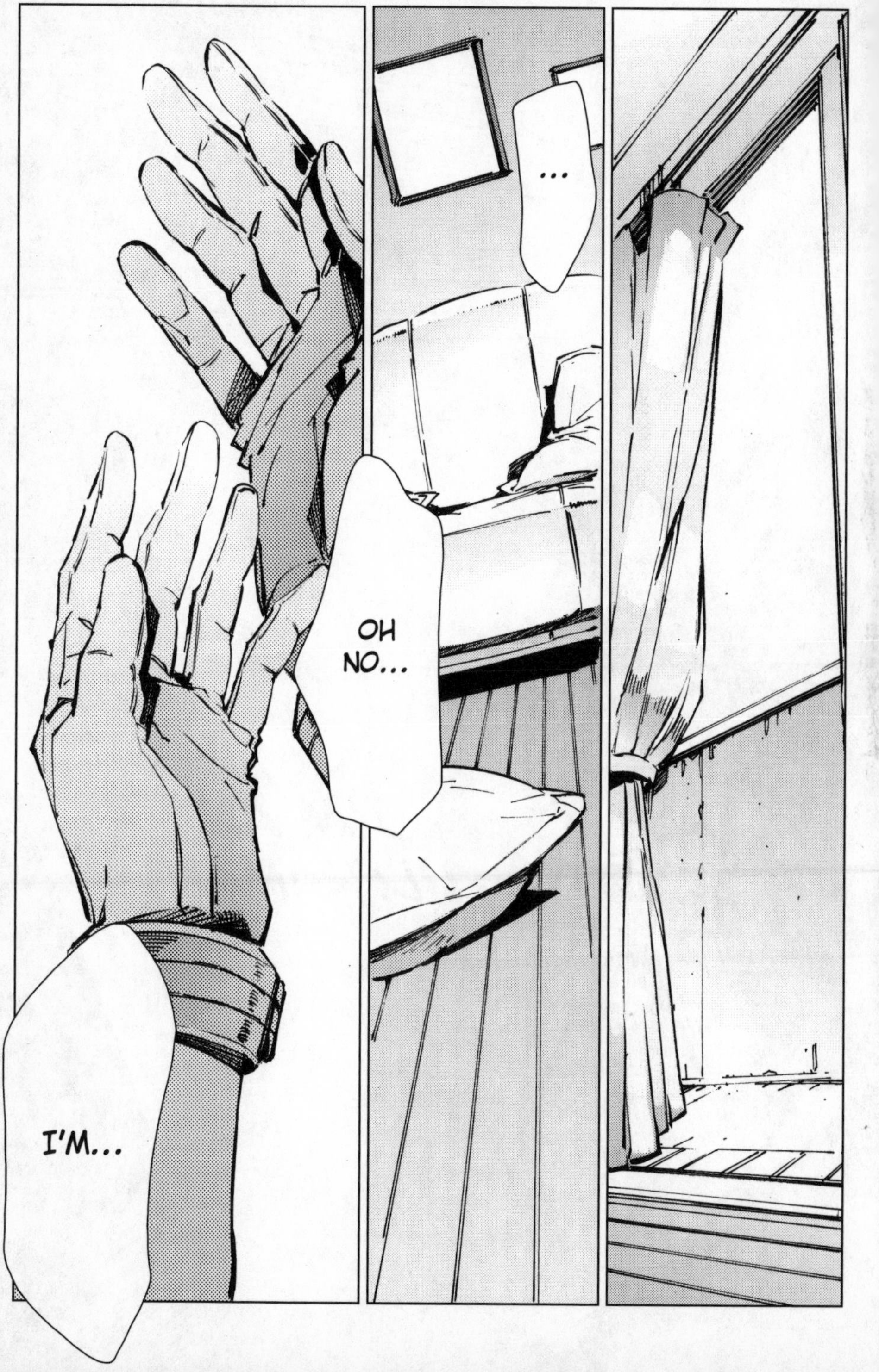
...
OH NO...
I'M...

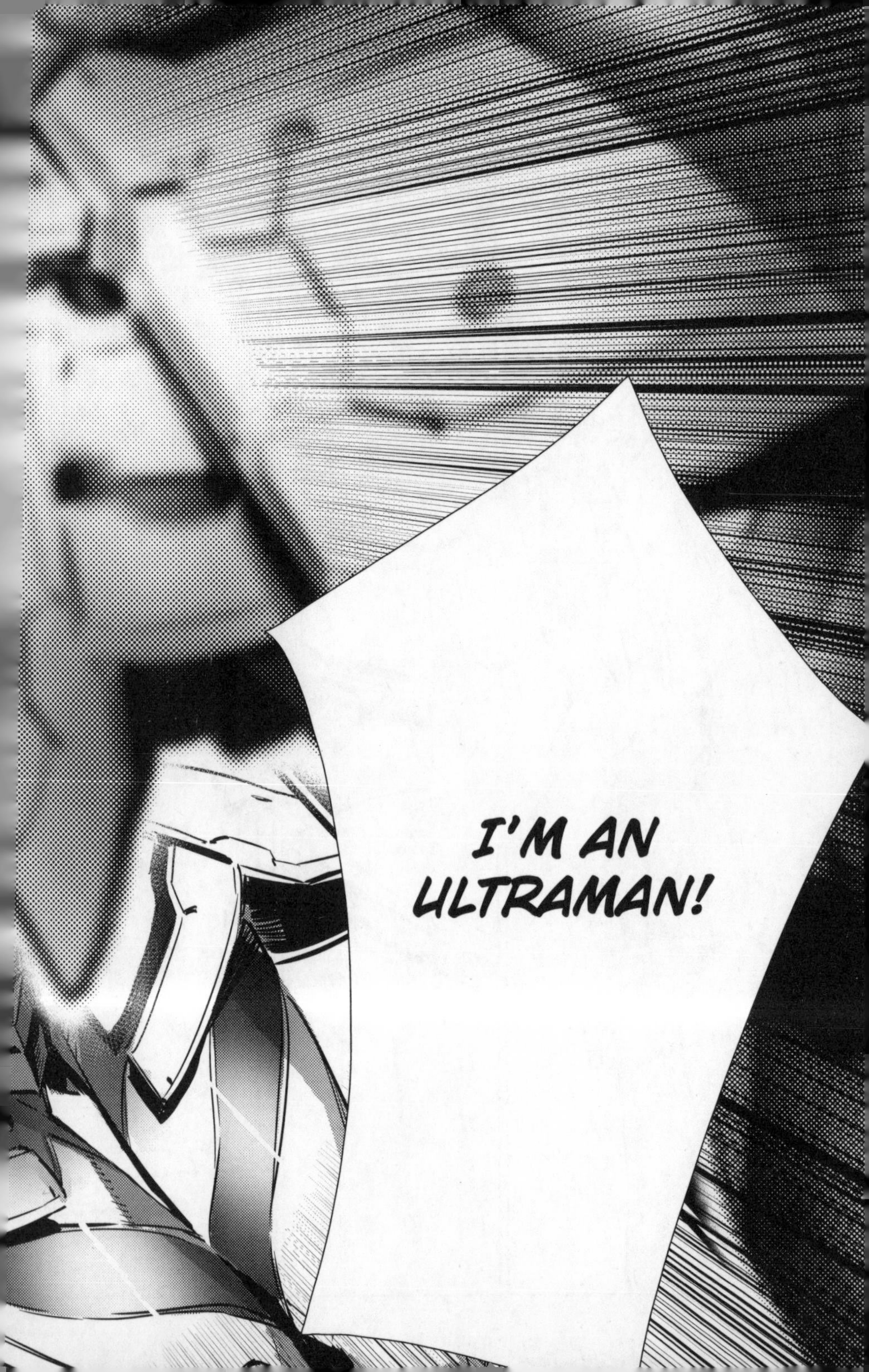
I'M AN ULTRAMAN!

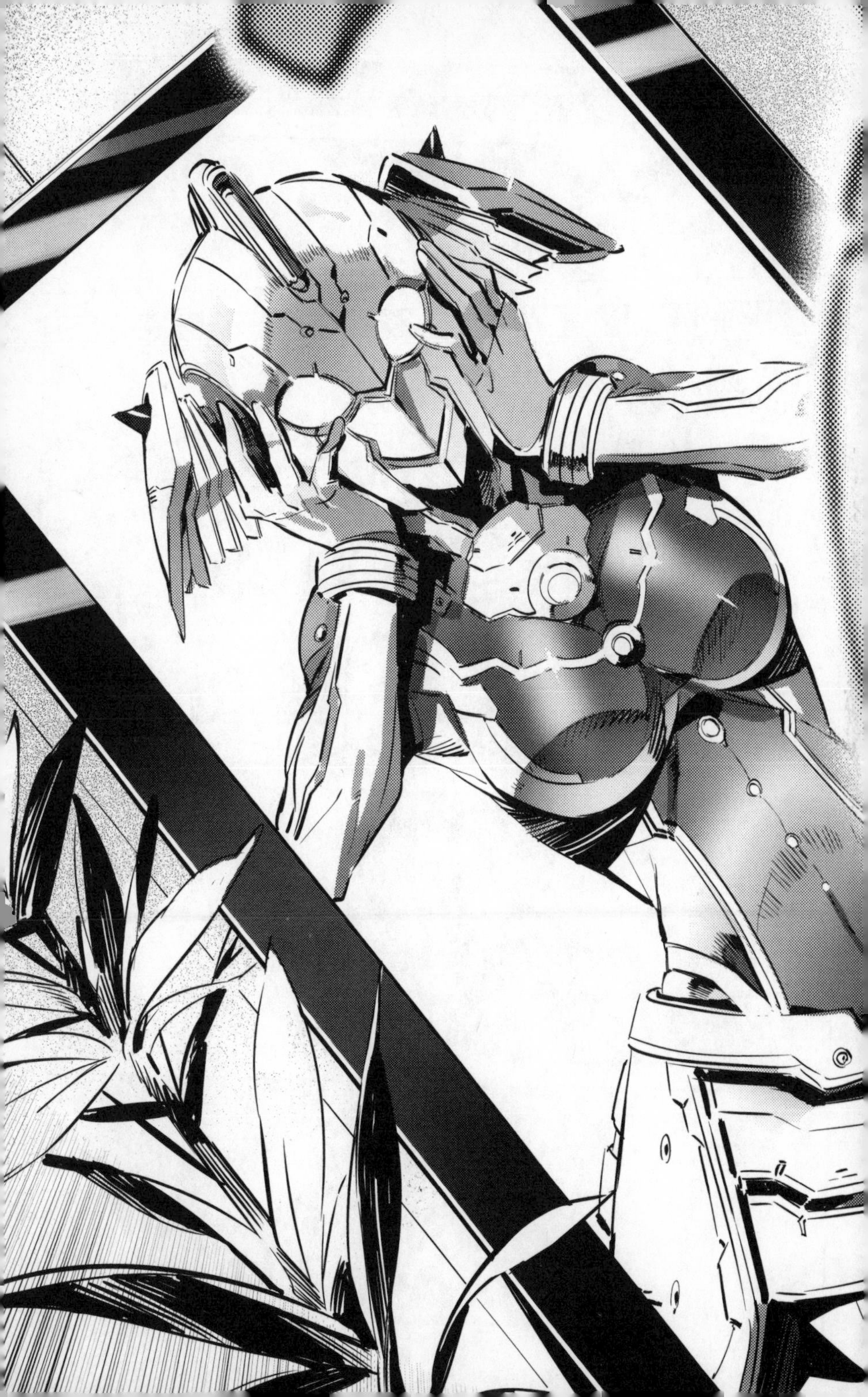

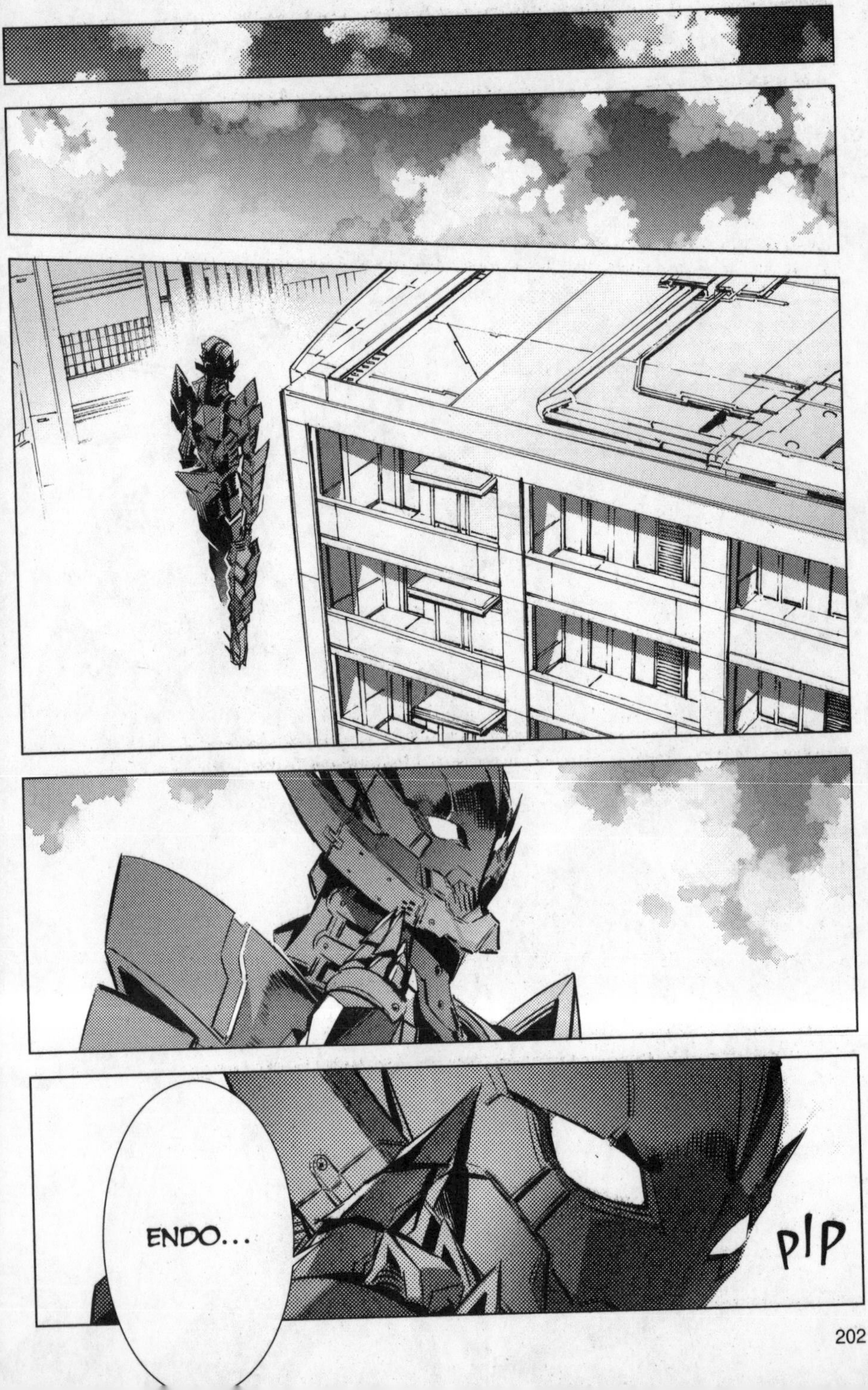
ENDO...
PIP

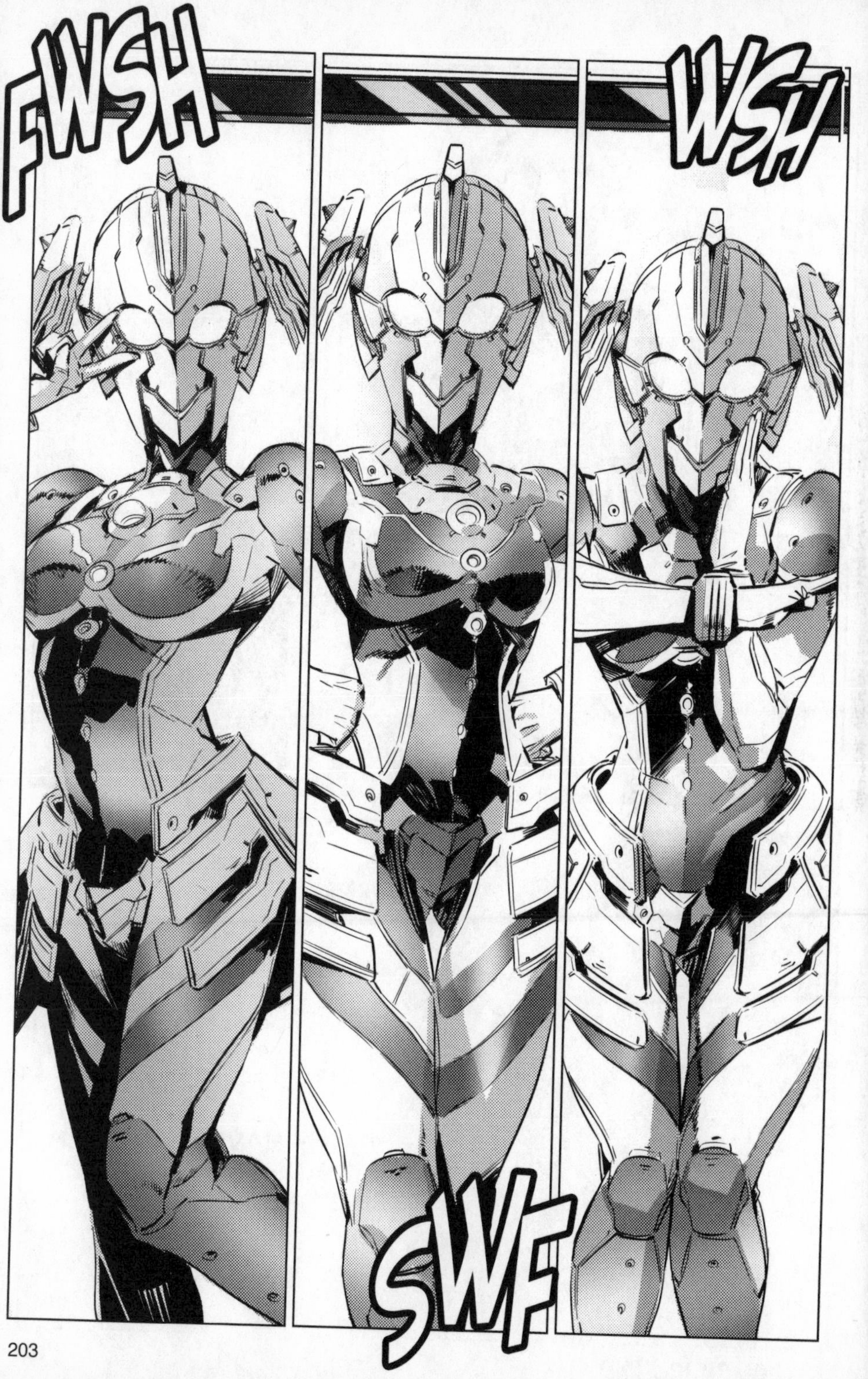
WSH
SWF
FWSH

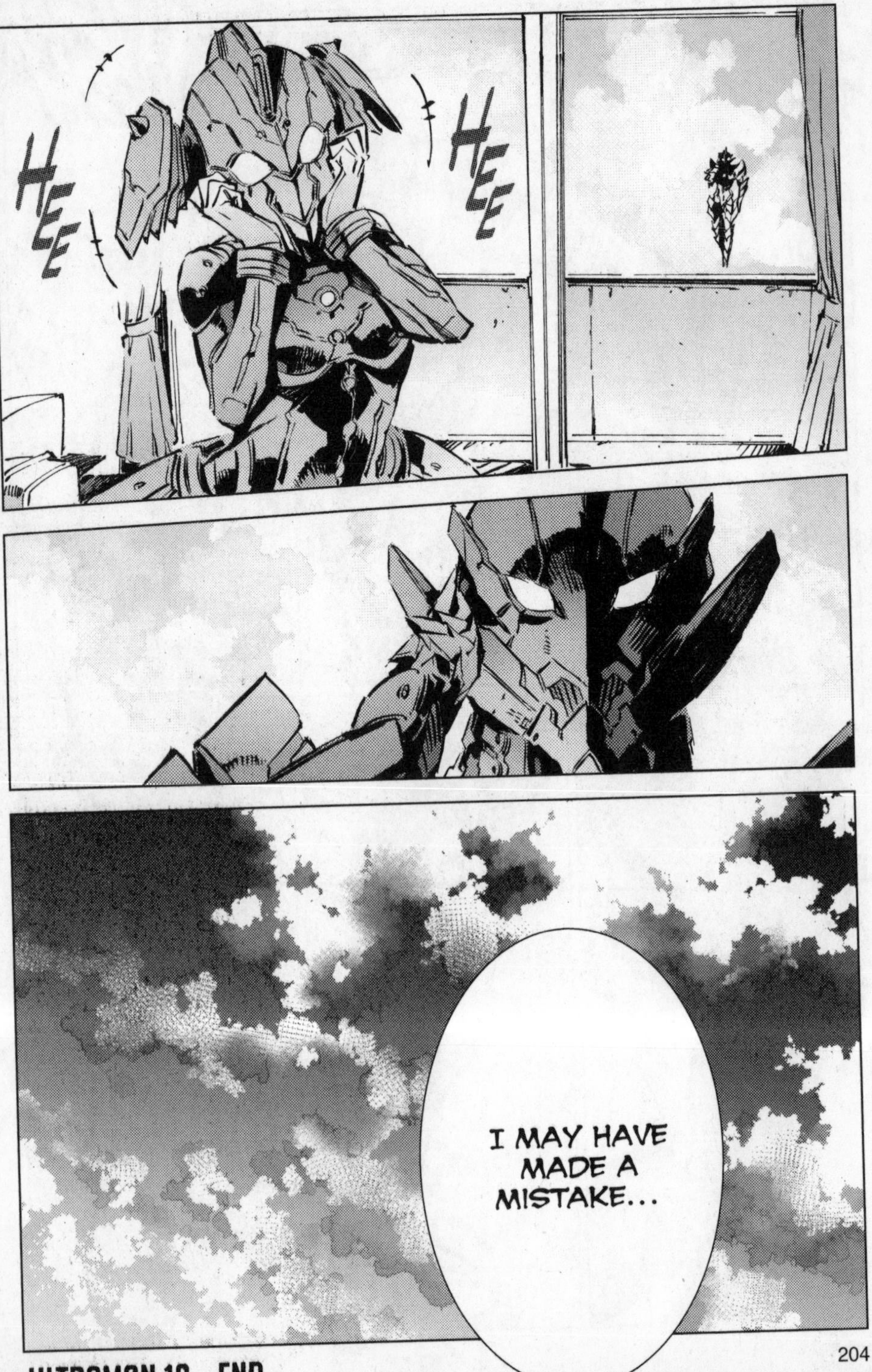
HEE
HEE
I MAY HAVE MADE A MISTAKE...

ULTRAMAN 16 - END

THIS IS THE BEGINNING OF A NEW AGE.

ZARAB ALIEN (RUNAWAY STATE) 1

■ A rogue Zarab alien. A covert operative from Planet Zarab working for Mephisto. Like Adacic aliens, Zarab aliens are considered highly dangerous by the Star Cluster Council and are not permitted to emigrate to other planets. He was smuggled to Earth by Mephisto.

ZARAB ALIEN

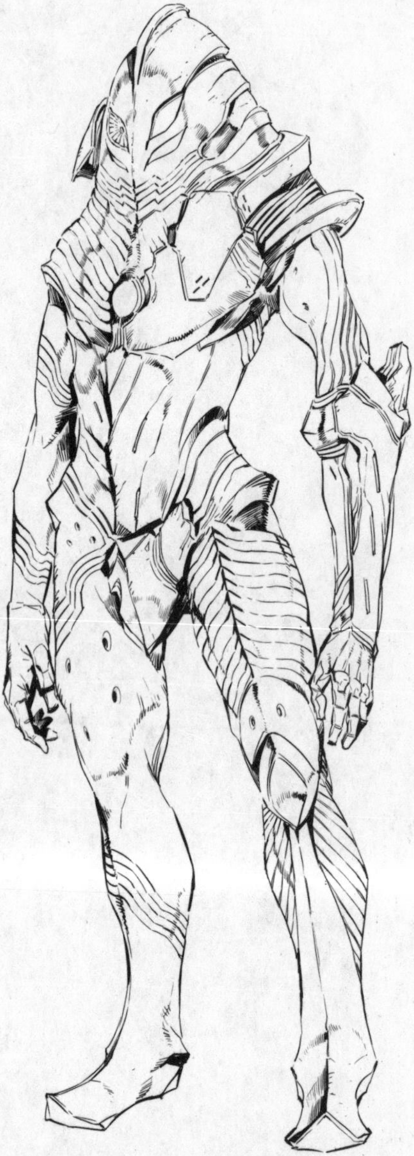

■ Like the Zarab aliens that came to Earth before him, he disguised himself as an Ultraman (in this case, Shinjiro). Due to a malfunction caused by the forced deactivation of his mimicry device, however, he took on a form as if he'd merged with the Ultraman suit. Edo ordered the forced deactivation of the mimicry device.

ADACIC ALIEN & UNKNOWN (RUNAWAY STATE)

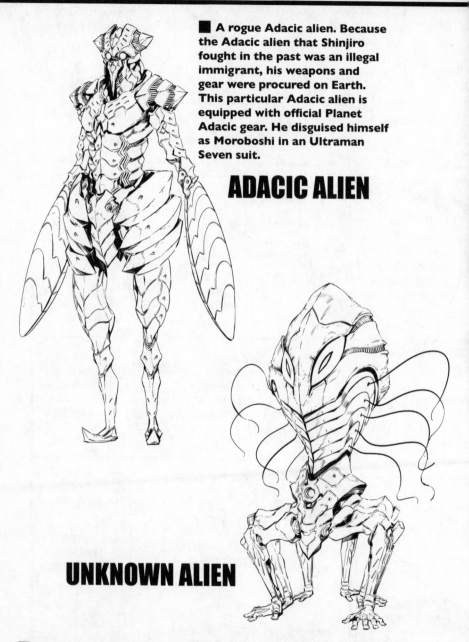

■ A rogue Adacic alien. Because the Adacic alien that Shinjiro fought in the past was an illegal immigrant, his weapons and gear were procured on Earth. This particular Adacic alien is equipped with official Planet Adacic gear. He disguised himself as Moroboshi in an Ultraman Seven suit.

ADACIC ALIEN

UNKNOWN ALIEN

■ A completely unknown and mysterious alien. He is believed to have been brought to Earth by the Zarab alien, but not even Mephisto knows the specifics. He disguised himself as Hayata in a Zoffy suit.

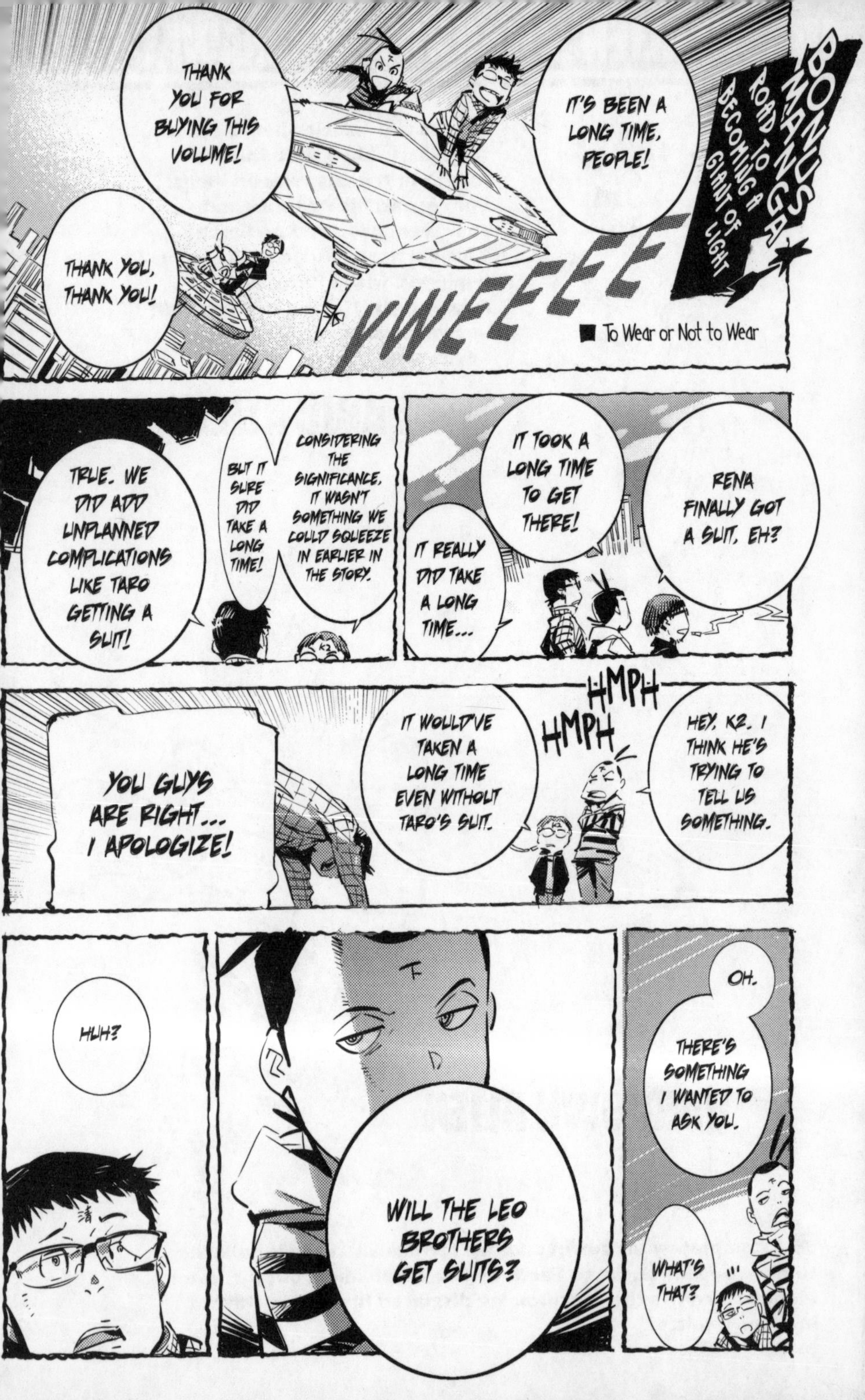
BONUS MANGA ★ ROAD TO BECOMING A GIANT OF LIGHT
■ To Wear or Not to Wear
IT'S BEEN A LONG TIME, PEOPLE!
THANK YOU FOR BUYING THIS VOLUME!
THANK YOU, THANK YOU!
VWEEEEE
RENA FINALLY GOT A SUIT, EH?
IT TOOK A LONG TIME TO GET THERE!
IT REALLY DID TAKE A LONG TIME...
CONSIDERING THE SIGNIFICANCE, IT WASN'T SOMETHING WE COULD SQUEEZE IN EARLIER IN THE STORY.
BUT IT SURE DID TAKE A LONG TIME!
TRUE. WE DID ADD UNPLANNED COMPLICATIONS LIKE TARO GETTING A SUIT!
HEY, K2. I THINK HE'S TRYING TO TELL US SOMETHING.
HMPH
HMPH
IT WOULD'VE TAKEN A LONG TIME EVEN WITHOUT TARO'S SUIT.
YOU GUYS ARE RIGHT... I APOLOGIZE!
OH.
THERE'S SOMETHING I WANTED TO ASK YOU.
WHAT'S THAT?
WILL THE LEO BROTHERS GET SUITS?
HUH?

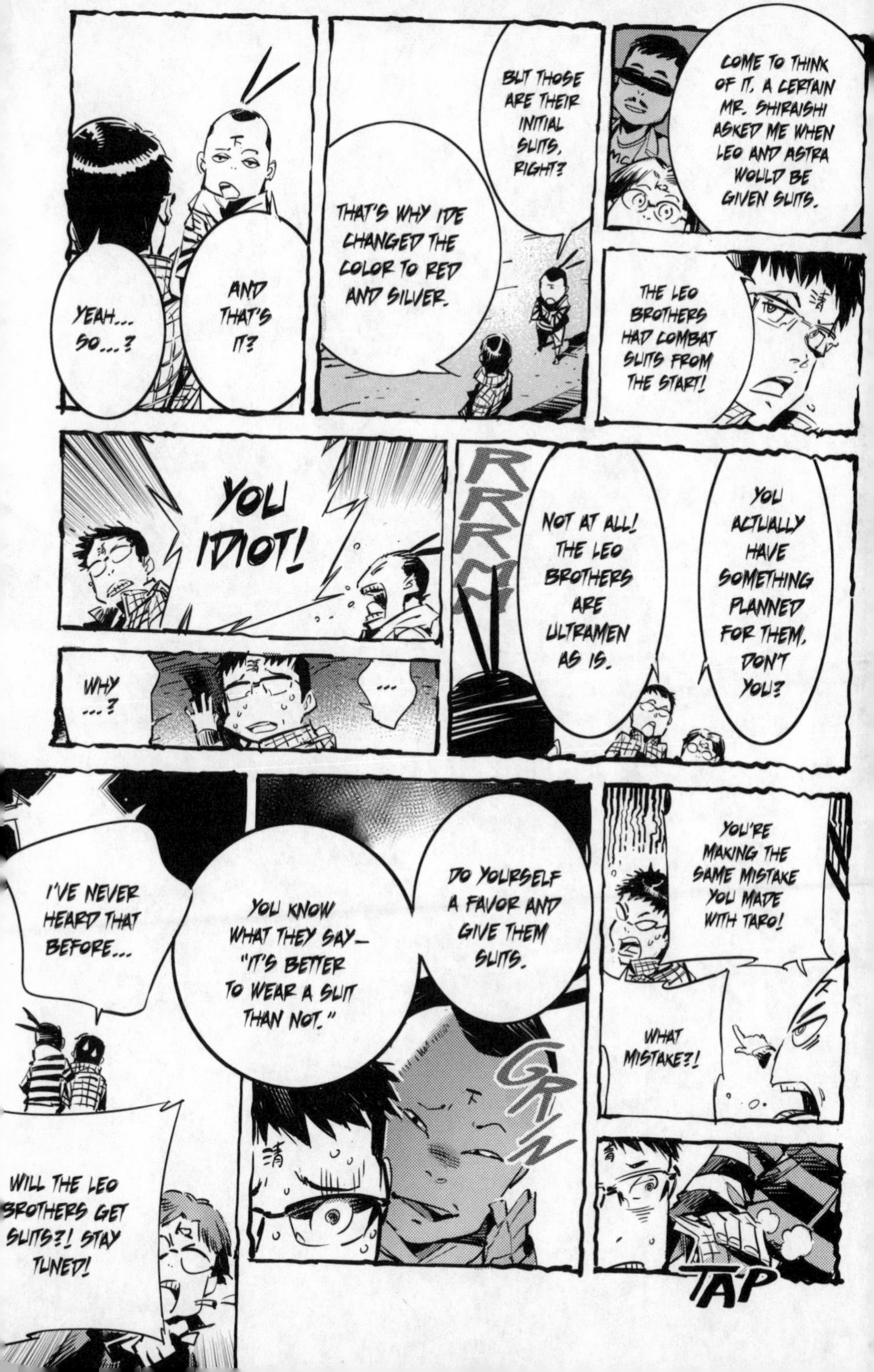
COME TO THINK OF IT, A CERTAIN MR. SHIRAISHI ASKED ME WHEN LEO AND ASTRA WOULD BE GIVEN SUITS.
THE LEO BROTHERS HAD COMBAT SUITS FROM THE START!
BUT THOSE ARE THEIR INITIAL SUITS, RIGHT?
THAT'S WHY IDE CHANGED THE COLOR TO RED AND SILVER.
AND THAT'S IT?
YEAH... SO...?
YOU ACTUALLY HAVE SOMETHING PLANNED FOR THEM, DON'T YOU?
NOT AT ALL! THE LEO BROTHERS ARE ULTRAMEN AS IS.
RRRG
YOU IDIOT!
...
WHY ...?
YOU'RE MAKING THE SAME MISTAKE YOU MADE WITH TARO!
WHAT MISTAKE?!
TAP
DO YOURSELF A FAVOR AND GIVE THEM SUITS.
YOU KNOW WHAT THEY SAY— "IT'S BETTER TO WEAR A SUIT THAN NOT."
GRIN
I'VE NEVER HEARD THAT BEFORE...
WILL THE LEO BROTHERS GET SUITS?! STAY TUNED!

EIICHI SHIMIZU ✕ TOMOHIRO SHIMOGUCHI

We're very thankful that in this volume we pass our 100th chapter! One hundred chapters—can you believe it? That's a hundred months (although we've taken some breaks, so it's actually more than a hundred months). That's enough time for a baby to grow up enough to be able to build model kits. At least that's what I did.

Finally, as we pass the 100-chapter mark, our heroine is ready for some action. (It's about time!)

ULTRAMAN
VOLUME 16
VIZ SIGNATURE EDITION

STORY/ART BY **EIICHI SHIMIZU** AND **TOMOHIRO SHIMOGUCHI**

©2020 Eiichi Shimizu and Tomohiro Shimoguchi ©2020 TSUBURAYA PROD.
Originally published by HERO'S INC.

TRANSLATION **JOE YAMAZAKI**
ENGLISH ADAPTATION **STAN!**
TOUCH-UP ART & LETTERING **EVAN WALDINGER**
DESIGN **KAM LI**
EDITOR **MIKE MONTESA**

Printed in the U.S.A.

Published by VIZ Media, LLC
P.O. Box 77010
San Francisco, CA 94107

10 9 8 7 6 5 4 3 2 1
First printing, January 2022

 MEDIA

viz.com   vizsignature.com

HEY! YOU'RE READING IN THE WRONG DIRECTION!

This is the END of the graphic novel

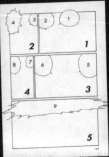

Follow the action this way.

To properly enjoy this VIZ graphic novel, please turn it around and begin reading from RIGHT TO LEFT. Unlike English, Japanese is read right to left, so Japanese comics are read in reverse order from the way English comics are typically read.

This book has been printed in the original Japanese format in order to preserve the orientation of the original artwork.

HAVE FUN WITH IT!

DECADES AGO, A BEING KNOWN AS THE GIANT OF LIGHT
joined together with Shin Hayata of the Science Special Search Party to save ~~...ters called Kaiju. Now, many years~~ ~~...ry, and the world is at peace. But in~~ ~~...ger that can only be faced by a new~~ ~~...~~ of **ULTRAMAN**...

The stunning revelation that Edo is the supreme chancellor of the Star Cluster Council stops the scheming Mephisto in his tracks, and he doesn't hesitate to save his own skin. Now that the real Ultramen have shown up, Mephisto's Ultramen imposters who are wrecking the city are about to get a hard lesson in why you don't mess with the defenders of Earth!

ЧЧЧР

SCIENCE SPECIAL SEARCH PARTY

~~...~~9 USA $17.99 CAN £9.99 UK

~~...~~n vizsignature.com

~~...~~lic ⊂ MEDIA *VIZ SIGNATURE* RATED TEEN

ISBN: 978-1-9747-2339-3

51299

9 781974 723393